GW00492762

Making Sense of a United Ireland

Making Sense of a United Ireland

Should It Happen? How Might It Happen?

BRENDAN O'LEARY

SANDYCOVE

an imprint of

PENGUIN BOOKS

SANDYCOVE

UK | USA | Canada | Ireland | Australia
India | New Zealand | South Africa

Sandycove is part of the Penguin Random House group of companies
whose addresses can be found at global.penguinrandomhouse.com

First published 2022
001

Copyright © Brendan O'Leary, 2022

The moral right of the author has been asserted

Set in 12/14.75pt Bembo Book MT Pro
Typeset by Jouve (UK), Milton Keynes
Printed and bound in Great Britain by Clays Ltd, Elcograf S.p.A.

The authorized representative in the EEA is Penguin Random House Ireland,
Morrison Chambers, 32 Nassau Street, Dublin D02 YH68

A CIP catalogue record for this book is available from the British Library

ISBN: 978-1-844-88605-0

www.greenpenguin.co.uk

Penguin Random House is committed to a
sustainable future for our business, our readers
and our planet. This book is made from Forest
Stewardship Council® certified paper.

To Lori, in memory of our year in Galway and Cushendall

Contents

Preface

Ever since the contested partition of Ireland in 1920, there have been regular demands for reunification. Sometimes these demands have been accompanied by threats of violence or sustained armed campaigns. This book does not *demand* Irish reunification, but it does *expect* it, with a high degree of probability, for reasons advanced in the first chapter. The ethos of the book is peaceful, and democratic – in keeping with the Belfast or Good Friday Agreement. Respect for the will and consent of majorities in both jurisdictions on the island is exhibited throughout.

Expectations of reunification have varied in intensity over the past century. The premise of this book is that reunification is more likely to occur within the next decade than at any juncture in the last hundred years. The year 2030 will mark a decisive tipping point, with the disappearance of a cultural Protestant majority in Northern Ireland among those entitled to vote across *all* age-cohorts – with the possible exception of those aged 85 or over.

Demography is not destiny, and this book is written without the results of the 2021 census in Northern Ireland, which will be published after it goes to press. But we do not need to wait for them; the brute demographic facts of the census of 2011 predict the future quite well. Nineteen years later, in 2030, the cohorts aged between 0 and 18 in 2011, assuming they are still living in Northern Ireland, will have joined the electorate as adults. They will decisively tip the balance against the historically dominant community, which will also have lost any advantage among the older age-cohorts that it had in 2011. The future of Northern Ireland will be in the hands of a non-Protestant majority.

This fact-to-be requires preparation, not premature exultation, and certainly not lazy deferral of its predictable consequences. Regrettably, some will persist in wishful thinking. Some will be saddened at the thought of this future fact; sadness, however, is not a political remedy. Others will be angered, but will want to think after their rage dissipates.

The need to prepare for the possibility of reunification affects all on this island, and it affects our diasporas. This book is a call for effective preparation, accurate information, and informed judgements. How will reunification happen – if it does? And how *should* it happen, so it can happen as well as possible?

Making Sense of a United Ireland was first drafted on a Fulbright scholarship in late 2021, between Delta and Omicron becoming the latest letters from the Greek alphabet to describe global threats to our public health. The manuscript was revised in early 2022 after close readings by numerous friends named in the Acknowledgements. The text was completed one hundred years after the establishment of the Irish Free State. The book accordingly may exhibit some of the collective pride widely felt in the recent accomplishments of independent Ireland. It will also be clear that I regard partition as an avoidable error, or series of errors, and that over the long run Northern Ireland, by any measure, has performed much less successfully than independent Ireland. Holding these opinions does not mean that I believe that Irish reunification is inevitable, or that it will necessarily be a success. It can be a success, but only if mistakes are avoided, and preparation to avoid them must begin now.

Plagues remind us of the fragility of all people, and that our most lethal enemies may not be humans. They also provide some of us with stilled moments to think about the future.

The book before you was written without certainty about the future, even though it seeks to avoid ambiguity. Fanatics and prophets, especially fanatical prophets, know the future with certainty. Usually, they are wrong. This book has been composed to reduce uncertainty: to address probabilities, possibilities, risks, and benefits, and to clarify what may happen, and what should happen. It aims to provide provisional and revisable answers to what the author judges to be the most looming questions obliged by our shared future.

A realistic portrait is offered of the possibilities of reunification, not a promise of a golden age. The focus is on feasible reunification. It is deeply important that reunification happens as smoothly as possible for *all* those affected – including those who vote against it. Long-term preparation is required now, not just the short-term improvisations for which Irish politicians are justly famous on both sides of the Atlantic.

Making Sense of a United Ireland addresses several audiences. It speaks to Southerners who are curious to know what may happen and what preparations are required – including those Southerners who don't like being called Southerners, for good geographic reasons – and to Southerners who thought that these questions were all settled. Addressed, with equal standing, are those British unionists and cultural Protestants in Northern Ireland who know or fear that they may shortly lose a referendum to preserve the Union that most of them, including their parents and grandparents, have sincerely believed has been in their best interests. My respect for their British identity is unequivocal, even as I discuss the possible dissolution of the Union of Great Britain, and that of Great Britain and Northern Ireland. I do not expect them to change their identifications, and certainly not because of this book. Northern nationalists are addressed, as the most immediately interested community. This book should remind them that they need to think through questions of goals, strategy, and alliances, without illusions. The book speaks about, to, and of the 'others' – those who identify with neither nationalists nor unionists. The 'neithers' and the 'nors', the undecideds, and the current 'don't knows' will likely determine Irish futures in referendums, especially in the North. Lastly, this book hopes to reach the Irish diaspora, and those with benign interests in Irish futures in Scotland, Wales, and England, as well as in the European Union, North America, and further afield. It has fainter hopes of reaching the British diaspora from Ireland – including the Ulster Scots, or the Scots Irish.

This book will not calculate the level of anyone's pension in 2032 or 2042 if Ireland reunifies. It will not tell you what the cost will be, if any, of a visit to a doctor or to obtain prescription drugs, or the length of waiting lists for non-emergency treatment. It will not predict your after-tax disposable income, nor your child's degree or technical qualifications. Anyone who claims to know precise answers to these questions eight to ten years out would be pulling your leg, as they say in both jurisdictions on the island. The book should, however, help thinking about ways to address these questions. Broad information and the outlines of policy directions on these subject matters will need to be answered in any referendums. The book will show that there are good reasons to expect a united Ireland within the European Union to create increasing and sustained prosperity, by contrast with the recent isolationist move of Ireland's eastern neighbour – a decision driven by a majority of English voters. The vote to leave the EU has reduced the comparative prosperity of Great Britain (or a rump UK) and will continue to do so.

It is impossible to write a relatively short book without assuming some background knowledge among readers. I have tried to be helpful, but without writing a parallel history of Ireland, North and South. Many of the judgements expressed here rely on materials explored in full in *A Treatise on Northern Ireland* (three volumes, 2020 paperback edition). *Making Sense of a United Ireland*, however, assumes you have not read these three volumes.

Making Sense of a United Ireland is informed by my discipline and specialism, but with an emphasis on accessible argument, and with some of the assumptions of a brand of power-sharing known as 'liberal consociational thought' – a style of thought that commends people's freedom to express their identifications politically, through self-determination rather than pre-determination by others. People's identities, to the extent that they matter, should be as freely chosen as possible.

In consociational thought, four principles are recommended for deeply divided places: parity, proportionality, autonomy, and veto rights. Parity implies equality in status and recognition, or full partnership. Proportionality suggests that a group's influence and benefits should be in accordance with its numbers. Autonomy requires that groups should be able to govern themselves on cultural matters of profound concern to them. Veto rights should exist, when necessary, to prevent tyrannous majorities maltreating minorities. These principles are in the Good Friday Agreement. These principles may not need to be so thoroughly applied in a reunified Ireland as they have been in Northern Ireland, yet they may need to be preserved if Northern Ireland remains in existence *within* a united Ireland.

Making Sense of a United Ireland is also informed by democratic republican thought developed on both sides of the Atlantic since its revival in Renaissance Italy. Republics of equal adult citizens are capable of significant self-government, free of domination by patriarchs, churches, capitalists, civil servants, and great powers. Hard-won pluralist conclusions are here too. There is not one best way of life. There are deep as well as shallow differences in cultures and mentalities, but these deep differences can be managed, even if they cannot be transcended or peacefully eliminated.

The book is written in the conviction that I have some standing to address reunification, because I am a Southerner by birth who became a Northerner by residence. In my adult life I have worked mostly in Great Britain and the USA, the two powers with Irish diasporas that have most affected both parts of Ireland. I have both left and never left Ireland. I am a professor of political science best known in my profession for working on power-sharing in deeply divided places. In 2009–11, I was the second person to be the senior advisor on power-sharing in the Standby Team of the Mediation Support Unit of the Department of Political Affairs of the United Nations. My predecessor was my school friend and regular co-author, Belfast-born John McGarry, who is now a Canadian citizen. My professional work on divided places partly stems from my autobiography – I grew up amid three civil wars, in Nigeria, Sudan, and Northern Ireland. I do not claim that arguments on Ireland's reunification are reducible to personal projection or experience, and I do not claim privileged insights, but unlike many Southerners and Northerners I am both, and perhaps that may help me to be read with some sympathy across the island.

Outline of the book

There are eight parts to this book:

- Why we are here
- Lessons from elsewhere
- How reunification may happen
- Models and process
- The government of a united Ireland
- The economics of reunification
- Securing Ireland
- Accommodating diversity

Part One sketches the scene in both parts of Ireland in 2021–22, paying most attention to the North. It explains the revived interest in reunification, why that question will form the political canopy of the rest of the decade, and why 'reunification' is the right word – even if it is not the only word to describe what may be expected. The conjunction of long-run demographic and electoral change and the ramifications of the UK's decision to leave the European Union are emphasized in accounting for the renewed likelihood of reunification.

Part Two asks what we can learn from the failure to reunify Cyprus by referendums in 2004, and from the comparative success of German reunification. The failures and successes of our European neighbours are instructive. We also have lessons to learn from our own pasts. We may make new errors, but we can at least avoid repeating some old ones. Lastly, we can learn from past referendums, including the UK's referendum of 2016. The key lesson is not that there should never be any referendums, but that referendums should have clearly defined outcomes, with credibly clear consequences.

Part Three looks at how reunification may happen – through the referendum process pledged in the Good Friday or Belfast Agreement. It highlights three important but neglected accomplishments of Irish diplomats in the drafting of that agreement, which will have significance in regulating the referendums to come. It sets out what needs to be done by way of preparation, planning, deliberating with mini-forums and citizens' assemblies, and polling – all with as much of an all-party consensus in the South as possible. A Ministry of National Reunification is recommended, as is the formation of a Sovereign Reunification Fund.

Part Four is the most technical part of the book, but it is presented as plainly as possible. What territorial models of Irish reunification are available, and when should these be chosen? Should voters in the Northern referendum know exactly what territorial model of a unified Ireland will emerge if they vote for it? Alternatively, should they vote on principle, for a process – a constitutional convention – that would reshape the island in a fresh start? Each of these key choices has costs and benefits. Much hinges on the answers to these questions, to which my friend,

Mayo-born John Garry,* and I – along with others – have devoted some of our recent attention, and some of our results from deliberative forums are reported in this book. I argue that the two most feasible models of a united Ireland are: (i) one in which Northern Ireland persists as a devolved government inside a united Ireland; and (ii) an integrated Ireland, in which Northern Ireland would no longer exist politically. It is possible to imagine that one model might precede the other, with a transition from one to the other. This part of the book also explains why certain models of our collective future are currently precluded by the Good Friday Agreement, or the Constitution of Ireland, or UK constitutional statutes, and sometimes all three. Bluntly, I argue that, barring radical changes, an independent Northern Ireland, a Confederation of Ireland and Northern Ireland, and repartition are politically impossible, or unwise. I also explain why the sharing of sovereignty over Northern Ireland by the UK and Ireland is increasingly improbable, even if the idea once had merits. Lastly, I explain why federalizing Ireland is increasingly improbable, rather than undesirable. No party with a significant mandate advocates federalization, and there are reasons why Southerners will not wish to risk the stability of the state they have built – they will want to recognize the state they have built in a united Ireland.

Part Five examines the government of a united Ireland. What changes, if any, will be required to the Irish presidency, the Government (the cabinet), the two chambers of the Oireachtas (the parliament), and the courts? Will there be a need to reconstruct local government – and if so, how? What institutions of the Belfast Agreement will persist in a reunified Ireland? Lastly, I will argue that the whole island should consider adopting some of the electoral arrangements developed in Northern Ireland – uniform electoral districts with the single transferable vote, and the d'Hondt method of filling cabinet portfolios. Unification should not be a one-way street: the South can and should learn from the North.

Part Six addresses the economics of reunification. Ireland is much

---

* John McGarry and John Garry are two different but equally likeable people.

better prepared for economic reunification than Germany was in 1990. The Republic is now more prosperous than West Germany was then, and Northern Ireland is more prosperous than was East Germany, and there are net gains to be made from reunification. I suggest that the costs of reunification have been significantly exaggerated, and the benefits understated, and I spell out the implications. This part also addresses the first efforts to model the consequences of Irish reunification, while warning that far greater research and capacity needs to be developed on this subject.

Part Seven is devoted to 'securing' a united Ireland. What has been done and what will need to be done to achieve a legitimate, representative, and effective policing service – or services – in a reunified Ireland? What needs to be done in the decade ahead for Ireland to have defence forces worthy of the name, capable of performing UN, EU, and internal security functions? What needs to be done to end paramilitarism, and to make any loyalist insurrection against Irish reunification unviable?

Part Eight focuses on the critical question of the accommodation of greater diversity – avoiding any coercive assimilation, preventing any regression in the improved rights-cultures in both jurisdictions, and managing fresh challenges to the organization of education, languages, and the coexistence of rival symbols of identity. It pays special attention to what rights, protections, and securities British people in Ireland and cultural Protestants may want – and should have – in a reunified Ireland.

In the conclusion, I address whether Ireland should reunify.

I do not expect anyone to agree with every last suggestion made here. I have, however, made every effort to be factually correct – and will happily accept evidence-based corrections. Above all, I hope to encourage the current and future Governments of Ireland over the next decade to do what is suggested here – prepare properly for the momentous possibility of reunification.

Brendan O'Leary, Cushendall, Galway, and Philadelphia, April 2022

PART ONE

Why We Are Here

1.   Six into twenty-six won't go – or will it?

6 into 26 won't go!

I saw that painted on a Belfast gable wall when I was a boy. Being a competitive little lad, I thought the graffiti author didn't understand fractions. After all, six goes into twenty-six 'four and a third times'. Of course, the statement was not about division, where it may have been correct according to certain schoolteachers, but about partition. The six counties of Northern Ireland could not, would not, and should not fit into the twenty-six counties of the Republic of Ireland. Monarchist, Protestant, English-speaking people could not live in the Republican, Catholic, and Gaelic nation-state. The statement was a slogan – a word derived from the Irish for 'war cry'. It proclaimed an 'impossibility'.

Irish reunification was long deemed impossible. For many it still is, especially because of the long conflict – or war, or 'troubles' – between 1966 and 2005, or 1968 and 1998. The dates and names are contested.[1] Yet reunification is now certainly possible, indeed highly probable, though not inevitable – at least, not yet. But even those who want it to happen are not prepared – at least not adequately prepared, even if they may think otherwise.[2] That includes Fianna Fáil, Fine Gael, Sinn Féin, the SDLP, the Irish Labour Party, the Greens, People Before Profit, and others.

The Government of Ireland Act of 1920, the instrument of partition enacted by the Westminster Parliament, was the most enduring gerrymander of the last century.* With some truculence, Ulster unionists accepted a six-county Northern Ireland, rather than one consisting of all nine counties of Ulster. Their local leaders had made a strategic

---

* To gerrymander is to draw boundaries deliberately to advantage one's own side, and to disadvantage the other. The expression derives from the early American republic. Governor Elbridge Gerry redrew constituency boundaries in Massachusetts in 1812. One looked like a salamander, so 'Gerry's salamander' became 'gerrymander'.

decision. In the words of James Craig, Northern Ireland's first Prime
Minister, they would secure those counties they could control, and
thereby create 'a new and impregnable Pale', behind which loyalists
could withdraw and regroup to maintain the Union with Great Britain.[3]
That control has now been lost, however. The ramparts of the new Pale
are long gone. Unionist control went in 1972 when the London government shut down the Northern Ireland Parliament, which the Ulster
Unionist Party (UUP) had dominated for fifty years. The ramparts
were the Royal Ulster Constabulary (RUC), the armed police force,
and the B Specials, its armed reserve. The former was mostly Protestant; the latter, originally recruited from the Ulster Volunteer Force
(UVF), entirely Protestant.

The most famous Ulster unionist slogan is 'No surrender', still cried
at the annual August and December parades of the Apprentice Boys
over Derry's walls – or Londonderry's.[4] The 'boys' are nowadays mostly
somewhat-matured men. The slogan means no surrender either to Irish
Catholics or to illegitimate British power. There have, however, been
several unionist surrenders – as well as British betrayals. Ulster unionists
parted with their Southern counterparts, who wanted all of Ireland
to remain in the United Kingdom, or in the British Empire, or in the
British Commonwealth. Southern unionists would have settled for
'dominion status' for the entire island in 1917–18 – so that they would
have been part of a larger minority, rather than the small one they
became.[5] They feared an Irish republic, but they did not want partition.
Ulster unionists preferred to leave Southern unionists behind rather
than bolster them in a sovereign united Ireland. As retreating generals
do, they cut their losses.

Ulster unionists had made a solemn covenant on 'Ulster Day' in September 1912. In it, they pledged loyalty to their brothers and sisters
throughout Ulster. The covenant was signed by more than 235,000
men, with a matching declaration signed by nearly the same number of
women. The three counties of Donegal, Cavan, and Monaghan, however,
had large Catholic and nationalist majorities. A nine-county Ulster would
have meant, according to the census of 1911, a Protestant-to-Catholic
ratio of 57 to 43 rather than the 66-to-34 ratio of what became Northern
Ireland. The UUP leadership's 'inner circle' effectively surrendered the

unionists of Donegal, Cavan, and Monaghan to what became the Irish Free State.[6] They might have had all of Ulster, and kept to their covenant, but then their demographic and electoral majority would have been highly unstable, and quickly reversible.

The British coalition government of 1918–22, made up of Conservative Unionists and Liberal Imperialists, and led by David Lloyd George, organized Ulster's 'downsizing'. The Ulster unionist elite were effectively allowed to pick their preferred Northern Ireland: six counties, four with cultural Protestant and Unionist majorities – Antrim, Down, Armagh, and Londonderry – and two without – Fermanagh and Tyrone. Unofficially, unionists would call these six counties 'Ulster'. Officially, UK Governments refused requests to rename Northern Ireland as Ulster, but they had no objections to the naming of the Royal Ulster Constabulary, or later to the Ulster Defence Regiment, or to 'the Ulster Banner'.[7]

Unionist-dominated Ulster is now over. A referendum in the North on Irish unity is likely at the end of this decade, to be followed by one in the South – if the rules of the Good Friday Agreement of 1998 are followed. That is because Northern Ireland's tectonic plates have shifted.[8] Its cultural Catholic population – those who are Catholic or come from a predominantly Catholic family formation – now outnumber cultural Protestants. Since the last quarter of the nineteenth century, such Catholics have mostly voted for nationalist parties with platforms that favour an autonomous or independent and united Ireland. Today, the largest of these parties are Sinn Féin and the Social Democratic and Labour Party (SDLP).[9] Not everyone who votes Sinn Féin or SDLP will vote for Irish reunification, if and when the Northern referendum happens. Like everyone with a vote, they will want to know what is on offer, and what the benefits and costs are – both for themselves and their families and for their peoples. But cultural Catholics will have a choice, and their votes will matter – with increasingly decisive importance over the rest of this decade. By 2030, as I shall try to show, the decision will be theirs to make. The Alliance Party and the Greens, the most significant of the current parties in the Northern Assembly that refuse to register as either nationalists or unionists, and who identify as 'others', also have significant cultural Catholic members and voters; perhaps a majority have that background. Many of these voters will strongly feel the appeal of Irish reunification in a referendum, as will a distinct minority of liberal Protestants who identify with Alliance or the Greens.

The shifting of the demographic tectonic plates

Look at Figure 1.1 in the colour plate section, which contains a series of figures. The lines on the graph show the percentages of the local population of the six counties who identify as Catholic, Protestant and other Christian, other religions, or as 'no religion', or 'not stated', or 'none' over the 150 years since the first regular census. The black bar across the middle marks the 50 per cent line. It is easy to see that the proportion of Catholics in the six counties fell before partition in 1920 – partly because Catholics out-migrated from a hostile Belfast region.[10] It is also easy to see that the proportion of Protestants peaked around World War Two. By 2011, however, Catholics were poised to surpass Protestants in raw numbers, and as this book goes to press almost certainly did so in the past decade. Today, a century after Northern Ireland's invention, its founders' descendants can no longer hold it on the strength of their own numbers.

This change has not occurred because Catholics quickly managed to 'breed' at the rate popes are said to recommend, while Protestants did not. Catholics had a higher average birth rate than Protestants, but that did not matter before 1971–81. Under the domination of the Ulster Unionist Party in the old Stormont parliament between 1920 and 1972, life was significantly more unpleasant, on average, for Catholics than it was for Protestants. And deliberately so. As David Trimble put it, when accepting the Nobel Peace Prize at Oslo with John Hume in December 1998, 'Ulster Unionists, fearful of being isolated on the island, built a solid house, but it was a cold house for Catholics.' Catholics emigrated from this cold house far more than Protestants, proportionally and absolutely. Trimble continued: 'Northern nationalists, although they had a roof over their heads, seemed to us as if they meant to burn the house down.'[11] Whether these fears of combustion were justified, and whether they remain so, is the subject of unresolved controversy. What did end eventually was disproportional Catholic out-migration.

The demographic ratios of the two major groupings changed slowly after 1972, partly because comparative rates of migration changed. Educational reforms by the post-war Labour government in London created a graduate class of Catholics by the 1960s that would spearhead the Northern Ireland civil rights movement. Political reforms made a difference, eventually, after the imposition of direct rule by Great Britain in 1972. So did the MacBride campaign, begun among the Irish diaspora in the United States under the auspices of the former Irish foreign minister, Seán MacBride, which begat the Fair Employment (Northern Ireland) Act of 1989, enacted by Margaret Thatcher's government, to replace the failed act of the same name of 1976.[12] The draft bill was effectively redrafted by Belfast-born legal scholar Professor Christopher McCrudden, then lead advisor on law to Kevin McNamara MP, the British Labour Party's frontbench spokesman on Northern Ireland. The Fair Employment Act proved to be remarkably effective legislation.[13] Among other accomplishments, it made cultural Catholics more likely to stay in Northern Ireland.

Did unionists lose their demographic majority for reasons beyond those of a partly reformed and therefore better Northern Ireland, higher Catholic birth rates, and eventually lower Catholic migration? Other factors have also been suggested. Protestants have been more likely to leave to take university degrees in Great Britain – and not return – especially when university tuition was free. It is a plausible story, but it is difficult to estimate the flows, and their endurance. What is clear is that Northern universities have cultural Catholic pluralities or majorities in their student bodies.[14] Another suggestion is that unionists left disproportionally because of the war officially launched by the Provisional IRA in 1971. That explanation is also difficult to evaluate, and faces a decisive objection: more Catholics died than Protestants in the conflict, proportionally and absolutely, and more violence and injuries took place in Catholic-majority districts of Northern Ireland.[15] So, if violence induced emigration, then, at the margin, Catholics should have been more likely to leave than Protestants. Many Catholics did leave because of violence – by the B Specials, the RUC, the Ulster Defence

Regiment, the British Army, and loyalist militia, as well as violence by republicans on their front doorsteps.

Whatever one's opinions on these contested matters, the two most powerful demographic consequences of the conflict, euphemistically known as 'the troubles', are agreed: the brain drain from all communities; and the reinforcement of voluntary segregation, sometimes because of intimidation.[16] People with skills and higher-education qualifications were more likely to leave, and people who stayed became even more likely to live with their own. Mixed areas became unmixed. Sometimes they were forcibly unmixed. Some remixing is now taking place after twenty-five years of peace.

Figure 1.2 in the plate section returns us to the demographic future. It contrasts the bottom and top of the demographic age-cohorts in Northern Ireland in 2011. Among nearly 125,000 young children aged 4 or under, 50 per cent were Catholic compared to 35 per cent who were Protestant – with a significant number, 14 per cent, of 'none' stated. By contrast, among the elderly who were aged over 85 in 2011, 69 per cent were Protestant and 30 per cent were Catholic.

Figure 1.3 presents a simple visualization of the cumulative advantage cultural Catholics had over cultural Protestants in raw numbers in the 2011 census. As shown, the Catholic cumulative advantage peaks in the cohorts below the age of 40 in 2011, and it declines thereafter, disappearing among the cohorts aged 70 and above.

Barring migratory transformations that none of us have noticed, we know broadly what the demographic picture in 2030 will be. By that date, most of those in the cohorts aged 70+ in 2011 will have died, while those aged 0–19 in 2011 will have joined the eligible electorate, producing a net advantage for cultural Catholics over cultural Protestants across *all* cohorts of voting age, with the possible exception of the over-85s.

The shifting of electoral alignments

The net demographic dominance of cultural Ulster Protestants across *all* adult age-cohorts will therefore be gone in 2030 – give or take a year or two. Unionists' electoral majority has already gone, earlier than some anticipated. Politically there are three minorities in the North – defined as groups which have less than 50 per cent of the vote – namely, unionists, nationalists, and 'others'. Whether there will be a future overall cultural Catholic electoral majority is unclear. It takes time for higher numbers of Catholic children who do not emigrate to show up as higher numbers of voters on electoral registers – eighteen years, in the case of those who were babies in 2011. The rising numbers of 'nones' who do not state their religion – or do not have one – may mean that a formal Catholic electoral majority will never exist. Yet we know from multiple sources, including the census, that high numbers of the 'nones' come from predominantly Catholic backgrounds, as well as from predominantly Protestant backgrounds, so it is reasonable to infer that a de facto cultural Catholic electoral majority will materialize in 2030.

The loss of the unionist electoral majority has partly occurred because significant numbers of liberal Protestants support the Alliance Party. That party used to be unionist with a lower-case 'u', but now it is formally neutral on whether the Union or a united Ireland should prevail. Alliance thereby keeps both cultural Catholics and cultural Protestants among its members and voters. We therefore cannot count Alliance voters as unionist or nationalist without further evidence. How they vote, and how other 'others' vote – notably the supporters of the Greens and the micro-socialist parties, and the children of new immigrants – may be decisive in a future referendum in the North.

Visible evidence of electoral change, partly flowing from demographic change, may be confirmed by looking at the outcome of Westminster elections in Northern Ireland since 1997. Figures 1.4 to 1.7 in the plate section demonstrate the change. Figure 1.4 shows that, in the year before the Good Friday Agreement, unionist parties won thirteen of Northern Ireland's eighteen seats in the Westminster Parliament, including three of the four seats in Belfast. By the 2001 elections, however, the west and south, and the entirety of Northern Ireland's border with independent Ireland, had greened. As Figure 1.5 shows, Sinn Féin won Fermanagh & South Tyrone and West Tyrone, and northern nationalists now held seven of the eighteen seats. Unionists were down to eleven.

The 2010 Westminster elections registered another decisive shift: the near-balancing of the blocs. Figure 1.6 shows that Alliance briefly held a seat in East Belfast after scandals immersed Peter Robinson, the leader of the Democratic Unionist Party (DUP). Belfast had a non-unionist majority of MPs for the first time. The major nationalist and unionist parties won eight seats each. An independent unionist won North Down, and the Ulster Unionist Party, which had founded Northern Ireland, was eliminated from Westminster. Unionists were down to nine seats.

In the 2019 Westminster elections, the results of which are displayed in Figure 1.7, the final blow to unionist pre-eminence was delivered. Nationalists won nine of the eighteen seats, while Alliance took North Down, creating the first-ever non-unionist majority delegation from Northern Ireland at Westminster. Unionists were down to eight seats; the DUP's Westminster parliamentary leader Nigel Dodds lost to John Finucane of Sinn Féin in North Belfast.

Westminster elections take place under the rule of winner-takes-all in single-member districts, so these visual representations of the winning parties are more striking than any visual representations of Northern Ireland Assembly elections would be. In the latter, proportional representation produces multiple winners in each constituency, so change would be less easy to present. But these visualizations exhibit the picture expected by the opening demographic analysis: a less unionist and a less Protestant-dominated electoral scene has been the big-picture story for more than two decades.

Polling evidence consistent with demographic and electoral shifts

The Conservative peer Lord Ashcroft, a unionist and Brexiteer, runs a reputable polling organization. I have selected his most recent poll in Northern Ireland, taken before this book went to press, because it is based on a large sample and cannot be accused of having been conducted with an Irish nationalist or a pro-European agenda. Between 15 and 18 November 2021, Ashcroft's organization ran an online poll of over 3,300 eligible voters in Northern Ireland, weighted to be representative of all adults. The results were striking.[17]

Excluding 'don't knows', the margin in favour of maintaining the Union with Great Britain was 54 per cent, compared to the 46 per cent who favoured a united Ireland. A clear majority affirmed that leaving the EU was not the right decision for Northern Ireland (63 per cent), including one in five of 2017 DUP voters. A full 13 per cent of the poll affirmed they now favoured a united Ireland, after Brexit, having previously favoured staying in the UK (including high proportions of SDLP and Alliance voters), while 9 per cent were now less sure that Northern Ireland should be part of the UK. Two-thirds of respondents thought Brexit had made Irish unification more likely in the foreseeable future – including 49 per cent who thought it was much more likely. More than two-thirds (69 per cent) of current voters in Northern Ireland said there should be a referendum on Irish unification at some point in the future: 85 per cent of those aged 18–24 agreed it should occur, with 72 per cent thinking it should be held within the next ten years.

Any referendum on reunification in 2030 may be decided by the currently undecided. They are, after all, one in ten in Ashcroft's poll. Alliance voters support a united Ireland by 35 per cent to 25 per cent, but the largest portion of them, 40 per cent, 'don't know'. This data is especially interesting. If Alliance, the largest party among the 'others', expands its vote share, especially at the expense of the SDLP, it will be read by many commentators as a fall in support for nationalism – and as making the Union safer. But that would be a premature judgement. The limited evidence suggests Alliance voters are more pro-reunification than they are pro-Union, but that the largest portion of them is undecided – swayable in a referendum. Differently put, the combined Sinn Féin and SDLP vote does not measure the ceiling of support for Irish reunification.

More than a quarter of voters (27 per cent) affirmed that they had changed their mind over whether Northern Ireland should stay in the UK at some juncture, including 16 per cent who had changed their minds more than once. We might label them the 'wobblies' – those with swaying preferences. Therefore the Northern referendum may be decided, according to Ashcroft's poll, by the undecided, Alliance 'don't knows', the wavering wobblies, and especially by women, who reported themselves six times likelier to be undecided compared to men (18 per cent compared to 3 per cent).

Protestants (86 per cent) were more likely than Catholics (64 per cent) to respond that they had never changed their mind about Northern Ireland's position in the UK, but as we have seen, Protestants are the declining demographic grouping. A less Protestant, more undecided, and partially fluid electorate will decide in the decade ahead. For now, however, the currently youngest electoral cohort wants change by a dramatic margin. Those aged 18–24 said they would vote for Irish unification as opposed to the status quo, by a supermajority margin of 71 per cent to 24 per cent. By comparison, among those aged 65 or over, the ratio is 25 per cent to 55 per cent. Expectations have also clearly shifted: 51 per cent responded that a referendum in ten years' time would produce a majority for joining the Republic, whereas 34 per cent disagreed.

Many in Ashcroft's focus groups sensibly affirmed that they would want to be sure of 'the package' before they voted. As one UUP voter put it: 'At the moment I don't think [my generation would] be interested in a united Ireland unless there were more benefits than negatives, regardless of religion.' Fears, however, persist among some Protestants. Another UUP voter said that 'if there was a united Ireland, there would be no Orange Parade, no 12th of July. They would shut Protestant schools. We'd be told to get off the land, they're taking it over. They would make life hell.' In Ashcroft's focus groups, many on all sides felt there was a growing number, particularly among younger voters, who would see a referendum according to 'practicalities' rather than religion, nationality, or tradition – or, as one participant put it, 'some will vote green or orange, but a lot of people will vote with their heads'.[18]

All parties, whether nationalist, unionist, or 'other', do not mobilize all their potential voters in normal elections to Westminster, Stormont, or to local governments in the North. The Northern nationalist vote has sat at around 40 per cent for nearly two decades. It is not fully clear why. Some cultural Catholics likely shifted to voting Alliance, because the SDLP was not viewed as sufficiently socially liberal. Sinn Féin's expansion is definitely hindered by its historic support for the IRA's 'long war'. It must be emphasized that though all elections provide clues as to how a referendum may go in the North, they offer no certainty. The Northern nationalist vote is a proxy, though perhaps an unreliable one, for how voters will decide in a referendum. That is because a much higher turnout can be expected in a referendum than in normal elections. The turnout in the Scottish independence referendum of 2014 was 85 per cent. Turnout will be high in a future Northern referendum, not only because the decision is momentous but because it is likely to be a close result.

Northern nationalists boycotted the first and only previous referendum held on Irish unity in the North, in 1973.[19] Another such boycott could occur if the UK Secretary of State for Northern Ireland calls a referendum when it is not justified. Conversely, unionists or loyalists could boycott a referendum, especially if they think they are certain to lose. The following questions therefore need further thought: when the appropriate time to hold a referendum might be; how to avoid a boycott among those who expect to lose; and what power-sharing 'securities' might be offered so that losing will not devastate the losers.

Whatever your thoughts on these matters, this chapter has demonstrated that it is plausible that a referendum in the North might be called around 2030, and that it is probable that it can be won by non-unionists.

2. The comeback of reunification after 2016

A united Ireland seems a simple concept to understand. The six counties and the twenty-six counties would become a single political unit, under one common sovereign government – six plus twenty-six equals thirty-two – after the agreement of the people of Ireland, North and South, in two referendums. The border created in 1920 would cease to be. The wound of partition would be over. Perhaps that is exactly what will happen, but as we shall see, there is another possibility – namely that Northern Ireland will persist within a united Ireland.

A word to the wise on reunification

'Reunification' is the right word, rather than 'unification', because the two units were created through the British partition of 1920. Some historians – not only unionist or 'revisionist' historians – argue that any future unification would not be reunification. They maintain that Ireland was never previously united – except under the Crown of England, later that of Great Britain, and later still that of Great Britain and Ireland. Relax; deep historical engagement over how unified Ireland was before Strongbow invaded – or was invited in by his collaborators in Leinster – will not be necessary. The short answer is that before the first English colonization started, Ireland was culturally but not politically unified – though state-building projects had begun.[1]

Nor need time be spent here evaluating the precise status of the Kingdom of Ireland before the Union with Great Britain was brought about in 1800 – indeed *bought* about.[2] The Kingdom of Ireland was territorially unified – albeit annexed to the Crown of England since Henry VIII's decree. And it was administered as a unified jurisdiction, with its own partly autonomous parliament.

'Reunification' is the correct legal, political, and historical word because of a different and often forgotten point. Under the provisions of 'the Treaty', or the 'Articles of Agreement for a Treaty', signed in 1921 and ratified in 1922, Great Britain recognized the Irish Free State as a dominion – as a state, domestically sovereign, with the foreign policy powers of Canada. And it recognized it whole, as one unified entity. The Treaty, however, gave the Northern Ireland Parliament the right to opt out, or to secede, from the Irish Free State after Westminster's ratification of the Constitution of the Irish Free State was complete.[3] So, in British law, and in international law – not just in Irish nationalist doctrine – two referendums, North and South, favouring a united sovereign Ireland would reverse partition, and would reunify Ireland. Nevertheless, if you prefer the expression 'unification', a 'united Ireland', or simply 'Irish unity', use these phrases instead.

Yet the yearning for unity partly rests on the idea that there is merit in *re*unifying. The urge recognizes that the peoples on the island, divided by colonial and religious legacies, have much in common, and may have much to gain, jointly, from reorganizing themselves under new auspices. Especially among Northern nationalists, the conviction is widespread that reunification will fully rejuvenate their fellowship within the Irish nation, with which they have a shared ethnic, cultural, and linguistic heritage. Unionists will often argue that they would prefer the reunification of the United Kingdom – through the return of Ireland to the Union. I have heard that response many times, but those same unionists have never gone on to say that Northern Ireland should become part of a restored all-island Kingdom of Ireland. After all, if they want to restore the unity of the UK, then they should favour the reversal of partition.

Reunification should be advanced because it is a good idea, not because it is inevitable or 'natural', though those claims are made – and will continue. It is true that, of the twenty largest islands in the world, there are just three divided by a sovereign border: New Guinea, Borneo, and Ireland. But geographic determinism does not, and should not, drive Irish reunification. The memory of a shared – albeit often divided – past and the prospect of a better joint future are what drives it, and should drive it.

Affirmative referendum results in favour of a united Ireland, in the

North and the South respectively, would restore a politically unified and distinct island-wide polity. Not under the Crown, however. Any role for the Crown and the British royal family would be confined to the Commonwealth, and that in turn would be subject to two provisos: *if* a united Ireland re-joins the Commonwealth, and *if* the British monarch remains its head.* A sovereign, democratic, and secular republic is the widely understood meaning of reuniting Ireland – certainly under Ireland's existing laws. In this expanded republic, there would be no religiously defined citizenship, or religiously defined head of state, and no established religion – unlike the UK, where the monarch cannot be a Catholic and the Church of England remains established.

The entire territory of Ireland (including its immediately adjacent small islands), as well as its territorial waters, would be united under the sovereign authority of its people. No sovereign border would cross the island, or its seas. Ireland would be one self-governing jurisdiction, fully free to organize its own internal jurisdictions – which could include keeping Northern Ireland as a devolved unit of government. The United Kingdom of Great Britain would be Ireland's neighbour, unless Scotland secedes from Great Britain. In that case, a united Ireland would have two neighbours, Scotland and England (incorporating Wales), and Great Britain would displace Ireland as one of the three top-twenty largest islands in the world that are divided into more than one state.

Last, but not least, a reunited Ireland would be *doubly* reunited. The South and North would be reunited as one Ireland: reunification one. But something novel would also happen – Northern Ireland would reunify fully within the European Union, this time as part of a different member-state: reunification two.

The Good Friday Agreement: mixed outcomes

It is now almost a quarter of a century since 10 April 1998, the morning the text of the Good Friday Agreement was agreed in multi-party and intergovernmental negotiations. The Agreement was finalized in

* See Chapter 24, pp. 268 ff.

Belfast, but negotiations had taken place in Dublin and London, and informally in Washington, DC. Though made in all these places, the UK Government and unionists called it the 'Belfast Agreement' because that is where the text took final form. I recall the moment vividly. Expected to be delivered on Thursday 9 April, deadlines were extended, and I continued broadcasting throughout the night and the following morning on the BBC World Service, well informed by contacts or friends in most parties and in both the British and Irish governments. As dawn broke over Belfast, it was easy to predict that the Agreement would be called the 'Good Friday Agreement'.

A light snow blew over the face of the UUP leader David Trimble as he began a defensive justification of the Agreement outside the Stormont parliament building. Though he should have been proud and happy, he was all to the contrary. His party delegation had split. Jeffrey Donaldson had walked out over the arrangements on prisoner releases, and doubts over whether the decommissioning of weapons would be required before republicans could participate in the new executive.

Earlier in the year, Ian Paisley Jr had told me, off-air, that he expected an agreement to be reached, which the DUP would oppose. He said that his father's party would focus on planning to defeat any agreement that would follow, not by winning an overall 'No' vote in the pledged referendum but by winning a majority of 'No' voters among Protestants. The DUP, he told me, would demand major revisions to the forthcoming agreement, not its complete destruction. Its goal would be to displace the UUP as the leading party of unionism. I recall that interaction not to show that Paisley Jr, like his father, has significant political realism and skill beneath the characteristic public bluster. Rather, the story warns us that any political agreement, including a future agreement on reunification, will be challenged by its prospective losers, who will seek to reshape whatever has been agreed – or to destroy it. The Good Friday Agreement (GFA) was targeted by the DUP for renegotiation even before it was signed, and it has remained the constant object of attempted renegotiation, rather like the more recently negotiated Protocol, which is intended to stabilize the GFA.

The political settlement of 1998 created new power-sharing institutions, in the three strands within which they were negotiated – namely, across the North, North–South, and East–West.[4] The peace process ended substantive armed conflict. It brought eventual demilitarization of the border and troop withdrawal by the British Army; eventual decommissioning of paramilitary weapons by the IRA, and by some loyalists; the release of paramilitary prisoners on licence; eventual reform of policing and the administration of justice; eventual substantive disbanding of the IRA; and an array of pledges on rights, safeguards, reconciliation, and the treatment of the victims of conflict. That last sentence is littered with 'eventual' to recall the slow and distrust-laden pace of implementation, and the last clause emphasizes *pledges* rather than *delivered outcomes*.

Simply put, neither the political settlement nor the peace process has been completely successful, or fully implemented. Jointly, however, they have delivered a radical improvement in public life, with mostly peaceful politics, albeit with a negative rather than a positive peace.[5] Excessive ingratitude or cynicism about the GFA is inappropriate, but uncritical admiration is not sustainable.

Seventeen years later, Northern Ireland had a peaceful Assembly election in 2016 with a low turnout. Sinn Féin and the DUP were returned as the leading parties of nationalism and unionism respectively. The political temperature was calm and unexcited. Political momentum on shared commitments was stalled, but it was hard to argue that 'the system' was in complete crisis. Within a year, however, the Assembly would be dissolved, after Martin McGuinness resigned from the deputy first ministership – precipitating a fresh election in March 2017 in which, on a much higher turnout, the DUP was nearly beaten by Sinn Féin in the competition for first place, in votes and seats, and unionists lost their political majority.

At the time the DUP was entrapped in a corruption scandal mostly of its own making. 'Ash for Cash' was the memorable name given to the renewable heating initiative approved by First Minister Arlene Foster in her previous ministerial portfolio.[6] But while the Ash for Cash scandal was the immediate precipitant of the breakdown in cooperation between Martin McGuinness and Arlene Foster, it was the European question which disrupted the sustained cooperation between their parties that had formally commenced in 2007. That may not have been inevitable, but the DUP made fateful choices in and after 2016.

The European question

The outcome of the 2016 referendum on UK membership of the European Union was largely driven by English voters,[7] but it overtly and vividly revived the question of Irish reunification. The project of reunification had never gone away, however. Reunification was provided for in the text of the Good Friday Agreement, which could not have been made, let alone ratified, without these provisions. Yet much of the focus of political life in Northern Ireland between 1999 and 2015 had been on establishing and stabilizing the new Northern institutions, and on implementing agreements arising from commitments given – or failing to implement them.[8]

The claim that but for 'Brexit' the issue of reunification would have remained dormant is not credible. Recall the demographic and electoral data in the previous chapter. Reunification would have incrementally suggested itself in this decade under all scenarios. Both Sinn Féin and the SDLP still proudly affirmed reunification as their goal, even if their attention was elsewhere during the eighteen years focused on the implementation of the GFA. Moreover, how the DUP had played its political hand in 2006–15 had begun to irritate nationalist patience with the status quo, while also frustrating the 'others'.

Quite simply, the UK referendum on EU membership brought reunification loudly back onto the political agenda because the result threatened to destabilize the GFA, and because, for nationalists, reunification became a solution to a new problem – Brexit – not just the old ones (partition, and the perceived and actual resistance of the DUP to egalitarian power-sharing). Reunification would mean rejoining the EU, not just reunifying the island.

The new world opened up by the UK's referendum result was appreciated in the Dublin government, which had been better prepared for Brexit than Whitehall and Westminster. An early prudent step into the future was taken by Irish Taoiseach Enda Kenny in late April 2017, just before negotiations between the UK and the EU began. At his initiative, the European Council of heads of states and governments formally agreed in their minutes that, in the event of Irish reunification, Northern Ireland would automatically return fully to the European Union.[9]

In the June 2016 referendum, the UK as a whole voted to leave by 52 per cent to 48 per cent, but Northern Ireland voted to remain by a more significant margin: 56 per cent to 44 per cent. The local result strongly suggested that the remain/leave division within Northern Ireland significantly coincided with the nationalist/unionist or cultural Catholic/cultural Protestant division, but not completely. Every Westminster constituency in Northern Ireland which had previously had a nationalist majority backed remain by over 8,000 votes. Remain's lowest margin of victory within safe majority-nationalist seats was in Fermanagh & South Tyrone (59 to 41 per cent). Remain won both swing seats in Belfast – comfortably in Belfast South, but by a whisker in Belfast North. All Westminster constituencies on the border voted to remain, as did urban voters in Belfast as a whole and in Derry. Strikingly, two of the then nine safest unionist constituencies voted remain: North Down and East Londonderry. The first has the lowest share of Catholics, the second may slowly be becoming a marginal seat. The leave side prevailed in two of the safe unionist constituencies by just over 500 votes. Differently put, nationalists were more solidly in favour of remain than unionists were in favour of leave.

This referendum result was replicated in both the European Parliament election of May 2019 and the Westminster election of December 2019. The combined vote in the latter election of the largest remain parties – Sinn Féin, Alliance, the SDLP, and the Greens – constituted 55 per cent. Remain MPs are currently a majority of Northern Ireland's Westminster delegation: ten out of eighteen. Nationalists, however, continue to punch underweight at Westminster. As long as MPs must take an oath of allegiance to the Crown to take their seats it seems unlikely that Sinn Féin will fully participate in that body, though that party has been burning many of its sacred cows since 1986.

The Alliance winner in North Down in 2019 was Stephen Farry, a cultural Catholic in a constituency with few Catholics – evidence of hostility to Brexit among unionists who are prosperous and educated professionals. Less noticed, in Lagan Valley the vote share of the incumbent MP, Jeffrey Donaldson, fell by 16.4 percentage points. Surging into second place behind him was the Alliance Party's Sorcha Eastwood, improving her party's previous performance by 17.7 percentage points. She too is a cultural Catholic. These contests demonstrated a significant swing to the pro-European Alliance among cultural Protestant voters. One question ahead is whether socially liberal Protestant remainers and socially liberal cultural Catholic remainers, who currently back parties designated as 'others' (notably Alliance and the Greens), will move jointly to favour Irish reunification within the European Union. If they do move in that direction, the pressure to hold a referendum on reunification will materialize sooner than many commentators currently expect.

In the UK's 2016 referendum, the Democratic Unionist Party, then the largest unionist party, endorsed Brexit. No other major party in the North did. The DUP's MPs at Westminster nevertheless eventually, and deliberately, chose to support a 'hard Brexit': a total withdrawal from the EU's institutions – its parliament, its court, its commission, and its ministerial councils – *and* its treaties and policies, especially the customs union and single market. A hard Brexit would automatically mean a new customs and regulatory border between the UK and the European Union. The DUP claimed it did not want a hard land border recreated on the island of Ireland, but then deliberately acted to promote that goal by refusing all 'soft exits' that would have kept the UK aligned with the EU in ways that would have avoided the need for regulatory or customs borders. Along with the Brexiteers in England, the DUP suggested that novel technologies – falsely claimed to be in active operation elsewhere – would resolve any teething problems. These 'alternative arrangements' were correctly diagnosed as 'unicorns' and dismissed by the Government of Ireland, and the European Union, and eventually by the UK Government. Special arrangements would, however, be required for Northern Ireland if restoring a hard border on the island were to be avoided.

The DUP had an opportunity to promote a softer UK exit from the EU, including full UK alignment with EU customs and regulatory policies, which would have avoided the need for any hardening of the border between the UK and the EU. From the summer of 2017 until the summer of 2019, a weakened Theresa May had a supply and confidence agreement with the DUP to support her government because it lacked a parliamentary majority. However, the DUP's MPs chose to go with the hardest Brexiteers and later to align themselves with Boris Johnson, who promptly betrayed them, making the Protocol with the EU – having agreed its substance with the then Irish Taoiseach, Leo Varadkar. He did so to 'get Brexit done'.

Brexit meant Brexit, not UKexit

'Brexit', initially, was a mistaken abbreviation, a misnomer.[10] The United Kingdom of Great Britain and Northern Ireland is the UK's full title. 'Britain' is not an accurate synonym for the UK. Great Britain is not the UK, period; it is the bigger part of the UK, Northern Ireland the smaller. The UK has two unions: the Union of Great Britain and the Union of Great Britain with Northern Ireland. Northern Ireland has very many British people in it, but it is not formally British – by name, by legal jurisdiction, or by geography. It is not 'Little Britain', though some unionists would like it to be. Yet, as it turns out, Brexit is what has happened, not a complete UKexit.

In the negotiations over the UK's withdrawal from the European Union, it was agreed in a Protocol – a legal text annexed to the UK's withdrawal treaty with the EU – that Northern Ireland would remain within the regulatory structure of the European single market for goods and agriculture.[11] While legally Northern Ireland would be part of the UK's customs union, for practical purposes it would remain within the European customs union for goods and agriculture because the UK–EU customs border would be administered at ports on the Irish Sea and the North Channel – and at airports. That is, at the boundary between Great Britain and Northern Ireland. UK officials would administer EU customs rules there. The Protocol also creates a novel process of consent: the Northern Assembly may vote to maintain the Protocol in 2024, for four or eight years, depending upon the level of support. If the Assembly votes to terminate the Protocol, it can only vote against

Articles 5 through 12, which deal with the substance of customs and single market regulations. That would set in motion fresh negotiations for their replacement, to be completed in 2026.[12]

The outcome of the protracted negotiations between 2017 and 2020 is simple to summarize: Great Britain is fully out of the European Union's authority, but Northern Ireland is not.* But behind that apparently simple statement lie layers of legal and bureaucratic complexity. The Protocol may be fairly described as a Heath Robinson or Rube Goldberg construction. It is highly elaborate machinery designed to achieve a simple objective: protecting the gains of the Good Friday Agreement.[13] Its critics say it violates the GFA. It does not; it was designed not to do that. What it does do, however, is add fresh layers of complex power-sharing to Northern Ireland's existing power-sharing arrangements. The UK Government and the European Commission now share authority in a Joint Committee that oversees the implementation of the Protocol. The EU must, however, be able to monitor the UK's compliance in order to secure the regulatory standards of the single market, which the UK has left. EU law still applies in Northern Ireland, along with UK and devolved law – what Gordon Anthony calls 'legal hybridity'.[14] This remarkable negotiating outcome is not yet stabilized, and it may become a pivot point towards reunification.

The Protocol does not create, or recognize, an economically united Ireland – except in electricity production and distribution. Tax regimes – income taxes, VAT rates, and corporation taxes – remain different on both sides of the land border across Ireland. Neither public nor private services – such as banking, insurance, or digital database storage – are covered by the Protocol. But the Protocol creates incentives for manufacturing and agri-food companies, domestic and foreign, to treat the island as a single regulatory unit. Northern Ireland, in principle, could have the best of both worlds: 'double market access' to Great Britain *and* to the European Union, which may appeal to local and foreign investors. Double export market access, but not 'double import' freedom. The Protocol creates new import barriers for

---

* Great Britain remains bound, however, by Part Two of its Withdrawal Agreement with the EU, which deals with citizens' rights.

Northern Ireland. Goods, plants, animals, and foods exported from Great Britain to Northern Ireland must comply with EU standards. Not because the EU has created new standards, but because Great Britain refuses to align with EU standards in future. Exporters from Great Britain must declare whether the final location of the goods is Northern Ireland (customs free), or whether they go to the European Union (liable to customs).

Table 2.1 sketches four scenarios, which deliberately simplify future possibilities in the decade ahead. They take the survival of the Protocol and some of the institutions of the GFA to be open questions. In the first scenario, the most benign, both the Northern Ireland Assembly and the Protocol function from late 2022 onwards. The EU and the UK resolve their difficulties in the implementation of the Protocol. Unionists, chastened by modest losses in the Assembly election of 2022, proclaim victory, live with the Protocol, and work the institutions. This scenario might put Northern Ireland on a benign glide path towards reunification referendums around 2030. Unionists might hope that if both the institutions and the Protocol are working, and if Northern Ireland is prospering – at least comparatively – then they could win the first referendum. Nationalists, by contrast, might hope that, having

Institutional possibilities	*The Northern Assembly and the GFA bodies function*	*The Northern Assembly and the GFA bodies do not function*
The Protocol functions	*Scenario 1* The NIA & Protocol both function GLIDE PATH to reunification referendums in 2030	*Scenario 2* The NIA does not function, but the Protocol does ROCKY ROAD to reunification referendums while UK direct rule is restored until 2030
The Protocol does not function	*Scenario 3* The NIA functions, but the Protocol does not; the NIA votes down the Protocol in 2024 ROCKY ROAD renegotiations commence under the shadow of reunification referendums in 2030	*Scenario 4* Neither the NIA nor the Protocol functions VERY ROCKY ROAD hard border has to be restored; UK–EU trade war if Protocol unilaterally ended by UK

Table 2.1: Four scenarios for the mid to late 2020s

proved that Northern Ireland is more prosperous largely outside the UK's internal market, the economic case for reunification will have been established. The unfolding of this scenario is in the best interests of responsible Irish and British governments, and the EU.

In the second scenario, the Protocol functions but some of the GFA institutions do not. This scenario would most likely occur after the EU and the UK have settled their differences on implementing the Protocol, but in circumstances where the DUP and/or other unionist parties refuse to go into the Executive. This refusal might occur because unionists cannot yet countenance a Sinn Féin First Minister, or/and because they continue to insist that the Protocol should be scrapped. Loyalist direct action may drive unionist politicians towards this stance in order to keep their supporters content. This scenario might also unfold *after* the Northern Ireland Assembly votes in favour of renewing the Protocol in 2024. In most run-throughs of this scenario, British direct rule would be restored, at least de facto. That would mean that any reunification referendums would occur without the key institutions of the GFA working – the Assembly and the North South Ministerial Council. In this scenario, a UK Government might be tempted to hold an early referendum – if only to legitimize direct rule.

If unionists are the primary aggrieved and alienated party in the second scenario, the tables would be turned in the third scenario. Here the institutions would continue to function, but the Northern Ireland Assembly would vote down the Protocol in 2024 – a scenario that is likely only if sufficient Alliance MLAs vote with all the unionist parties to do so. In this admittedly currently unlikely scenario, the Protocol would not immediately come to an end, with a reversion to the status quo. By treaty and by law, the Protocol would continue for a further two years, until 2026, while negotiations on alternatives to parts of the Protocol would continue – between the UK, the EU, and the affected parties. Nationalists and the Government of Ireland would adamantly resist a restoration of a hard border on the island, and likely become more enthusiastic for early reunification referendums.

In the last scenario, neither the Northern Assembly nor the Protocol functions successfully after late 2022. An early breakdown of the Protocol could occur because of a unilateral UK decision to suspend or terminate it – taken by Brexiteers in the London government, with the support of unionists. In this world, unionists might refuse to enable the Assembly or the Northern Ireland Executive to function – to avoid a vote on the Protocol in 2024. A trade war between the UK and the EU cannot be ruled out if this scenario unfolds – one in which Ireland would be obliged to defend the EU's single market and customs union, and perhaps restore customs and regulatory controls on the border with Northern Ireland against its will. In this scenario, an outraged nationalist population, along with some of the others, may well demand early reunification referendums, with support from across the border.

Judging possibilities

Given the number of governments and political agencies involved, and their abilities to shift tactics and strategies, I would be a fool to predict precisely what will happen, though I have suggested broad future paths that could be either benign or rockier. What can be said is that unionists face riskier horizons than nationalists. If they try to break both the GFA and the Protocol they could precipitate early referendums, which they might lose because they would be held responsible for pushing cultural Catholics into a corner.

The novel special arrangements of the Protocol clearly stick in the throats of activist loyalists and unionists. They are read as detaching Northern Ireland from Great Britain by a sea border, which they partly do. Unionist politicians chose not to see them as an economic opportunity, though Arlene Foster briefly seemed minded to do so.[15] Unionists are hardly consoled when so many Irish nationalists agree with them. Baroness Kate Hoey, Jim Allister, Jeffrey Donaldson, and many other unionists also claim that the Protocol violates the Good Friday Agreement and the UK constitution. These claims, however, are simply untrue, as Justice Adrian Colton declared in June 2021 when finding against the baroness and the leaders of all the unionist parties in a case before the Belfast High Court,[16] a decision unanimously upheld by the Northern Ireland Court of Appeal in February 2022.[17] Whether unionists continue to flirt with extra-constitutional fire remains to be seen. If they do, however, it will hardly build support for their cause in Great Britain. As I write, the DUP and TUV (Traditional Unionist Voice) are demanding that the UK Government repudiate two international treaties shortly after they have come into force – and want the UK to risk a trade war with the EU in order to impose their minority preferences on Northern Ireland. Otherwise, they say, they will refuse the devolutionary settlement which they negotiated in 1998 and renegotiated in 2006.

Symptoms of political morbidity within Ulster unionism

The Protocol has destabilized Northern Protestant cohesion. Liberal Protestants who supported remaining in the European Union, but not necessarily Irish reunification, now have the Alliance Party as their principal political outlet. Alliance, with a popular leader, Naomi Long, is currently happy to make the Protocol work. The DUP, by contrast, is campaigning to scrap it, with an unstable leadership. The party has had four leaders in six years: Peter Robinson, Arlene Foster, Edwin Poots, and Jeffrey Donaldson. Jim Allister's TUV, the faction which broke away from the DUP because Ian Paisley agreed to share power with Sinn Féin after the St Andrews Agreement of 2006, advocates non-compliance with the Protocol by unionist ministers. That is, the TUV favours civil disobedience and treaty-breaking – as do some loyalist paramilitaries.

Meanwhile, the UUP, the second-ranked unionist party in electoral support when the referendum was held in 2016, has performed a partial volte-face. It has had three leaders since 2017: Robin Swann, Steve Aiken, and Doug Beattie. Having been in favour of remaining in the EU, it has accepted that withdrawal from the EU has happened and suggests that all must now live with Brexit. It too is attacking the Protocol, though in a more measured manner, and it (correctly) blames the DUP for the Protocol as much as Boris Johnson's government.

As I write, the latest DUP leader, Jeffrey Donaldson, has obliged his party's First Minister to resign, thereby disabling the Northern Executive and partly paralysing the Assembly. A fresh Northern Assembly election is scheduled for May 2022. Unionists with a capital 'U' will go into these elections with a precarious political plurality, but whether they will retain it remains to be seen.

Over the coming decade, we will learn whether nationalists will edge ahead as the leading bloc, or whether the 'others' will expand at the expense of both unionists and nationalists. Will Northern Ireland journey towards ratios of 50:30:20 among nationalists, unionists, and others respectively, or rather towards 35:35:30? Or somewhere in between? These are open questions, including whether the nationalist bloc expands. They will be decided partly by the political skills of the respective party leaderships.

Will Sinn Féin, as seems likely, win the right to nominate the First Minister, having become the largest political party in seats won? Can Alliance move decisively ahead of the ageing SDLP? To whom will voters give their transfers? Is it possible that both nationalists and unionists will lose support to the 'others'? Can the UUP recover its former status as the leading party of unionism? Will Allister's voters transfer their ballot papers to the DUP? Some of these questions will have been decided by the time this book is published, but the exact answers do not matter for our purposes. The fact these questions are being posed shows that the political equilibrium of 2005–15 is over, partly because the DUP's risk-taking has damaged its standing.

Going forward, Ulster unionists, of all varieties, desperately need allies. Their core voters are older than those of their nationalist rivals. To win a future referendum on the status of Northern Ireland, unionists need to keep existing cultural Catholic support for the Union with Great Britain, and then to win *increasing* support for that idea among cultural Catholics as the leading and advancing demographic category in the electorate. They would also benefit from support among new minorities – from the South Asian, Brazilian, Caribbean, Chinese, Lithuanian, and Polish diasporas – and their children, who may acquire UK or Irish citizenship, or both. Otherwise, unionists will lose the coming referendum.

I am suggesting that unionists' future is mostly slipping from their hands. 'Not an inch' and 'This we will maintain' lack 'staunch' conviction. The current strategy of unionist politicians, if 'strategy' is the right word, has worsened their prospects of reaching out and building alliances beyond their historic core.[18] Their actions over the European question and the Protocol have been counterproductive: aversion therapy for the Union with Great Britain. They have also done little to accommodate new minorities – the new Northern Irish. The converse would be more accurate: loyalist militias have frequently displayed racist or religious contempt for the newcomers.

Unionists, in short, give every sign of being in an advanced state of political decay, on top of their declining demographic and electoral base. In this century they have lost their local majority in elections to Westminster, the Northern Ireland Assembly, and Belfast city – the city founded by Protestants and built by Presbyterians. The DUP hitched a ride with English nationalists to reduce the sharing of sovereignty over the island of Ireland, a project that has backfired for them – at least for now. Northern Protestants divided over the European Union in ways that may have given a long-term boost to the Alliance Party, though that is not certain. What is certain is that unionists are in danger of losing their liberals, their graduates, and their professionals to Alliance.

Cultural Protestants are divided across four principal parties; cultural Catholics across three. The competition among the DUP, the UUP, and the TUV is set to make Sinn Féin the largest political party in upcoming Assembly elections. Calls for pan-unionist unity seem unlikely to succeed. Each of these unionist parties is remarkably small in formal membership. Their joint future is not bright as they scramble for leadership of their bloc. One of these three parties is likely to die; the question is which one.

Loyalist militias no longer look like plausible vanguards of future military resistance to a united Ireland. Rather, they advertise the symptoms of the organic decay of the unionist bloc. The failure to police these criminal militia out of existence speaks poorly of British policymakers, and of the devolved administration of justice and policing since 2010. The ever-larger July bonfires, overseen by these militias, seem like a metaphor for unionist anxiety and decline. Culturally brutal, hazards to life and limb and the built environment, these bonfires are designed to be burned by loyalists. Their collapse is expected, and endangers those who build them.

Irish reunification, however, cannot and should not simply rest on the organic decay and political disarray of Ulster unionism, or casual assumptions about loyalist militias, or presumptions of growth in the nationalist bloc that may not be fulfilled. Reunification should offer a positive fresh start for all, a reset on our island, an opportunity for joint renewal of our institutions, our relationships, our policies, our international alliances, our economic, cultural, and social policies, our freedoms, and our rights. In later chapters we shall come to that appealing vista, which need not be visionary, but first we should look elsewhere for guidance.

PART TWO

Lessons from Elsewhere

3.   The failed reunification of Cyprus

When faced with any political question, it is useful to think comparatively. There have, however, been few in-depth studies of unifications after partitions.[1] The most useful comparative cases for our subject are democratic reunifications within the context of European integration. There have only been two so far: the failed reunification of Cyprus, and the successful reunification of Germany. Before we look at these cases, a word of warning about partitions and their aftermaths.

British colonial administrators and politicians discussed and implemented two major partitions: in Ireland (1911–25); and in India (1940–47). The partition of India was extraordinarily bloody and involved three sub-partitions: of Punjab, Kashmir, and Bengal.[2] Subsequently, three major successor wars have been fought between India and Pakistan, while a fourth was avoided through US mediation in 1999. British colonial administrators and politicians also discussed and considered partitioning Mandatory Palestine (1937),[3] but they quit Palestine and left its formal partition to the young United Nations – and to war, many wars. Since 1948, Israel has fought eight wars and faced at least two Palestinian insurrections (intifadas). Fiercely contested projects to reunify Palestine continue: the Palestinian version would abolish Israel; the Israeli version would annex the entirety of the West Bank and dispense with the Palestinian Authority. There is no significant political project to reunify South Asia, and Kashmir remains politically and militarily disputed.[4] Not much positive instruction from the aftermath of these partitions is available for our island, at least for now.[5] Indeed, they may suggest that partition is not generally justified because, thus far, it has led to more violence than it was proposed to avoid, as was true in Ireland – though, fortunately, the absolute levels of collective violence experienced here were on a lower scale.

India and Palestine may suggest the irreversibility or impossibility of unification after partition. Yet, it is not so. There have been unifications after partitions. Germany reunified at lightning speed in 1990. Vietnam reunified through military force after the American exit from South Vietnam in 1973. Unification by conquest, as in Vietnam, provides no desirable role model for us to follow.* Korea was partitioned in 1945. The Japanese surrendered to the Americans below the 38th parallel; the Soviets and the Korean Communist Party took power above it. No one doubts that Korea would rapidly reunify if the despotic Kim dynasty, dressed in a Leninist shroud, were to collapse in the North. The Republic of Korea (South Korea) has a Ministry of Unification and a specialist unit on women's affairs, two good Korean ideas worth importing to Ireland.[6]

Reunification after a complete political collapse of Northern Ireland cannot be ruled out, but it seems unlikely. The bewildering incompetence of the Johnson government may encourage the successful secession of Scotland from Great Britain, but the subsequent utter collapse of the North would still be unexpected.† It seems improbable that politicians from Great Britain will simply quit Northern Ireland, as their precursors quit Palestine. After all, they fought a thirty-year war, which the British Army called 'Operation Banner', to avoid doing just that. Improbable, but not beyond the bounds of possibility: British derelictions have happened, in Palestine and India. So the Irish, North and South, need to be ready for the possibility of British, especially English, irresponsibility. It is in our collective interests, South and North, that any reunification be orderly, and carried out with the cooperation of a responsible British Government (or its English successor). Complacency is not an option. Preparing for the possibility of a disorderly collapse and/or a chaotic British withdrawal is essential. With luck, such contingency planning won't be needed, but we shouldn't gamble on our luck.

* See Chapter 5, p. 69.
† England and Wales would be the successor state sovereign over Northern Ireland if Scotland seceded from Great Britain.

The story of a failed reunification

In April 2004, the Annan Plan to reunify Cyprus, organized under the auspices of the then Secretary-General of the United Nations, went to a referendum in the Republic of Cyprus, the internationally recognized sovereign authority of the whole island. Technically it was put to two referendums, one in each community, not to two separate territorial entities, but in practice it was the latter. 'Southern Cyprus', mostly Greek Cypriot, has been controlled by the Republic of Cyprus's government since Turkey partitioned the island by force in 1974, while the so-called Turkish Republic of Northern Cyprus, mostly Turkish Cypriot, was created after that partition. So-called, because that republic is recognized only by Turkey.

Remarkably, 'Northern Cyprus' voted 'Yes' to the Annan Plan, even though its citizens would constitute roughly just over two in every seven persons in a reunified Cyprus: 65 per cent of them voted in favour. They particularly liked the prospect of joining the European Union, and the constitutional securities they were pledged. Equally stunningly, Greek Cypriots voted 'No': 76 per cent preferred to render the Annan Plan 'null and void'. The turnout was extraordinary: 89 per cent in Greek Cyprus, 88 per cent in Turkish Cyprus, practically a full turnout when we consider the very aged, the infirm, and those who don't care – who exist in every political system.

The question, which both communities voted on in their respective languages, was as follows: 'Do you approve the Foundation Agreement with all its Annexes, as well as the constitution of the Greek Cypriot/Turkish Cypriot State and the provisions as to the laws to be in force, to bring into being a new state of affairs in which Cyprus joins the European Union united?'[7] Clearly it was a complicated question, on a detailed plan: note the reference to all those annexes. That was the exact question, as phrased in English. I am told it did not read any easier or more elegantly in Greek or Turkish.[8]

The two referendum votes took place simultaneously, perhaps influenced by the procedure for ratifying the Good Friday Agreement in 1998.[9] Cypriots were formally voting to reunify as a two-unit federation, and in effect to endorse three constitutions: that of a unified Cyprus and of the two entities of which it would be composed. The Annan Plan on which they were simultaneously voting would have preserved some of the laws and treaties of the Republic of Cyprus, and, in effect, offered the provisions of a peace treaty, which included possible settlements of compensation and property disputes created by expulsions and flights. The plan would also have taken (a reunified) Cyprus into the European Union. The new state of affairs would replace the older Republic of Cyprus and the so-called Turkish Republic of Northern Cyprus. That was a reasonable conclusion, even if it was not exactly stated as such. Partition would technically have been over.

There are some clear lessons for our future selves from this failed reunification project. A carefully negotiated unification plan, even one supervised by the United Nations, may be rejected by the people of one of the prospective partners. Such a plan may not survive a referendum campaign, especially when the downsides of reunification may be described with some accuracy. Holding both referendums on the same day may have costs, because each partner is voting 'blind', uncertain whether the other will accept the compromise package. Ambiguities in a negotiated text can have negative consequences. Turkish Cypriots believed they were voting to join the European Union. Greek Cypriots believed that all of Cyprus would legally accede to the European Union, irrespective of the outcome of the referendum, and that if they joined as they were – as the Republic of Cyprus – then European Union law would formally apply throughout the island.[10] Many of them considered their state a success, and vehemently disliked the idea of abolishing it, especially if the new state came with very strong power-sharing provisions, in which the Turkish Cypriots, believed to be puppets of the Turkish government, would have a veto over Cypriot foreign policy and over constitutional change.

Greek Cypriots voted 'No' to the Annan Plan for these and many other reasons, including their conviction that there could be a better negotiated plan in future. In particular, they objected to voting rights being extended to Turkish settlers – illegal immigrants under international law, brought over by Turkey after 1974 to consolidate the new Turkish entity. Greek Cypriots regarded as unjust the absence of any plan for the repatriation of these settlers. They feared there would be no obstacles to further Turkish settlers coming to the island. Above all, Greek Cypriots rejected provisions allowing for a continuing Turkish military presence on the island, which would violate the sovereignty of an independent Cyprus. They disliked the presence of Turkish troops, who had bloodily executed the partition of 1974, and they also disliked the 1960 Treaty of Guarantee, which the decolonizing UK, Greece, and Turkey had signed, and under which Turkey claimed the right of intervention on the island. Equally, they objected intensely to the stake that Turkey and Britain (through its so-called sovereign bases) might acquire in natural resources in Cypriot territorial waters.

Greek Cypriots were also not enthusiastic about the power-sharing arrangements in the Annan Plan. Legally, they resented the idea of a Supreme Court based on parity of judges from the two new constituent entities – with three foreign judges likely holding the casting votes.[11] Parity in decision-making power for a minority of one in four, based on historic citizens, or for a minority of over two in seven, if the illegal settlers were to become citizens, strongly clashed with the principle of proportionality: one person, one vote of equal value. Nevertheless, the power-sharing provisions would have been acceptable to most Greek Cypriots had the Turkish troops and bases been withdrawn, the right of Turkish intervention voided, and had there been a satisfactory settlement of property disputes and a fair line of division between the two entities.

Greek Cypriots feared that the settlement might in effect render European Union law void, at least for a period, regarding freedom of movement and property rights.[12] This prospect would prevent Greek Cypriots from repopulating the North and acquiring fresh property in that location. At least for a while, the obvious consequences of partition could continue. Symbolically, there would be no acknowledgement, let alone atonement, by Turkey for the loss of lives and forced expulsion that accompanied partition.[13] Complex quotas for 'returns' did not satisfy Greek Cypriots. Any compensation for the victims of partition would come through the treasury of a reunited Cyprus, not from Turkey. Since Greek Cypriots were significantly richer than Turkish Cypriots, this prospect felt like Greek Cypriots compensating themselves for human rights violations by the Turkish government and army. No wonder the Greek Cypriots voted 'No'. What is surprising is how many voted 'Yes', presumably in the conviction that reunification would get better over time.

Could the island of Ireland repeat the Cypriot pattern, with the North voting 'Yes' and the South voting 'No' to reunification? The answer must be 'yes', but it is much less likely in our case. To begin with, according to the Good Friday Agreement, voters will vote on making a 'sovereign united Ireland'.[14] A sovereign Ireland could not have British military bases – even if a British Government raised the demand – unless the Irish Government agreed, which it would not, if it had any interest in keeping office.

We no longer have a current settler-colonial question. The settlers of British origin arrived in Ulster in the seventeenth and eighteenth centuries, not in living memory as in the Cypriot case, and no serious Irish party or politician disputes the rights of their descendants to vote as equals in an exercise of Irish self-determination, North and South. Since the late eighteenth century, Irish independence and republican political projects have supported uniting all under common citizenship. In Irish law and political discourse, Northern Protestants are fully entitled to be equal citizens. No Irish people are seeking compensation for the large-scale land confiscations executed in previous centuries, because the historic 'land question' is settled. No one is seeking compensation for damages occasioned by partition in 1920, though the farmers on the border have taken to court cases against the security forces of both the UK and Ireland. The European Union will not be an ambiguous subject in a vote on unification. In joining a sovereign united Ireland, Northern Ireland and its people would return fully to the EU and the jurisdiction of EU law. If the Protocol functions, there would be no changes regarding market regulations in goods and agriculture. These are some important reasons why the Southern Irish are less likely to oppose reunification than were southern Cypriots. What will be offered in Irish referendums will bear little resemblance to the Annan Plan.

The failure of Cypriot reunification nevertheless merits attention. The southern Cypriots did not want to make their existing state 'dysfunctional'. They feared that they would no longer have a unified voice in foreign and international relations. No plan of Irish unification would look good to Southerners if Ulster unionists, and their successors, were granted a veto in the foreign and international relations of a united Ireland. The Irish Free State and the Republic of Ireland, for all their faults, are historic successes, legitimate, and achievers of widespread development. Southerners will be prepared for compromise and change, but not, I think, for the disabling of the existing Republic. The Irish Republic will need to be recognizable after reunification, even if there is a new 'replacement constitution'.

Greek Cypriots disliked the strong over-representation of Turkish Cypriots proposed for the reunified Cypriot parliament, and did not warm to Turkish Cypriot veto rights in a collective presidency. Likewise, a plan for Irish reunification would have a hard time in a Southern referendum if it led to significant over-representation of Northern Protestants in Dáil Éireann, the first chamber of the Irish Parliament, or the Government. The Annan Plan effectively would have made Cyprus into a state with a weak federal government – so weak that the federation's legal and political supremacy over the two entities would not have been clear. To many Greek Cypriots, it resembled dressing up partition by another name. Again, the Southern Irish would likely reject a model of reunification in which the existing Republic and Northern Ireland were federal entities subject to a weak federal government, and in which there was over-representation of the North, and a Northern veto – especially if that over-representation was of a minority within the North. They might also reject a model of reunification if it resembled window-dressing partition.

Greek Cypriots fear Turkey more than the Southern Irish fear Great Britain. Greek Cypriots remain concerned that any unification settlement will give what they call 'Ankara's puppets' – the Turkish Cypriots – a veto over everything a unified Cyprus might do, and could conceivably create mechanisms through which Northern Cyprus could lawfully secede and then achieve international recognition. A Turkish client-state would then be entrenched on the island. In the alternative, they fear Turkey might annex Northern Cyprus. By contrast, no one in the Republic of Ireland currently has rational grounds to fear that Great Britain would support Irish reunification as a means to control the island through

Northern Protestants. British public opinion certainly harbours no such ambition. We shall explore later why majorities in both communities in the North, and across the island, reject the idea of an independent Northern Ireland.

Political scientist Joana Amaral has compared the negotiation of the Annan Plan and the Good Friday Agreement. She argues that *how* political settlements are negotiated may affect the outcome when they are put to a referendum. The negotiations of the Good Friday Agreement, compared to the Annan Plan, 'were comparatively more open, representative and inclusive, which increased public information, political party support and civil society campaign mobilization for the "yes" vote'. Whereas 'in Cyprus, the secrecy of the negotiations left Greek Cypriots dependent on information from political leaders'.[15] The much less inclusive process from which the Annan Plan emerged failed to mobilize Greek Cypriot civil society, though there was debate and mobilization within the Turkish Cypriot community. Amaral argues for 'the benefits of including civil society in peace negotiations', adding that its 'early engagement with the negotiations is important to . . . later mobilization in support for the peace settlements in the referendum'. Amaral would probably agree that both the *content* of settlements and *how* they are negotiated matter in shaping the outcomes of referendums. The content of the Annan Plan *and* how it was negotiated killed its prospects among Greek Cypriots, not least because parts of the Annan Plan were written by the UN without the joint agreement of the principal negotiators from both communities.

There are lessons for our future reunification. To do better, we need a robust reunification plan that is negotiated and developed in ways that can attract widespread support across political parties and civil society. A transparently developed plan, for and in the North, as well as for and in the South, may be crucial to its success. However, while ensuring civil society is fully informed, and fully heard, is an admirable aim, granting civil society a full seat at the negotiating tables is another matter. The largest civil society organizations in the North, if we exclude churches, are the Orange Order and the Gaelic Athletic Association (GAA). They should certainly be heard and informed, but elected representatives should have the authority to design and negotiate the details of the reunification plan, openly. Ireland, fortunately, has recently developed expertise in the use of citizens' assemblies and deliberative forums to address complex and demanding political and ethical questions. These assemblies and forums can be even better and more democratic ways of gauging representative opinion *and* facilitating the public to become better informed than traditional modes of civil society organization and consultation.[16] However, it is not a case of either/or. We can and should organize citizens' assemblies, deliberative forums, *and* engage civil society, North and South.★

A last word on the Cypriot case. Almost no Greek Cypriots were left in the so-called Turkish Republic of Northern Cyprus after the Turkish invasion and partition. Northern Cyprus has since had its own internal divisions – including between old Turkish Cypriots and new Anatolian settlers – but it has consisted almost entirely of Turkish speakers. Here there is no analogue with Northern Ireland. The North's population is mixed. Politically, among nationalists, unionists, and 'others'. Religiously, among Catholics, Protestants (of numerous varieties), adherents of other religions, as well as atheists and agnostics. The religious vary significantly in their intensity and enthusiasm. Ethnically, the population divides among those mostly descended from Irish Gaels, and those mostly descended from Scots and English settlers. The Gaels and the old English became Irish Catholics; Scots Presbyterians and English Churchmen became Ulster Protestants – though there are, of course, fusions and hybrids. There has been some mixed marriage down the centuries across the Irish/British and Catholic/Protestant lines of division. Linguistically, in the North, almost everybody speaks and writes English, though some also have Irish, or Ulster Scots, as well as heritage languages among the new minorities. Yes, Northern accents differ from Southern ones, but accents are not languages, and not all 'Nordies' speak in 'Norn Iron', just as all Southerners do not talk in the poetic but slightly impenetrable cadences of Kerry playwright John B. Keane. Mutual unintelligibility is greatly exaggerated. I can swear as if I am from Cork or Belfast – and be understood.

More positively put, accommodating Northern Ireland for the

★ See Chapter 13, p. 152.

Southern Irish would be very different from accommodating Northern Cyprus for Greek Cypriots. Northern Ireland contains large numbers of co-nationals, co-ethnics, and co-religionists who actively want to be part of a reunified Ireland. Though Northern Ireland's population is mixed, it is also partly segregated, in location as well as pre-tertiary educational institutions. Where it is segregated, it is in small units, which makes creating homogenous ethnic or religious territorial cantons unviable. Proposals for Irish reunification need to be sensitive to the North's distinctive plural as well as its pluralist geography: the plural emphasizes the historic division and segregation; the pluralist emphasizes the mixity.

We must learn from the Cypriot case how to avoid failure in the double-referendum requirement for Irish reunification. We need an inclusive, planned, publicly deliberated account of how we intend to deliver a workable model of reunification when the referendums occur, *or* of the constitutional process that will follow successful referendums to choose that workable model. The plan of Irish reunification must be sufficiently attractive that the North will vote for it, and that the losing minority in the referendum can accept it – and later flourish under it. Our plan must expansively accommodate the prospective losers. But not too much. The plan must be sufficiently credible that Southerners will not fear for the stability of their hard-won constitutional republic. A workable polity, with adequate power-sharing provisions, must be our goal. A dysfunctional state must be avoided. We will have to think through whether to amend or replace our constitution, before, during, or after reunification, but avoid the errors of the Annan Plan, which would have replaced the more successful of the two polities in Cyprus.

4. The successful reunification of Germany

German reunification was an astonishingly big and swift-moving surprise to most Europeans, including most Germans. The Berlin Wall was breached and broken on 9 November 1989, and by 3 October 1990 German reunification was formally complete. On that day, the Federal Republic of Germany officially integrated the people and the five reconstituted *Länder* – federal regions – of the former German Democratic Republic (DDR).[1] It is now a public holiday, German Unity Day. All told, the population of the German federation expanded by a quarter; the territory of the republic by over 40 per cent. The DDR ceased to exist, voted out of existence by parliamentary resolution. No new constitution for a reunited Germany was drafted. No constitutional convention took place. No referendums occurred. Rather, the entire united Germany was incorporated under the *Grundgesetz* – the 'basic law' of the Federal Republic, perhaps better translated as 'the fundamental law', rather like the Bunreacht na hÉireann, the Constitution of Ireland.[2] Even more rapidly than the domestic incorporation of the East, Germany's exterior borders were scheduled for reaffirmation, and ratified afresh in international treaties with Poland and the Union of Soviet Socialist Republics.

The lightning pace of German reunification benefitted from an historically unique conjuncture. The Soviet Union under Mikhail Gorbachev had just repudiated the Brezhnev Doctrine. The peoples of Eastern Europe were now free to support or reform their regimes without the threat of Soviet tanks. Without exception, their peoples protested the status quo, and took to the streets to overthrow the Soviet implants imposed across the East after 1946. The implosion and disappearance of the DDR were therefore just one huge fissure in the political earthquake that ran across Eastern Europe.

Many Western European leaders, Margaret Thatcher in particular, wanted to resist or at least brake the pace of German reunification. They failed – utterly. Resounding democratic majorities across the partition line – and across the divided city of Berlin – strongly supported German unity. '*Wir sind ein Volk!*'* swept aside the New Forum that had focused on democratizing the DDR. The Western superpower, the United States, strongly favoured German reunification – but within NATO.[3] And that was the outcome, despite significant support for neutralism and pacifism within German public opinion.

Another unexpected outcome was that the European Economic and Monetary Union (EMU) would become a central feature of the European Union-in-the-making: EMU was the insurance policy that France extracted on behalf of the rest of Europe.[4] Germany's most envied institution, the *Bundesbank*, its federal bank, would be subordinated (rather than sacrificed) to a future European Central Bank, though this new central bank, the ECB, would reside in Frankfurt. Astonishingly, all that happened – within a decade. There were sceptics and opponents – there still are – but EMU happened, and it survives.

More than thirty years later, the warp speed of German reunification and its aftershocks amaze those of us who lived through it. But as this capsule history suggests, Germany was almost completely unprepared for these events. Its universities, and its civil servants, were taken aback. Germany's intellectuals, in the main, had neither expected nor predicted reunification. In the West they were writing of 'a post-national Germany'. In the East, some were building a novel historical tradition – Luther, Frederick the Great, and Bismarck were becoming retrospective East Germans.

In different ways, German scholars on either side of the iron curtain had come to agree that the two Germanies were permanent fixtures.[5] However, as two famous Germans once put it, all that is solid may melt into air; major unanticipated change can happen; and minds must remain open to the multiplicity of choices and outcomes that cannot be reliably predicted.

Our first German lesson therefore is that we Irish need to avoid any equivalent shocking surprise. We need to be prepared, and to be ready to help manage an equivalently huge change – our prospective reunification.

---

* 'We are one people.'

Many German transformations occurred at lightning pace and were partially regretted later. Unlike the Germans, however, we have some reasonable advance notice. Moreover, unlike Germany we will not have great powers to appease. To the contrary, there will be immense goodwill in the USA towards the prospect of Irish reunification. More cynically, neither Russia nor China is likely to want to preserve the UK. Our existing Republic is also part of the greatest soft power in Europe, the European Union. Our friends include the Germans, the French, the Italians, the Spaniards, and the Poles, along with twenty-one other medium- and small-sized European member-states. We have sought and often achieved cooperation and goodwill with the UK, notably since the Anglo-Irish Agreement of 1985, but also previously, such as in the free trade agreement negotiated in 1965, and in the quasi-formal management of the Common Travel Area. Our relations with Great Britain can be positive partly because, as many unionists know, the British aspiration to maintain the union with Northern Ireland is of 'low intensity'.

Are we complacent about the endurance of the UK? It is not the Soviet Union, but it may dissolve in the decade ahead. In 2021 Scotland re-elected the Scottish National Party as the largest party in its parliament, with a mandate to hold a referendum on independence – they are in coalition with the Scottish Greens, who also favour a second referendum. In 2014, 45 per cent voted for independence, 55 per cent against.[6] A decade later, this result could be reversed. Welsh nationalists too are rejuvenated by Brexit; they want to return to the EU.

Great Britain has had three distinct party systems for over a decade. The Conservatives are pre-eminent in England; the SNP in Scotland; and Labour, for now, in Wales. Four parties compete across Great Britain – the Conservatives, Labour, the Liberal Democrats, and the Greens – but their support is heavily territorially skewed, and Scottish Greens support Scotland's independence and return to the EU. In short, our neighbour, Great Britain, a former great power, is not politically stable. The Union of Great Britain has not looked so uncertain since the Jacobite rebellions and the repression of our cousins in 1715 and 1745. And the Union of Great Britain and Northern Ireland, the successor to the failed Union of Great Britain and Ireland, also looks uncertain. If

Scotland exits, can Northern Ireland be far behind? While Irish reunification will be easier than German reunification because it will raise far less international anxiety, the instability of the UK may complicate its arrival and implementation.

Any assessment of German reunification should not assume that it has been a total success – nor, conversely, a total disaster. It *is* a success. It has happened. Germany is no longer partitioned. There is no secessionist movement in the former East Germany. German unity – *Deutsche Einheit* – has not been easy, however; some would say it remains uneasy. 'Internal reunification', to translate a phrase in use, is a work-in-progress. Germans talk of 'walls in the mind' that survived the fall of the Berlin wall. We might ask, how could that not be the case? Thirty years is less than half of a normal European life expectancy. We would do well to unify as well as the Germans have done, but most informed Germans would agree that we should aim higher, partly because we have more time to prepare, and because Northern Ireland will be in better shape at reunification than was East Germany in 1990; and the Irish Republic will be in better shape at reunification than was West Germany.

There have been remarkable successes in German reunification. Angela Merkel, though born in Hamburg, was brought up – and regarded herself – as an East German. She was Chancellor of a united Germany from 2005 until 2021, and the leading European statesperson of our times. In 1991, the capital of a reunited Germany was moved, by a parliamentary vote, from Bonn in the West to a reunified Berlin in the East. (West Berlin had special status, though closely linked to the Federal Republic.) The revival and youthful buzz of Berlin are known to every tourist. Its architectural reconstruction has generally been tasteful, and sensitive to the worst as well as the best of the German past. Politically, the main German parties of the West quickly organized in both parts of the reunited country.

German reunification has had its failings too. East Germans, *Ossis*, are significantly under-represented in top positions in the German polity, economy, and public culture. *Mutti Merkel* (Mummy Merkel) was a striking exception. Some East Germans compare their incorporation with the Third Reich's coercive takeover of Austria in 1938 – the infamous *Anschluss*, the historic word for 'union'. That is over-the-top rhetoric: Helmut Kohl, Gerhard Schröder, and Angela Merkel were and are no Hitlers. But there were positional 'takeovers'. The leadership of public administration of the East, including its universities, was allocated to *Wessis* (Westerners). Western civil servants were given a financial incentive to leave to live and work in the East – a *Buschzulage* (bush allowance), an expression from Germany's colonial past.[7] The Trust Agency, the *Treuhandanstalt*, was assigned the task of deciding the privatization or liquidation of 8,000 public sector enterprises in the East. It was heartless, generating mass unemployment amid 'shock deindustrialization'. Liquidation was the order of the day – ironically made more 'logical' by the generosity of German monetary unification, in which East Germans had received an exchange rate of 1:1 for their marks. That rate, unfortunately, rendered most of their enterprises, and their wage bills, domestically and internationally uncompetitive. The East gives proportionally more votes to the *Alternative für Deutschland* and *Die Linke*,* at the far right and far left ends of the spectrum respectively, a signal of its incomplete integration.

Ireland will not face equivalent problems. Monetary unification of the North into the Euro can take place with comparative ease. On the appointed day, converting all bank accounts and salary payments from sterling to euros will be technically feasible – with securities to ensure that Northerners do not lose, or that any gains they make will be modest, and that they can keep sterling accounts if they wish. If we still have paper and coins to convert, that will not be complex, except for those who have hoarded sterling cash away from the UK revenue authorities. The middle-aged and older Southern Irish can recall the relative painlessness of the transition from punts to euros in 1999, experienced in coins and notes in 2002; despite predictions of 'price-gouging', the transition was smooth. True, the European Central Bank is not run with conspicuous attention to Ireland's needs, but then the Bank of England hardly focuses on the needs of Northern Ireland. Monetary integration will not immediately make Northern enterprises economically unviable. Income and cost-of-living differences will be addressed later in the book. The question of the British 'subvention' – the gap between public

---

* Respectively, 'Alternative for Germany' and 'The Left'.

expenditure in Northern Ireland and what is raised there in taxation – is also addressed later.★ The questions are not trivial, but are incomparably easier to address than the questions posed for West Germany by the East German economy of 1990.

Old-style public sector enterprises are mostly gone from Northern Ireland, though its public services are large in relation to the local population. Coal production ceased to have significance in the last century. The smokestack and 'brownfield' heavy industries are dead. Shipbuilding and major chemical and engineering works are departed. The Titanic Quarter is a tourist site, overlooked by enormous and largely disused cranes. The site of Mackie's steel, munitions, and engineering works, once Belfast's largest employer, is being promoted as a solution to social housing needs.[8] A much-reduced aerospace sector survives; Short Brothers, a pioneering aircraft company founded in London, is now owned by Spirit AeroSystems, a US company that hopes to supply profitable business and military jets – and military drones! By contrast, the linen industry of earlier centuries and the artificial-fibre industries of the 1960s are at best heritage enterprises. The departed enterprises left poor environmental and unemployment legacies, but not on the East German scale of the 1990s. Deindustrialization upended the loyalist working class of the Lagan Valley. They have lost many of their skilled occupations, and these roles have not been replaced with sufficient new apprenticeships or with a strong cultural commitment to modern education for flexible role performances, as has developed in the South and to a significant degree in the Catholic schools of the North.

Northern Ireland has had previous severe bouts of repression and insurgency, notably at its foundation, and it underwent a grim internal civil war that ended in 1998. Northerners refer to 'legacy' to summarize the unresolved questions from the most recent and deepest conflict, notably the absence of an exact truthful account of who, individually, was culpable for each killing and injury. This legacy won't go away in the next ten years, though its intensity may fade as the relatives and friends of victims and survivors themselves pass away. In 2031 it will be

★ See Part Six, Chapters 22 and 23.

sixty years from 1971, the year of escalation by all sides, and it will be thirty-three years since the Good Friday Agreement.

Comparative horror should not be engaged in lightly, but Northern Ireland does not have the double legacy of Nazism and Stalinism, East Germany's distinct path and burden. Mass lustration – the removal and exclusion from public office of those who broke the DDR's own laws and of those who populated the highest ranks of the Communist Party and the Stasi, the secret police – will have no analogue in a reunified Ireland. Harsh judgement of the UUP government from 1921 until 1972, and of the operation of British military and police intelligence agencies, including their collusion with loyalist militia, is appropriate, but the scale of their repression – and crimes – scarcely approaches the lowest foothills of the deeds of the Stasi or the Gestapo. There will be no administrative purge upon Irish reunification, both because it would not be justified and because it would be counterproductive. Reunification should be accompanied by the opening of the archives, if we are lucky or unlucky enough to acquire them, but not for judicial retribution. Northern Ireland also experienced republican insurgents who committed major human rights violations of their own, another difference from East Germany that marks our past.

Among what the Irish, especially civil servants, should learn from German intellectuals and public officials is what they think in retrospect. What, especially, do German constitutional lawyers, economists, political scientists, historians, and professors in the humanities think could have been done better – a little better, or far better? What did they say at the time? What painful policies were pursued? Were they worth it, or should they have been avoided? What better options were not taken? Where should the pace of internal reunification have been slowed? Where should it have been accelerated?

It may seem preposterous to compare the possible future trajectory of our small island with a total population closing on 7 million, with the recent fate of the most powerful state in the heart of the European Union – Germany has the largest economy, and a population of 83 million.[9] But there is a strong case to be made for the value of this comparison. Some will insist that Northern Ireland, historically divided by ethnicity and religion, bears no relationship to the DDR. Certainly, many of the citizens of either region would be mutually insulted to be compared in the same sentence. However, if the Republic were to integrate the people and land of Northern Ireland under its existing constitution – following the German model – then the Republic's population would grow by nearly two-fifths; and its territory by over 20 per cent. These raw numbers suggest that the proportionate scale of the task of Irish reunification in accommodating new numbers of people may even exceed that commenced in Germany thirty years ago.

These raw numbers are starting points for an informed and instructive comparison with Germany, regarding the economic scale, costs, benefits, and dynamics of the possible integration of the two Irelands into one state within the European Union. Neither the worst nor the best should be presumed, and both grim and glowing economic scenarios merit full scrutiny. In 2019, before the global pandemic, the World Bank ranked the Republic of Ireland as the ninth richest country in the world in Gross National Income (GNI) per capita, estimated at $67,050.[10] Germany was in sixteenth place; the United Kingdom in twenty-third. In the 2018 Eurostat reports of Gross Domestic Product (GDP) per capita data, in which the then EU-28 average was normalized at a scale of 100, the UK stood at 106 in its last year as a member of the EU, Germany at 124, and Ireland at 181.[11] So, at first glance, Ireland seems far better placed than Germany was in 1990 to absorb the costs of reunification and to focus on how to organize the benefits. Ireland's republic is richer per head than *today's* German republic, let alone the West Germany of thirty years ago. Sovereign Ireland has a post-industrial knowledge-based economy, extensive and long-term multinational enterprises invested here, and is without a significant legacy of deindustrialization to manage.

In 2018, Northern Ireland's regional economy was estimated to have a GDP per capita of €28,500, and €24,900 in PPS (purchasing power standard), making Northern Ireland, perhaps surprisingly, richer than Wales or North East England.[12] The Republic of Ireland's equivalent figures were €66,700 and €57,500 respectively. For comparison, Germany's respective figures were €40,300 and €37,000.[13] On some estimates of Northern Ireland's GDP per head, the North currently ranks behind the *current* five *Länder* of the former East Germany – one of which now includes a united Berlin. That is an indicator of the magnitude of the task of Irish reunification, but also of the success of German reunification. Moreover, within the Irish Republic growth has been uneven: the north-west has yet to match the economic performance of the rest of the country.

None of us knows whether the global coronavirus pandemic, supply-side crises, and the repercussions of the Ukraine war will produce a sustained depression of the world's economy – and, if so, who will perform comparatively better or worse in harsher times. But let us simply register advance notice of the argument of Part Six: Irish economic reunification will be easier than some claim, and easier than German reunification. The North is not a basket case, as is sometimes alleged, and the South is rich enough to manage reunification, though it has pockets of poverty and squalid deprivation and a housing crisis that need priority attention in the decade ahead.

Ireland was one of the few countries in Western Europe to exhibit no official opposition to German reunification. To the contrary. Official Ireland was robustly warm to the principle of democratic self-determination – inspired partly by its own widespread memory of the costs of an externally imposed partition. Ireland held the presidency of the European Community during the momentous year of *Deutsche Einheit*. It deliberately facilitated the immediate entry of the entirety of the new Germany into what would soon become the European Union. Twenty years later, Ireland received official German gratitude in writing for that perceived act of kindness.[14] Yet today's official Ireland has not sought to examine the lessons of German reunification in any depth. There is also a surprising dearth of English-language translations of major studies of German reunification; that must be put right.

The partition of Germany was executed by its neighbours, an experience Germany shares with us, though we were not responsible for two world wars. German reunification, however, took place with the consent of its neighbours, and by internal democratic consent. Mutual consent was expressed by the democratically elected parliaments of West and East. The DDR's first freely elected parliament voted for the dissolution of East Germany. A future Northern Ireland Assembly may vote to request the sovereign governments to initiate such referendums – even though it has no authority to initiate or hold referendums itself. There were no referendums in the German case, however. No referendums to unify, and no referendums to make a new constitution, or to enact constitutional amendments. The federal states of Germany, the *Länder*, may conduct referendums, some under citizens' initiatives, but under the basic law the German federation allows national referendums under two circumstances only: ratifying a new constitution, and confirming territorial changes to the external border of Germany. An aversion to plebiscites remains common in German political culture because they are associated with Hitler's Nazism and with Ulbricht's Communism (the constitution of the DDR was endorsed with 98 per cent support in 1968).[15] Our case will be different. Our agreed mechanism for reunification is through double referendums, but we must consider whether our constitution is fit for the purpose of reunification, and whether the German decision to avoid a constitutional convention was a good one.

German questions arising for us

Constitutional, political, and economic questions arise for our prospective reunification from reflecting on the German case. There was no major constitutional reconstruction of Germany. The fundamental law, intended as provisional in 1948, was extended to all of Germany in 1990, which poses the question whether we should do the same: by simply applying Bunreacht na hÉireann to all of Ireland. That was what Éamon de Valera intended — though he allowed for two options, as we shall see.* The Germans modified the Preamble to their constitution. Should we? Our Preamble has been described as tribal and sectarian. Is that fair? Even if it is not, do we need to change the Preamble? What problems, if any, were created in Germany by not having a convention to consider constitutional replacement?

Ossis have been 'fitted' into a reunified Germany. They have joined pan-German organizations. The successor to the Communist Party of the East, the Party of Democratic Socialism (PDS), eventually dissolved

* See Part Four, p. 132.

in 2007. *Ossis* are a minority in a unified Germany, sometimes identifiable by their accents, their education, and by their different experiences under a communist dictatorship. Not much of 'the best of the East' was preserved in reunification. *Wessis* persistently regard *Ossis* as lazier, less efficient, and prone to nostalgic whining. Does that predict future Southern estimation of all 'Nordies' – not just Northern Protestants? Will Southerners treat Northerners in such ways that they will generate nostalgia for Northern Ireland's past place in the UK? *Really?* Will a united Ireland require anti-discrimination laws, affirmative action, or quotas for Northerners? Or for Northern Protestants? How has Germany managed all its new minorities – *Ossis*, *Volksdeutsche*,* guest workers, refugees, and EU residents (or metics)? A united Ireland will face equivalent questions.

German citizenship laws and multicultural and integration practices have developed amid a notable division: between the 'super-diversity' of some German cities and the comparative cultural homogeneity of the countryside.[16] What lessons are there for us? East Germany was historically almost uniformly Protestant – or Marxist atheist. The return of East Germans to the Federal Republic looked as if it would reshape the balance between Catholics and Protestants in favour of the latter, but most East Germans in fact have no religion, and Protestantism in the West has been losing adherents at a faster rate than the Catholic church. In our case, might Protestantism in the South recover some of its historic vibrancy after reunification? Older German practices, such as the funding of religious welfare institutions through taxation, persisted after reunification. Collectively, will we want to prop up the historic presence of religious personnel in schooling, healthcare, and social care? After all, the churches, North and South, have disgraced themselves in these domains – not just the Catholic church.[17] Or will we decide to secularize these domains fully – or to have a mixed formula? Answers to these questions will be needed before and during the referendums.

---

* Loosely translated as 'ethnic Germans', the expression has been used to include both those Germans expelled from Central and Eastern Europe between 1944 and 1950, and ethnic Germans who moved to Germany after the collapse of Communism in the Soviet Union and Eastern Europe.

The comparative positions of the respective economies of the two Germanies were not fully known on the eve of reunification. Some matters were correctly appraised, but other difficulties were underestimated. The DDR's economy was heavily public-sector, built under a model of command planning, and it was a branch economy of the wider communist bloc, specializing in military production – and surveillance of its own citizens.[18] East Germany had developed the highest standard of living within the communist bloc by the 1960s – a testament to German rather than communist efficiency. And it had become a bridge between the Soviet-led COMECON (Council for Mutual Economic Assistance) and the then EEC (European Economic Community). West Germany created a special economic relationship with the East as part of its *Ostpolitik*, partly intended to ease future reunification. That facilitated the transfer of EEC goods to the East. The Federal Republic, by contrast, developed a thriving market-economy with large numbers of dynamic medium-sized enterprises (the famous *Mittelstand*). At reunification it was decided that the Eastern model would go: the West would be the model for the East.

We should think about the consequences of such an approach. 'Shock' economic liberalization and privatization would hardly ease Irish reunification, and who would vote for it? In any case, the policy would not be warranted, because the starting points would be so much more similar between the North and the South.

The net welfare effects of German reunification are contested. Social policy specialist Gerhard Ritter argues that German reunification took place at the expense of the previously more generous welfare state, suggesting that reunification encouraged a neo-liberal turn in West Germany, and in Germany as a whole – one that disadvantaged the weakest.[19] Would we want to follow that path when the average Southern voter may well be turning away from an overdose of neo-liberalism? Ireland's welfare state, however, is less generous than West Germany's was in 1990. Yet the UK's welfare state has been significantly retrenched since 1979, so arguments that suggest that Irish reunification must necessarily be accompanied by a deep retrenchment of existing welfare benefits in the North should be challenged. Germany was described as 'the sick man of Europe' in the late 1990s. No one speaks that way today, but does its experience suggest we will have to go through an economically painful reunification before we emerge on a better and mutually beneficial growth path?

Collectively, we have much to learn from the German case. The major difference between German reunification and our prospective unification, however, is simple: people. In 1990 Germans could say '*Wir sind ein Volk*' without embarrassment. East Germans were Germans. 'We' Irish cannot yet make that claim. Some Northern Irish people are British. Differently put, not all Northern Irish are Irish. Wise policy must treat people as they are and not as we would have them be. If there is a positive vote for reunification in the North, it will signal that a political majority want to be fully Irish, but even among that majority there will be those who have a Northern Irish or Northern identity – not surprisingly, after a century of different historical experience. As importantly, among the losers in the referendum there will be those who will insist, in large numbers – and we should not disbelieve them – that they are British, or Northern Irish, or, indeed, that they are Irish people who wish to remain British.

The British-designed sovereign border across Ireland will be gone, but there will be a British question in a united Ireland – even if Great Britain dissolves – and that question requires deep and careful consideration. The rest of this book unfolds in the light of this question. The losers of the Northern referendum will be disproportionately British Protestants. They will not be like East German Protestants, because the latter voted overwhelmingly for parties that supported German reunification. Northern Protestants, who are not homogenous, differ from Southern Protestants, who are also not homogenous. Will the latter act as welcoming guides to the former? Social liberalism has just triumphed in the South. How will the South address the prospective infusion of Northern social conservatism among some of its Catholics and its Protestants, or will that cultural lag disappear over the next decade?

From Germany we can see the benefits, and the costs, of a programme of integration without specific territorial or cultural accommodations, and of reunifying without significant constitutional change in the larger and historically more successful entity. We must ask ourselves: is that what we want? If so, can we do it even better than the Germans, a people notoriously excellent at most things to which they set their minds? Or would it be more prudent to have a less shocking integration than the Germans have gone through, perhaps with the transitional preservation of Northern Ireland as a devolved polity within a reunified Ireland – allowing for, but postponing, a fuller integration? These are among the German-inspired questions that shape the rest of this book.

5.   Lessons from our past

Irish reunification will, if it happens, be distinct from all other cases of unification, attempted or fulfilled. We, North and South, will inevitably do things our own way – well, or badly, or with mixed outcomes. But if we learn from others, notably Germans and Cypriots – about what not to do, as well as what to do – we will be truest to ourselves. Or rather, our multiple historic selves.

We have distinct lessons to learn from our own past about how to accomplish reunification. Among the most obvious: avoiding brutal majoritarianism – domination by a majority over a minority or several minorities. Our reunification, if it happens, will and should draw from ideas and experiences beyond Ireland, North and South, as already suggested, but should also build upon our own best practices, North and South – as well as those from elsewhere. Constructive Irish nationalism has always borrowed from abroad, and locally adapted policies and strategies for its purposes. It needs to continue to do so, or it will stagnate. Critical review and renewal are constant political obligations, precisely because the results of borrowing and adaptation will not always be successful.

It can't just be ourselves

Sinn Féin has been translated as 'We Ourselves' or 'Ourselves Alone', but I have seen the organizational title translated as 'Self-determination', a more apt account of its historic mission. Currently, the three largest parties in the Republic, and on the island, as measured in raw numbers of voters, are Fianna Fáil, Fine Gael, and Sinn Féin. All originated in the second Sinn Féin (1917–23), which led the independence movement politically but divided into three by 1926. Cumann na nGaedheal broke from Sinn Féin to support the Treaty, and later became Fine Gael.

Fianna Fáil broke from Sinn Féin to participate in the institutions of the Irish Free State and to remake it. The rump, or the third Sinn Féin, rejected both the Treaty and participation in the institutions of the Free State (and its successor). The rump would much later split into Official Sinn Féin and Provisional Sinn Féin, in 1969–70. The former morphed into the Workers' Party while the latter took the old name. In due course, this Sinn Féin abandoned its opposition to participation in Stormont and Leinster House, and in signing up to the Mitchell democratic principles in making the Good Friday Agreement, it ceased to support political violence.[1]

As I write, Sinn Féin is the leading party of the left in the Republic and the leading party of Northern nationalism, and it leads opinion polls in both the North and the South. But reunification cannot happen through Sinn Féin alone. Optimistic though the party may be in its current horizons, led by its president, Mary Lou McDonald, it is highly unlikely to become a majority party, in either the North or the South. Irish reunification therefore can only occur through a multi-party coalition, formal or informal, that works collaboratively towards that objective over the next decade and manages to win the two referendums required. A coalition, perhaps informal, of parties from the historic Sinn Féin family – including Fine Gael and Fianna Fáil – and the parties outside it – Labour, the Social Democrats, the Greens, the SDLP, and perhaps Alliance – is required. To play a leading role in such a coalition, which need not be a governmental coalition, Sinn Féin will have to exhibit further practical and policy flexibility.

Building broad alliances

The very first Sinn Féin, founded by Arthur Griffith, sought independent Irish development – independent of England – because, Griffith argued, that was the best way for Ireland to progress, especially economically. Griffith also advocated institutional compromise, a 'dual monarchy' – namely, a common monarch for two kingdoms, Great Britain and Ireland, modelled on the settlement reached between Austria and Hungary in the Habsburg Empire.[2] Some claim his original vision materialized in the Treaty of 1921. Returning to the idea of the dual monarchy will not be among my proposals.

The first Sinn Féin also advocated standing in elections but abstaining from participating in the Westminster Parliament. The intention was to imitate how the Hungarians had accomplished a separate parliament in Budapest – peacefully, with the eventual concurrence of Vienna. This abstentionist policy was a strategy, not a dogma. It worked in 1919–21, in conjunction with the IRA's War of Independence. It has not worked since. Today's Sinn Féin will need to reconsider its position on Westminster, e.g. taking up its seats at Westminster to argue for a referendum, especially if there is no party with a governing parliamentary majority in London. It may also wish to consider being present to vote on legislation that carries through the UK's treaty obligations on the terms of reunification, or on matters related to the Protocol. It may need to show further flexibility on matters of principle, e.g. on the type of a united Ireland to be advocated, or built.

The Irish Free State started with a civil war over the terms of the Treaty. It was a war over roads to sovereignty, a war of green against green.[3] The victors built the Free State by winning support from the parties outside Sinn Féin. The losers eventually built Fianna Fáil, but to succeed that party had to reduce opposition to itself amid fears that it would return the country to civil war. It only became a party of government with the support of the Irish Labour Party. The conclusion is simple: Irish nationalism succeeds best in broad-based coalitions. Current Sinn Féin should take note.

Sinn Féin, in its original founding, was not an inward-looking, insular, and reactionary movement, though it would attract people with these dispositions, and Griffith's then customary anti-Semitism and racism permanently stained his reputation.[4] At its best, Sinn Féin, in its various incarnations, sought to develop as well as to protect Irish culture – just as other European nations did with their own cultures, and continue to do – without refusing modernization, including scientific and educational progress.[5] The numerous projects to have an autonomous and developmentally successful Irish polity – Henry Grattan and Henry Flood's Patriots, Wolfe Tone and the United Irishmen, Daniel O'Connell's Repeal Movement, Thomas Davis and

Young Ireland, and John O'Mahony's Irish Republican Brotherhood, right up to the first Sinn Féin – drew inspiration from the wider world, especially but not only from France, America, and Germany, successively seen as exemplars of different 'modernities' to that of Great Britain.

An outward-looking orientation

The first Sinn Féin sought to protect the Irish economy – to develop it, and make it competitive, not to preserve its backwardness in amber. Irish nationalists were inspired by the German economist Friedrich List, who plausibly argued that underdeveloped countries needed to protect infant industries to develop their capacities, and replace imports with domestic production.[6] Seán Lemass pursued this strategy at the helm of economic policy under de Valera. This 'import substitution' strategy, as it was later called, has had its successes in certain places and times, notably in nineteenth-century Germany. As economic historian Kevin O'Rourke has shown, however, that strategy could not work quite as well in independent Ireland, because the latter was too dependent on and interconnected with the slow-growing British market, even after it established its own industries.[7] The policy of import substitution was eventually revised and abandoned – after 1958. Sovereign Ireland's economic development took off through European integration, notably later European integration – with the Single European Act of 1987 and the formation of the European Union in 1992. Fully opening the Irish economy to extensive foreign and direct investment, a switch towards an emphasis on export-led growth, and an embrace of foreign and multinational enterprises that would deepen capacities and skills within the Irish economy proved to be the right formulae. This switch, facilitated by changes in Europe and the world economy, and with a post-industrial focus on applied science, technology, and services, has been a striking success.

One primary economic lesson, going forward, is that Ireland should not risk that success – either by creating a hostile environment for foreign direct investment or by becoming Eurosceptic. Equally, it is vital that reunification is pursued peaceably and constitutionally – as at present. Ireland lives, makes, services, and sells between Boston and Berlin. The EU is Ireland's largest market (37 per cent of its exports by value in 2021). The US is next (32 per cent).[8] Amazingly, the tall kingdom that has stood over Ireland's shoulder throughout modern history has just disabled its ties to the world's largest single market. England's difficulty has become Ireland's opportunity – in economics.

To become prosperous, Ireland learned many things, including to educate as many as possible – scientifically, not clerically. The most important lesson is that western Atlantic isolation is a recipe for stagnation and the export of Irish citizens. Having arrived in the UN, and then the EEC and its EU successor, no reversion to isolation makes sense. Ireland must remain attractive to outsiders, and sufficiently attractive to our diaspora that it will continue to want to return.

Reunification by dual majority consent

Bitter experience has taught that reunification through conquest, insurrection, demanding a unilateral British withdrawal, or a war of national liberation is impractical, counterproductive, and ethically wrong. Some learned these lessons earlier than others, but now only the last stranded platoons of 'dissident republicans' reject this hard-won knowledge.

Conquest has been outlawed by the Constitution of Ireland since 1937.[9] Article 29 pledged the state to peaceful international relations, firmly opposed to conquest:

1. Ireland affirms its devotion to the ideal of peace and friendly co-operation among nations founded on international justice and morality.
2. Ireland affirms its adherence to the principle of the pacific settlement of international disputes by international arbitration or judicial determination.
3. Ireland accepts the generally recognized principles of international law as its rules of conduct in its relations with other States.

Any attempt to conquer Northern Ireland, or to incorporate it without the consent of the UK Government, is, and was, unconstitutional. In 1937, in international law, territory could be peacefully transferred from one country to another, provided that the relevant sovereign states agreed. That was one of de Valera's policies: if Northern unionists could not be persuaded to negotiate reunification, then Dublin could ask London to cede Northern Ireland. The possibility that Great Britain would reach such an agreement with Ireland numbered among the dashed hopes of de Valera, but it remained quasi-official Irish policy until 1973.

In the Sunningdale Agreement of 1973 – and later, more significantly, in the Anglo-Irish Agreement of 1985 – the Government of Ireland agreed with the United Kingdom that there was only one way that a change of status in Northern Ireland could take place: through the consent of a majority of the people of Northern Ireland. In the 'Agreement between the Government of Ireland and the Government of the United Kingdom (The Anglo-Irish Agreement)', Article 1 of the Irish version stated:

The two Governments

(a) affirm that any change in the status of Northern Ireland would only come about with the consent of a majority of the people of Northern Ireland;

(b) recognise that the present wish of a majority of the people of Northern Ireland is for no change in the status of Northern Ireland;

(c) declare that, if in the future a majority of the people of Northern Ireland clearly wish for and formally consent to the establishment of a united Ireland, they will introduce and support in the respective Parliaments legislation to give effect to that wish.

The then 'status of Northern Ireland' remained controversial, however, especially for unionists, because Article 2 of Ireland's Constitution declared that the 'national territory' consisted of 'the whole island of Ireland, its islands, and the territorial seas'. This statement was considered 'irredentist',* even though the following Article 3 restricted the

---

* Irredentism comes from the Italian *irredenta*. 'Italia irredenta' was Italian land unredeemed from neighbouring powers, so an irredentist pursues 'unredeemed land'.

laws of the Irish Parliament and Government to the territory of the Irish Free State. The reason is that Article 3 was qualified as 'without prejudice' to the right of the Irish Parliament and Constitution to 'exercise jurisdiction over the whole of' the territory of the island, its islands, and its territorial seas.

The idea that the transfer of Northern Ireland could occur without local majority consent was completely and finally repudiated by the two votes, North and South, in favour of the Good Friday Agreement in 1998. Whatever the exact meanings of the old Articles 2 and 3, they were replaced in the amending of the Constitution of Ireland that gave effect to the Good Friday Agreement. Articles 2 and 3, as amended in 1999, now state:

2. It is the entitlement and birth right of every person born in the island of Ireland, which includes its islands and seas, to be part of the Irish nation. That is also the entitlement of all other persons otherwise qualified in accordance with law to be citizens of Ireland. Furthermore, the Irish nation cherishes its special affinity with people of Irish ancestry living abroad who share its cultural identity and heritage.

3.1. It is the firm will of the Irish nation, in harmony and friendship, to unite all the people who share the territory of the island of Ireland, in all the diversity of their identities and traditions, recognising that a united Ireland shall be brought about only by peaceful means with the consent of a majority of the people, democratically expressed, in both jurisdictions in the island. Until then, the laws enacted by the Parliament established by this Constitution shall have the like area and extent of application as the laws enacted by the Parliament that existed immediately before the coming into operation of this Constitution.

3.2. Institutions with executive powers and functions that are shared between those jurisdictions may be established by their respective responsible authorities for stated purposes and may exercise powers and functions in respect of all or any part of the island.

These solemn constitutional pledges bind the Government of Ireland, and all Irish citizens. The Irish nation must seek 'to unite' all who share the island 'in all the diversity of their identities and traditions'. Consent to unification is now doubly pledged. It must flow from a majority in the North *and* a majority in the South – i.e. the consent of the people in two referendums, North and South, respectively. A united Ireland will not just happen if the North wants it.

It has been suggested that the South could express its democratic consent simply through Dáil Éireann and Seanad Éireann, the second chamber of Ireland's parliament, and the President passing and ratifying legislation. That *would* be a democratic expression of support, but the members of the Oireachtas, Ireland's democratic parliament, are not 'the people of Ireland', merely its representatives. These constitutional details are vital in preparing for reunification and will demand our further attention.

Uniting Ireland in all the diversity of its identities and traditions

Historically, Irish nationalism pitched the historic Irish nation – largely a fusion of Irish Gaels and old English Catholics, with occasional support from radical Protestants, especially Presbyterians in the 1790s – in a struggle for autonomy within, or to be free from, the British Empire: home rule within, a republic outside. During its growth the British Empire had conquered and reconquered Ireland, outlawed the island's principal religion, and colonized it with plantations of varying demographic success, comprising Scots, English, and Welsh Protestant settlers. The most successful of these plantation projects were in Ulster. The power of the British Empire, including its power of neglect – never more obvious than during the Great Famine – led to English becoming the language most Irish people speak and read. Ireland's historic culture – with its flaws and virtues like any other – was partly eradicated by imperial power, neglect, and policy.

These are among the many reasons why it has been difficult for Irish nationalists to achieve outreach to Ulster unionists. The latter celebrated the British Empire. They also often despised native Irish culture, though there were notable exceptions, such as the poet and antiquarian Samuel Ferguson.[10] Since partition, in the South the coexistence of diverse identities and traditions has been much easier, partly because Irish Protestants of British stock were proportionally smaller in number. They have largely been successfully integrated – as equal citizens – and many have assimilated. By contrast, in the North, the Ulster Unionist Party presided over an overtly discriminatory regime, in which Northern Catholics and nationalists were deliberately disorganized and disadvantaged. Historic antagonisms have remained fiercer in the North than in the South, because the long-run imperial and colonial legacies have more palpably marred the present, and local mentalities.

Despite and because of this past and present, a successful project of Irish reunification must be more inclusive than recent nationalist projects. Irish reunification must overcome the colonial legacies. The historic settlers must be both treated as natives and facilitated in preserving their culture – in all its variety, reformed or otherwise. To commence this task, the future securities guaranteed for Ulster Protestants and British unionists – in their full internal diversity – will have to be made clear in advance. The diminution of a culture of contempt among Ulster Protestants towards Irish Catholics will make this task easier, but it will not be easy. The Irish nation has been built on the premise that the norm is to be of Irish stock, Catholic, and favourably disposed towards the Irish language. This premise will have to be refurbished. Ulster unionism has been constructed in opposition to Irish nationalism: it will resist what it will see as its final defeat.

In James Joyce's *Ulysses*, published one hundred years ago, 'the citizen' declares in the 'Cyclops' passage that the Irish language is on the march, and he goes on, 'To hell with the bloody brutal Sassenachs and their *patois* . . . The curse of a goodfornothing God light sideways on the bloody thicklugged sons of whores' gets! No music and no art and no literature worthy of the name. Any civilisation they have they stole from us. Tonguetied sons of bastards' ghosts.'[11] It is not clear whom Joyce's citizen had in mind as the Sassenachs – the English, or the lowland Scots who settled Ulster and who did not speak Gaeilge. I suspect the latter. Joyce's citizen here represents Irish cultural prejudices in satirical form. Yet the Irish do tend to claim fluency of the tongue, and defensively to assert the heritage of an older and superior civilization. In the century ahead, the Irish nation will have to learn to be much more civil with the allegedly 'tonguetied' sons *and* daughters of 'bastards' ghosts' who will wish to preserve their civilization.

The Good Friday Agreement has a clear credo and ethos. In 1998, its authors – two governments and eight parties – declared that 'we firmly dedicate ourselves to the achievement of reconciliation, tolerance, and mutual trust, and to the protection of the human rights *of all*'. They declared their 'total and absolute commitment to exclusively democratic, and peaceful means of resolving differences on political issues, and our opposition to the use or threat of force by others for any political purpose'. They also emphasized their commitment to 'partnership, equality and mutual respect as the basis of relationships within Northern Ireland, between North and South, and between these islands'.[12] Reunification must realize these commitments, or it will not be worth pursuing.

6.   Lessons from other referendums

Since 1789 the number of 'sovereignty referendums' – used to address the status of territories and peoples – has been variously estimated at between 150 and over 600.[1] We are interested here in the relevance of previous referendums to the possible transfer of sovereignty over Northern Ireland and its people from the United Kingdom to Ireland. As we shall see, there is a strong argument for the uniqueness of our future case. It will trigger a pair of self-determination referendums, with just two possible outcomes; Northern Ireland has no right to independence. There are guarantees of enduring (and inheritable foreign) citizenship rights, and commitments to impartial government of diverse and equal citizens under either option in the referendum question. The recurrence of the same referendum in the North, if the reunification option loses, is allowed every seven years.* These provisions are combined with the possibility of a matching but perhaps sequentially later referendum in the South. This distinct bundle of elements is certainly internationally and comparatively unprecedented. However, some of the future individual attributes *do* have precedents. The future referendums will fit within the category of lawful referendums in which a transfer of sovereignty may take place under democratic conditions.

Sovereignty referendums

The provision for a future referendum as part of a peace agreement is not a unique feature of the Good Friday Agreement. Similar provisions were built into the Comprehensive Peace Agreement in Sudan,[2] and to settle conflict in and over Bougainville in Papua New Guinea. However, these agreements, both of which were signed in 2005, precisely

* See Chapter 7.

timetabled a referendum, providing a future choice between union and secessionist independence. These referendums have since been held, under a simple majority formula, with secession endorsed on both occasions: South Sudan became independent in 2011; Bougainville is negotiating its independence, having voted for that in a referendum held over the last two months of 2019.

When the people of a territorially defined unit vote on whether to join another state, it may become a *unification*, or an *incorporation*, or an *accession* referendum. The appropriateness of these three near-synonyms depends on whether a united Ireland will be unitary, federal, or confederal,★ and whether Northern Ireland will persist as a political entity within these governmental forms. An 'incorporating union' would generally imply a unitary state, but it could be compatible with the persistence of a devolved Northern Ireland, or other Northern Ireland institutions. 'Accession' is normally reserved to describe becoming a member of an international organization or a confederation (a state composed of sovereign states).

The term 'unification' is less confined in scope: it covers both the expansion of a unitary state (with or without a devolved Northern Ireland) and the formation of a federation. Accession is therefore the least appropriate description of a future Northern Ireland referendum, because that would require Northern Ireland to become an independent, sovereign state before acceding to an Irish confederation (and the European Union). I will argue that will not happen in our case.† So, following standard usages, the Northern referendum will be a unification or incorporation referendum,[3] though the case for calling it a reunification referendum is equally historically strong; and the same naming will apply to its Southern twin.

There have been six types of unification or incorporation referendums in modern history. One is the holding of a referendum to legitimize *the unification of existing independent entities to form a union or a federation*. In 1958, postcolonial Syria and Egypt unified as the United Arab Republic in simultaneous referendums while also electing Nasser

★ For more on these political concepts see Part Four, Chapters 11–16.
† See Chapter 14, pp. 157–9.

as their president.[4] The endorsement through referendum of the new and more federalized Swiss constitution of 1848, replacing the previously more confederal arrangements, also fits this category.

The second is *the unification of dependent polities, under colonial conditions, to form a union or federation* that would subsequently become domestically independent, and later fully independent. The formation of the federal Commonwealth of Australia (1898–1901) as a dominion is a clear example. There were two rounds of referendums among the future states, because the first round ended after New South Wales failed to meet the quota set by its parliament.

The third is *the joining of a dependent polity to a state-in-the-making*, e.g. the referendum held in Western Australia in 1900 to join the Commonwealth of Australia. The referendum in Natal, on a racist franchise, to join the Union of South Africa in 1909, was otherwise similar. The failed referendum held in Cyprus, administered under the auspices of the UN in 2004, is another illustration.

The fourth is *the upgrading of a dependent polity to full membership of an existing state*. The referendums held in Alaska and Hawaii to promote shifting their status from territories to states and to join the US federation are illustrations.[5] Washington, DC and Puerto Rico have passed referendums in the same cause but have failed to achieve congressional approval – because US Republicans believe that would disadvantage them.[6] We may also think of these referendums as ways of acquiring a full share in collective sovereignty.[7]

The fifth is *that pioneered amid the making of the Treaty of Versailles, where sovereignty and borders are adjusted*. The Versailles treaty – and other treaties made in other French chateaux after World War One – authorized referendums, all then called plebiscites, to be held in specific territories. *But* in some of them the aggregate majority vote was not decisive in allocating the entire territory. Rather, voters' preferences were used as information to apportion sub-units of the place(s) in which the vote had been held to revise the boundaries of the neighbouring states.[8]

The sixth and last type of unification referendum, and the one which fits our case, is *the transfer of a dependent polity from one sovereign to unify with another*. The pioneering plebiscites in Avignon and the Comtat Venaissin, which led to their incorporation into France (1791), are the paradigm cases.[9] It is almost universally acknowledged[10] that the French revolutionaries thereby initiated the practice of conducting referendums on territorial unification.[11] The Newfoundland referendums of 1948, held under the modernized secret ballot, fit this type,[12] as do three referendums to join India, held in Junagadh, Chandernagore, and Sikkim in 1948, 1949, and 1976 respectively, and the decision by British Togoland to join Ghana in 1956.

Northern Ireland may be a coequal partner in the Union in one construal, but it is constitutionally dependent in all standard readings. In UK law, its government is devolved, i.e. the Westminster Parliament reserves full sovereignty over it, including the right to suspend it or abolish it (or indeed, unilaterally cede Northern Ireland to Ireland).[13] That was demonstrated when Peter Mandelson suspended the Assembly in 2000. In short, a future Northern Ireland referendum may lead to the transfer of a dependent polity from one sovereign to unify with another, in which it may be incorporated as a devolved unit or it may be unified (or integrated) with Ireland.

No authoritative list exists of referendums of the sixth type. What we need to know, however, may be gleaned from diverse sources.[14] There have been referendums which have led to the transfer of a dependent polity to another sovereign state (*either* after a plebiscite by commune or primary assembly, *or* after a referendum by secret ballot) and there have been referendums where the population in the relevant territory voted *against* the transfer of sovereignty. The outcomes have gone both ways. Referendums on these questions are normal, and both nationalists and unionists have cause to hope they may win the Northern referendum, provided it is fairly conducted, while the 'others' have reason to believe their votes may be decisive.

In the overwhelming majority of these cases, the referendum posed one question with two options. The exceptions were in Newfoundland in 1948, where three options were available in the first referendum; in Saarland in 1955, where the third option of joining France received less than half a percentage point; and in Singapore in 1962, where three modes of incorporation into the Federation of Malaysia were available. In all these cases, a simple majority was the decision rule. In Newfoundland, a second run-off referendum ensured that confederating with

Canada won with 53 per cent of the vote, defeating the restoration of dominion government, which had won the most votes in the first referendum but was short of a majority.[15]

In most cases, the results of such referendums have endured. Where the French revolutionary armies produced highly questionable outcomes, the results did not endure – notably in Belgium. But Savoy and Nice voted twice for incorporation into France after they had been lost in the Napoleonic Wars, and Alsace and Lorraine were recovered twice from Germany, having been annexed by German conquest in 1871. Of the three provinces recovered by Ottoman Turkey in 1918 after a plebiscite held under the Treaty of Brest-Litovsk, Republican Turkey lost one, namely Batumi, to the Soviet Republic of Georgia (the Treaty of Moscow ratified Bolshevik military successes). There has been only one secession after lawful incorporation by referendum, and even that case may be questioned: in 1965, Singapore arguably was expelled from – rather than seceded from – the Federation of Malaysia.[16]

Comparative analysis of these precedents reveals two dominant historic norms. Referendum questions regarding the transfer of sovereignty generally provide two options, and they are determined by simple majority rule. These provisions are in the Good Friday Agreement: the two options of a united Ireland or the maintenance of Union; and simple majority determination. In the same historical record, improvement in fair referendum processes may be traced over time – the secret ballot has replaced head counts, and regulations to improve the democratic character of deliberation before voting occurs, and as it occurs, have become far more evident, especially since Versailles. Progress in these standards, and upholding them, has not, however, been linear.

Informed planning

Ill-judged and ill-prepared referendums can be disastrous, as the world saw in 2016 in the UK's referendum over whether to retain shared sovereignty within the European Union, or to retake it to Westminster and withdraw or secede from the EU. The UK's decision to hold a referendum on membership of the European Union with an unclarified substantive question, and inadequate procedural protections, produced a poor debate and an institutional and policy mess. I am carefully *not* saying that the UK had no right to hold such a referendum. After all, its membership of the EEC had been confirmed by referendum in 1975.[17] Responsibility for the folly rests with the Prime Minister who called the referendum, David Cameron, who favoured remaining within the EU. He called the referendum to discipline his own party, taking a gambler's risk. Seeking to bias the outcome in favour of remain, he deliberately instructed his civil servants to make no preparations for a leave victory. That was irresponsible: he thought that divisions over what 'leave' might mean would help the remain side. He also neglected UK constitutional norms. What would the role of parliament be in implementing the outcome; and what would happen in the event of different outcomes in different parts of the UK? Most significantly, for Irish people at least, Cameron neglected to consider the implications for another treaty that had been endorsed by referendum – the Good Friday Agreement of 1998. So, of course, did the leaders of those who advocated leave, the Brexiteers. In sum, it was a referendum held largely in the interests of one party, without any effort to build a serious all-party remain campaign.

The most important lesson for Ireland from the Brexit referendum is that the Government of Ireland and Irish parties, North and South, need to plan to ensure that any referendum on reunification, if and when it is held in the North, meets the best standards of preparation, procedural propriety, *and*, above all, clarity. The South, to remint a phrase, cannot stand idly until a Northern referendum is initiated by a UK Secretary of State for Northern Ireland. The South must prepare, on an all-party basis, to clarify what reunification will mean. It would be the height of irresponsible risk-taking to leave clarification to the morning after a pro-reunification vote. Clarity would also help legitimize a narrow vote in favour of reunification. In the UK, the lack of prior agreement on the meaning of 'leave' gave remainers what they regarded as good cause to seek a second referendum to reverse the narrow outcome of the first – though they failed in that endeavour.

Northern and Southern Irish voters will want to know what they are voting for or against. The choice between a united Ireland and maintaining the Union with Great Britain is insufficiently clear on its own, even if this is the choice that may well be specified on the referendum ballot paper. According to existing UK law, the independent Electoral Commission of the UK must ratify any question or questions in any referendum. That is one reason why the British-Irish Intergovernmental Conference, an underused body from the Good Friday Agreement, must be kept active. It would be bizarre if the two governments failed to use this forum for referendum preparation – for example, to finalize the wording of the question. They will also need to address such matters as whether the responses available will be 'Yes' *or* 'No' to reunification or, 'Remain in the United Kingdom with the Protocol' *or* 'Reunify with Ireland within the European Union', or some other wording.[18]

It is the duty of the Government of Ireland to ensure that, when a referendum is held, Northerners will choose between two well-defined alternatives, A and B, and not as in the UK's referendum of 2016 between A, the status quo, and not-A, where not-A was allowed to mean every possible mode of UK existence outside the EU. Failing to define 'leave' was the most irresponsible political decision in the holding and conduct of the referendum – for which Cameron, not Boris Johnson, was culpable. As Joseph Fouché, Napoleon's Minister of Police, said of his emperor's murder of the Duc d'Enghien: 'It was worse than a crime, it was a blunder.'

'Leave' was allowed to mean everything for the voter, bar staying in the EU. Two leave campaigns fought for influence – that effectively led by Dominic Cummings, and that led by Nigel Farage, even after the first was made the 'official' leave side.[19] As Michael Heseltine, a remainer and former Deputy Prime Minister of the UK, has put it:

> We all have a clear memory of the Brexit campaign and what was said. That we were being run by Brussels. That European restrictions were holding back our economy and lowering our living standards. That we could keep all the benefits of the single market and customs union, while negotiating trade deals with faster-growing countries in a world that was shifting east. That we had to regain control over our borders. That there would be no new border between Northern Ireland and mainland Great

Britain, and that the Good Friday Agreement, having ended years of strife, would be fully honoured.[20]

Heseltine is pro-European, but he is not wrong.

The Irish Government, Irish political parties, and Irish civil society, interacting as fully as possible with their Northern – including their unionist – counterparts, must define B, a united Ireland, properly in advance, in documented detail. It will be up to the unionists to define remaining in the Union – according to the status quo, or some credible improved offer on the status quo. Ensuring that a united Ireland is well defined can occur in two ways. *Either* by the careful elaboration of a specific model, *or* by credibly specifying a clear constitutional process to follow a result in favour of reunification. These choices will be elaborated in Part Four. Meanwhile, referendum matters must be probed in greater depth.

PART THREE

How Reunification May Happen

7.   Referendum matters

Let us turn now to how reunification may happen. Simply put, there must be referendums in favour of reunification, North and South, followed by the transfer of sovereignty over Northern Ireland from the UK to Ireland. In this chapter, I address this first step. To change the sovereign status of Northern Ireland, a simple majority is required in a referendum in the North, in which the choice is between maintaining the Union with Great Britain or creating a sovereign united Ireland.

The most important referendum rule is stated five times

Majority rule has two obvious virtues: it is neutral between change and the status quo, giving each voter an equal opportunity of being decisive, and it is the regular rule in international relations for deciding the transfer of sovereignty. A simple majority is truly simple: 50 per cent of those who vote, plus one, must vote, in both jurisdictions, to unify as a sovereign united Ireland before that can happen.

The rule is stated, in the text of the Good Friday Agreement, five times. The first three occasions occur among the 'constitutional issues' agreed by the makers of the Agreement. They state that they:

(i) recognise the legitimacy of whatever choice is freely exercised by *a majority*★ of the people of Northern Ireland with regard to its status . . .

(ii) recognise that it is for the people of the island of Ireland alone, by agreement between the two parts respectively and without external impediment, to exercise their right of self-determination on the basis of consent, freely and concurrently

★ This set of italics and all italics in (i) to (iii) are this author's.

given, North and South, to bring about a united Ireland, if that is
their wish, accepting that this right must be achieved and
exercised with and subject to the agreement and consent of *a
majority* of the people of Northern Ireland;
(iii) acknowledge that while a substantial section of the people in
Northern Ireland share the legitimate wish of a majority of the
people of the island of Ireland for a united Ireland, the present
wish of a majority of the people of Northern Ireland, freely
exercised and legitimate, is to maintain the Union and,
accordingly, that Northern Ireland's status as part of the United
Kingdom reflects and relies upon that wish; and that it would be
wrong to make any change in the status of Northern Ireland save
with the consent of *a majority* of its people . . .[1]

The fourth and fifth mentions in the Agreement are just as significant. The UK Government pledged the draft clauses (or schedules) that
would be incorporated into future British legislation. These draft clauses
state:

(1) It is hereby declared that Northern Ireland in its entirety remains
part of the United Kingdom and shall not cease to be so without the
consent of *a majority*⋆ of the people of Northern Ireland voting in a poll
held for the purposes of this section in accordance with Schedule 1.
(2) But if the wish expressed by *a majority* in such a poll is that Northern
Ireland should cease to be part of the United Kingdom and form part of
a united Ireland, the Secretary of State shall lay before Parliament such
proposals to give effect to that wish as may be agreed between Her Majesty's Government in the United Kingdom and the Government of
Ireland.[2]

The Northern Ireland Act (1998), incorporating the Good Friday
Agreement into UK law, followed up that pledge, with exactly those
words, under the heading 'The status of Northern Ireland', which
opened the Act.[3] The legal language used needs some unpacking. That
Northern Ireland 'in its entirety' remains part of the UK, until a

---

⋆ All italics in (1) and (2) are mine.

majority consents to leave it, means that there can be no lawful repartition, or cession, of any part of Northern Ireland in UK law. Equally important, Northern Ireland's options on status are confined to two: remaining part of the UK or becoming part of a united Ireland.*

Mistaken readings

The UK legislation is sometimes misread. Some think it implies that the Government of the United Kingdom and the Government of Ireland have a veto over reunification, because legislation will be required in Westminster and Dublin to give effect to the referendum result. An understandable mistake. The Good Friday Agreement is a treaty binding on both governments, and their states.[4] The wording of the GFA recognizes that Ireland's right to self-determination, North and South, is to be exercised 'without external impediment'[†] and according to the principle of consent for Northern Ireland. In international law, the Westminster Parliament cannot lawfully block the will of the people of Ireland, North and South, and neither can the Government of Ireland. The two governments will, however, have to agree the practicalities of the transfer of sovereignty.

What is now Section 1(2) of the Northern Ireland Act 1998 is worded to reflect the UK's tradition in legal drafting. The Westminster Parliament regards itself as sovereign: no parliament can bind its successor, and therefore ministers lay proposals before parliament when fulfilling international legal obligations. The principle of parliamentary sovereignty means that the UK Parliament could as a matter of UK law break the treaty incorporating the Good Friday Agreement, and international law, by refusing to give effect to a referendum result favouring Irish reunification. There would be a price, however. This action would render the UK's status over Northern Ireland internationally unlawful.[5]

The UK Government's pledge to lay proposals before parliament to

---

* See Chapter 14.
† See Chapter 8, pp. 99–100.

give effect to the referendum result as an act of self-determination by the people of Ireland, North and South, is now solemnly expressed and ratified in *two* international treaties. It is in the original treaty between the UK and Ireland,[6] and it is reaffirmed as part of the UK's Withdrawal Agreement with the European Union. In the Protocol on Ireland/ Northern Ireland,[7] the European Union and the United Kingdom affirm that:

> [The] Good Friday or Belfast Agreement of 10 April 1998 between the Government of the United Kingdom, the Government of Ireland and the other participants in the multi-party negotiations (the '1998 Agreement'), which is annexed to the British-Irish Agreement of the same date (the 'British-Irish Agreement'), including its subsequent implementation agreements and arrangements, should be protected *in all its parts*.*

'All its parts' includes giving legislative effect to a referendum in favour of Irish reunification. It is reinforced by Article 1 of the Protocol, where 'all its dimensions' is the phrase.

If the UK failed to give effect to referendums in favour of Irish reunification, the UK would violate its treaty with Ireland and the spirit and letter of its withdrawal treaty with the European Union, and would invite the wrath of Irish Americans and others in the US Congress.

However, the UK remains sovereign over Northern Ireland for now, and the *legal* initiative in starting referendum proceedings rests exclusively with the UK Secretary of State for Northern Ireland.[8] She or he is obliged to hold a referendum if the test in the Northern Ireland Act is met. The opening to Schedule 1 to the Northern Ireland Act 1998 reads:

> 1. The Secretary of State *may*＊ by order direct the holding of a poll for the purposes of section 1 on a date specified in the order.
> 2. Subject to paragraph 3, the Secretary of State *shall* exercise the power under paragraph 1 if at any time it appears likely to him that a majority of those voting would express a wish that Northern Ireland should cease to be part of the United Kingdom and form part of a united Ireland.

＊ Italics are mine.

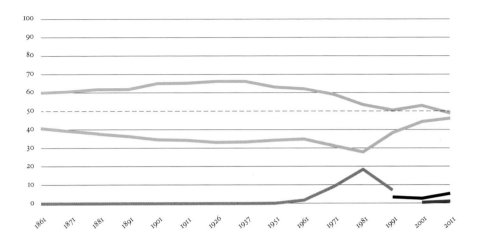

Protestants and other Christians

Catholics

Not stated

None

Other religions and philosophies

Figure 1.1: The shifting percentages of those who identify with the two major religions in the six counties that became Northern Ireland, 1861–2011

(i) The 2001 and 2011 census reports assign many of the 'none' and 'not stated' to 'community background' or 'religion brought up in' (based on answers given by respondents) and are then classified as 'Catholic' or 'Protestant' as appropriate, along with those who identify as such. So the Protestant and Catholic lines exaggerate religious identification from 2001 onwards, and cannot be taken as a guide to the numbers of believing or practising Catholics or Protestants.
(ii) The 1981 census was subject to a partial boycott.

Sources:
1861–1991: The Northern Ireland Census 1991, Religion Report: Table I, 1993, p. 1
2001: The Northern Ireland Census 2001: Table KS07b, 2002, Community background
2011: The Northern Ireland Census 2011: Table KS212NI, 2012, Religion and religion brought up in

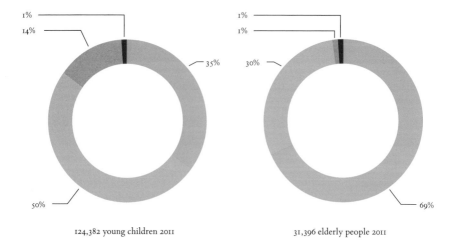

1% ——
14% ——

35%

50% ——

124,382 young children 2011

1% ——
1% ——

30% ——

69%

31,396 elderly people 2011

▬ Protestants and other Christians
▬ Catholics
▬ None
▬ Other religions and philosophies

Figure 1.2: Bottom and top of the demographic age-cohorts in Northern Ireland, 2011

Sources: The Northern Ireland Census 2011: Table DC2254NI

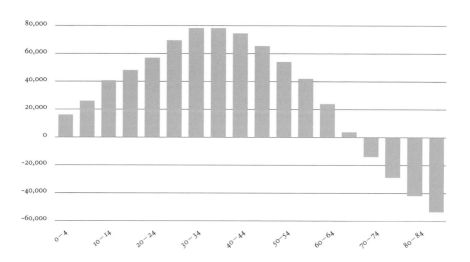

■ Cumulative Catholic demographic lead

Figure 1.3: The cumulative Catholic demographic advantage across age-cohorts in 2011

Sources: Author's calculations from the Northern Ireland Census 2011: Table DC2254NI

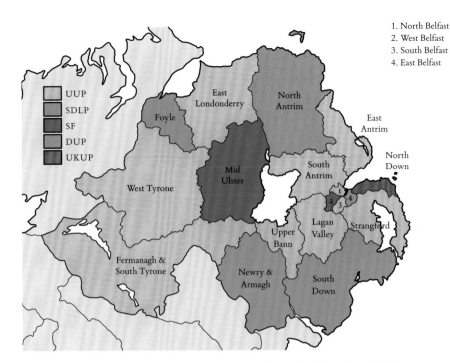

1. North Belfast
2. West Belfast
3. South Belfast
4. East Belfast

Figure 1.4: The 1997 Westminster elections in Northern Ireland: largely UUP light orange, with green patches

Sources: ARK website (previously Nicholas Whyte's website on NI elections, donated to ARK); adapted from a map by Conal Kelly

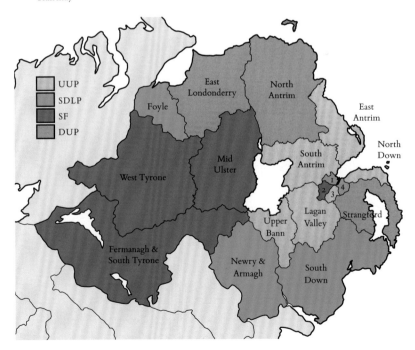

Figure 1.5: The 2001 Westminster elections in Northern Ireland: the greening of the border seats

Sources: ARK website (previously Nicholas Whyte's website on NI elections, donated to ARK); adapted from a map by Conal Kelly

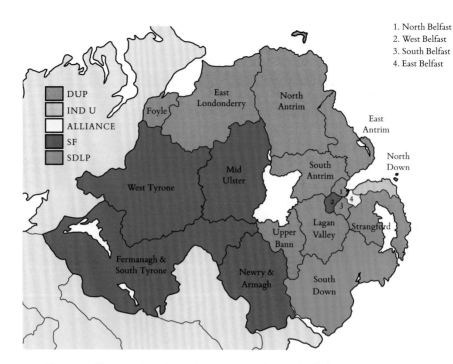

1. North Belfast
2. West Belfast
3. South Belfast
4. East Belfast

Figure 1.6: The 2010 Westminster elections in Northern Ireland: the near-balancing of the blocs

Source: ARK website (previously Nicholas Whyte's website on NI elections, donated to ARK); adapted from a map by Conal Kelly

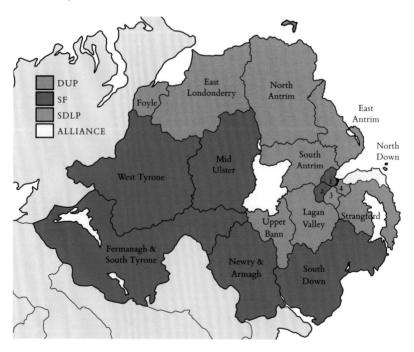

Figure 1.7: The 2019 Westminster elections in Northern Ireland: the greening of Belfast, and a non-unionist majority

Source: ARK website (previously Nicholas Whyte's website on NI elections, donated to ARK); adapted from a map by Conal Kelly

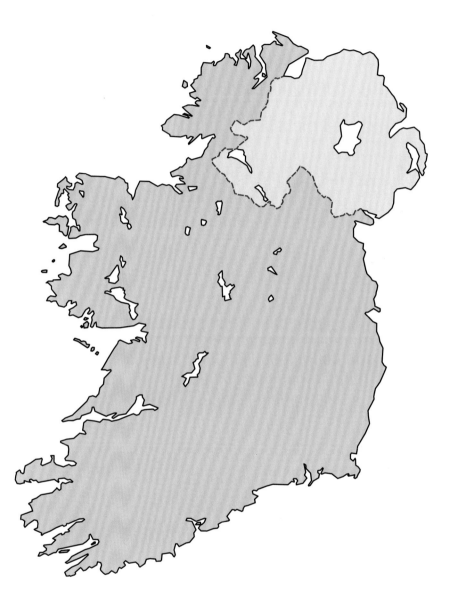

Figure 11.1: Visualization of Model 1: the persisting Northern Ireland or the full transfer model of the Good Friday Agreement

Under the persisting Northern Ireland model, there would no longer be a sovereign border across the island demarcating states: Ireland and the UK. Partition would end, but the border created in 1920 would mark the extent of the autonomous powers of the Northern Ireland Assembly, though these powers would be granted and recognized by Ireland's National Parliament rather than by Westminster. Northern Ireland would have 'home rule' within a united Ireland.

Figure 12.1: Visualization of Model 2: an integrated Ireland

An integrated Ireland, with the minimal transfer of the GFA. This model of a united Ireland distinctly resembles and incorporates the traditional conception held by many Northern nationalists and Irish republicans – namely, 'a thirty-two-county unitary Irish Republic'.

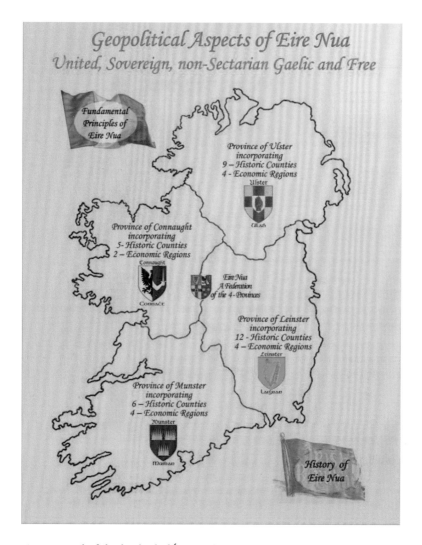

Figure 16.1: The federal Ireland of Éire Nua (1972)

An immediate question for any Irish federation would be its federal units. The traditional answer would reconstitute the four historic provinces of Ireland: Leinster, Munster, Connacht, and Ulster. In Éire Nua (New Ireland) in 1972, the late Ruairí Ó Brádaigh suggested exactly that. (The late Desmond Fennell may have been involved in this proposal.) This four-unit federation was Sinn Féin's formal objective until 1981, when the policy was abandoned. The idea remains attractive to some republican micro-groups.

Source: Éire Nua blog

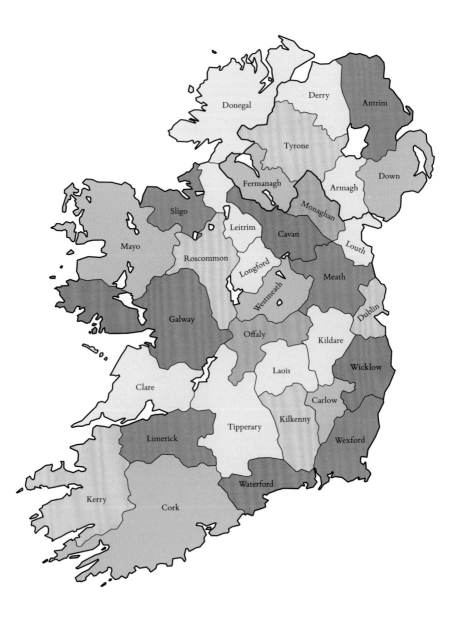

Figure 16.2. An Irish federation based on thirty-two counties

A federation could in principle be built around the thirty-two counties. Scale, in principle, should not exclude this idea: Switzerland has twenty-six cantons. But in such a federation there would be only two counties with a secure cultural Protestant majority (Antrim and Down).

3. The Secretary of State shall not make an order under paragraph
1 earlier than seven years after the holding of a previous poll
under this Schedule.

So, the Secretary of State *may* order a referendum at any time, provided it will be held seven years since the last one, but *shall* order one
when the test is met: when it appears likely that a majority favouring
the end of the Union has emerged.

What objective evidence would enable the Secretary of State to make
that assessment? That is not stated. Perhaps a resolution favouring
reunification endorsed by a majority of Northern MLAs, or by a majority of Northern Ireland's Westminster MPs, or a credible run of surveys
or polls suggesting the requisite shift in opinion may constitute sufficient objective evidence. The Secretary of State has some discretion,
but is constrained by established UK public administration and norms
of legality, fairness, and reasonableness in the exercise of his or her
function. The constraints would come into effect if the decision to hold
or not to hold a referendum was questioned in a court of law. It would,
of course, be sensible for there to be British and Irish political consultation before any referendum, but it would be improper, under
existing UK law, for the Secretary of State to grant a veto to the South
over whether a referendum should be held – that would require fresh
enabling legislation, and modification of the GFA.

What about the other way around? May an Irish government refuse
to give effect to positive referendums? Article 3.1 of Ireland's revised
Constitution reads:[9]

> It is the firm will of the Irish Nation, in harmony and friendship, to
> unite all the people who share the territory of the island of Ireland, in all
> the diversity of their identities and traditions, recognising that a united
> Ireland shall be brought about only by peaceful means with *the consent of
> a majority of the people, democratically expressed,*★ in both jurisdictions in the
> island. Until then, the laws enacted by the Parliament established by this
> Constitution shall have the like area and extent of application as the laws

★ All italics are mine.

enacted by the Parliament that existed immediately before the coming into operation of this Constitution.

Differently put, Irish reunification is a firm constitutional objective, subject to all the specified conditions, so it would be unconstitutional for any Irish Government to refuse to give effect to consent for reunification, and to attempt to block its accomplishment. True, Article 3.1 does not explicitly mandate a referendum in the South, and nor does the text of the GFA, but how else would the consent of a majority of the people in the South be democratically expressed, if not by referendum?

The sole plausible answer is that the two chambers of the Oireachtas could authorize reunification by a majority vote (on legislation). Though the Oireachtas is democratically composed, and abides by democratic norms, it is not 'the people' as named in this constitutional clause. It is reasonable, I conclude, to insist that Article 3.1 obliges a Southern referendum to match that in the North. It must also be doubtful whether the Government, or the Oireachtas, could resist a case brought before the Supreme Court demanding a referendum on Irish unity after a Northern 'Yes' vote.[10]

So, Irish reunification would be accomplished in the South by passing legislation giving effect to a referendum in the North and one in the South that jointly support reunification. In both cases, a simple majority of votes will be sufficient. The Government of Ireland has no veto on Irish reunification. It cannot stop a UK Government determined to hold a referendum on the subject, and it would be inappropriate for it to request halting such a referendum if the conditions for holding one had been met. Equally obviously, the Government of Ireland needs to be prepared for the surprise calling of a referendum in the North, one held without sufficient evidence of significant change of public opinion in the North – a stratagem that may appeal to unionist tacticians eager to win such a referendum and postpone further choice for seven years. In the end, it is those who will vote in Ireland, North and South, who will decide or have a veto on reunification. They can vote against reunification in a referendum, and in the South, citizens can also refuse to endorse any constitutional amendments proposed to give effect to reunification. It is the people, North and South, who will exercise self-determination, not their governments.

Mistaken and unhelpful suggestions

Some have suggested adding qualification to a majority, or a process of parallel consent, instead of the simple majority rule requirement in a referendum in the North (and the South).[11] These proposals, to be explained, are unhelpful – even if they are motivated to achieve greater consent among unionists for a united Ireland.

Start with an obvious paradox. A unionist who votes for Irish reunification is, by that very act, ceasing to be a unionist. So, there can formally never be any unionist support for Irish reunification – as most unionists will tell you politely, if asked politely. But they have accepted the procedural principle of consent: that the sovereign status of Northern Ireland should be decided by the will of a majority.

Moving the goalposts from the existing rule would profoundly disrespect the 1998 referendums. The Government of Ireland has just argued that the UK's withdrawal from the EU should not jeopardize any part of the hard-won GFA. If the South initiated or agreed a major change to the GFA's sovereignty rule, it would appal the Irish in the North and the Irish diaspora and would surprise our allies in Europe. It would also be unworkable because it would have to start through a review of the 1998 Agreement and would be firmly opposed by organized Northern nationalists. No prudent Irish government would adopt such a policy.

In 1998, Irish nationalists, North and South, agreed to stop emphasizing that the will of the majority of the Irish people as a whole in 1918 had been overridden by the partition of 1920. They agreed to put aside the fact that Northern Ireland had been unjustly territorially defined. In return, however, major reforms of policing and the administration of justice, and a battery of equality rights and commissions, were pledged. And unionists accepted three new power-sharing arrangements (within the North, North–South, and East–West). But a core part of the package was the entrenchment of the possibility of reunification by majority consent.

In 1998, the makers of the GFA accepted that reunification required majority consent in the North – *not* the consent of the majority of the unionist community, and *not* the consent of a qualified majority.

Changing the rule would not just be imprudent but unjust. After the Ireland Act of 1949, Northern nationalists were assured by successive British governments that Irish reunification required majority consent by a Belfast parliament. Since 1973 that has been replaced by a majority of those voting in a referendum. A change to require a qualified majority vote for the North to reunify with Ireland would logically require that a qualified majority vote be required to sustain the status quo. If a qualified majority for the Union with Great Britain were not present, then joint British and Irish sovereignty would be the fair response, not the maintenance of the Union.★

To suggest the requirements of a qualified majority in the North for Irish reunification, but not for the maintenance of the Union, is an argument for minority rule. That makes no sense. As Judge Richard Humphreys has noticed: 'Generally, people who say that one cannot coerce hundreds of thousands of unionists into a united Ireland have no real problem with coercing hundreds of thousands of nationalists into a United Kingdom. If one takes equal respect seriously, one has to accept the consequences of a reciprocal test.'[12]

Proponents of a qualified majority are usually imprecise. What, we might ask, do they think a better threshold for consent should be? Fifty per cent plus a specified proportion of unionists (or former unionists)? What proportion though? And how would that be measured, and when?[13]

Imposing a threshold requirement on turnout is a bad idea because it would encourage a boycott by the expected losers. The Venice Commission's Code of Good Practice on Referendums is clear. It is advisable not to provide for a turnout quorum (threshold) or minimum percentage, because it treats voters who abstain as the same as 'No' voters. Equally, to impose an approval quorum (a qualified majority)

★ See Chapter 15 for a discussion of shared sovereignty.

is bad, because that would risk creating a difficult political situation if the proposal is approved by a simple majority that does not meet the threshold.[14]

There is no British precedent for altering the established rule for a reunification referendum from a simple majority to a qualified majority. UK practice in referendums has almost invariably been 50 per cent plus one – with no minimum turnout requirement. The National Assembly for Wales, later renamed Senedd Cymru (the Welsh Parliament), came into being after a 50.3 per cent 'Yes' in the 1997 referendum, on a 50.2 per cent turnout. The UK's exit from the EU occurred after 51.9 per cent voted leave, on a 72.2 per cent turnout.

The late Seamus Mallon's proposal for parallel consent to be applied in the Northern referendum would have equally unacceptable, and more bizarre, consequences. He proposed that a majority of nationalists and of unionists, in the North, should agree before reunification would occur. To work, that idea might require voters in the polling booth to designate as nationalist or unionist. If so: what would stop a unionist designating themselves as a nationalist and voting 'No' to unification, or a nationalist designating as a unionist to favour reunification? Alternatively, the proposal would require all voters to self-designate in advance on separate electoral registers. How else, after all, would one measure parallel consent? Even if that could be done, a simple objection would arise. Are *three* majorities to be required – namely that of nationalists and unionists respectively, and overall? Or four? That is, a majority overall, and majorities among nationalists, unionists, and the 'others' respectively?

There is another decisive objection to Mallon's proposal. Imagine if, between 2022 and 2032, the proportion of the electorate that votes unionist were to fall to roughly 30 per cent, from roughly 40 per cent now. Then, under Mallon's proposed rule, unionists numbering 15 per cent of the voters in Northern Ireland, plus one, would have the right to block reunification. That would be an absurd unionist veto, one that no unionist leader has ever demanded. Revealingly, the party that Mallon once led, the SDLP, has never endorsed his proposal to change the principle of consent.

There is, in short, no wisdom in modifying the existing decision-rule, only unworkable and unjust paths that would confirm the most extreme claims of 'dissident' republicans. The best way to allay fears about a narrow majority for reunification is to make a united Ireland as desirable, or at least as acceptable, as possible for most non-Catholics and non-nationalists. Historically rooted security anxieties throughout the island must also be credibly addressed in planning for reunification.

Premature calls for the Northern referendum should be avoided

The Northern referendum is not a 'one-off'. It can be held twice, or more; indeed, there is only one restriction on further referendums. If the vote for a reunited Ireland does not obtain a simple majority, the same referendum question may be posed no earlier than seven years later.[15] Even though this provision for numerous referendums exists, it would be unwise to call for a Northern referendum, as Sinn Féin leaders have sometimes done, before public opinion clearly favours both a referendum and a vote for reunification.

Personally, I would define 'clearly favours' to mean reliable surveys, or polls, running at a steady 50 per cent favouring reunification,* or a majority resolution by the Northern Assembly, or by a majority of Northern Ireland's Westminster MPs, provided the legislators or MPs have jointly won 50 per cent of the votes cast in the last election. That would both preserve the letter and the ethos of the GFA and be good politics. Losing a reunification referendum, even closely, may damage support for the idea.[16] It would be much better to win a reunification referendum on the first occasion, having spent the interim preparing for all the issues likely to feature in the referendum campaign.

---

* All relevant surveys and polls within their respective margins of error should count and be averaged. For some polls, support for reunification running at 47.0 per cent and above would count as affirmative evidence for a referendum to be called, but as averaging occurred, to make a 'poll of polls', the margin of error would narrow.

The ethos of planning: winning losers' consent

Unionists should be politically treated now, and in the future, with consistent respect and dignity. They should be invited to participate in all deliberative forums and citizens' assemblies devoted to matters related to reunification, and to address committees of the Oireachtas. They should be encouraged to specify which models of a united Ireland they like least, or to say what they would choose if obliged by a referendum loss to consider various versions of a united Ireland. Respect, however, means recognizing that, more likely than not, most unionist leaders will maintain their identifications, and refuse to engage, until they have lost. Their voters are another matter.

There is far more amenable ground for persuasion in the build-up to a referendum to be found among those who, when asked in surveys, self-identify as neither unionist nor nationalist – as well as among those who answer with 'don't know' or other responses. My friend Professor John Garry believes the 'neither/nors' are of three types: weakly committed unionists who do not want a united Ireland, and who vote for unionist parties but don't want to identify with them; cultural Catholics who do not actively want a united Ireland but vote for nationalist parties to champion Catholic interests; and the genuine neither/nors who want nothing to do with the divisive politics of Northern Ireland.

Much should be done to offer strong unionist identifiers and regular voters multiple opportunities to be heard, to participate in citizens' assemblies or constitutional conventions, to negotiate appropriate securities, accommodations, and rights, and to signpost clear and fair processes governing their individual and collective futures. But realists should not expect any significant shift among those who vote unionist before they have lost in a referendum.

The appropriate policy towards strong unionist identifiers may be summarized in a simple formula known to political scientists as 'obtaining loser-consent', or simply 'losers' consent'. Unionists have the same problem. They want nationalists to consent to the union. Nationalists did so by voting for the GFA, but they kept the opportunity to change the sovereign status of Northern Ireland in future. The necessary condition of a successful democratic process is that the losers accept the outcome – or, more realistically, that enough of the losers accept the outcome, so that the outcome can be implemented. In the marshalling of preparations, of managing reason and emotion, those who favour or who simply expect Irish reunification must endeavour to ensure, as best they can, that unionists accept that, when they have lost in a referendum, they have lost fairly, under the provisions of the GFA; and, in addition, that upon losing, they have not lost everything – their identity, their interests, and their cultural preferences. Their British citizenship rights will be respected in the reunified Ireland. Their proportionate collective voting power will be greater in a united Ireland than in the UK. They will be equal citizens and face no discrimination or exclusion – under the protection of European Union law and the European Convention for the Protection of Human Rights and Fundamental Freedoms – and they may enjoy many other negotiated positive or collective rights.

It would be tragic if Irish reunification took place with *zero* support from cultural Protestants – that is, if reunification was entirely dependent upon the votes of cultural Catholics. Such an entirely 'sectarian' result is, however, highly improbable. Right now, there are cultural Catholics who are content with the Union, even if they do not identify as unionists (or nationalists), and there are also smaller numbers of cultural Protestants who recognize that independent Ireland is now very different to William Cosgrave's or de Valera's Ireland, and that the Republic is significantly more secularized than Northern Ireland. They carry Irish passports, not entirely instrumentally, support the Irish rugby team, male or female, and they have experienced exiting the European Union as a loss. In short, there are already some cultural Protestants and cultural Catholics respectively lined up for a united Ireland and for the Union with Great Britain. And then there are the neither/nors.

To win more support than 50 per cent plus one solely based on sectarian origin, and to facilitate losers' consent, the period ahead must be carefully used to make reunification more attractive to the 'others', particularly to cultural Protestants among the others and the self-identifying neither/nors, long before as well as during and after the referendum. It is also necessary to think about a soft landing for those unionists shocked by a vote against the Union. The South has a duty to prepare properly for a 'Yes', and to learn and know what that 'Yes' will mean. The Government and the Oireachtas must begin preparations now – admittedly much earlier than some expected before the UK referendum of the summer of 2016 or the global health crisis that began in the spring of 2020. The horrors of the pandemic and its economic fallout, followed by the Russian invasion and attempted conquest of Ukraine, should not be allowed to obscure the imperative to prepare for a foreseeable outcome and momentous referendum(s).

8.   Three expressions that will still matter

Three key expressions in the Good Friday Agreement, inserted through the successive efforts of Irish diplomacy, have received insufficient attention in the context of discussions about reunification. When drafted, their significance was partly future-oriented, but that future will face us in the decade ahead. They are 'without external impediment', 'the people of the island of Ireland alone', and 'rigorous impartiality'.

In the 1998 Agreement, the governments of the UK and Ireland, and the other participants, recognized that:

> *it is for the people of the island of Ireland alone*, by agreement between the two parts respectively and *without external impediment*, to exercise their right of self-determination on the basis of consent, freely and concurrently given, North and South, to bring about a united Ireland, if that is their wish, accepting that this right must be achieved, and exercised with and subject to the agreement and consent of a majority of the people of Northern Ireland . . .[1]

In the same long sentence, the two sovereign governments affirmed that:

> whatever choice is freely exercised by a majority of the people of Northern Ireland, *the power of the sovereign government with jurisdiction there shall be exercised with rigorous impartiality* on behalf of all the people in the diversity of their identities and traditions and shall be founded on the principles of full respect for, and equality of, civil, political, social and cultural rights, of freedom from discrimination for all citizens, and of parity of esteem and of just and equal treatment for the identity, ethos and aspirations of both communities . . .⋆

⋆ All italics in the above passages are mine.

Without external impediment

The second of these three italicized phrases, 'without external impediment', derives from Book IV of Aristotle's *Politics*.[2] Aristotle was considering arguments for a good polity: it should be most in accordance with our aspirations; appropriately adapted to circumstances; and developed without external impediment – that is, by other polities and empires.

In the long negotiations that preceded the GFA, Ireland's officials in the Department of Foreign Affairs (DFA) familiarized themselves with the international law of self-determination.[3] David Donoghue, a senior official in the 'Anglo-Irish Division' and later Ireland's ambassador to the UN, has told me that they saw:

> merit in going back to the hallowed formulations around self-determination under international law, beginning with Woodrow Wilson in 1918–19 and the League of Nations and extending up to UN texts and resolutions from the 1960s–1970s onwards (when there was a strong emphasis on anti-colonialism and preventing colonial powers from exerting unwelcome pressure, to inhibit a people/nation from carrying out an act of self-determination). Sometimes, as I recall, the phrase which appeared in UN texts was 'external interference', and sometimes it was 'external impediment'.[4]

The 'Declaration on Principles of International Law concerning Friendly Relations and Cooperation among States in accordance with the Charter of the United Nations'[5] issued in 1970, states that:

> By virtue of the principle of equal rights and self-determination of peoples enshrined in the Charter of the United Nations, all peoples have the right freely to determine, *without external interference*, their political status and to pursue their economic, social and cultural development, and every State has the duty to respect this right in accordance with the provisions of the Charter'.★

★ All italics are mine.

Simply put, no 'external interference' by the former colonial powers, or of great or regional powers, should affect the exercise of any people's right to self-determination. 'Without external interference' and 'without external impediment' are synonyms in the customary international law on self-determination,[6] which binds both the UK and Ireland.

'Without external impediment' was introduced into the 1993 Joint Declaration on Peace by a key Irish official,[7] Ireland's former ambassador to Washington and to Berlin, Seán Ó hUiginn.[8] He has told me it was 'a polite way of saying there should be no British finger pressing the scale against unity, i.e. a reinforcement of the British neutrality pledge'.[9] Ó hUiginn emphasizes that the 1993 Declaration was, among other matters, a solemn pledge of British governmental neutrality in the choice between the options of a united sovereign Ireland or the Union, and on any agreement put to referendum, North and South.[10] That pledge is preserved in the GFA. 'Without external impediment' has legal significance because it is a synonym for 'without external interference' and was understood as such by Irish diplomats – and by their British opposite numbers. The future external 'impedimentor' was understood to reference, politely, the historic and the most likely future source of the frustration of Irish self-determination, namely Great Britain.[11]

Martin Mansergh, former advisor to Taoiseach Albert Reynolds, and a skilled historian, seems to think the British obligation is confined to not impeding the holding of a referendum, whereas others, including me, see the UK state and government, though not British political parties, as legally obliged to be fully neutral, i.e. not to intervene to tilt the scales, or to impede a free choice – in the event of a future referendum or referendums, *before*, *during*, and *after* the referendum(s). The difference may seem subtle, but Ó hUiginn is right: the phrasing is intended to preclude any UK/British governmental finger pressing the scale against reunification.[12]

The people of the island of Ireland, alone

On 15 December 1993, in the Joint Declaration on Peace,[13] UK Prime Minister John Major agreed that '*it is for the people of the island of Ireland alone*, by agreement between the two parts respectively, to exercise their right of self-determination on the basis of consent, freely and concurrently given, North and South, to bring about a united Ireland if that is their wish'.★ This wording reappeared in the GFA, but now as part of an international treaty. The right of self-determination of the people of the island of Ireland is to be exercised *alone*. Not with Great Britain. No power outside the island of Ireland may interfere with the exercise of self-determination by the people of the island of Ireland.

The British had pushed back against Sinn Féin's demands in the Hume–Adams talks. The documentary record – both private and public – shows that neither the Irish nor the UK Government entertained the Sinn Féin and IRA proposal that the UK Government be obliged to pledge to become active 'persuaders' for Irish unity.[14] Great Britain was not to interfere in either direction – pro-reunification or pro-Union.

Constructive pledges were first heard in speeches from UK Secretary of State Peter Brooke. He stated that 'it is not the aspiration to a sovereign, united Ireland against which we set our face, but its violent expression'.[15] Britain had no 'selfish strategic or economic interest'[16] in Northern Ireland, and it would accept Irish unification if a majority of the people of Northern Ireland wanted it – a version of the commitment to procedural neutrality on constitutional status that the SDLP argued was already manifest in the Anglo-Irish Agreement of 1985. The statement materially assisted John Hume in encouraging Sinn Féin's Gerry Adams to deliver an IRA ceasefire.

Rigorous impartiality

'Without external impediment' and 'the people of the island of Ireland alone' are explicitly tied in the same sentence in the GFA with a commitment by the sovereign government – as long as it exercises jurisdiction in Northern Ireland – to exercise 'rigorous impartiality'[17] regarding local identities, traditions, and the 'ethos'[18] and aspirations of 'both communities'.

★ All italics are mine.

This commitment to 'rigorous impartiality' is not pious waffle. It is confined to the sovereign government: the UK for now, and it will apply to the Irish Government in the future we are considering. No qualifying restriction is placed on the obligation of the incumbent sovereign government to exercise rigorous impartiality. The most reasonable reading is that the incumbent sovereign must be rigorously impartial regarding the holding of a referendum – when the specified conditions are met – *and* in the conduct of that referendum. Otherwise, the 1998 Agreement would allow for bias in the UK administration of the referendum. The tradition, identity, ethos, and aspirations of Northern nationalists include, perhaps above all, the desire to reunify with the rest of Ireland. By contrast, the tradition, identity, ethos, and aspirations of Ulster unionists include, above all, the desire to retain the Union with Great Britain. It is over their contrasting identities, traditions, ethos, and aspirations that the UK Government must be rigorously impartial, throughout the period of the conduct of the referendum.[19] The obligation is asymmetrical: the Government of Ireland is not the incumbent sovereign and may actively support reunification, but it must prepare to be a sovereign government that would be rigorously impartial.

The upshot

My interpretation of these expressions does not impose – and could not impose – any restriction on the free speech of parties or persons outside the island of Ireland. But the exercise of self-determination by the people of Ireland, North and South, alone, without external impediment, places restraints on the appropriateness of external funding of campaigns, especially but perhaps not only from Great Britain – certainly from UK public funds. Either both sides in the referendum should be equally publicly funded, or not publicly funded at all. No other mode of accomplishing rigorous impartiality is possible.

The island of Ireland cannot be isolated from regional or global opinion or media sources. Free speech off-island about the choice between Irish reunification and maintaining the Union with Great Britain cannot easily be regulated by the Secretary of State, other UK authorities, or the authorities in the Republic. But the obligation placed on the sovereign UK Government and the UK state is clear. Political parties are another matter, especially parties organized on the island of Ireland. It may not be easy to keep a bright line between governmental actions and those of political parties, but the Irish Government must hold the British Government, and its successors, to that line.

It must persistently oblige UK ministers to administer their functions with rigorous impartiality. British party leaders may well be in favour of keeping the Union, and may express themselves in that manner enthusiastically, but not when they are acting in their official capacities, as Prime Minister, Secretary of State, or ministers – or as Leader of the Opposition. It would be a breach of faith, and of the Good Friday Agreement, if the UK Government, Prime Minister, Cabinet, or state officials were to act as partisans in their official governmental capacities, especially in the context of a referendum. If the British Government, as such, were to use the machinery of government to take sides, or distort the channels of public communication, then that would be a violation of pledges solemnly and jointly made in 1993, 1996, and 1998, and reaffirmed through recent international commitments to protect the Good Friday Agreement 'in all its parts'.

In short, these three expressions forbid three sets of actions:

a) outright bias in administration;
b) ambiguous or threatening external impediments to free choice by the people of the island of Ireland, North and South;
c) the subversion of self-determination.

These prohibitions are spelled out below.

Outright bias in administration

Outright bias in administration is forbidden, including biased wording of the question to be posed in the Northern referendum; preparing for the referendum with an opaque decision-making style; choosing an irresponsible moment to initiate the Northern referendum, e.g. when there is a severe natural disaster or pandemic, or nearby armed conflict;

encouraging, or colluding in, partiality among taxpayer-funded public broadcasting and media organizations. Also forbidden is selectively releasing government-sponsored research or information that 'tilts the scales' in favour of the Union; deliberately exaggerating the short-, medium-, or long-term costs of Irish unification – economic, political, and cultural; publicly and abnormally inflating the current and future performance of the Union's economy, Northern Ireland's economy, and current and future scales of public service provision. As are selectively endorsing partisan unionist private media, including social media; propagating or encouraging false beliefs in the low capabilities of the Irish state, or in its record of economic management; and casting unreasonable doubts on the protection of the rights, beliefs, and traditions of Protestants, and of non-Catholics, in the current and future public and private life of Ireland.

Ambiguous or threatening external impediments to free choice by the people of the island of Ireland, North and South

This activity would include British governments threatening to deny or actually denying their obligations under the Good Friday Agreement to maintain the British citizenship rights of people born in Northern Ireland after the transfer of Northern Ireland and its people to the sovereign jurisdiction of Ireland in the wake of a 'Yes' vote for re-unification. British governments are also prohibited from denying the counting of Northern Ireland's monetary share of UK assets in the event of its decision to leave the Union, *or* from declaring their unwillingness to count such assets in an appraisal of Northern Ireland's assets and liabilities. The UK Government may not obstruct or threaten to obstruct how the transfer of sovereignty proceeds, not just regarding citizenship rights and outstanding financial obligations (e.g. pensions) but on the maritime boundaries between the UK and Ireland, or between the UK and the EU, or by linking good UK governmental behaviour on such matters to irrelevant international behaviour by Ireland. Lastly, the UK Government may not threaten non-cooperation in the transfer of sovereignty if the result of the referendum is close, but in favour of Irish reunification.

The subversion of self-determination

The subversion of the free exercise of self-determination by British officials and politicians is forbidden, such as encouraging – quietly, surreptitiously, or publicly – loyalist militia to threaten or use violence to undermine the Good Friday Agreement (or the Protocol created to protect the achievements of the 1998 Agreement); or to frustrate the holding, fair counting, or implementation of a referendum; or encouraging a movement for a unilateral declaration of independence within any or all of Northern Ireland before, during, or after the Northern referendum. It is also forbidden to subvert the GFA to change the rule on the transfer of sovereignty from simple majority rule to some qualified majority rule, or by adding a threshold; to play deliberately upon societal fears, prejudices, or stereotypes in the run-up to or during the referendum; to discourage the police or other security officials from cooperating in preserving public order before, during and after the referendum on the potential transfer of sovereignty; to question the legitimacy of a future referendum outcome, by suggesting that it is a result of fraud, or solely influenced by past violence by militant Irish republicans. It also undermines the GFA to treat peaceful advocates of Irish reunification as subversives, traitors, extremists, or as simply irresponsible, and the choice of Irish reunification in a referendum as irrational. To place Ulster unionist partisans on referendum commissions in an unbalanced manner, or on the boards of British public broadcasting media, would also be a biased subversion of the pledge to observe rigorous impartiality. So would over-representing pro-reunification voices within public broadcasting in Great Britain.

These are negative lists, bleak hazard warnings. I regret having had to compose them. However, the UK's referendum on EU membership of 2016 was an education; so too has been the conduct of the Johnson administration since 2019, as well as Johnson's previous conduct as a campaigning Brexiteer, and Foreign Secretary. Considering this very recent past it would be irrational for any Irish person, North or South, simply to trust in some nostalgic idea of British fair play, especially but not only that of Conservative governments. The torrent of irresponsibility towards Ireland that has flowed from Great Britain since 2016 is a clear and present warning. Irish planning for reunification must take place with open consideration of these bleak possibilities.

It should become the duty, and prepared commitment, of both the British and Irish governments to ensure that unlawful external impediments to free choice do not happen. Ireland can hope for a more principled UK Government than the current one, but it cannot rely on that prospect. Irish Governments must seek procedural safeguards in advance and use the British-Irish Intergovernmental Conference to elaborate agreed rules of conduct, and misconduct, regarding future referendums. It may seem regrettable to appraise the future relevance of the GFA in this manner, but it is wise to do so. We should not be faint-hearted or down-hearted, however: the hard-won accomplishments of previous cohorts of Irish diplomats and politicians are there to be built on.

9.   Preparation: planning, deliberation, and polling

On average, humans are optimistic about our own lives but pessimistic about our countries – and the planet.[1] We are optimists about what is local and seems in our control, but not about matters on a larger scale, or out of our control. The late Albert Hirschman suggested that to generate progress we need to be irrationally optimistic about our capabilities: those who have a wholly rational sense of their ability to do things are depressed.[2] Martin Seligman, my colleague in the Psychology department at the University of Pennsylvania, links control and optimism: the more we think we can control matters, the happier and more optimistic we can be.[3] Seligman is an unusual psychologist because he studies human happiness. 'Miserabilism', however, is the norm among intellectuals and in folk wisdom. To judge that the world is accelerating its descent into hell is considered proof of high intelligence, even though the net evidence in favour of human progress remains significant.[4]

There is a tendency among Irish intellectuals especially to be bleak about the prospects of reunification. The message of this chapter is that we Irish and the British in Ireland, North and South, should be happy with our net progress – in the South since the 1960s, and in the North since the 1990s. I say *net* progress, as there has been plenty of intermittent regress, failure, and shame all round, and we should not be complacent. Increased secularization has been generally good for our happiness. Largely gone is the grim focus on the next world as the site of possible well-being in compensation for this vale of tears. Even those who believe in a hereafter believe we can do better in the here and now. It is in this spirit that our prospective reunification can and should be prepared for and planned.

Reunification will start with two democratic events – the two referendums – and we must get ready for both. The two feasible models of reunification, and the choice between models or the process to pick a model, will be outlined in the next part of the book. Whichever model or process is chosen in the South before the Northern referendum should be extensively researched, publicly deliberated, and scrutinized – tested by the fire of public opinion, public debate, and public reflection – with as much engagement of the peoples in the North as possible, British, Protestant, and Unionist, Irish, Catholic, and national-ist, as well as the neither/nors.

We can do that. We have just enough time if the likely date for the referendums is around 2030. Not to do so – not to research, deliberate, and plan – is either a decision to avoid reunification or a decision to postpone serious choices until after these referendums. The majority in the deliberative mini-publics that John Garry and I have held, North and South, strongly concur with the view that they need to know what they will be voting for – or against. This view has been greatly influ-enced by the Brexit referendum.

The prospects for the chosen model will be brightest if a cross-party consensus can be built around it in the South. That is not an outlandish hope. A complex subject – transforming healthcare – resulted in such a consensus in the project of Sláintecare.[5] It is a ten-year plan, and every party from Fine Gael through to Sinn Féin signed up to it. It is, of course, not without controversy; nevertheless, the policy consensus survives on what is to be done.

The time has arrived for a genuine debate in the South about what form of Irish reunification would and should be on offer as and when such a ref-erendum is held in the North. It is the minimal courtesy owed to potential future citizens among Northern unionists, nationalists, and 'others'. It is better that they hear the Southern conversation in its full range, including the naysayers and those observing, of difficulties and trade-offs. Whispers to the effect of 'don't frighten the horses' should not put people off. Nor should the advice to focus solely on cross-border cooperation, without ref-erence to the possibility of Irish unification, be followed – though that is the direction in which Micheál Martin is perceived to have taken the recently established Shared Island Unit inside the Taoiseach's department.[6] The trajectory of the Shared Island Initiative is difficult to assess because it is new. Its projects should be supported, with the proviso that, as currently projected, they will not be enough. The initiative may be adapted to allow conversation on models of a united Ireland.

To debate and prepare is not to prejudge or prejudice the outcome, still less is it to harass prospective future citizens. Rather, preparation is required to avoid chaotic, fast-paced, crisis decision-making at some future date, and to allay legitimate anxieties in advance, as well as possible. Quite simply, Ireland cannot afford a magnified version of the Brexit referendum. Namely, an irresponsible referendum, irresponsibly debated, saturated with disinformation, without proper planning for either outcome, and with shady funding. Debate must occur and endure, even though unionist politicians, for coherent strategic and tactical reasons, will likely decide not to debate the possibilities of reunification, or to attend conferences and forums, or to participate in media events, until, from their perspective, an adverse referendum outcome occurs. Every effort must be made to ensure that unionist politicians cannot say they were never invited, nor consulted, nor given an opportunity to comment on plans, white papers, contingent legislation, or contingent (or actual) constitutional amendments. Retired unionist politicians are another matter – Peter Robinson has indicated that unionists need to prepare for a referendum.[7]

Southern politicians and civil society need to consider in deliberative depth what changes, if any, they would like to make to the Constitution *either* in advance (e.g. to encompass the identities, rights, and interests of new minorities, including a large British minority) *or* that would go into effect contingent upon reunification. They need to start at the very beginning of the Constitution.

Start at the beginning, with the Preamble

Take the Preamble, which is not an operative part of Ireland's Constitution, but which has symbolic significance, and which will be brought to the attention of any conscientious person, North and South, before the referendums. It reads:

> In the Name of the Most Holy Trinity, from Whom is all authority and to Whom, as our final end, all actions both of men and States must be referred,

We, the people of Éire,

Humbly acknowledging all our obligations to our Divine Lord, Jesus Christ, Who sustained our fathers through centuries of trial,

Gratefully remembering their heroic and unremitting struggle to regain the rightful independence of our Nation,

And seeking to promote the common good, with due observance of Prudence, Justice and Charity, so that the dignity and freedom of the individual may be assured, true social order attained, the unity of our country restored, and concord established with other nations,

Do hereby adopt, enact, and give to ourselves this Constitution.[8]

The goals sought in this Preamble – the common good, and the dignity and freedom of the individual – are not controversial. Likewise, concord with other nations. Importantly, however, after reunification unity would be restored or established, by definition, and therefore part of the Preamble would be immediately redundant.

But anyone can read that the Preamble is neither inclusive nor pluralist. Even its democratic and republican spirit is questionable. It derives all authority, curiously, from the Most Holy Trinity, rather than God, though in Catholic and much Protestant theology they are one and the same. It defines 'the people of Éire', not the people of the whole island of Ireland, as adopting and enacting the Constitution. It recalls the religious as well as the national oppression of the Catholic Irish, and their religious oppression before their national oppression. It is Christian but does not sit well with Christians who are not Trinitarians (including Protestant Unitarians). It has no room for unbelievers, agnostics, and atheists, who would not accept any religious source of authority, and are arguably the fastest-growing demographic category, South and North. And there is no overt place for exponents of non-Christian religions (though Jews were protected elsewhere in the original text). As for our fathers, or forefathers, were they always heroic or unremitting in their struggle? And who were those fathers? Did we have no mothers? Some would even quarrel with the idea that we *regained* as opposed to *gained* our independence.

The Preamble is therefore outdated, redundant, and offensive to proportionally far more people than it was in 1937. What is to be done? Here is one possible preamble, more appropriate to our present, and our future reunification:

We the people of the island of Ireland and its islands;

Mindful of all past dissension, and determined to avoid its recurrence;

Seeking to promote the common good while assuring the dignity and freedom of the individual;

Determined to respect and accomplish the full equality of all men and women;

And to protect and cherish all our children equally;

Respecting all the languages of our island: Irish, English, and Ulster-Scots – and the heritage languages of our newcomers;

And recalling all those who sought to establish a free and self-governing Irish nation, who sought to establish an independent democratic republic based on the equality of all its citizens in the full plenitude of their diversity, those who left our shores to avoid hunger and hardship or in pursuit of greater freedom and opportunity, those who sought to improve our health, our well-being, and our prosperity, those who stewarded our lands and waters, those who advanced our cultures, those who sought to establish the rights and dignity of those who work and care, those who were killed or maimed in our civil wars and conflicts with our neighbours in Europe, those who sought religious, secular, intellectual, and sexual freedom, and those who sought to reduce cruelty in our public and private lives;

Embracing in full respect for their identity and ethos in common citizenship, Nationalists, Republicans, Unionists, Loyalists, and others, the Travellers, and all those of English, Scots, Welsh, or British heritage among us who have been part of our shared island for centuries, or who have joined us more recently, who are new Irish from elsewhere, & those who will become new Irish in future;

Rejecting all national or religious exclusivism or sectarianism while respecting the religious liberties of all, including the freedom to have no religion,

Respecting the separation of our State from all churches and religions,

Abhorring all racial, ethnic, and sectarian hatred, and negative racial, ethnic, or sectarian discrimination;

Fully respecting the equality, and intent on securing the flourishing of people with disabilities, the elderly, and the infirm;

Determined to steward our beautiful island and its islands for future generations;

To promote peace, democratic freedoms, and human rights at home, and within our common European home, and in the wider world;

To be unified and sovereign amid our past, current, and future diversity,

Do hereby adopt, enact, and give to ourselves this Constitution.

Feel free to amend, emend, or delete this suggested alternative. It is simply one replacement draft for discussion, to show what could be done. It is not written in the expectation of immediate universal assent. Simply ask, however, whether the tone and timbre, drafted for possible use in 2030, would be better than that drafted under de Valera's auspices in the 1930s.

In a possible, spare, and simpler alternative, what of the following?

Ireland's citizens do hereby adopt and enact this democratic Constitution.

Those who prefer concision will be happier with this brief preamble.

The appropriateness of the existing Preamble is but one among the numerous questions for which detailed and credible answers about the Constitution will be required in the referendum campaigns. There will be, as I will elaborate, a strong case for a 'mix and match' approach to reunification, in which the best of Northern and Southern practices and policies would go into a united Ireland. The point is that specifying exactly which practices are best can only be done after extensive research, deliberation, and planning, and through detailed and credible sectoral analysis and research, accompanied or followed by deliberative forums and assemblies.

In planning reunification, we can do more than we are doing now, and better. What is required, well before any possible Northern referendum, is for the Oireachtas and the civil service to clarify the two feasible models elaborated in Part Four of this book (or indeed any model not considered here, including those proposed by others with different views to my own), and then to decide which model will be advanced in the referendums – if any. If a decision is made to postpone the choice of a model to a constitutional convention after the referendums, then the transitional model of a reunified Ireland will have to be specified.

Work needs to be done on clarifying the benefits and costs of each model. Domestic, international, and comparative expertise should be openly sought out. The initial estimations of the benefits and costs should be continually updated. Minimally, transitional legislation and contingent constitutional amendments, along with a transition fund, would have to be prepared for the chosen model. A reunification bill, and any necessary amendments to accompany the Southern referendum should be 'lawyered', and written as accessibly as possible (admittedly a paradoxical injunction).

The duty of parties organized in the South

All major political parties in the South favour a united Ireland. In addition, the Greens, People Before Profit, and Sinn Féin are organized in both the North and the South. Here is Fine Gael's manifesto pledge from the general election of 2020: 'Bunreacht na hÉireann affirms our national aspiration for territorial unity. Fine Gael, the United Ireland Party, shares that aspiration, based on the principle of consent and a majority, north and south, being in favour.' No planning commitments followed.

Sinn Féin declared in its manifesto that it would seek the full implementation of the GFA, publish a white paper on Irish unity, establish a joint Oireachtas Committee on Irish unity, and that it would 'secure' a 'referendum, North and South, on a United Ireland'. The planning components were reasonable commitments, but the party, even if it led the government, cannot 'secure' the holding of a Northern referendum while remaining within the provisions of the GFA, because the initiation of such a referendum rests with the UK.

In its manifesto, Fianna Fáil has a full passage under the heading 'Protecting the Good Friday Agreement & Strengthening North-South Links after Brexit'. The manifesto declares that Fianna Fáil believes that 'unity within a shared state' would be to 'the social, economic and cultural benefit of all the people of our island', though it does not define such a shared state. The manifesto warns: 'The future constitutional status of Northern Ireland cannot be allowed to become a party-dominated issue, exploited for short-term reasons. Fianna Fáil believes that the unity of hearts and minds cannot be achieved in an aggressive, partisan manner. We believe that the focus in the next few years must be a neutral and factual discussion of the impact of various approaches to Northern Ireland's future.' That may seem reasonable, especially regarding matters of tone, but Fianna Fáil cannot be fully neutral if it truly believes in unity within a shared state. In government since 2020, the party's ministers have not focused on reunification as one of the various approaches to Northern Ireland's future. They have, however, paid some attention to other approaches, notably through the Shared Island Initiative, which is promoted as without prejudice to reunification or the status quo.[9]

While both Fine Gael and Fianna Fáil are short on detail, and unwilling or reluctant to start their planning homework, Sinn Féin seem overeager to speak of planning without recognizing its scale and to 'secure' the first referendum, which is not within their discretion. All three major parties will have to change if they are to engage and collaborate in mature planning. The same injunction applies to the Greens, Labour, the Social Democrats, and People Before Profit. Sinn Féin's commitment to a joint Oireachtas Committee must be matched with Fianna Fáil's commitment to detailed factual analysis, which cannot be neutral because of the parties' shared commitment to the objectives in the Constitution. Fine Gael's aspirations must be rendered as operational plans, built with others. The smaller parties, as the initiation of Sláintecare shows, are quite capable of helping build a considered consensus on difficult questions posed by reunification, but must be allowed to do so.

Financing the transition

One immediate matter on which the parties in the Oireachtas could agree is simple, though the legislation will require care. A transition fund could and should be started now. It is exceptionally difficult to estimate the exact costs of the transition, especially eight to twelve years out, and I will discuss possible costs and benefits further in Part Six, but it would be foolish to assume the costs could be covered with ease out of current borrowing at the time of reunification. Although that possibility exists, it should not be taken for granted. It would be deeply unwise to propose or to implement across-the-board tax rises at the time of reunification because, other things being equal, that could dampen economic growth – and promising a recession is a bad way to promote the political birth of reunification in a referendum, not just bad economics. It would also aid the unionist cause in a referendum.

Borrowing now at low interest rates, which may remain at historically low levels even as the European Central Bank is mandated to control inflation, would be prudent. Even the war over Ukraine, which started in February 2022, is not going to lead to very high levels of interest rates, though the future will be there to correct me. These borrowed funds would be put into a hypothecated (or targeted) sovereign wealth fund. The dividends from the sovereign wealth fund could be used for two purposes only:

– to finance capital expenditure projects that are all-island or
  cross-border in character
– to address the costs of transition at reunification.

Capital expenditure should be construed as covering traditional infrastructure (roads, railways, airports, ferries, seaports, and electricity) and new infrastructure (digital and new environment-friendly energy programmes). It should also cover the infrastructure of the public services that will have an all-island character, especially those related to the North South Ministerial Council. Specialist medical units would be one reasonable focus. Legislation should be written deliberately to block the diversion – or virement – of the sovereign fund for other purposes by ministers. A 'sunset clause' of twenty years could be included to address the possibility that reunification may not occur or may be voted down twice. After the establishment of this fund through initial borrowing at relatively cheap rates, it should be annually topped up with 1.00 per cent of annual governmental revenues, perhaps on a quarterly basis. For comparison, 0.70 per cent of GDP is what is globally recommended for development aid.[10] If we cannot manage a little more than that for the momentous possibility of reunification, we will not be planning.

A national strategic reunification plan

It would be impossible for me to address here all current and future domestic public policy questions (health, housing, education, taxation) attached to a united Ireland, and those externally focused on international alliances, and the numerous symbolic questions – including those internally focused on flags, emblems, anthems, and parades – though I will make suggestions later.* But I emphasize that policies should not be proposed amid hasty decision-making in a coalition cabinet just before the referendum is called, when short-term party interests could be too much to the fore.

Ireland requires a developed national reunification strategic plan that is as all-party in its development as possible. Not one person's plan. Not one party's plan. Not a rigid plan, with a single critical path, or a diktat, but a plan based on large-scale and intensive consultation and research, and one capable of surviving scrutiny from friendly and ferocious fire; a strategic plan that will be published as a credible text, and one that can undergo regular review and revision but which will define a united Ireland – so that it will no longer be an abstraction by the time it is voted on.

* See Part Eight.

Democratic expression on reunification requires a matching Southern referendum, as I argued earlier, but it need not take place on the same date as the Northern referendum. Concurrent referendums must address substantively the same question; they need not be held on the same day, or indeed have exactly the same words on the ballot paper.★ As I will argue in Part Seven, it is likely better that the Southern referendum should occur after the Northern one. One consideration is simple: if the Northern referendum fails, what need would there be to put the South through unnecessary transformations? If the Northern referendum has not passed, or is not expected to pass, why would the Southern public engage fully with the issues at stake? Whatever one's judgement on these matters, it surely needs to be clarified by the Government of Ireland, with legal care, that there *will* be a Southern referendum, or referendums – or *not*; and exactly when one (or many, if there are to be a series of constitutional amendments) should take place after the Northern referendum. There is, in places, a right to silence, but, going forth, silence on these subjects is not sensible; posterity will deem it irresponsible.

Those who do not want reunification to happen, North and South, are and should be entirely free to say so, and no doubt will do so. During the referendums they can campaign for the status quo as vigorously as they wish – peacefully. It is far, far better that their objections are known and addressed in the decade ahead, and appropriately accommodated as justly and efficiently as possible. It will be best, however, if politicians and public opinion in the South do not hide for another five years under what an old satirist called the 'principle of unripe time' – namely, 'that people should not do at the present moment what they think right at that moment, because the moment at which they think it right has not yet arrived'.[11]

★ The reason the words need not be identical is that the South may be amending its Constitution through the referendum, and the UK and Ireland have different conventions on the design of question wording in a referendum.

A Ministry of National Reunification

A ministry with a mandate to prepare for the possibility of national reunification, and to remain in place after reunification has been ratified, should be established through legislation, given the scale of planning required, to provide continuity across changing Irish governments; and because, lest we forget, the GFA allows for a reunification referendum seven years later if there is a 'No' vote in the North on the first occasion. Irish reunification should not be a matter exclusively for the Department of Foreign Affairs, or left in a small sub-unit of the Taoiseach's department devoted to all-island matters – though that is a welcome upgrade of attention. Ambitious civil servants, with strong track records and high-calibre profiles from across numerous departments, are required. They need to be resourced to conduct their own work, and to commission fundamental research from outside their ranks. Irish reunification, if it happens, will cut across every dimension of Irish public life, so nothing short of a ministry is necessary to create the right kind of coordinated planning for a change of this order.[12]

Just as draft legislation is proofed for its conformity with our existing human rights commitments, so the Ministry of National Reunification should comment on the implications of all draft legislation for reunification. The cabinet handbook should be amended so that this new ministry is among the few that vets all new legislation (to assess its implications for reunification). A Brexit department was mooted and rejected recently, but reunification is of an order of magnitude greater in significance for all of Ireland.

The ideal ministry would not, however, be a traditional one, at some remove from the public. Rather, it would work to include citizens in engagements over the choice of a model or a process; and to support research, deliberation, and citizens' assemblies. It would be tasked with coordinating and operating the national strategic plan for reunification. Successive citizens' assemblies or a preparatory constitutional revision convention could address and refine the models proposed here (and possibly others), and questions that will arise irrespective of the model or process chosen for reunification. Clarity, for example, is required on the franchise – who will have the right to vote in the referendums, in the North and South respectively.[13] Detailed consideration of the proper rules and best practices on campaign conduct, financing, and media regulation is imperative. The ideal aim, never capable of full realization, should be to accomplish a common Irish deliberative space, North and South, both actual and virtual, free from all external impediment – including Russian bots and other forms of disinformation.

A cautionary warning on citizens' assemblies. John Garry and I agree that citizens' assemblies are of most value when convened to address a well-specified choice between two plausible but distinct alternatives, where the public is known not to be fully informed or known not to be entrenched in its positions. Citizens' assemblies are good for deliberation over choice A or B, on policy or constitutional question X. When conducted well, they tell us what the public is likely to think when it is better informed. They are much less good as all-purpose meetings on subjects without clearly defined binary choices. Specifically, I am not commending citizens' assemblies on Irish reunification, but rather citizens' assemblies on defined questions related to the possibility of reunification, such as 'Should the Government of Ireland define a model of a united Ireland before the Northern referendum, or should it allow that referendum to take place as an answer to a question of principle, leaving the definition of a model to a constitutional convention?'

A standing forum

Ireland held a New Ireland Forum in 1984. Unionists did not attend. Ireland hosted the Forum for Peace and Reconciliation in 1995 – in which 'others', not just nationalists, participated. It is now time to consider a sitting Forum on Irish Futures that is all-party, i.e. with standing invitations to all political parties on the island committed to democratic and peaceful means. Indeed, it should not be confined to political parties. It could sit in plenary for every business day in one month in every year, and in the interim commission research, take hearings, and invite whomever it wishes to address it. It could be resourced and organized under the auspices of the Ministry of National Reunification. It should be part of the duty of the ministry to poll and survey regularly, with or without focus groups or deliberative forums, to identify enthusiasm, hostility, or indifference to holding unification referendums, and to identifying the chief obstacles to support for unity, North and South, and the chief reasons for support. Such information will assist governmental and party communications and could lead to a decision to switch the initially chosen model of reunification. The ministry should be the responsibility of a Minister of State, perhaps within the portfolio of the Taoiseach or the Deputy Prime Minister, the Tánaiste (it could be the department of that important post).

Referendum security

Cyber-security is not among my fields of competence, but the sustained experience of external interference in elections and referendums across a range of democracies provides advance warning to the Government of Ireland. The conduct of the future referendums needs to be protected by recruiting from the numerous digitally savvy technicians available on the island – through advance planning and building standing capacity. Doubtless long before 2030 greater security in these domains will have been legislated for and provisioned.

Unifying Ireland in referendums must be done carefully to avoid civil war, let alone state collapse. Preparation is key, as I have emphasized. The biggest danger is a loyalist insurgency that may begin before and during the Northern referendum and continue up until, and after, the Southern referendum. A much smaller danger is that radical republicans, so-called dissidents, might exploit instability or a loyalist insurgency to attempt to seize power following the dreams of previous cohorts of republican revolutionaries. What can be done to minimize these dangers? The Government of Ireland must plan for reunification through democratic consent, North and South, but it must systematically prepare for action against those who will not accept a democratic procedure or outcome. It must prepare, ideally in cooperation with the British Government, to provide adequate policing and cyber-security during and after the referendums, not least in securing the transparent conduct of the counts.

There is a security case for having the unification referendums, North and South, on the same day, but there is a better case to have them sequenced, both for constitutional reasons already given and security reasons. The security case for sequencing is that the two governments can focus on the site of the relevant referendum, because direct action, including bombings and killings, would likely be targeted to shape the views of voters in the place where the next referendum is due. Yes, both the grim and the positive have to be countenanced: hope for the best, prepare for the worst. We shall return to security questions,* but we must first address some of the key choices about which we all need to deliberate.

* See Part Seven.

PART FOUR

Models and Process

10. A critical choice: offering a model, or a process to pick a model?

Northerners and Southerners will vote concurrently on reunifying Ireland – they will co-decide, on the same substantive question, but that decision need not be simultaneous. Simultaneous or not, voters will need to know the structures, the financing, and the policy arrangements into which they will be incorporated. Not every minute detail of the national reunification plan will need to be known, but the future citizens of a united Ireland will minimally need significant and stable information, elaborated in a concise version of that plan. The appropriate knowledge to enable informed voting in the referendum can be acquired either through a modelling or a process approach – or perhaps both.[1]

The modelling approach

In the modelling approach, a specific model for reunification will be drafted after issues have been extensively deliberated through the work of citizens' assemblies, deliberative forums, committees of the Oireachtas, government-sponsored policy forums, and after ministerial-led planning, preferably coordinated through a Ministry of National Reunification, as discussed in Chapter 9. The fundamental purpose of elaborating the model of reunification will be to clarify exactly what kind of united Ireland will be on offer during the referendums, and to provide an implementation plan in the event of a joint vote for reunification. The relevant model will be offered by the Government of Ireland, on behalf of the Southern citizenry, after having taken in-depth and sustained soundings of Northern opinion. The model will be published before the North votes, and it will have to be endorsed by the South when it votes subsequently in its matching referendum.[2]

If the modelling approach is followed, then two feasible models are the most likely to emerge. I will outline these two models in Chapters 11 and 12. The two feasible models are variants of a *unitary state* – a state in which the people, through their central legislature, are fully sovereign. Unitary states can make, remake, and break their regional and local governments. By contrast, in a *federal state*, sovereignty is shared and divided between the federal government and the federative regions that compose the federation. The federal government cannot break the federative regions, and the federal constitution protects the initial pattern of sharing and division: constitutional amendments are usually difficult to make.

Unitary states vary in their degrees of centralization, however. France, for example, was once one of the most centralized republics in Europe. At the other end of the scale are decentralized unitary states: Sweden and Denmark are good examples. A state can be unitary but constitutionally protect its chosen pattern of decentralization – that is, it may require constitutional amendments to modify that pattern. So constitutionalized decentralized unitary states can come to resemble federations, while the legal primacy of the sovereign people remains intact.

The two models elaborated in the next two chapters are feasible because they flow from Ireland's existing constitutional, institutional, and treaty heritages. In one, Northern Ireland persists as a devolved entity within a united Ireland; in the other, Northern Ireland is dissolved into an integrated united Ireland. Each of these models can be tweaked in numerous ways, and each is sufficiently flexible that it could respond to future desires for constitutional, institutional, and policy change. A key advantage of both models is that the Republic will not have to engage in grand-scale constitutional replacement. Both are compatible with the Constitution of Ireland and the Good Friday Agreement, so each is consistent with existing constitutional pledges to Northern Ireland. The argument developed in these chapters deliberately attempts to focus attention on these two choices. Later chapters consider other options.

The process approach

The process approach, by contrast with the modelling approach, asserts that the future referendums, North and South, should not focus on a precise model of a united Ireland, put forward by the Government of Ireland, or on providing the institutional and policy detail attached to that model, sector by sector, body by body, in an abundance of annexes. Rather, it insists that only the 'question of principle' should be decided in the referendums – namely, whether Northern Ireland's union with Great Britain is to continue, or whether there is to be a sovereign united Ireland. Only after that question of principle is decided should the modelling commence. The process approach suggests we should post-pone the choice of model until after the referendums, but it could include limiting the range of models that will be available.

The process approach is based on principled and pragmatic consider-ations. The principled argument is that the South should not choose for the North, in the way, for example, that the Federal Republic of Ger-many chose the model of unification for the former DDR. Rather, all of Ireland, after reunification, should choose together. Two pragmatic arguments are also made. Most unionists will not engage on their pre-ferred model of a united Ireland until they have lost in the referendum, so we should halt discussions of a possible model until they have defini-tively lost. It is also suggested that the modelling approach, with its clarity, might alienate potential nationalists, North and South, who might otherwise support the principle of reunification. The suggestion is that the modelling approach will encourage people to think ego-centrically – 'What's in it for me, and what will I lose?' – as opposed to altruistically – what is best for Ireland, North and South?

Advocates of the process approach typically suggest that, after the principle of reunification has been endorsed, there would have to be a democratic, all-island, constitutional convention, elected by pro-portional representation and convened to propose a brand-new replacement constitution, or to propose extensive or minimal amend-ments to the existing Constitution of Ireland. This convention is where the model would be decided.

The process approach accepts that the modelling approach asks most of the right questions. Unitary state? If so, with a continuing Northern Ireland or not? Federation? If so, with what federal regions? Power-sharing securities for the new unionist, culturally Protestant, and British-identifying minority, or not? If so, which ones? Transitional or permanent accommodations? If so, which ones? The process approach insists, however, that all these appropriate questions should be discussed, deliberated fully, and negotiated *after* the referendums – when Northerners are in a reunified Ireland.

Advocates of the process approach usually concede that there must be a transition. Northern Ireland could not wait in a UK layby until the constitutional convention delivered the tarmac of a united Ireland. The existing Constitution of Ireland would have to remain in force, pending renewal or replacement. An immediate decision, however, would have to made about the transition – namely, whether to recognize the continuation of the Northern Assembly and Executive until the constitutional convention decides their fate, or dissolve them, even if they might be reactivated by the convention's decisions. Another matter could not be avoided. The Oireachtas would have to be expanded proportionally, bringing in Northern deputies, again pending the outcome of the constitutional convention. Those deputies would have to be freshly elected.

In the process approach, the transitional arrangements, unavoidably, would have to take place under the existing Constitution of Ireland. But these transitional arrangements would have to be clear before the referendum. You can see where this discussion is headed. There is no *pure* process approach: a transitional model will have to be advocated, and the transitional arrangements will likely predict the final model.

The process approach does not mean that preparatory work would have to be postponed: it does not let any current or future Irish Governments off the hook. Preparatory work will have to be done by the South, both in justifying the process approach and in preparing the grounds for a successful constitutional convention. The key and immediate difficulty is that, before they vote in the referendum, Northerners, whether unionist, nationalist, or 'other', will not know the outcome of the constitutional convention. That is equally true of Southerners, but there is an important difference. Southerners will comprise two-thirds or more of the convention under any rule of proportional representation. Southerners' critical concerns are therefore unlikely to be neglected, and the default will be the Irish Constitution as is. If the convention fails to agree a constitutional report or replacement constitution according to its own rules of procedure, or if the public votes down the replacement constitution painfully agreed at the convention, then the default would be Bunreacht na hÉireann – with or without a recognized subordinate legislature in the North. Differently put, by default Dáil Éireann would choose the model in these circumstances, by voting on whether to recognize the Northern Assembly as a subordinate legislature.

The uncertainty in the process approach would be very high. One of my correspondents, Kieran Bradley, a Northerner who became a Southerner, and then an EU judge, has described the process approach as 'like voting for an engine without seeing the car'.[3] Securities or guarantees would have to be given *before* the referendums about how the constitutional convention would work, what its decision rules would be, and who would chair or co-chair it, for example. The convention, for these reasons, would have to work under a set of principles, and to operate under the constraint of guaranteeing that a set of rights, and affirmative governmental duties, would be in the final draft constitution written at the convention. These provisions would have to be published well in advance by the South, as its solemn pledges, before the Northern referendum. All Northerners – unionists, nationalists, and 'others' – would then be able to know their minimal future rights and expectations. So, it would be impossible for a credible process approach to avoid some preliminary modelling.

A possible mechanism exists to make credible the commitments on rights and principles to be given by the South about the functioning of a constitutional convention before the referendums. Ireland could follow a variation on the approach used in the transition from apartheid to a democratic South Africa.[4] Namely, the judiciary, comprising a panel of the Irish Supreme Court and an equally sized panel of the judges from the Northern Ireland Court of Appeal, would be tasked to read and confirm that any draft constitution produced by the convention – or set of amendments – is fully compliant with the principles and rights pledged by the South before the referendum. If the judges did not approve the text – subject to a decision rule to be agreed – then the draft constitution would not go before the people for ratification until suitably amended by the re-seated convention.[5]

That is a sketch of how the process approach might work. To preserve constitutional order, Ireland's current Constitution would remain as the default until it was renewed or replaced. No advance guarantees could be given that the constitutional convention will succeed in drafting a new constitution or amendments which would then be approved by the public. If such guarantees could be given, then the convention would be redundant. The default would be the existing Constitution of Ireland, with its existing opportunities for the two feasible models – but with one of them already in operation. The integrated model is the default unless and until Dáil Éireann and the Senate vote to recognize the Northern Ireland Assembly as a subordinate legislature. If the convention failed, or if its draft constitution was rejected by the people, then the Oireachtas would decide, by normal legislation, which of the two feasible models went into effect.

So, there is a nested choice here. Should the South offer a model of reunification to the North before the referendums, or should it offer an opportunity to pick a model jointly after the referendums? Offer a model, or a process to pick a model? Before we consider that question in depth, greater clarification is required about what I have called the 'two feasible models'.

11. Model 1: A continuing Northern Ireland

The first model may be called, to spell out its implications, the 'persisting Northern Ireland model', or the devolved model. The version of the continuing Northern Ireland model developed here may also be called the 'full transfer of the Belfast or Good Friday Agreement model' (or simply the 'full transfer model', if you prefer). In this model of a united Ireland, Northern Ireland would continue to exist, but not as a devolved entity inside the United Kingdom. Instead, it would become a devolved unit within a reunited Ireland, as visualized in Figure 11.1 in the colour plate section.[1]

Constitutional background

This model has been constitutionally available ever since Ireland became sovereign. Indeed, the idea of a continuing Northern Ireland has a significant republican pedigree. That may surprise some readers. Yet Article 44 of the Constitution of the Irish Free State (1922) had the following provision: 'The Oireachtas may create subordinate legislatures with such powers as may be decided by law.'[2] This possibility was requested by Michael Collins, as the head of the provisional government. He wanted a compromise mechanism readily available to incorporate Northern Ireland in a reunited Irish Free State.

There were three drafts of the Free State constitution: A, B, and C. All fulfilled Collins's instruction. Drafts A and B allowed the Oireachtas to create subordinate legislatures, while Draft C permitted an 'Irish Congress' to delegate to 'local representative assemblies' such 'derivative authority in legislative administrative, cultural and economic affairs, as is compatible with the unity and integrity of Ireland'. Draft B was chosen and, with some modifications, became the final constitutional text.[3]

Draft A, by Darrell Figgis, focused more fully on the powers that should *not* be devolved by the Oireachtas. Namely, military security, citizenship, the currency, market regulations, customs and excise, and communications. His list significantly overlaps with Westminster's current lists of 'excepted and reserved powers' over Northern Ireland, though the latter are more extensive.[4] Figgis drafted in this way to enable Northern Ireland to have generous devolved powers over policing, the administration of justice, health, education, agriculture, roads, ports and airports, and taxation (though not customs and excise), all within an all-island single market and polity.

Fifteen years later, Éamon de Valera kept open the option for 'subordinate legislatures' when he replaced, by referendum, the Constitution of Saorstat Éireann (the Irish Free State) with Bunreacht na hÉireann (the Constitution of Ireland). So, both Collins and de Valera, and their followers, agreed with the idea of allowing for the possibility of a continuing Northern Ireland.

Article 15 of the Bunreacht provides that:

2.1° The sole and exclusive power of making laws for the State is hereby vested in the Oireachtas: no other legislative authority has power to make laws for the State.
2.2° Provision may however be made by law for the creation or recognition of subordinate legislatures and for the powers and functions of these legislatures.[5]

There is a clear difference between the provisions in the two constitutions. Under Ireland's current Constitution, a law may be passed by the Oireachtas to *recognize* an existing subordinate legislature. This textual change allowed for the recognition of the Northern Ireland Parliament, which had been running for some sixteen years when Bunreacht na hÉireann was ratified. So, in short, the same clause could be used to recognize the current Northern Ireland Assembly as a subordinate legislature.

How might it work in practice?

Under the devolved Northern Ireland model, *mutatis mutandis* (that is, with the necessary changes having been made), the full package of arrangements agreed on 10 April 1998 could transfer into a united Ireland, including both the Northern Ireland Assembly and its power-sharing Executive. The institutions would transfer as they were at the time of reunification – including the changes made at St Andrews in 2006, and subsequently. The biggest institutional changes would happen at the all-Ireland level, to which we will come in due course.*

Under the persisting Northern Ireland model, there would no longer be a border across the island demarcating two sovereign states: Ireland and the UK. Partition would end, but the border created in 1920 would continue to mark the extent of the autonomous powers of the Northern Ireland Assembly, though these powers would be granted and recognized by Ireland's National Parliament, rather than by Westminster. Northern Ireland would have 'home rule' within a united Ireland. The border would retain legal and institutional significance, as suggested in Figure 11.1, because the Assembly would exercise authority inside Northern Ireland for those powers for which it had been delegated responsibility, and its laws would have force there. But the border itself would have no infrastructure, no customs or excise, no police or soldiers patrolling it, and no immigration officers demanding documentation. There would be complete freedom of movement for citizens, permanent residents, and those validly here on visas. The border would not be visible.

The all-Ireland Oireachtas and Government would exercise powers in and over Northern Ireland – roughly speaking, those powers currently exercised over Northern Ireland by the Westminster Parliament and UK Cabinet, known in the UK as 'excepted' and 'reserved' powers. They include the currency, overall fiscal policy, the head of state, foreign policy and external security policy, and the intelligence services. The existing devolved arrangements could transfer without major complication. The Northern Assembly would perform its existing functions, and its existing statute book would remain in place, though its laws would be subordinate to the jurisprudence of the Irish Constitution, Irish Supreme Court rulings, and the Court of Justice of the EU.

A full scrutiny of the Constitution of Ireland, alongside the GFA,

* See Chapter 17.

would be required to accommodate the spirit of a full transfer, which might lead to proposals for constitutional or institutional change. Ireland's Constitution, as we have seen, allows the Oireachtas to recognize a subordinate legislature and its 'powers and functions'. The devolved powers could be defined residually, as Darrell Figgis sought to do, by naming the powers that would be reserved to the Oireachtas. (Residual powers are those powers of government not specified in a constitution; constitutional designers have a choice as to which tier of government has them.) The devolved powers could, by contrast, be defined specifically, by naming in legislation all the powers and functions of the Northern Assembly as these exist at reunification; that would be to 'enumerate' the devolved powers. The former approach, granting the residual powers to Northern Ireland, would be more generous in spirit. There is sufficient existing constitutional flexibility to add or subtract powers to the existing capacities of the Northern Assembly that would meet with local widespread consent. If, for example, it was proposed to have a uniform Irish national health service – publicly owned and run, funded through general taxation, and supervised by a central ministry – then the Assembly's powers in this domain might be reduced. Conversely, if it was proposed to allow the Northern Assembly to apply different VAT, income tax, or corporation tax rates than in the rest of the island, then the Assembly's powers would have to be expanded.

A continuing Northern Executive?

Missing in the existing constitutional provision to recognize subordinate legislatures is an explicit mention of the ability of the Oireachtas to recognize a subordinate *executive*. Constitutional lawyer Professor Oran Doyle has argued that Irish courts have strictly disciplined any delegation of executive power, and maintains that a constitutional amendment would be required to allow the Northern Executive to persist alongside the Assembly.[6] If he is right, then a constitutional amendment will be required to make this model work as a full transfer of devolved powers under the GFA. Without an enabling amendment, the Assembly would have to operate without a formal executive.

This issue raises the possibility of offering a model of reunification with a continuing Northern Ireland Assembly but without its existing Executive, perhaps replacing the latter by a series of committees with specific powers. That is a possibility, but it would mean weakening the protections which unionists have in the current design of the Executive – guaranteeing them one of the first ministers, and a veto within the Executive. No amendment will be required for the executive powers of the North South Ministerial Council and its implementation bodies, because they have been constitutionalized since 1999.

Constitutionally protected autonomy within a decentralized unitary state is fully compatible with Ireland's existing Constitution and the GFA. To secure that vista in full would require a constitutional amendment that gave constitutional standing to the subordinate legislature – and executive – and which recognized the institutions of Strands One and Three of the GFA (the Assembly, the Executive, and the British-Irish Council). The question of how that constitutional protection could be secured against a potentially hostile majority across the island that would want to amend the Constitution could also be the subject of deliberation and possible negotiation.

This model of reunification would be constitutionally and institutionally conservative with a small 'c'. Ireland and Great Britain would swap places as sovereigns, but all other institutions, commissions, and policies mandated by the GFA would stay the same – or more accurately, would develop under existing rules. This model would enable Northern Ireland to persist with different educational, health, and welfare state policies, and to keep its own police service and its own courts – though a constitutional amendment would be required for formally devolved courts to continue.[7] There could be a separate Northern Irish regiment in the Irish Defence Forces, but loyal to a united Ireland.

The continuing existence of Northern Ireland, albeit within a united Ireland, would recognize unionists' local patriotism towards Northern Ireland, and facilitate numerous ways of enabling Northern Ireland to remain, or become, different from the rest of the island, all while being part of a sovereign, united Ireland. For that reason, we might expect unionists to prefer this model to the other feasible model, which I shall sketch in the next chapter. Equally, however, we might expect Northern nationalists to be less enthusiastic about the continuing Northern Ireland model. The 'others', by contrast, we might expect to be divided. An 'institutionalist' might predict that this model will be picked because it is the 'path-dependent' option, which is a slightly pompous way of saying it is the least dramatic option. But the Southern public will have a say on the matter, and they may prefer the more dramatic option, as may Northern nationalists.

Tricky questions about Model 1

Several tricky questions arise in thinking through this model of a continuing Northern Ireland. What is called the 'West Lothian question' in Great Britain would materialize on a much bigger scale.[8] Initially in the UK's devolutionary settlement of the late 1990s, Scottish MPs voted in the Westminster Parliament on laws that affected England and Wales, and Northern Ireland, but English, Welsh, and Northern Irish MPs did not vote on matters devolved to the Scottish Parliament. Applying a similar arrangement will be a much bigger problem in this version of a united Ireland, because Northern Ireland would provide roughly over a third of the population of a unified Ireland, and therefore roughly over one third of the deputies in Dáil Éireann.

Proposals to address this question would have to be known before the referendum if this model were to be put forward as Ireland's plan. The question raises the problem of 'dual majorities'. We can imagine a coalition government being formed in Dublin with the support of an all-island majority in Dáil Éireann. But what if that coalition majority had a decisive majority among Northern deputies but did not have majority support among the deputies from the twenty-six counties – let us say it had the support of half the Southern deputies, one short of a majority? If the twenty-six county deputies could not vote on Northern matters, but Northern deputies could vote on Southern matters, the all-island and Northern majority would decide Southern laws and policies without a Southern majority.

Would the solution be to reduce Northern Ireland's number of deputies in Dáil Éireann, following the original British precedent in 1920 of reducing Northern Ireland's number of MPs at Westminster? Surely not. That would hardly be a welcoming note to defend in the referendums, and it is a brutally ad hoc rather than a proportionate or proportional solution.

A much better solution would be to legislate so that Northern deputies could not vote on subjects in Dáil Éireann affecting the South that are devolved to Northern Ireland, thereby matching Southerners' inability to vote on devolved Northern matters. That proposal would have the virtue of balance. The two parts of Ireland would therefore enjoy autonomy on the Northern devolved subjects.

However, the all-island majority that included a Northern but not a Southern majority, including its cabinet, could not give effect to all its preferred policy programmes in the twenty-six counties. Dáil Éireann could have within it two different majorities, an all-island one for non-devolved functions, and a twenty-six-county majority for functions devolved to Northern Ireland. The Irish Government would have a legislative majority across the island but not have a Southern legislative majority to implement its programme. Some will use this difficulty to argue for a federation,* others for an integrated unitary state, and yet others for 'devolution all around', with possible devolved governments in Leinster, Munster, and Connacht–Ulster, for which there is no current demand.

There are other tricky issues attached to the full transfer model. Would there be a Minister for Northern Ireland, appointed by the coalition government in Dáil Éireann, to fill the place previously held by the UK Secretary of State? If so, could he or she be a Northerner by constituency? If not, would that not be a denial of Irish unity? If so, would that lead Southerners to argue that the Taoiseach – and the Tánaiste – would have to be Southerners under this model of what is technically called 'asymmetric devolution'? Again, this hardly paints a picture of unity. What about a messy compromise in which the Taoiseach would be a Southerner and the Tánaiste a Northerner? This pattern of thought fits poorly with the idea of a common citizenship in a united Ireland. It

* See Chapter 16.

would be more elegant, and just, to avoid these questions by not having a Northern Ireland minister to replace the Secretary of State. Instead, North–South coordination should be left to the North South Ministerial Council, with regular summits at prime-ministerial level between the Northern first ministers and the Taoiseach and Tánaiste to address difficulties and pursue common purposes.

The mediation role played by the Secretary of State should not be re-institutionalized in a united Ireland. After all, that secretarial post, created in 1972, was originally envisaged as an impartial *outsider*. If a mediator is temporarily required, it could be part of the duties of the Taoiseach and the Tánaiste. The British foreign minister could assist in mediation within the British-Irish Intergovernmental Conference (BIIGC), as the Irish foreign minister has effectively done since 1985. Ireland's presidency and Council of State could also be repurposed for mediation, addressing disputes between the Northern Executive and the Government of Ireland, or between different designated parties in the North.* When thinking about mediation, the question arises: what would happen if the leading party within one of the designated communities in the North collapsed the Executive? Would the Oireachtas have the right to suspend the Northern Assembly? Yes, because it is a subordinate legislature, but no if it was constitutionally protected. If the latter were the case, a constitutional amendment would be required to give the Oireachtas that power. Analogously, should there be provision for 'direct rule' over the North from Dublin? Would the Oireachtas have the right – and the duty – to legislate for the North while the institutions were not functioning? Would the Taoiseach spend his or her days negotiating with, say, Ulster unionists to go back into the Executive? Advocates of the other feasible model, which we shall shortly explore, would simply riposte: if a devolved Northern Ireland cannot function beyond an allotted transitional period, why persist with it?

There are further tricky questions regarding the appropriate division of powers between Dublin and Belfast. Keeping the existing division of powers might lead to efficiency losses. Two education systems, two health systems, two social security systems, two different language

---

* See Chapter 17, p. 179.

policies, and two police services, for example, would generate at least some coordination difficulties, and questions about duplication in procurement and other governmental functions. Economies of scale would suggest that the all-island provision and procurement of at least some public services would be better than two parallel services – if economics is allowed to trump the value of local control.

Lastly, economic policy and funding would raise special questions regarding the division of powers. Would the two parts of Ireland be free to pursue rivalrous strategies regarding attracting foreign direct investment? How would the all-island government coordinate despite such a rivalry? Would the Northern Assembly have the right to vary taxation from that elsewhere in Ireland, and have the right to issue bonds and borrow on the money markets? Would there be a fixed formula in which Northern Ireland received a block grant from the Oireachtas, in proportion to the population of Northern Ireland, or would there be some redistributive 'equalization formula' to help Northern Ireland out, at least initially?

The continuing Northern Ireland model, filled out as the maximal transfer of the Good Friday Agreement, would therefore have distinct difficulties. These are not, however, impossible to manage – just difficulties. Such difficulties exist in all polities with what is called 'asymmetric devolution', such as the kingdoms of Spain and Denmark, and the United Kingdom. They may be more difficult when there is just one devolved unit, and two units of territorial government relatively similar in population size – one with 5 million people, including non-citizens, and the other with nearly 2 million. Where one entity is very large compared to the other, as with Tanzania's mainland population of 56.5 million compared with Zanzibar's 1.5 million, policy differences and accommodations are much easier to manage than they may be in our case.

12.   Model 2: An integrated Ireland

The second model we may call an 'integrated Ireland'. It distinctly resembles and incorporates the traditional model of a united Ireland held by many Northern nationalists and Irish republicans – namely, 'a thirty-two-county unitary Irish Republic'. It is visualized in Figure 12.1 in the colour plate section.

In this model, those entitled to vote in a united Ireland will elect Dáil Éireann and the President. There will be no subordinate legislatures or executives, though there will be local government.* Northern Ireland would be dissolved as a political entity. After the referendums, Northern Ireland would voluntarily be absorbed into a unitary Irish state. Laws, institutions, agencies, and public services of the South would extend to cover what is now Northern Ireland, though subject to new Northern influence through Dáil Éireann and the Senate, and with some possibility of 'pick and mix', i.e. adopting the best of the North, or the best of the South, or some fusion of the two. The existing Irish statute book and EU laws will be in force – except where transitional arrangements have been made. Symbols, the national flag and national anthem, and language regulations† will be as promised in the referendums, or subject to post-unification negotiation. They will default to current arrangements in the absence of commitments made in the referendums or agreement on new legislation.

All existing political institutions would be affected by the integrated model. The all-island parliament in Dublin would have to expand – this being the easiest way to incorporate the North proportionally. Government would operate on an all-island basis. The organization of Southern political parties into the North would likely follow, and some extension of some Northern parties into the South, alongside the possible

* See Chapter 18.
† See Part Eight.

formation of new parties (or mergers). As a rough estimate, between one in six and one in seven voters in a united Ireland would be cultural Protestants, most of them from the North.

The provision of public services, major public policies, and the organization of security under the integrated model would become the same across the island. Not overnight: policies and plans would be needed to achieve convergence. A common civil service would fuse the two existing services, pending a review of public administration. Competence requirements in the Irish language would be reviewed. The existing ministerial departments in Northern Ireland would cease to be departments; their functions and their civil servants would be incorporated into the relevant all-island departments. To avoid fear, chaos, and pre-emptive departures at reunification, all public officials should be offered transitional security in their positions for five years until a thorough review of public administration is carried out. This review would be all-island; it would not be confined to the North. Its task would be to organize the public services for reunification and for continuing membership of the European Union. Nothing in this model would preclude deconcentrating public administration – with different governmental departments, for example, headquartered in Belfast, Derry, Athlone, Cork, and Galway.

In this model there would be an integrated health service, either the Northern or Southern health model, or something new, with a transition period to merge the existing two. There would be common provision for Catholic, Protestant, and non-denominational primary/ secondary schools, and an integrated higher education sector (again, with a transition period). There would be a single social welfare system. Public pensions, unemployment and social benefits would become the same throughout Ireland (with a transition period). Common infrastructure, planning and environmental policies would apply across the island. Monetary, fishing, and agricultural policies would be determined within the EU, as would issues relating to single market regulation and the customs union. Access to abortion, and rights for same-sex couples, would be subject to the Irish Constitution and Supreme Court decisions. The Police Service of Northern Ireland would be merged into the Garda Síochána, with a common code respecting both traditions and those outside the traditional nationalist and unionist blocs.[1] The Irish Army would be recruited on an all-Ireland basis, with no separate Northern regiment. In the integrated model Ireland would have one army, one navy, and one air force – with full facility for Northerners serving in the British Armed Forces to join and, where feasible, to preserve their existing ranks, years of service, and pension entitlements.

What GFA provisions would persist in the integrated model?

Some key provisions from the Good Friday Agreement would carry over in the integrated model, but not everything, so we might call this the 'minimal transfer model' – in contrast to Model 1, which we outlined as a full or maximal transfer.

The relevant GFA obligations need not require constitutional amendments. The Irish Government would be legally obliged to conduct itself impartially across diverse religions, nationalities, and ethnicities; the same rights would have to be protected across the island, as previously pledged by both the Irish and British governments; and there would have to be cross-border institutional relationships with British islands, likely through the British-Irish Council. The Irish state's fundamental rights provisions would apply across the island – subject to possible modifications by the incorporation and elevation of the European Convention on Human Rights and by European Union law. The minimum package of rights would be that required by our existing Constitution, and treaty commitments, and by our obligations under the GFA. That would be the floor, not the ceiling.

The dissolution of the Northern Ireland Assembly and its Executive may disappoint some, but it would create an architectural opportunity. A fine set of parliamentary buildings would be available for use at Stormont. They could be repurposed as the site of a reformed all-island Senate.* To replace the power-sharing securities in the North,

* See Chapter 17, pp. 182–4.

formal or informal power-sharing securities, inspired by the GFA, could be offered in the integrated model.

Later, I will advocate the application of the d'Hondt rule – in use in the North because of the GFA – to help compose coalition governments supported by a majority in Dáil Éireann.★ More expansively, this rule could be used to provide the opportunity for all significantly sized political parties to win places to participate in the cabinet, and to sequence their choice of ministries and junior ministries, in accordance with their success in elections. If, by contrast, the Irish cabinet, as now, is to be comprised of voluntary coalitions – and serious fears exist, or materialize, of the permanent exclusion of parties based on the historic Ulster unionist community – then a constitutional or legal quota should be considered. Any constitutional quota would require a constitutional amendment. An appropriate quota, in my opinion, would require a minimum of five elected from Northern constituencies and a minimum of two persons of cultural Protestant formation (or with British or British and Irish identification) to be present in every fifteen-person Irish cabinet, transitionally – say for twenty years. This quota would require deputies to designate their identities. If a permanent quota is considered better, then it would be best to make the size of the quota proportionate to the share of the former Northern Ireland population in a united Ireland, and/or the share of Northern British passport holders, and/or the share of cultural Northern Protestants in the census. That way the quota would rise or fall in accordance with the principle of proportionality.

In the integrated model, the Northern judiciary and legal profession will fuse with their Southern counterparts, under existing Irish law. Credible arrangements would need to be proposed before the referendums to ensure a representative judiciary, in which lawyers of cultural Protestant background, and those of Northern background, would be proportionately represented in the higher ranks of the all-Irish judiciary.

Similarly, all the professions, from accounting through to veterinary services, would likely fuse, and harmonize, through the joint action of

★ For explanation and elaboration, see Chapter 20, pp. 210–17.

their incumbent senior executives and professional associations. Coordinating principles for their fusion would have to be advertised. The South should recognize all existing Northern professional qualifications and accreditation bodies, pending reviews within each profession to ensure harmonization with current EU best practices and to enable Northerners to retain their credentials with British professional bodies.

The upshot

Unlike the full transfer model, the integrated model is not institutionally conservative. It will entail dramatic change for Northern Ireland: its abolition as a political entity, and as a set of political institutions. The border will cease to have legal or policy significance; it will be terminated. There will be no preservation of dual and devolved institutions and policies. Fusion will be the order of the day.

Bear in mind, however, that logically there are three possibilities of integration, and each of these possibilities may occur in different domains. Integration could take place with the best Southern practices moving North, with the attendant danger that Irish reunification could be seen as a Southern takeover. Conversely, Northern practices could move South. Lastly, amalgamation could lead to some novel practices. Sensible integration can take place along each of three different patterns, sector by sector, institution by institution, policy by policy.

Without advance planning, engagement, and deliberation, a Southern takeover is what will happen ubiquitously if the integrated model is chosen. A Southern takeover would be the likely outcome of a last-minute, improvised, and ill-considered reunification. In some instances, the South currently has the best institutions and polices, and these should be extended to the whole island, but that should never be the automatic presumption. With planning and democratic deliberation, the best of the North could also certainly be extended to the whole island. And, of course, some fresh joint beginnings may and should be possible. A successful and realistic reunification plan would envisage all three of these possible modes of integration across a range of functions and practices. An expansion of the Irish primary and secondary education systems, an Irish national health service modelled on the North's, and fresh policies on languages would be just one package consistent with all three patterns of integration.

Tricky questions for Model 2

Model 2 will have different problems to Model 1. Most obviously, the abolition of Northern Ireland would be an extremely painful experience for Ulster unionists. As already mentioned, in 1948, Newfoundland voted in a referendum to end its dominion status, and in a subsequent referendum to join Canada. Black flags of mourning were hung out by the households on the losing side in the first referendum.[2] That is the very least of the emotional reactions we should expect from losing Ulster unionists. The locus of their political and symbolic identity since 1921 would be over. Having been a dominant majority in Northern Ireland between its foundation in 1921 and 1971, they would become a minority within a united Ireland. In the integrated model, no special territorial recognition of the place they built and presided over, and which some call 'our wee country', would persist.

How would unionists react? We should expect most of their leaders and followers to be opposed to the integrated model precisely because it abolishes Northern Ireland as a political entity. Reunificationists would have to persuade unionists to accept the new order, democratically accomplished in fair referendums; to ask them to participate in the new all-island democratic republic; and to test to the full the new rights secured for them in the national reunification plan, with or without constitutional amendments. Peaceful integration was achieved with the bulk of Southern Protestants after 1922. That could happen again, but this outcome cannot be guaranteed, and it is not the only possibility.

Unionists could emigrate, as Arlene Foster has said she would, and as some Southern Protestants did between 1911 and 1926. As British citizens, all unionists would be entitled to relocate to Great Britain, should they choose to do so. Some may, but most will not. After all, the geographic north of Ireland is their home too, and was for centuries for many of their ancestors. Their motherlands are in Great

Britain – Scotland and England – and long ago. Scotland may have become independent by 2030. To the irritation of most cultural Protestants, the English invariably treat those from Northern Ireland as Irish, whatever their self-identification, so relocation would not be easy. Emigration will be an unwelcome idea to many. Most unionists will want to stay, as Peter Robinson, Mike Nesbitt, and Jeffrey Donaldson have indicated they would.[3] And that must be a key objective of reunification: to make unionists feel welcome and secure in their own homeland, homes, and places of work and leisure.

Unionists might create a movement to demand home rule for Northern Ireland within a united Ireland – that is, to transition from Model 2 to Model 1. Perhaps, but if they try to mobilize such a movement, Northern Ireland will have a non-unionist majority which has just voted for reunification. Would unionists downsize their ambition, as their ancestors did in 1911, and seek autonomy for a Northern Ireland Mark 2, carved out of four north-eastern counties or fewer? Possibly, but such a move would splinter their community.

Unionists could *in extremis* support an attempted loyalist insurrection – to create a new and smaller independent Northern Ireland. Later I will explain why a loyalist insurrection is likely to fail, but the prospect must be contemplated – and planned for.

Advocates of the continuing Northern Ireland model would say that concern about the possible unionist reaction to the abolition of Northern Ireland should lead us to delay the integrated model. Unionists, if not their leaders, will need to be engaged, and their public's likely reactions carefully evaluated. The point may become this: rather than a fast-paced transfer to an integrated Ireland, the preservation of Northern Ireland within a united Ireland for a transitional period may be considered the more prudent judgement.

Reunification under the integrated model could be experienced by unionists like some East Germans experienced German reunification – as a complete takeover. With the Northern Assembly and Executive dissolved, there would be no principled case for Northern ministries, or departments, or for the civil servants working within them, though they could of course be repurposed within Southern ministries. If this model were proposed in a referendum, Northern public officials, who include many cultural Catholics, might be fearful of job losses. This fear could be met by promising the incorporation of all existing Northern public employees into the amalgamation of public services in the Irish state for a specified period. That would have implications for the initial expected costs of reunification.

Leaving aside specific questions of policy, what will matter for the future referendums, if the integration model is chosen, is the need for clear and publicly available plans on how integration will be begun, and developed, sector by sector.

13.   Questions for both models

Three key matters need attention in the two models I have just outlined: the GFA requirement that the newly incumbent sovereign Irish Government be rigorously impartial over the diverse people of the North; British citizenship rights in Northern Ireland, especially their extent and scope compared to Irish citizenship rights; and whether Northern Ireland should have the right of secession to reunify with Great Britain through a referendum.

The rigorous impartiality, identity, and citizenship requirements

Upon reunification, and becoming the incumbent sovereign, the Irish Government has pledged to administer Northern Ireland 'with rigorous impartiality' on behalf of all the people 'in the diversity of their identities and traditions'.[1] The other obligation is that the people of Northern Ireland would continue to have the right 'to identify themselves, and be accepted, as Irish or British or both', and would continue to have 'the right to hold both British and Irish citizenship'. Let us call that the 'identity and dual citizenship requirement'.[2]

Treating these obligations with the gravity they deserve has consequences for planning a united Ireland. If Ireland became the sovereign government in Northern Ireland, it would be under an obligation – in international law – to ensure that its domestic laws respected these obligations. So, if the current Constitution of Ireland is inconsistent with these obligations, it would need to be amended, upon or after reunification. There can be no judicial resolution of this question because the Irish courts cannot enforce unincorporated treaty provisions, and because Ireland does not recognize the jurisdiction of the International Court of Justice in any legal dispute with the UK regarding Northern Ireland. We must therefore do the best we can to interpret the principles ourselves.

Let us look first at citizenship. Currently the franchise for constitutional referendums and presidential elections in Ireland is confined to Irish citizens. A constitutional amendment was passed in 1985 that allows non-citizens, including British citizens, to vote in elections for Dáil Éireann, just as Irish citizens resident in Great Britain may vote, in Westminster elections in the UK, as if they were Commonwealth citizens. The franchise in Ireland was deliberately not extended to non-citizens for presidential elections, or for referendums on constitutional amendments. That restriction makes sense from the perspective of classical republican and democratic political theory. The state, including its head and its constitution, should be controlled by its citizens, and not by non-citizens. It is, however, reasonable for the Oireachtas, local governments, and our Members of the European Parliament to be elected on a wider franchise, and Ireland has allowed for that. This franchise enables non-citizens who pay taxes to vote and to have representation, and it enables us to grant reciprocity to the citizens of fellow EU member-states, and to grant reciprocity to the UK's citizens resident in Ireland.

I argue later in this book that Ireland's existing constitutional provisions are compliant with the Good Friday Agreement, and that no constitutional amendments are required regarding citizenship and rigorous impartiality.* It might, however, be a good idea to propose to entrench respect for *dual* citizenship constitutionally, through a duty of recognition, and to welcome British and unionist people into a united Ireland. But people in the North with British citizenship who wish to run for office in either chamber of Ireland's parliament, to vote in future referendums on constitutional change in Ireland, or to run for the presidency, should accept, in addition, the Irish citizenship to which they will be automatically entitled. Not everyone will agree with these arguments, but these subjects need to be resolved in deliberation and planning, and perhaps in legislation and contingent constitutional amendments.

The requirement of rigorous impartiality was not incorporated into UK domestic law, so there is no reciprocal obligation upon Ireland

---

* See Chapter 28, pp. 293–6.

to incorporate it into its domestic law. The principle could feature in a draft reunification of Ireland bill, to be enacted after reunification, expressing a generous and permanent commitment. Consideration could be given to whether the requirement should be incorporated into the Constitution, to show good faith regarding future conduct by the Irish Government and Parliament. It should, after all, be part of Ireland's collective mission to meet and exceed British performance in respecting international obligations under the GFA. If this reasoning is accepted, then at least one constitutional amendment will be required, but that should only be proposed after a thorough assessment is made of how its incorporation will affect other provisions of the Constitution.

Right of secession, or right to return to the UK?

Should Northern Ireland have the right of secession from a united Ireland? You may think it is a curious question, but comprehensive planning is required. Granting a right of secession would not be an obligation flowing from the GFA. The GFA permits Northern Ireland just two options: the preservation of the Union with Great Britain, or a sovereign united Ireland. If reciprocity were invoked, the argument would have to be that Northern Ireland should have the right to reunify with Great Britain in the same way that it currently has the right to reunify with Ireland. So that would be after referendums held in Northern Ireland *and* Great Britain, with a simple majority in each case. Whether the people and government of Great Britain would wish to entertain this prospect will be up to them, but neither the British Government nor unionists made any request for texts to this effect in the making and negotiation of the GFA.

Northern Ireland's self-determination is constrained to two options because the injustice of the partition of 1920 was effectively recognized in the GFA. Ireland's right to self-determination had been violated by the Government of Ireland Act. The GFA was a form of reparation and allowed for the reversal of partition. Analogously, Northern Ireland may acquire the right to reunify with Great Britain if its citizens consider it to be unjustly governed in a future united Ireland.

There may, indeed, be a pragmatic reason to establish the right of secession. Namely, to provide a peaceful and democratic method to reverse reunification, and thereby to make the reality of Irish reunification easier for unionists and loyalists to accept. Unionists, after all, should have the right to campaign for reunification with Great Britain, peacefully and democratically. Supporting the Union is part of their tradition and ethos, and its restoration would be a predictable aspiration in the event of Irish reunification. It would, however, be up to the government of a united Ireland to decide under what circumstances secession could occur – presumably, in the devolved model, after a majority resolution of the Northern Assembly passed, a referendum on the subject could be held, with the decision-rule being a simple-majority level of support in a referendum among eligible voters in the six counties. That possibility would not exist in the integrated model of reunification, where the Northern Assembly would not exist and where survey evidence would be required of opinion in the six counties.

Crucially, it would also be up to the Government of Ireland and the Oireachtas to decide, with Great Britain, the circumstances under which the United Kingdom of Great Britain and Northern Ireland would be restored. This possibility could also form part of a review of reunification, which could be built into the reunification act.

The upshot

In summary, two actions are required if Models 1 and 2 are to respect the Good Friday Agreement, and a third is required for Model 1 to be a full transfer of the GFA. A clear citizenship law, which could be enacted now – a constitutional amendment is not required, though that view may be disputed – and a constitutional duty to recognize dual Irish and British citizenship may be proposed. A pledge of rigorous impartiality in administration by future Governments of Ireland must be in the reunification statute that would take effect after the referendums – a constitutional amendment could be proposed, but it is not essential.

And, to implement Model 1 as a full transfer of the GFA, a constitutional amendment is required to allow the persistence of a Northern Executive, along with the Northern Assembly – in which case the question would be whether this amendment would be bundled with the referendum question on reunification in the South.

Opinion on the two models

John Garry and I have led 'deliberative forums' on these two models, in the North and in the South. Such forums are small samples of the general citizenry tasked with deliberating over a policy question, following an objective guide to the relevant subject matter by an expert presenter or presenters. They are miniature versions of citizens' assemblies, with which many in the Republic became familiar during the debates over constitutional amendments on marriage equality and abortion.[3] I was the presenter at all the forums, North and South. We have since scaled up this work into large annual surveys that are to take place, North and South, organized by ARINS (Analysing and Researching Ireland, North and South) and the *Irish Times*.[4] The surveys are accompanied by focus groups. One of our central goals is to judge what the publics, North and South, currently think about reunification, especially about the two models sketched out here – and why they think that way.

These forums have been too small to predict outcomes in referendums, but they are a good guide to what questions animate citizens. In our 2019 study, cultural Catholics in the North preferred an integrated Ireland to a continuing Northern Ireland. The same was true of Southerners in a deliberative forum held in the Republic in 2021. In the 2019 forum, cultural Protestants who were obliged to choose which model of a united Ireland they would prefer – an unpalatable choice for most of them – generally supported a continuing Northern Ireland, the option which promised or threatened less change. So far, no surprises.

Unexpectedly, however, *after* deliberation, support for the devolved option fell among cultural Protestants. What appeared to drive the shift was recognition of the dysfunctionality and division that have characterized contemporary Northern institutions. The forum took place when neither the Assembly nor the Executive was running. What may also have mattered, at the margin, was that, in a devolved Northern Ireland inside a united Ireland, cultural Protestants would be a double minority. They would be a minority inside the North, and in Ireland as a whole. Confronted by this scenario, some cultural Protestants, likely able to elect at least one-seventh of a future Dáil Éireann, may prefer the more fluid coalition politics of an integrated Ireland, including the possibility of alliances with Southern parties – perhaps especially the more conservative of these parties.

In short, two things are clear from our deliberative forums. Cultural Catholics across the island prefer an integrated Ireland. Cultural Protestants, obliged to choose, prefer a devolved Northern Ireland within the UK to any model of a united Ireland, but their views on this matter may be more amenable to discussion and modification than currently assumed. Could there be a future convergence – a sweet spot – namely, a devolved Northern Ireland inside a united Ireland as a transitional arrangement, provided that it is fully intended to lead to an integrated Ireland? That remains to be seen. It would have its own numerous complexities. How long would the transition last? How could it be ended? A devolved Northern Ireland within a united Ireland may reduce cultural Protestant antipathy to a united Ireland, but at the cost of reducing the enthusiasm for Irish reunification among cultural Catholics, North and South.

People's preferences are partly shaped by institutional opportunities. When invited to reflect on different possible futures, numerous citizens, North and South, can shift from entrenched positions. What protections would Protestants, unionists, and British citizens want to see within a continuing Northern Ireland within Ireland, or in a reunified and integrated Ireland? Likewise, what accommodations and changes would citizens of the Republic and Northern nationalists be willing to make to accommodate a formerly dominant minority?

A deliberative forum held online during the pandemic in the spring of 2021, led by John Garry and me, found that discussion of these matters by Southerners produced a substantial increase in support for specifying the particular model of a united Ireland on offer *before* any referendum, compared to before the deliberation began.[5] The findings suggest that an Irish Government that acted in line with the views of the citizens in this forum would explicitly indicate, significantly before any referendum, that an integrated united Ireland would follow from affirmative referendums in favour of reunification. Deliberation also led to a very substantial decrease in support for holding an immediate referendum, before 2023, and substantially increased support for a five-to-ten-year time frame.

Learning and deliberation over the two models did not decisively change Southerners' views on the relative merits of these possible models of Irish unity. Our Southern participants were more in favour of the integrated model than the devolved model, both before and after deliberation; perhaps, however, they felt better informed about why this preference would be the better one. Many of our participants changed their minds, however, regarding *when* a model should be specified. There was a majority both before and after deliberation preferring model specification *before* any referendums. But the majority in favour of specification before the first Northern referendum was much larger after the participants had learned about and discussed the issues. Learning and reflecting on the issues relating to a possible referendum did not make our Irish mini-public less in favour of holding a referendum, or less in favour of a united Ireland, however. It did make them much less in favour of holding an *imminent* referendum.

In contrast to the continuing Northern Ireland model, participants saw the integrated Ireland model as consistent with the conventional understanding of a united Ireland, clear in allocating political responsibility, provided beneficial all-island policies, and did not continue an historically divisive border. The perceived advantage of the continuing Northern Ireland model – as potentially more acceptable to some Northerners – was not sufficient to dampen participants' strong preference for the integrated model, though several participants thought that if the continuing Northern model was proposed as a transitional path to the integrated model, it would be more acceptable. Similarly, while there were some perceived advantages to the process approach, most notably that it might be more inclusive of Northerners and lead to an outcome more acceptable to them, these opinions were not sufficiently strong to stop a substantial increase in support for pre-referendum model specification, which was seen to have the crucial and overriding advantage of providing clarity in what would be involved in the vote.

The prioritization of clarity was the key feature emphasized in discussions on referendum timing, with participants highlighting the need for sufficient time to be spent by all in moving on from Brexit and Covid, preparing, and providing relevant details to voters.

These findings – on models, process, and timing – pose important questions for the Irish Government. What model of a united Ireland does the Government – or the Opposition – prefer, and how and when does it prepare for it? Strategically, when should the Irish Government reveal its institutional preference – before or after any referendum? And how should it test and check that preference?

'What model?' and 'When to choose the model?' are distinct questions, but crucially overlap to form a formidable challenge. If the Irish Government were to act in line with the considered views of Southern citizens, as observed in our deliberative poll, it would explicitly indicate, significantly before any referendum, that if people in the North and South respectively voted for Irish unity, the form of reunification would be an integrated united Ireland. The Government of Ireland may, however, have a constrained opportunity, if it wishes, to try to lead the public towards the idea of a continuing Northern Ireland model, as a compromise. To succeed in that endeavour, however, it would likely have to promise that it would be transitional towards an integrated Ireland.

If the Government of Ireland, and its successors, remains silent on the questions of 'What model?' and 'When to choose the model?' that unavoidably will position it in favour of a vote on the broad principle of a united Ireland, rather than on a specific model, and in favour of a post-referendum constitutional convention, which would decide the specific model.

14. What won't happen: an independent Northern Ireland, confederation, and repartition

Ireland used to prepare its amateur rugby union international team by playing its 'probables' against its 'possibles'. The two most probable options for Irish reunification have been discussed. The possibles must now be considered, because some readers quite reasonably will have other ideas about how the island of Ireland should be governed in future.

An independent Northern Ireland

The GFA envisages a constrained exercise of self-determination. Northern Ireland is not fully free to determine its own political status. A majority in Northern Ireland, under the GFA, has no right to create a new sovereign and independent state.[1] Neither is any 'right to independence' granted in UK or Irish constitutional law. The 'principle of consent' does not include this option. Northern Ireland may choose between just two alternatives: keeping the Union with Great Britain, or joining a sovereign united Ireland. That's it. No ifs, no buts, no third ways.

The same is true in relevant international law. Northern Ireland was not among the territories scheduled for decolonization after the formation of the United Nations. In international law, any future Northern referendum will *not* formally be about decolonization.[2] It will also not formally be about secession – understood as the withdrawal of a territory and its people from a confederation, a federation, or a union, to create an independent sovereign state.[3] Rather, the referendum will be about the potential 'transfer of sovereignty'.

Proposals to create an independent Northern Ireland were advanced by loyalists in the 1970s, the former UK Prime Minister James Callaghan in 1981, and various independent figures, North and South, in the 1970s and 1980s.[4] The best arguments in favour of independence were advanced through academic reviews and outsider reports, rather than by the advocates themselves.[5] For the outsiders, the proposal has the virtue of tough love. Neither nationalists nor unionists would get what they most want – respectively, a united Ireland or maintaining the Union. Making everyone equally unhappy was, we should recall, the alleged virtue of British direct rule.[6] It was not true. Advocates of independence say the two communities would have to swim together, coexist through power-sharing, or sink one another in civil war. But are these risks of joint drowning worth taking?

Independence suffers from insuperable objections. It is not the first preference, or second preference, of either community, and would have to be enforced upon the entirety of the population, and against treaty obligations to the Irish Government. The two sovereign governments, the UK's and Ireland's, have rightly judged independence an unstable outcome. Without the oversight of the two sovereign governments, it is unclear whether power-sharing would persist, let alone improve. Independence would leave Northern Ireland outside the European Union, divided over whether to apply for membership. Jointly, these objections predict a rapid social and economic collapse.

Independence may, however, be the goal of last-resort or 'last ditch' loyalists, to recall Roy Bradford's novel.[7] They may contemplate a unilateral declaration of independence before, during, or after a referendum on reunification if they expect to lose. Such a bid would take place against the will of a majority in Northern Ireland, and to be viable for any duration it would require an accompanying military capacity and a militia policy of brutal ethnic expulsions, disguised as 'transfers', with the goal of repartition, which I will discuss in a moment.

The confederation of Ireland and Northern Ireland

There has been limited discussion or advocacy of the creation of an all-island confederation based on two states – a new sovereign Northern Ireland state, and the existing Republic of Ireland.[8] A confederation is a union of member-states that delegate their revocable sovereignty to share power within confederal institutions set up for that purpose. The EU is a strikingly large-scale and successful confederation,[9] though Brexiteers do not agree.

For there to be an Irish confederation, Northern Ireland would first have to become a sovereign and independent state, as discussed above. Possibly building upon or expanding the current North South Ministerial Council, the two states would have to delegate power and authority to bodies with all-island jurisdiction, by treaty. Northern Ireland could remain internally governed by its existing power-sharing arrangements, with the authority to modify its institutions in accordance with current norms, through cross-community consent. Since the member-states of a confederation retain the right of secession, either Northern Ireland or Ireland could secede from an Irish confederation.

For these reasons, a confederation is incompatible with the GFA. A proper confederation requires a sovereign independent Northern Ireland state to exist and join in a treaty of confederation with the sovereign Republic of Ireland. Unless the Irish Government were to declare it so, and persuade its public of the fact, confederation is also not a 'sovereign united Ireland', and an Irish Government trying to implement this option would violate Ireland's Constitution, because it may not be compatible with the new Article 3.* The formation of a confederation would involve the inhabitants of Northern Ireland agreeing to make it a sovereign state *and* Ireland's recognition of a sovereign and independent Northern Ireland before the two entered into a treaty of confederation. That Northern Ireland, however, would have to enter two confederations – that of Ireland, and that of the EU – and Ireland would have to grant Northern Ireland the right to leave the Irish confederation, if it so desired, at some point. Since joining the EU is likely to be part of the attraction of voting for reunification, it is simply far easier for the North to join an Irish unitary state, or an Irish federation, within the EU, rather than to become independent and then seek separate admission to the EU.

The UK's exit from the EU has therefore double-bolted the closed

---

* See Chapter 5, p. 71.

door on a confederal Ireland. The GFA, protected in all its parts by treaty, does not allow for an independent Northern Ireland. An independent Northern Ireland outside the EU could not confederate with ease or sense with the Republic, which is within the EU.

Repartition

Restructuring the border was envisaged in the Treaty of 1921. The boundary commission it mandated was set up late, however, partly because it was subverted by the UUP government and the Conservatives at Westminster, and the Labour government lacked an appetite and a parliamentary majority.[10] In any case, the commission's report was buried by both the Free State and the UK Government in 1925. The Free State leadership refused to contemplate the loss of any of the twenty-six counties to meet the unjust proposals of the commission's head, Justice Feetham, which ignored popular preferences, and verged on absurdity. The idea of repartition was subsequently ruled out in UK law by the Ireland Act of 1949, though Margaret Thatcher asked her officials to review its possibilities in 1984, shortly before she signed the Anglo-Irish Agreement.

The sole systematic treatment of repartition as a serious policy proposal was advanced in 1986 by the Southern-born economic historian Liam Kennedy, a professor at Queen's University Belfast and a campaigner against republican violence.[11] His work and his maps were appropriated – without his consent or approval – in the Ulster Defence Association's doomsday plans of the early 1990s. These sketched out a programme for downsizing Northern Ireland in the event of a unilateral British withdrawal, or a British-Irish deal to enforce a united Ireland against the wishes of 'the majority'.

If repartition was ever an idea worth considering, its merits have long gone.[12] Demographic change and the patterns of segregation that have developed since the 1960s render it impossible to accomplish without an abundance of fresh coercion. Four of the six Northern counties are contiguous to the border, and Down overlooks Carlingford Lough. Nationalists consistently win elections in border districts. Drawing a new 'clean' line would be difficult, leaving too many of the 'wrong' people on the 'wrong' side of the border.

The crucial demographic, geographic, and political problem is Belfast. The North, South, and West Belfast constituencies are currently held by nationalists, and a downsized Northern Ireland without Belfast, or half of Belfast, matches no unionist imagination. Linking North, West, and South Belfast to the Republic would create an Irish West Berlin, a Green space surrounded by an Orange heartland. Could East Belfast or Craigavon be the capital of a Northern Ireland Mark I? Conversely, in any repartition, Derry would be lost to the Republic.

Whoever advocates repartition, or an independent Northern Ireland, is really advocating either chaotic ethnic expulsions or 'agreed' population transfers. Without these brutal means it would be impossible to create a more compact and more Protestant Northern Ireland, free of exclaves and enclaves. Executing a fair repartition is therefore nigh on impossible. Repartition would materialize as a messy and bloody choice if – and only if – loyalist militia are allowed to arm on a significant scale; if Irish reunification plans are, or are made to appear, deeply unattractive to cultural Protestants; and if unionists prefer the risk of a loyalist insurrection to emigration or remaking their political lives in a united Ireland.

15.   An increasingly improbable model: shared sovereignty

The logical space, institutionally and chronologically, between the maintenance of the Union of Great Britain and Northern Ireland and a united sovereign Republic of Ireland is haunted by an idea. Known variously as 'joint (or shared) sovereignty', or 'joint (or shared) authority', or as a 'condominium' (from 'co-dominion'), the core idea is that Great Britain and Ireland should be co-sovereigns over Northern Ireland, recognizing that both have co-nationals there and shared interests in its stability. Would joint sovereignty take the form of joint direct rule, however, with no region-wide democratic legislature? Or would it involve shared sovereignty over a 'democratized condominium' in which the Northern Irish would participate in the making of laws, and in the executive? And would this model be permanent, or transitional?

Only fanatics define sovereignty or authority in such a way that it can never be shared or divided, and there are both colonial and European precedents for joint sovereignty.[1] The Anglo-Egyptian condominium over Sudan was admittedly far more Anglo than it was Egyptian, but the French and the British co-managed a condominium in the New Hebrides. The condominium over Andorra in the Pyrenees lasted centuries. Sovereignty over the principality was jointly held by the Spanish/Catalan Bishop of Urgell and the King of Navarre, who became the King of France; the power has passed to the President of France. The two remain constitutional heads of state, but Andorra is otherwise independent. Bosnia and Herzegovina arguably came under the joint authority of the EU and NATO in the Dayton Agreement of 1995, and it remains so.

Joint sovereignty for Northern Ireland was advanced by the SDLP in 1972, shortly after its foundation. Taoiseach Garret FitzGerald ran with the idea in the New Ireland Forum in 1984, and in negotiations with Margaret Thatcher's government.[2] In 1992, John Hume put forward a paper to the Brooke–Mayhew talks in which a six-person executive was proposed for Northern Ireland – consisting of a British, Irish, and EU commissioner, and three politicians elected in Northern Ireland by the single transferable vote system of proportional representation. It helped bring the talks to an end. In between 1972 and 1992, several academics and intellectuals considered the idea.[3] They sought to address how to make a British-Irish condominium internally democratic. They rarely addressed the institutional or funding arrangements in any detail. Kevin McNamara's team did.

I was part of that team (along with Jim Marshall and Tom Lyne). In preparation for the possibility of a British Labour government in 1992 we developed a policy text with two plans. Plan A was based on Irish unity by consent, which was party policy: the consent of a majority in Northern Ireland would be required before reunification could occur. A Labour government would seek to encourage both the formation of a devolved power-sharing government in the North and enhanced North–South cooperation – if necessary, by relying on the two sovereign governments cooperating through the British-Irish Intergovernmental Conference. The thinking was that devolved power-sharing would facilitate eventual reunification by consent, thereby respecting and staying within the remit of party policy. All this planning was possible within the framework of the Anglo-Irish Agreement. Looking back thirty years later, Plan A was not far from what was agreed in 1998.[4]

But we also developed a Plan B, a system of joint sovereignty with an opportunity for a power-sharing devolved government to function. Plan B had a triple function: as a fallback policy if Plan A failed; as a possible incentive for unionists to accommodate Plan A; and, lastly, as a possible long-term constitutional compromise. I was the principal drafter of this part of the argument, along with Tom Lyne. The detailed policy proposal went in McNamara's and Marshall's names to Neil Kinnock's office. McNamara hand-delivered it to Kinnock's office and told us it had been approved. After Labour unexpectedly lost the election, and John Smith took over as Labour leader, I led a team, at Kevin's suggestion, that published *Northern Ireland: Sharing Authority* in 1993, under the auspices of the Institute for Public Policy Research, widely regarded as Labour's think tank though it was then independent of party control.[5] My co-authors were Tom Lyne, Jim Marshall, and Cambridge economist Bob Rowthorn. We tackled hard questions and sketched a workable model, both as a policy option and as a credible incentive.

The existence of a coherent proposal, and fears that it might be adopted, may have encouraged unionists to contemplate devolved power-sharing more seriously from 1994–95 onward, as they had not done since 1974–75. So, our work may not have been wasted. It prepared some unionists for power-sharing – for fear of something worse. When Peter Hain, with whom Kevin's team retained friendly relations, became Labour Secretary of State for Northern Ireland in 2005, he adopted the threat of joint sovereignty as part of his strategy to encourage Ian Paisley to accept power-sharing and work within the Good Friday Agreement.[6]

Given my involvement in these initiatives and endeavours, I cannot and do not argue that British and Irish joint authority or shared authority over Northern Ireland is impossible. It is, however, improbable, and more improbable than it was. It would require deep and sustained British-Irish cooperation. That idea is much less credible than in 1992, when both states were members of the new European Union, with a strong shared interest in peace which would respect both British and Irish people in Northern Ireland. If the Northern Ireland Protocol causes heartaches for the UK's sovereignty sensibilities, real or alleged, imagine the coordination difficulties involved in operating full joint sovereignty over Northern Ireland, with one co-sovereign in the EU and the other outside. In McNamara's team we were modelling with reasonable pro-European Conservatives as the outer limit of British possibilities. We never contemplated a Tory Brexiteer government. In fact, we had rejected John Hume's proposed European commissioner in our model of an executive, both because we thought it unlikely that the EU would welcome this poisoned chalice, and to assuage anti-European sentiment among unionists. We were also aware of British Eurosceptics within both the Conservatives and Labour.

Shared sovereignty in four respects would be easier to accomplish today: there is peace; Ireland is immeasurably richer than in 1992; Northern Ireland has reformed policing and the administration of justice; and, ironically, the UK and the EU are sharing authority in the management of the Protocol. But in most respects, it would be more difficult. Even with an abundance of goodwill, which is currently lacking, the UK outside the EU will inevitably have more policy tensions with Ireland within the EU. The Protocol advertises this tension.

Shared sovereignty is also contrary to the GFA, in which each of the two states retains its own sovereignty and is solemnly bound to an agreement under which sovereignty over Northern Ireland can be changed in a referendum by a simple majority vote. Ironically, however, unionist interest in joint sovereignty may be expected to increase the likelier it seems to be that Northern Ireland will vote to reunify with Ireland. Some may put it forward as a transitional arrangement, though that too is not strictly compatible with the GFA. Some will put forward joint sovereignty along with the idea of a raised qualified majority threshold for change in the sovereign status of Northern Ireland. Again, though, this thinking is not compatible with the GFA, as I explained in Chapter 7. Last-ditch proposals of this kind are to be expected, but by then reunification referendums and their consequences will be upon us.

16.   An Irish federation?

An Irish federation is improbable rather than impossible. It would meet the requirements of a sovereign united Ireland, and would therefore be compatible with the GFA.

Continental Europe has five federations: Belgium, Germany, Austria, Switzerland, and Bosnia and Herzegovina. The first four function very well. The last does not: it lives under international supervision as a protectorate of NATO and the EU, as 'a European Raj'. I have experience in the establishment of federations in difficult places. In 2004–05 I advised Kurdish negotiators in the making of Iraq's federal constitution of 2005; and earlier advised the Somalis of Puntland engaged in the federal reconstruction of their war-torn polity. When on the Standby Team of the United Nations Mediation Support Unit, I wrote reports after site visits, notably on Nepal's federalization and Sudan's break-up.[1] As these cases suggest, federations are often proposed, attempted, and break down.

As in all federations, a federal government in Ireland would have key exclusive functions. These powers would likely include foreign and defence affairs, EU functions, the currency regime (delegated to the European Central Bank), sovereign economic, commercial, and fiscal policymaking, national infrastructure, and probably health and tertiary education. The federal regions would either have specified or enumerated powers or they would retain all the powers not specifically granted to the federal government. Alternatively, the federal government could retain the residual powers not named in the constitution. Lastly, residual powers could be shared between the federal and regional governments.[2] A federation could certainly solve the problem of asymmetric devolution we identified with Model 1: all regions would have the same powers, and those deputies voting in the federal parliament could only vote in areas of federal governmental competence.

How would an Irish federation's units be composed?

An immediate, and perhaps insuperable question, for any Irish federation would be its federal units.

The four historic provinces?

The traditional answer would be to reconstitute the four historic provinces of Ireland: Leinster, Munster, Connacht, and Ulster. Using them
for a federalization project was sketched by the late Ruairí Ó Brádaigh
of Sinn Féin in the Éire Nua (New Ireland) proposal in 1972.[3] This four-
unit federation was Sinn Féin's formal objective until 1981, when the
policy was abandoned. The idea remains attractive to some republican
micro-groups (see Figure 16.1 in the colour plate section).

The four provinces have been significant in GAA organization, and in
the successful rescaling of Irish rugby union, but it is hard to envisage
their political reconstruction, which remains an abstract proposal. They
have never been democratic self-governing units, and there is no strong
impetus to remake them as such. Currently, no elected republicans in any
part or party of Ireland are pushing to recreate historic Ulster, a nine-
county entity. Most Northern Irish Protestants prefer keeping the
six-county Northern Ireland to restoring the Ulster that their precursors
chose to relinquish. Restoring historic Ulster as a federal region would
make them an even smaller minority than they are scheduled to become
in Northern Ireland. Unionists like the name 'Ulster' – they used to lobby
to have Northern Ireland renamed as Ulster – but no prominent unionist
advocates nine-county Ulster's restoration. There seems little point in
rebuilding the four historic provinces as federal units if neither Sinn Féin
nor any of the unionist parties displays any enthusiasm for the idea.

In any case, as can be seen in the map, a serious balancing problem
would arise with the four historic provinces. Leinster would be very
dominant in number of counties incorporated (12/32), in population,
and in wealth production. Would it also have the capital, Dublin? A
nine-county Ulster would not be far behind in population, but it would
be in wealth.

A modern federation built on city-regions?

A modern federation could alternatively be built around city-regions, determined by the intensity of each region's economic and communicative networks. These would, however, be novel federal entities. Each federal region would have at least one big city with its surrounding suburbs and countryside. In one sub-variant of the city-region model of federation, Northern Ireland would remain as a large city-region, with Belfast as its capital, organized with the transfer of the GFA institutions, while the South would be decomposed into three or four regions. But which ones? In another variant, which would help serious decentralization, both the South and North would be restructured. The cities in the city-regions could be Belfast, Dublin, Waterford, Cork, Limerick, Galway, and Derry on the coasts, with Armagh (or Craigavon) and Athlone in the interior. Jointly, they would comprise a nine-region federation. How county governments, or other local government districts, would fit into these city-regions would be one issue; whether they should be abolished would be another. And the rage from residents of the cities and towns excluded by this sketch from being capitals of city-regions can already be heard before this sentence is completely read.

Like the historic four provinces, this idea of a federation is abstract: it is neither the cause of a political party, movement, or think tank, nor an obvious means of smoothly accommodating the North. Decomposing the North will be difficult enough without having to re-engineer the South at the same time. Recall how Greek Cypriots had little enthusiasm about decomposing their successful entity in the cause of reunification. The same arguments would be put against building an Irish federation around geographic regions, whether city-regions or major waterways and watersheds, as suggested by Professor Breandán Mac Suibhne of the University of Galway.

Swissing Ireland?

A federation could in principle be built around the thirty-two counties (see Figure 16.2 in the colour plate section). These counties already retain collective identities, loyalties, and flags, especially but not only in GAA sports. Scale, in principle, should not exclude this idea. Switzerland has a population of 8.5 million people – 7 million citizens and about 1.5 million others, including guest workers who hold multiple citizenships. The Helvetic Confederation, as it is officially known, though it is a federation, has twenty-six cantons and some 2,300 communes! Its historic religious communities include Protestants, Catholics, and Jews, though the Swiss are currently hostile to Muslims – having voted by referendum against allowing minarets to be built. Switzerland has three major language communities – German, French, and Italian speakers – and a minority language, Romansch. Its cantons respect history, language, and religion.

Could Ireland imitate or learn from Switzerland?[4] Perhaps, especially in its principles of pluralism and toleration among Christians and Jews, and its diverse languages, but the learning would be largely abstract. One problem is that county government has disappeared from the North: its eleven local government districts have been in place since 2014; ten are of roughly comparable size (Belfast, the eleventh, is the largest), and nationalists and unionists are majorities in roughly the same number of units.★ Another is that in a federation based on reformed county government, unionists could be assured of majorities only in Antrim and Down, i.e. one-sixteenth or 6.25 per cent of the total counties in a united Ireland, hardly a proportionate share of self-government for a people potentially more than one-seventh of Ireland's population.

Importing Swiss practices would not be easy, in any case, because they have deep foundations in strong democracy at the communal level, which both parts of Ireland lack. Ireland should also steer clear of many Swiss practices: Swiss banking regulations; the practically permanent exclusion of guest workers from citizenship; the allocation of citizenship by votes in the commune; the absence of free trade between cantons; referendums on everything; and Switzerland's regular refusal to join pan-European institutions. None of these traits are intrinsically connected to Switzerland's federal structure, but they suggest a distinct public culture that it would be difficult to import. What we *can* learn from Switzerland, however, is the principle of having a power-sharing

★ See Chapter 18.

executive that is religiously, ethnically, and linguistically inclusive of its citizens.

A two-unit federation?

Lastly, a two-unit federation could be created, with Northern Ireland and the existing Republic as the constituent units. Some say this is the solution to the problems of asymmetric devolution found with Model 1, a continuing Northern Ireland. A two-unit federation cannot be recommended, however, because of the extraordinarily poor track record of the form.[5] Think only of Pakistan and Czechoslovakia, and the failure to reunify Cyprus. A two-unit federation would be unbalanced: the South would be two and a half times larger than the North in population, and better resourced.

Considering federation

The decision on federation, of course, is not mine to make. It would be that of a constitutional convention, though previously it could have been considered in citizens' assemblies and deliberative forums. That convention should be informed of evidence that suggests that federations can only cope with genuinely deep communal divisions where there are many units in the federation, preventing domination by one unit, and where a party system develops which provides political linkages across internal regional boundaries.[6]

All federal designs – two, four, nine, or thirty-two federal regions – would necessarily differ from what I have called the two feasible models of a continuing Northern Ireland and an integrated Ireland, because sovereignty would be shared between the federal government and the federal regions. Crucial here would be the allocation of powers between the federal government and the new regional governments. New difficulties would be added by construction of the senate of the federation, which would replace Ireland's existing Senate. Would the federal units have equal numbers of senators, and would this new senate be as powerful as Dáil Éireann, and would it be directly elected or appointed by the federal regions? Establishing an effective federal supreme court would be a further institutional task.

Federation is unlikely to be formally offered by the South before the Northern referendum – except as a theoretical outcome from a constitutional convention. Pragmatic, not just constitutional, reasons explain why a federal Ireland, however desirable, would be unlikely to materialize. How and when would the South be decomposed to create comparable federal units, given that two-unit federations have a very poor track record? How would Southern opinion on this option be taken, or expressed? What would Donegal's preference be? (Almost certainly, north Donegal would want to be in the same federal unit as Derry, while south Donegal would want to be connected to Enniskillen.) How could one create new federal units in advance, before being certain that reunification is to occur? Radically restructuring the state through federalizing *before* reunification is secured seems highly unlikely. Who would argue, successfully, for extensively disrupting the South for an outcome that may be defeated in a referendum in the North? Federation could only materialize *after* an all-island constitutional convention.

Voluntary federations can evolve from pre-existing institutions of comparable status 'coming together', as with the thirteen US states in 1787–88; or through a decision by an existing state to federalize as a mechanism to 'hold together', as with Iraq in 2005 or, to take a more inspirational case, Belgium. The first condition does not apply to our case – Northern Ireland is not independent – and the second could only apply *after* Ireland unifies.

These remarks are not intended to close discussion on a federation. Some successful small countries with good habits of coexistence have federations. As mentioned above, Switzerland has twenty-six cantons; and Belgium has three territorial and three community governments (the Flemish merge theirs). But if the South, collectively, is to propose a federation as its model of a united Ireland, then the division of powers and the process of federalization must be considered in advance, and a decision made on whether Northern Ireland will be a single federal unit – and if so, what the other units will be; or, in the alternative, whether there will be multiple new units across the entire island. Detailed thought will have to be given to how they are chosen, and their powers.

Current demand, and supply, for these thoughts is at exceptionally low intensity. Not a single political party currently advocates for an Irish federation. Ireland has significant numbers of Euro-federalists among its intellectuals and politicians, but no significant advocates of internally federalizing the Irish member-state. For now, therefore, a federal Ireland is not a viable model of a united Ireland.

PART FIVE

The Government of a United Ireland

17.   The central government: separating and sharing powers

Now that we have considered various models for reunification and narrowed our choices to the two most feasible models, we must turn our attention to what this new united Ireland might look like at central and local levels. Whether integrated or with an autonomous Northern Ireland within it, a united Ireland will have a central government, based on the form of government in the existing Republic.

Currently the Republic has a president as its head of state, and a prime minister, deputy prime minister, and cabinet as its executive. The two chambers of the Oireachtas form the legislature. The courts ensure that the executive and the legislature respect the Constitution, Irish law, European law, and the rule of law. What changes to these bodies are needed to facilitate a smooth transition to a united Ireland, before or after the required referendums? The symbolic charge of the Irish names of these bodies will be discussed later. Let us focus here on their functions.

The presidency and the Council of State

The presidency, fortunately, has never been religiously or ethnically exclusive. Even in the highest tide of Catholic clerical influence, two Protestants served as President of Ireland. The first President, Douglas Hyde (1938–45), was Protestant. The fourth President, Erskine Childers (1973–74), who was born in England, was also Protestant. The presidency was initially an elderly male preserve, but those days are over. Two middle-aged Marys occupied the President's residence in Phoenix Park for twenty-one years: Mary Robinson (1990–97) and Mary McAleese (1997–2011), both serving with distinction.

A candidate for President of Ireland must be at least thirty-five years of age, which is reasonable given the expectations of patient dignity and restraint attached to the role, and accords with a large majority of recent opinion.[1] Ireland's directly elected head of state is chosen by the single transferable vote.[2] This method and the number of parties with significant support across the island make it highly unlikely that any future presidential candidate will be elected solely by supporters of one political party. A new winning candidate will often need vote transfers from other parties' supporters. Ireland therefore has a good system for electing a President with cross-party support. True, a popular incumbent President may win on the first count without the need for transfers, as Michael D. Higgins did in 2018; similarly, Mary McAleese was so popular in 2004 that she was 're-elected' unopposed. Both these Presidents demonstrated independence of their parties of origin and won widespread public respect.

The Constitution requires the President of Ireland to take office with a declaration that begins, 'In the presence of Almighty God . . .'[3] An amendment is required to allow a President who does not believe in an almighty deity to take office in good faith, and must allow for a President who does not believe in the making of oaths or equivalent vows. That is true, famously, of some Protestants, and other non-Catholics, notably the Quakers.[4] More appropriate would be the early replacement of the oath, and the reference to an almighty god, with a pledge of office to uphold the values in Article 3 of the Constitution.* The new pledge of office, to be taken by all cabinet ministers, could be based on that taken by members of the Northern Ireland Executive, with appropriate modifications.[5]

The President is primarily a symbolic figure, who holds office for seven years and may serve one more term. The President is the supreme commander of the Defence Forces;[6] possesses the 'right of pardon';[7] and can appoint members of the Council of State, which advises the President – and can also dismiss those whom he or she has appointed.[8] The President's status is spelled out in one key provision: 'The powers and functions conferred on the President by this Constitution shall be exercisable and performable by him only on the advice of the Government,

---

* See Chapter 5, p. 71.

save where it is provided by this Constitution that he shall act in his absolute discretion or after consultation with . . . the Council of State . . . or . . . any other person or body.'[9] Judges, for example, are appointed by the President, but only on the advice of the Government.[10] In recent years Governments have become more relaxed about the scale and depth of their controlling advice to Presidents, who are recognized as having mandates of their own, and since Mary Robinson onward Presidents have been more assertive in carving out a civic leadership role, not subject to governmental advice. For example, in 2021 the Government left it to President Higgins whether to attend a centennial church event marking partition and the formation of Northern Ireland. He chose not to go.

The President has a limited but important role as a guardian of the Constitution and the people's rights. The President may convene a meeting of either of the two houses of the Oireachtas, a provision intended for emergencies; a national address to the houses or the nation still requires governmental approval. The President may halt a Taoiseach seeking to abridge the process of making legislation on grounds of alleged urgency.[11] If a majority of Seanad Éireann and not less than a third of the deputies of Dáil Éireann petition the President not to sign a bill that has gone through both chambers, the President may accede to the request and initiate a referendum on the measure.[12] Given the Government's historical control of the Senate, this provision has never been activated. Strengthening the independence of the Senate from Ireland's government of the day would make this power significant.

After consultation with the Council of State, the President may refer the constitutionality of parliamentary bills to the Supreme Court.[13] Presidents may, however, prefer not to question the constitutionality of bills because they think it better to leave that to be decided in the courts.

Lastly, the President has 'absolute discretion' to refuse to dissolve Dáil Éireann on the advice of a Taoiseach who has ceased to retain the support of a parliamentary majority.[14] This right has never been used.

The President, so far, has played no role in government formation and seems blocked from doing so. Only Dáil Éireann can nominate the Taoiseach. The President has no formal role in finding a Taoiseach after an election in which no party or coalition has won a majority in Dáil Éireann.[15]

Should the President's powers be enhanced beyond these limited domains during or after Irish reunification? Yes, a little. If the Senate is strengthened (see later in this chapter), then the President is more likely to initiate referendums. Encouraging the President to give an annual address on the state of human and minority rights protection, and on the progress of Irish unity, might be authorized by legislation, provided the presidency is resourced with the staff to make such an annual statement credibly informed. The President may also be requested in law to report annually on any concerns regarding the duty of the Government to preside with rigorously impartial administration over the major identities and traditions. The President should also have a role in senatorial nominations, as I will argue below.

After Irish reunification, will the rules for nominating the President need to be tweaked? The first rule for a non-incumbent needs no change: support from no less than twenty persons who are members of one of the houses of the Oireachtas. Unionist candidates will be able to muster that level of support. The alternative route to nomination does need to be changed. Namely, support by 'not less than four of the Councils of administrative Counties (including County Boroughs) as defined by law'.[16] Unless county and borough governments are restored to the North, the law will need to be modified to treat Northern local governments as the equivalent of county or borough councils. Northern councils would then appropriately acquire the right to nominate presidential candidates.

Should a united Ireland have a Vice President? There is a case for change even if Ireland is not reunified. Currently, death in office, resignation, or incapacity lead to the formation of an awkward three-person commission to perform the President's role before fresh elections can be held.[17] As the President is often abroad, a Vice President could perform some domestic duties in her or his absence. A vice presidency would require a constitutional amendment. Any such Vice President should be elected jointly with the President so that the voters endorse the ticket rather than face the possibility of experiencing an unexpected successor, or two people at odds with one another. No strong case exists for institutionalizing a requirement that someone from Northern Ireland must be on each joint ticket. A Northerner has already won the presidency (Mary McAleese). Choice of running mate should be left to the presidential candidates. They will have incentives to attract first or lower preference votes from Northerners of all backgrounds. The existing all-island parties – the Greens, Sinn Féin, and People Before Profit – will already be motivated to run both Northerners and Southerners. A Fianna Fáil candidate might want to run with an SDLP candidate; a Fine Gael candidate might want to run with a UUP or Alliance candidate; Labour and the SDLP might want to run on a joint ticket. The possible permutations are numerous.

Persons who are not Irish citizens should not have the right to become President (or Vice President) or to vote for the President.[18] Nothing should prevent dual Irish and British citizens running for the presidency, or those who hold any other citizenship, but the winner should deactivate his or her other citizenship(s) while holding office – as is normal in many countries. The Irish state is rightly obliged to recognize the right of people in Northern Ireland to identify as British, and to hold British citizenship. It is not obliged to grant British citizens the right to vote for the President (and a possible Vice President) unless they take out Irish citizenship. We should make it easy to take out Irish citizenship for those Northerners who have previously held only British citizenship. Those who argue that people who are solely British citizens should be able to vote for the President or run as presidential candidates would have to propose a constitutional amendment, one which I cannot see passing.

The current prime function of the Council of State is to advise the President. In a reunified Ireland, the Council may be advising more frequently on the constitutionality of bills, especially if there is a strengthened Senate. Therefore, whether or not there is a devolved Northern Ireland inside a reunified Ireland, it would be important to include in the Council all former first ministers and former justice ministers from Northern Ireland, as well as serving first ministers, the Speaker of the Assembly, and the Northern Attorney General, if Model I is chosen. That could be done simply through presidential discretion under existing powers, or as part of a constitutional amendment.

The Government: Taoiseach, Tánaiste, and the rest of the cabinet

There is no strong case for reforming the status and powers of the Prime Minister, the Deputy Prime Minister, or the cabinet. I will, however, advocate one radical change. The d'Hondt rule of proportionality,* used to fill committee places in the European Parliament and to fill places in the Northern Executive, should be used to help in future cabinet formation in Dublin.

The size of the Government, as the Irish cabinet is officially known, is capped by the Constitution, fixed between seven and fifteen ministers (fifteen is the current number). In comparative perspective this is a reasonable number, albeit on the low side. Denmark currently has twenty-five ministers (it used to have eighteen), Finland has nineteen, and Sweden twenty-two. The Attorney General also attends the Irish cabinet, though not as a voting member of the Government: s/he is there to advise. So does the Chief Whip. The Secretary General of the civil service attends and takes the minutes. So, there are eighteen people in the room. With questionable constitutionality, a 'super junior' minister has recently attended cabinet, which improperly circumvents the limit of fifteen.[19] Outside the cabinet room, Ireland currently has twenty Ministers of State, previously called 'junior ministers'. Together with the cabinet ministers, Ireland therefore has thirty-five ministers! Differently put, more than one in five deputies, of a current total of 160, is a minister. 'More Ministers means fewer disgruntled backbenchers,' writes Oran Doyle.[20]

Given that Dáil Éireann will expand upon reunification, likely to roughly 250 deputies, it may be wise to cap the total number of ministers at the current level: thirty-five, including the fifteen in the cabinet (with no 'super junior'). Alternatively, the reunification of Ireland bill should limit the total number of ministers – full and junior – to 14 per cent of the total number of deputies in Dáil Éireann: $250 \times 0.14 = 35$.

Quotas, as I will discuss, could ensure Northern representation in the cabinet.† If a devolved Northern Ireland persists, it would not be

* See Chapter 20, pp. 210–17.
† See Chapter 20, p. 216.

appropriate to have a Minister for Northern Ireland, as explained above.* Under the integrated model of a united Ireland, existing departments and public bodies in the North would fuse with or be reallocated to the appropriate Southern ministries. In the interim, a Ministry of National Reunification should be assigned to the Taoiseach or the Tánaiste, to signal its fundamental importance, with a junior minister responsible for its daily functioning.†

Dáil Éireann and Seanad Éireann

In a reunified Ireland it is vital that the National Parliament, the English name for the Oireachtas, be a vibrant and inclusive body. The Standing Orders of Dáil Éireann can be modified by that body, and it is the most appropriate body to do so. A coalition government determined to empower backbenchers is required if Dáil Éireann is to become more vibrant, with more powerful committees. Capping the ratio of ministers to deputies at 14 per cent, or one in seven, will create a pool of backbenchers with an interest in a more effective committee system. Dáil Éireann committee places should be allocated by the d'Hondt rule, just as committee places are allocated in the European Parliament and in the Northern Assembly, with a standing committee for each ministry, and a committee for each appropriate function handled by the relevant ministers who attend the European Council of Ministers, with fusion where appropriate. The proportionality rule will ensure that no committees are off limits to Ulster unionists or Protestants. To avoid Euroscepticism – not an exclusively English affliction – Dáil Éireann should be able to ensure its ministers are held to account for their decisions in Europe. Irish Members of the European Parliament (MEPs), who will expand in number upon Irish reunification, need to be invited to regular meetings of Dáil Éireann, or made senators, as I will suggest below.

The Irish Senate has been described as 'a crèche, convalescent

---

* See Chapter 11, pp. 137–8.
† See Chapter 9, pp. 118–19.

home and retirement community' for professional politicians.[21] It need not be so. Originating in home rule bills, which would have kept veto powers for anxious landed aristocrats, the Senate materialized in the Irish Free State partly to ensure a place for Protestants in an upper house: W. B. Yeats was the most famous Protestant senator. The Senate of the Irish Free State later became a site of resistance to de Valera's programme to unwind the Treaty of 1921, and it was constitutionally dissolved in 1936. Nevertheless, de Valera created a new Senate in the Constitution of 1937. In 2013, Irish citizens, albeit narrowly, voted to maintain the Senate, partly because they suspected a governmental power grab, and because of all the complicated changes to the Constitution that abolition would have triggered with uncertain consequences. Abolition is therefore not likely to be proposed this side of reunification.

There are defensible reasons to have a senate in a unitary state: to provide a delaying check and some balance in the legislative process; and to create a chamber with special responsibilities, especially the protection of minorities. This can be so, provided that the senate is based on different constituencies to that represented in the first chamber – otherwise it would merely mirror the first chamber. Ireland's Senate is not fit for purpose according to these standards, and it is relatively toothless. The Government dominates the Senate because the Taoiseach makes eleven nominations (over 18 per cent of the chamber). The Senate is extraordinarily subservient to Dáil Éireann, with minimal powers of delay, and is recomposed after a Dáil election. The rules for choosing senators are 'bizarre and anachronistic',[22] driven by a corporatist vocational model of representation that was never realized. The current Senate therefore does not meet reasonable reasons for its existence. It will need to be reformed while reunifying Ireland. I expect to receive fierce resistance from some existing deputies in Dáil Éireann to what follows, but such a debate is necessary.

The Senate needs to be expanded to 84–90 members, in accordance with the increased population of a united Ireland, and to allow for some creative changes. The minimal qualifications of senators should be the same as those required for nomination to Dáil Éireann, but the provision that allows the Taoiseach to nominate eleven senators should be abolished.[23] Instead, the President, who stands for the whole state – not the Taoiseach, who is a party leader – should make eleven nominations; among other eligibility criteria, nominees should be people who have not stood for elected office in the previous decade, and who have not donated more than €1,000 to a political party or candidate in any of the previous three years. The President should nominate at least five women and at least five men. The old panels should be abolished, but in partial respect for the old model, the President should nominate from the employers' organizations, agriculture, and the trade unions (one senator each), and the social professions, especially health and education (three senators), and from visible and invisible minorities, including Travellers and disabled people (five senators). In composing the eleven nominations, the President could be required by law to consider geographical representation and diversity of origins. That would account for eleven of the ninety senators.

The Republic currently has thirteen MEPs, a number that will rise to between fifteen and seventeen upon reunification, so let us say sixteen. Linking MEPs to the Senate would enhance informed treatment of European questions in the Oireachtas. This suggestion in turn would require the Senate to be elected (or nominated) at fixed intervals of five years, coincident with European Parliament elections – which could improve turnout. Decoupling the filling of the Senate from elections to Dáil Éireann, together with abolishing the Taoiseach's nominations, would enhance the independence of the Senate from the Dáil.

The remaining Senators, sixty-three, should be directly elected from nine constituencies: (1) Belfast, (2) Dublin, (3) Connacht (perhaps including Clare), (4) North Leinster (minus Dublin), (5) South Leinster (minus Dublin), (6) Munster (minus Clare, if included in Connacht), (7) North and East Ulster (minus Belfast), (8) West Ulster, and (9) the diaspora (perhaps in five electoral colleges in the US, Great Britain, the EU, Canada, and Australia). The boundaries of West Ulster would include counties Donegal, Cavan, Monaghan, Londonderry, Fermanagh, and Tyrone. The boundaries of North and East Ulster minus Belfast would include Armagh, Antrim, and Down. The number of diaspora senators should be fixed at five – to avoid the diaspora vote overwhelming the vote of those who live on the island. The question of defining the diaspora and its voting rights will not be discussed further here. But fixing the number of diaspora senators at five would leave the remaining eight constituencies to elect fifty-eight senators. The number of senators for each of these eight constituencies should be apportioned every five years according to the size of the registered electorate. They would be elected by the single transferable vote system of proportional representation.

In summary, under this model the reformed Senate would consist of fifty-eight senators directly elected from eight constituencies; sixteen senators who are Ireland's directly elected MEPs; eleven presidential nominees; and five senators directly elected from a college or colleges of diaspora citizens.

This suggested composition of the Senate could be endlessly tweaked. This proposal would deliberately weaken the Taoiseach's and the Government's control over the Senate. It would eliminate panels, and the university graduate senators whose existence is democratically indefensible – unless all universities or third-tier institutions are included *and* all non-graduates separately elect an equivalent number of senators. Proportionality would ensure democratic representation for unionist or cultural Protestant candidates, and equal worth for the votes and transfers of cultural Protestants. By directly electing senators at fixed five-year intervals from different constituencies to those of Dáil Éireann, this style of Senate would not mirror Dáil Éireann, and it would not be subservient to the latter, or to the Government. But it would not and should not be so powerful as to block Dáil Éireann indefinitely.

What would the reformed Senate do?

The Senate should scrutinize legislation with enhanced capacities for delay and be able to initiate legislation on non-money bills. The Senate's ability to delay non-money bills for 90 days should be extended to not less than 180 days, but not more than one year. A reformed Senate would become more likely to initiate a referendum on draft legislation on a controversial or neglected subject, with the support of a Senate majority and one-third of deputies in Dáil Éireann. The Senate might be empowered to require the convention of a citizens' assembly on a specific item of legislation or clear policy choice, to report back within four months. That would enable the Senate to test what informed public opinion is like on a subject that might go to referendum. The numbers of such assemblies per parliamentary session should be capped. Senators should be able to have regular question sessions with ministers.

Most importantly, there should be a Senate committee on public appointments beyond the civil service, with at least one senator from each of the constituencies identified above. Reviewing public appointments with the increased glare of Senate proceedings would help assure the public that clientelism, cronyism, and corruption are minimized, and competence prioritized.[24] The Governor of the Central Bank of Ireland and the Commissioner of An Garda Síochána and their colleagues would be among the suitable candidates for senatorial scrutiny. No individual senatorial veto or delay should ever apply to public appointments – an abusive US practice. Appointment processes would be scheduled allowing for due diligence but not inordinate delay. Appointment committees should vote publicly, giving reasons, and identifying any conflicts of interest of committee members.

Minority protections in the legislature[25]

The foregoing measures should ensure fair representation of cultural Protestants, Ulster unionists, and British citizens, provided they stand and vote. They cannot, however, guarantee fair treatment. Other provisions may do that, as should legislation, such as applying the Irish Employment Equality Act – or extending Northern Ireland's Fair Employment Act to the entire island.

Some constitutions allow a minority in the legislature to delay legislation pending further review and scrutiny. In Sweden, legislation affecting fundamental rights can be delayed for one year at the insistence of as few as 10 of 349 MPs.[26] This delay can be overturned by the votes of five-sixths of the MPs, so any party or group of parties having more than one-sixth of the seats can force a delay. They cannot stop such laws from being passed: a simple majority vote, in the end, is decisive. What they can do, however, is oblige public debate on such legislation and require the majority to justify its actions more carefully. The existence of this mechanism, even if it is not used, may have a moderating effect. Governments, aware of the potential for the Opposition to impose delays, may modify their proposals to accommodate specific objections or concerns. Such a rule discourages knee-jerk legislation and encourages the government to respond more deliberately to events, with some attempt to build consensus before legislating.

Adding a rule enabling such a minority delay would require a constitutional amendment in Ireland. An appropriate threshold for a fundamental rights review would be nine of the fifty-eight directly elected senators on the island. That number would be just over one-seventh of the directly elected senators, and would approximate the number of the British or cultural Protestant minority in a reunified Ireland, but it would require them to be unified in their sense of a pending injustice. Such a rule should be considered.

Denmark has a similar rule to Sweden, although the scope of the provision for delay is broader while the threshold for triggering the delay is higher.[27] In Sweden, the delay mechanism applies only to legislation affecting fundamental rights, while in Denmark two-fifths of the legislature can delay any bill – except money and citizenship bills, and emergency legislation – but for a mere twelve days. Nevertheless, it prevents legislation being rushed through by the majority without at least an opportunity for the opposition to scrutinize it, and it may serve to bring public and media attention to contentious legislation that might otherwise have gone unnoticed.[28] Having a reasonably empowered Senate, as suggested above, would obviate the need to imitate this feature of Danish democracy.[29]

Minority-veto referendums

The Constitution of Denmark makes provision for 'minority-veto referendums'.[30] One-third of MPs may suspend a bill that has been passed by parliament but that has not yet received royal assent, pending approval by the people in a referendum. Ordinarily, a petition signed by one-third of the parliamentary members must be submitted to the speaker within three working days of the bill's passage. The referendum must be held between twelve and eighteen working days after the publication of the bill, a short time to prepare a campaign. The government may avoid a potentially embarrassing referendum defeat by withdrawing the bill. If the referendum goes ahead, and if a majority of the votes cast in the referendum are against the bill, and if those voting against it account for at least 30 per cent of all those eligible to vote, then the bill does not receive royal assent.[31] So, turnout matters. This minority-veto referendum procedure cannot be invoked for money bills, citizenship bills, bills giving effect to existing treaty obligations, or bills concerning succession to the throne.

The Danish mechanism would seem a recipe for paralysis, making it nearly impossible to pass legislation, because there is little limit on the ability of the opposition to demand a referendum. Yet only two referendums have been held under this procedure since it was introduced in 1953. Its real effect is to act as a moderating mechanism. The governing majority has an incentive to cooperate to dissuade the opposition from invoking it. The final decision is majoritarian: there is no absolute minority veto, just a route by which the opposition may appeal to the popular majority rather than the parliamentary majority.[32]

For that reason, in a united Ireland the existence of such a provision may be of little value to Northern cultural Protestants or British people – initially about one-sixth of the population of a united Ireland *if* we include Southern Protestants in our count of Protestants. They would be appealing to the public over the heads of a majority of elected deputies and senators and might receive a frosty response. Therefore, some of their rights, for example their right to British citizenship, need to be protected from removal by amendment. That would require 'a non-amendable amendment'.

Right of the legislative minority to appeal to the Supreme Court[33]

Some democracies permit a legislative minority to refer a bill to the supreme or constitutional court for a ruling on its constitutionality. The Constitution of France enables any sixty members of the National Assembly or of the Senate, as well as the President, the Prime Minister, or the president of either chamber of the legislature, to refer legislation to the Constitutional Council. This process must take place after a bill has been passed but before it is ratified. Even if a constitutional reference is not made, the legislative minority can use the threat of this procedure to draw public attention to a bill, to highlight issues of controversy and perhaps to encourage the government to accept amendments to the bill.

In Ireland, the President already has the power to refer the constitutionality of any bill to the Supreme Court. In a reunited Ireland, perhaps a provision should be added by law or constitutional amendment to enable a minority of senators to petition the President and the Council of State to consider the constitutionality of a bill – a minority of nine senators.[34]

The courts

In light of the two feasible models of reunification advanced in this book, two different futures for the courts of Northern Ireland may be envisaged. They may remain the courts of a devolved Northern Ireland, but with final appeals to an expanded, all-island Irish Supreme Court under the supremacy of the Irish Constitution, Irish law, and EU law, where appropriate and to be decided. In the integrated model, by contrast, the courts of Northern Ireland would have to be fused with their Southern counterparts. In both models, it would be reasonable to ensure the Supreme Court adopts proportional Northern representation.[35] A quota for twenty years might be appropriate, with nominations from the North made by a judicial appointments commission and ratified by the Irish Senate – to avoid the Irish Government of the day controlling the courts. The quota should be either based on religion of origin, national identification, or place of birth, and with slight over-representation for the new minority – with one-sixth of places across the island held for those Northerners who identify as British or as British and Irish. Judges may have dual citizenship, but not, I think, while they are judges on the Supreme Court. Ireland's Supreme Court, currently headed by Chief Justice Donal O'Donnell, born in Belfast, will know that it will need to have justices knowledgeable in Northern Ireland law.

18. Local government

What of local government in a united Ireland? The Republic has retained county government. There are thirty-one elected local authorities in total, as laid out in Figure 18.1 in the colour plate section, consisting of twenty-six county councils, two city and county councils, and three city councils. In the integrated Model 2 the question would arise: should Northern local government be remodelled on the Southern pattern, restoring county or city government as appropriate? Or would it be better to retain the existing Northern arrangements of eleven local governments, as in Figure 18.2 (see the colour plate)? The latter approach would minimize institutional disruption, and there would be no constitutional obligation to impose county government throughout the island. 'Integration' need not mean 'utter uniformity'.

Over many decades of travel throughout the island, I have been struck by the persistence of 'county patriotism'. It is found strongly in rural Ireland, North and South. It is not confined to GAA sports, or to cultural Catholics: after all, counties were an English administrative creation. Is there any case for restoring six county governments and two city-boroughs in Belfast and Derry? The consequences would have to be considered very carefully, and I would advise against. A restoration of county government could reduce unionists to majority status in just two of thirty-two counties, Antrim and Down, and without majority status in any of the city governments on the island – given that Belfast and Derry cities, however defined, may well have non-unionist majorities – unless Craigavon were to be made a city-borough. This suggests a strong case for keeping the existing eleven local governments in the North – in which unionists currently have majorities in six (see Figure 18.3 in the colour plate section) – as a balancing measure. Under the existing organization of local government, unionists also enjoy majorities in several urban zones in central and east Ulster: Antrim & Newtownabbey, Craigavon, Coleraine, Lisburn & Castlereagh, and Newtownards.

Should local governments, however they are territorially organized, have their powers enhanced in a united Ireland? This question applies to both feasible models, but perhaps it has greatest force for those who advocate Model 2, an integrated Ireland. The objective case for greater decentralization in a united Ireland will be even stronger than it is now. In 2031 there will be a population of 7.5 million or more citizens in a possible united Ireland, by comparison with the fewer than 3 million who inhabited the Republic in 1961, at its demographic trough.

Local authorities in the Republic are partially responsible for the provision of housing, planning, roads, environmental protection, fire services, and maintaining the electoral register. Councils play a supportive role in economic development. The South is heavily influenced by the 'city manager' model, transplanted from the United States, as an insurance policy against corruption. Councillors deliberate on policy; the chief executive and his or her staff implement.

The delayed reform of local government in the North went into effect in 2014. The current eleven districts replaced twenty-six, each with a much larger average size of population than before. These councils have fewer powers than those in Great Britain or Ireland, partly because Northern Ireland's devolved government delivers region-wide, which often pre-empts local government. Local governments, after bitter experience, are not trusted with the electoral register.

Since local governments were the site of the most visible and entrenched sectarian and ethno-national bigotry, quasi-governmental public bodies often displaced elected local governments under British-sponsored reform programmes. The Housing Executive, Northern Ireland's single public housing authority, was set up in 1971. The Department for Infrastructure (DfI) is the region's sole road authority. The Education Authority is responsible for educational and library services. The provision of social care is overseen by six trusts. These public bodies are partly accountable to the Northern Ireland Executive, but not to local councils. These questions will therefore arise: to whom will these bodies be accountable in a united Ireland – and should they persist, if Northern Ireland is abolished? Under the integrated model they would be merged with their Southern equivalents.

Within a united Ireland there will be a demographic and a democratic case for more decentralization than currently flourishes on either side of the border, provided local authorities are constrained by appropriate financial and legal controls, and by political competition, which should inhibit corruption and reduce the risk of discrimination. The fate of local government, and related public bodies, could be postponed until after reunification, but, if so, I suspect the prospects of deeper decentralization would be diminished. Advocates of greater decentralization should use the prospect of reunification to advocate their case amid the deliberations over the appropriate model of a united Ireland.

Take policing as an example. Would advocates of decentralization wish to give local governments a role in holding the police to account? Would they consider a two-tier police service, with the central tier focused on crimes against the person, organized crime, and terrorism prevention, leaving all other policing organized at local level or by function (roads, ports, and airports), with local police accountable to local councils?

Many Irish intellectuals, of whatever national, religious, or ethnic background, fear that decentralization would lead to cronyism, clientelism, and corruption – or should that be further cronyism, clientelism, and corruption? That debate, and especially the financing of local government, should be engaged before reunification, because the latter moment will offer an opportunity for democratic revitalization.

One focus that will merit attention for harmonization is proportionality. The number of elected local authorities in the Republic is thirty-one, with 949 elected councillors,[1] but the number of councillors per authority varies widely. Northern Ireland, by contrast, has a much more uniform model: forty councillors for each local government district, except Belfast, which has sixty. Consideration might also be given to enabling, by law, a set of contiguous electoral districts to opt out of an existing local government district to set up its own local government district, subject to some threshold of viability and to approval by local referendum. That opt-out option would give scope for diversity in local policymaking and restrain councillors from neglecting areas where their vote harvest is low.

19. Repurposing the institutions of the Good Friday Agreement

In early 2022, the formal institutions established in the Good Friday Agreement were functioning: the Northern Ireland Assembly and its power-sharing Executive; the North South Ministerial Council; the British-Irish Intergovernmental Conference; and the British-Irish Council.

In May 2022, the seventh Northern Assembly since May 1998 will be elected. Yet both the Assembly and the Executive that it elects have been and remain fragile. The Assembly has been suspended in total for nearly eight years after it was first activated in December 1999 – formally suspended under the unilateral UK Suspension Act of 2000, which broke the GFA, on four occasions between 2000 and 2007 – and was informally preserved between January 2017 and January 2020 without a formal act of suspension when there was no agreed executive formation. As I write, the Assembly and Executive have functioned for just over two-thirds of the time available for them to do so, and the latest leader of the DUP, Jeffrey Donaldson, has just withdrawn the DUP from the institutions with the threat that he will continue to do so until the 'sea border' of the Protocol is scrapped.

Whatever the outcome of this decision, and Donaldson's extreme demand, the question will become: should we preserve all or some of these institutions before, during, and after the reunification of Ireland? Under Model 1 all will be kept, subject to agreed revisions; under Model 2, the Assembly and its Executive would go.

The British-Irish Council

The British-Irish Council should occasion no extended thought or debate. Since 1999 the Council, which brings together the two sovereign governments, the devolved governments of the UK, and the Crown dependencies of Jersey, Guernsey, and the Isle of Man, has met thirty-five times in summit format, albeit increasingly without the participation of British Prime Ministers.[1] At worst, the Council is harmless. It was created as part of constitutional balancing, to give British unionists an east–west linkage to match the north–south linkage created by the North South Ministerial Council. Originally marketed under the name of the 'Council of the Isles', its importance is largely symbolic – unlike the North South Ministerial Council, it lacks implementation bodies – but it is important in order to avoid unnecessary symbolic offence. So, it should stay in all futures. Like the Nordic Council of our Scandinavian neighbours, the BIC can facilitate cooperation among neighbours within and outside the European Union. It may, however, need to be renamed if Scotland secedes from Great Britain. Maybe not though. The naming issue may be decided by how many Scots will still want to be called 'British'.

The British–Irish Intergovernmental Conference

The successor of the Intergovernmental Conference of the Anglo-Irish Agreement played a vital role in the stabilization of the new Northern arrangements between 1998 and 2007. Its formal meetings were co-chaired by Ireland's foreign minister and the UK's Secretary of State for Northern Ireland. Its secretariat of public officials ensured follow-through. Between February 2007 and July 2018, no meetings of the BIIGC took place. Both the British and Irish governments, unwisely, stopped regular meetings, mothballing the Conference and its secretariat, partly to encourage the local Northern parties to govern on their own, but also to appease unionist, especially DUP, sensibilities.[2] The communiqués of the restored BIIGC can be banal,[3] but its meetings ensure that the UK Government is obliged to hear the voice of the Irish Government in a structured setting on all non-devolved subjects. It should be preserved at least while partition persists, and Irish Governments should be vigorous in ensuring its activity, especially when the Assembly and Executive are not functioning.

In the decade ahead, Irish Governments must breathe life into the BIIGC, and not just for the sake of preserving the GFA 'in all its parts'. The BIIGC could play a vital role before, during, and after reunification, provided that Great Britain still exists – not a trivial afterthought. Even if Scotland secedes, the remainder of the UK (England and Wales) would be the successor state to the UK and would inherit Great Britain's international obligations and memberships. On the assumption that Great Britain will persist, the BIIGC is the obvious vehicle for rational deliberation and planning on future possibilities, long before a UK Secretary of State for Northern Ireland calls a referendum. No other formal forum exists in which the two sovereign executives, and their officials, can discuss and contingently plan the modalities of the potential transfer of power, and later implement them. These transitional matters will include citizens' and permanent residents' rights; the demarcation of maritime boundaries; the assessment of assets and liabilities; and security cooperation. These matters can only be effectively addressed by the sovereign governments.

Such planning does not mean that either government must presume just one outcome of a future referendum. Both should plan for either outcome. They can also jointly roll out projects and policies that should happen anyway, whether there is reunification or not – such as full motorways between Derry/Londonderry and Dublin, and high-speed rail between Belfast, Dublin, Cork, Galway, and Limerick; all-island public health planning; the strategic coordination of tertiary education; and ensuring representative, accountable, and cooperative police services.

After Irish reunification, the BIIGC could be repurposed to provide a role for the British Government equivalent to that currently enjoyed by the Government of Ireland – namely, the right to regular timetabled conferences and consultation on policy matters affecting Northern Ireland that are not devolved to the Northern Assembly. Such a role, however, would presume the continuing existence of the Assembly. If, in contrast, an integrated Ireland materializes, then it would be more sensible to transfer any remaining relevant functions of the BIIGC to the British-Irish Council, especially if Scotland secedes from Great Britain. Each government within these islands, for example, could pledge itself to annual reporting on rights protection within its jurisdiction, laying itself open to questions from its opposite numbers.

In the decade ahead, Dublin governments, because it is their treaty right and duty, should seek to be consulted on all aspects of non-devolved functions affecting Northern Ireland *and* on formally devolved functions *if* the Northern Executive and Assembly fail to function or are suspended. The all-island and cross-border aspects of rights, justice, prisons, and policing remain part of its agenda. The devolution of functions in these domains does not remove the entirety of these matters from the Conference's remit. The BIIGC must also keep under review the international treaty and the machinery and institutions 'established under it'.

The North South Ministerial Council

The North South Ministerial Council oversees six fields in which common policies may be agreed but separately implemented in the two jurisdictions: transport, agriculture, education, environment, health, and tourism.[4] The NSMC delegates to six implementation bodies: the Foyle, Carlingford and Irish Lights Commission; the Food Safety Promotion Board; the North/South Language Body, with its two agencies (Foras na Gaeilge and Tha Boord o Ulstèr-Scotch); the Special European Union Programmes Body (SEUPB); the Trade and Business Development Body (also known as InterTradeIreland); and Waterways Ireland. The SEUPB continues with EU peace and cross-border programmes despite the UK's exit from the European Union.

When the Assembly and Executive were suspended, the North South Ministerial Council did not meet, though the six implementation bodies operated.[5] Since the NSMC was formed, it has remained strictly delimited and technocratic in character. Its powers and capacities have not been extended. Unionists have persistently combined to stunt its capacities for growth, by using their veto powers against Irish or Northern nationalist initiatives. In a positive scenario in the decade ahead, it is possible to imagine increased North–South economic cooperation, channelled through the NSMC, especially over infrastructure – particularly if the Protocol stabilizes, and if the island becomes a preferred site for investors with interests in the markets of both Great Britain and the EU. In a bleaker scenario, we should expect the continuation of the status quo, punctuated by unionist refusal to work the institutions, whether the Assembly is functioning or not.

The question to be addressed here is: what role would there be for the NSMC in a reunified Ireland? Clearly, an integrated united Ireland – Model 2 – would not need such a cross-border body, or a set of such bodies. However, if Northern Ireland persists as a devolved political unit within a united Ireland – Model 1 – then there would be a strong case for preserving the NSMC, not least to avoid too much centralized policymaking in ministries currently run from Dublin.

The councils and conferences

To sum up, the BIC should survive, but perhaps restructured, and renamed if Scotland becomes independent. The fates of the BIIGC and the NSMC will depend upon the persistence of the Northern Assembly, certainly under continuing UK sovereignty, but also under future Irish sovereignty. These intergovernmental and inter-ministerial bodies could be eliminated upon Irish reunification, if we reunify along an integrationist path (Model 2). In the alternative, these councils may be repurposed if a devolved Northern Ireland persists within a united Ireland. The symbolic and practical functions of the councils would change, however. British unionists might be assured by continuing British institutional interest in their fate in the intergovernmental council, and the ministerial council could function to facilitate both meaningful devolution and more ambitious all-island cooperation.

The Northern Ireland Assembly

The Assembly has been effective when it sits. It passes legislation at rates close to that of the Scottish Parliament.[6] Four-fifths of legislation goes through with simple majority voting, without the 'petition of concern' being invoked. Upon receipt of a petition of concern by thirty

Members of the Legislative Assembly (MLAs), voting must take place by 'cross-community consent'. Namely, with the concurrent consent of a majority of nationalists and unionists respectively, as well as an overall majority – sometimes referred to as the '50:50:50 criterion'[7] – *or* with a qualified majority of 60 per cent of the MLAs, including at least 40 per cent of registered nationalist and unionist MLAs respectively.

The petition of concern is widely lamented, including by those who use it, but bear in mind that the use of the petition initiates a cross-community consent vote; it is not an immediate veto. The higher threshold of support required for a cross-community consent vote may sometimes be appropriate. Usage of the petition could, in principle, be regulated by the Assembly's Speaker, and the three Deputy Speakers, to avoid it being tabled for matters that do not directly affect questions of national, ethnic, religious, or linguistic identity or equality. Use of the petition is most galling when one party has thirty MLAs or more, and deploys it as a party veto – especially on matters that have nothing to do with equality, or national, ethnic, religious, or linguistic identity concerns. But the Assembly recently has been reduced in size, from 108 to 90 MLAs, while the number required for a successful petition, thirty, has remained the same. So, since no party is currently likely to win over 33.3 per cent of the first-preference vote and an equivalent number of seats (30/90), the risk of an abusive party-veto has receded – for now. In New Decade, New Approach – the 'settlement' that restored the institutions in January 2020 – the parties agreed to reduce the use of the petition, confining it to the most 'exceptional circumstances and as a last resort', and agreed that it could only be triggered 'by members from two or more parties'.[8]

Recent surveys indicate that the public in Northern Ireland, though divided, wants the Assembly and its Executive to function. Preference for British direct rule never rose above 12 per cent in the last four surveys conducted before elections to the Westminster Parliament in 2019. Support for the Assembly and the Executive exists among voters in all three political blocs: nationalists, unionists, and 'others'. Sizeable majorities in both major communities, albeit with significant numbers of 'don't knows', believe that both nationalists and unionists should be in the power-sharing Executive together, and that legislation should enjoy support in each community. Rather realistically, however, as reported by Professor Jonathan Tonge, just over a quarter of the public believe the parties have cooperated well in the Executive.[9] These people are realists, or they have low expectations, or both.

It is common to hear that power-sharing makes the Assembly impotent in holding ministers to account, and prevents the public from targeting irresponsible ministers or parties with their votes. These complaints have, however, been successfully questioned by political scientists: Richard Conley has shown how questioning of ministers can be effective; while John Garry has shown how voters are able to hold party incumbents responsible for their decisions.[10] The Ash for Cash scandal, however, showed the failure of the Executive, Assembly, Assembly committees, parties, the civil service, and the media to get in early to address manifest failures in oversight.[11]

The indelicate question is whether the Assembly can survive likely crises in the decade ahead. Whether one favours the Union or Irish reunification, it will be better if the Assembly does survive and function.[12] Its survival would enhance the prospects of the Union with Great Britain functioning according to the Good Friday Agreement. Its survival would also materially assist Irish reunification, while highlighting an institutional path to a united Ireland in which the institutions of the Good Friday Agreement persist.

The collapse of the Assembly will not enhance the Union's prospects. It will bring direct rule, modified by the BIIGC. The collapse of the Assembly would also make the integrationist path to reunification more credible. After all, the questions would become: Why restore dysfunctional institutions? If the power-sharing institutions cannot function within the Union, why should they work better within a united Ireland?

The Northern Ireland Executive

Whatever one's judgement on the politicians who have filled the Northern Ireland Executive, it has been a fascinating institution.[13] It has two central innovations, the dual premiership and the d'Hondt executive, which are often misunderstood.

The dual premiership

In the 1998 negotiations, the SDLP and the UUP made a fundamental compromise. They agreed to create two first ministers, identical in their powers. Both would lead the new government, preside over its executive committee (or cabinet), run a joint office, and jointly represent Northern Ireland externally. They would be elected together on a joint ticket. The Northern Assembly would vote them into office, with a concurrent majority of nationalists and unionists, and a majority overall. The majority in one bloc could veto a candidate of the other bloc. This linkage would, it was hoped, encourage the nomination of mutually acceptable candidates. The two post-holders would differ solely in their official titles: First Minister and Deputy First Minister. This was a concession made by the SDLP to the UUP.

The SDLP and the UUP also agreed that the death or resignation of one of the first ministers would trigger the resignation of the other within six weeks, obliging fresh Assembly elections. This rule was intended to bind the two office-holders together, but quickly resulted in an unanticipated consequence. Both Seamus Mallon and David Trimble used the rule to stop the functioning of the institutions. Mallon did so when the institutions were in 'shadow form', to protest the failure to get things moving. Trimble did so when the institutions were up and running, to protest the IRA's refusal to start decommissioning its weapons. Avoiding the details of both controversies, what matters here is that these two men, regarded as moderates within their respective political communities, had a formidable institutional weapon: they could force an unwanted election on their partner.

The Secretary of State for Northern Ireland, Peter Mandelson, passed legislation through Westminster in 2000 granting his office the right to suspend the Assembly. This power was not part of the text of the GFA, or its spirit, and was therefore its first important breach.[14]

The DUP and Sinn Féin became the largest parties in their respective blocs in the 2003 Assembly elections. Though the DUP was prepared, with qualifications, to share power with Sinn Féin, it did not want to vote for Martin McGuinness. Among other lines on his CV, McGuinness had organized the bombing of Derry's city centre, represented the

IRA in talks with the British Government in 1972, and later was reputed to have been the organization's chief of staff. Sinn Féin, for its part, was prepared to share power with Ian Paisley, albeit reluctantly. Paisley's CV included roles in the formation of the Ulster Protestant Volunteers and the UVF in the 1960s, and of Ulster Resistance in the 1980s.

To resolve the impasse, the rules for electing the First and Deputy First Minister were changed in the St Andrews Agreement (2006). The Northern Ireland Act 1998 was amended. This enabled the DUP to claim it had renegotiated the GFA. The rules in force now read:

> 16 (4) The nominating officer of the largest political party of the largest political designation shall nominate a member of the Assembly to be the First Minister.
>
> (5) The nominating officer of the largest political party of the second largest political designation shall nominate a member of the Assembly to be the deputy First Minister.[15]

But there is an important qualifying clause:

> 16C (6) If at any time the party which is the largest political party of the largest political designation is not the largest political party –
> (a) any nomination to be made at that time under section 16A(4) or 16B(4) shall instead be made by the nominating officer of the largest political party; and
> (b) any nomination to be made at that time under section 16A(5) or 16B(5) shall instead be made by the nominating officer of the largest political party of the largest political designation.[16]

Translated, this qualifying clause means that the largest party always nominates the First Minister, irrespective of its designation. The concurrent majority rule was thus abolished. Ian Paisley and Martin McGuinness became First and Deputy First Minister without their parties having to vote on a joint 'investiture'. The two men had a brief period as the 'Chuckle Brothers' before Peter Robinson replaced Paisley and the chuckling stopped.[17]

No party or bloc can now veto a party entitled to nominate one of the two premiers. The new rule does something more. The largest party, or the largest party of the second-largest political designation, could be the Alliance Party if it won enough votes and seats. This creates the possibility that either unionists or nationalists could be excluded from these top two posts if their bloc's support falls sufficiently.

The d'Hondt rule for executive formation

The Executive Committee of Northern Ireland Ministers, by law, must have between six and ten ministers. Recently, excluding the first ministers, it has had eight. The Executive Committee is nominated by party officers in the Assembly through the application of the d'Hondt rule, named after a Belgian mathematician who devised this rule of proportional representation that is widely used across Europe, especially in the allocation of committee places in the European Parliament.[18]

In his memoirs, Tony Blair suggests that the d'Hondt rule is formidably complicated. It is not.[19] Let me illustrate and justify it, because I believe the d'Hondt rule should be kept for the Northern Ireland Executive if it persists – including if it persists in a united Ireland – because it works. More surprisingly perhaps, with qualifications it may provide a helpful rule for future coalition formation for the central government of a united Ireland, as I will argue in the next chapter.

The d'Hondt rule does two things. First, it awards ministries to parties in proportion to the seats they have won. It could be used to award ministries according to the first-preference votes parties win, but seats make more sense because MLAs have legislative power. The rule is slightly more favourable to larger parties, but that is a good thing because governing with very large numbers of small parties is difficult. Second, the rule allocates choices of ministries to parties in sequential order of their proportionate strength. They get to pick ministries according to how well they have done at the hands of the voters.

Now, a worked example. Imagine ten ministries in the Northern Ireland Executive Committee must be filled. Imagine too that the parties have won the seats listed in the second row of Table 19.1 (see over). Dividing the number of seats by one obviously leaves all the seat totals the same.

Making Sense of a United Ireland

	Sinn Féin		DUP		UUP		SDLP		Alliance		TUV		Greens
Total seats	28		16		13		12		12		7		2
÷ 1 =	28	M1	16	M2	13	M4	12	M6	12	M5	7	M10	2	
÷ 2 =	14	M3	8	M8	6.5		6		6		3.5			
÷ 3 =	9.3	M7	5.3											
÷ 4 =	7.0	M9												
÷ 5 =	5.6													
Total ministries	4		2		1		1		1		1		0

Table 19.1: Hypothetical allocation of ministries under the d'Hondt rule in Northern Ireland. M = choice of Ministry in sequential order

Step two: award the first ministry to the party with the largest seat total – in this case it is Sinn Féin (M1) – and then divide its seat total by two, so it now has 14 remaining seats available for selecting further ministers. Sinn Féin got the 'first pick' among the ministries (M1) because it has the highest total of seats.

Now look for the party with the next largest seat total. It is the DUP, with 16. Award it the next ministry (M2), and divide its share of seats by two, leaving it with 8. It gets the second 'pick'. Each time a party wins a seat, its total share is divided by the next appropriate integer in column 1.

Look for the next largest number: it is Sinn Féin with 14. Award it a ministry (M3) and divide its seat total by three, leaving it with 9.3 (recurring). Now, when we inspect the table the next largest number, 13, is held by the UUP. Award it a ministry (M4) and divide its seat total by two, leaving it with 6.5.

We now come to award the fifth ministry. There seems to be a problem. Alliance and the SDLP both have 12 seats. The makers of the Northern Ireland Act 1998 thought of that. The tie is broken in favour of the party with the higher number of first-preference votes. Let us imagine it is Alliance in this case, so it would get the fifth ministry (M5) while the SDLP takes the sixth (M6). Both parties then have their seat totals divided by two, to be left with 6. What is the next largest number which has not been allocated a ministry? It is Sinn Féin with 9.3 (recurring), so it gets the seventh ministry (M7). The DUP with its remaining seat total of 8 gets ministry number eight (M8), a numerical coincidence. Its seat total is divided by three leaving it with 5.3 (recurring). There are two remaining ministries to be allocated, but Sinn Féin and the TUV are tied with 7 seats each. Sinn Féin gets to pick before the TUV because it has a higher number of first-preference votes (after all, it won four times as many seats).

Look now at the last row: total ministries. Nationalists have won five ministries, Unionists have won four, and Alliance has one. The result is quite proportional across blocs as well as parties. Nationalists have 40 of the 90 seats, 4/9ths, and they have 5/10ths of the ministries. Unionists have 36 of the 90 seats, 4/10ths, and they have 4/10ths of the ministries. The 'others' have 14 of the 90 seats, 1.4/10ths, and they have 1/10 of the ministries. Ministries are not perfectly divisible. A party can't be awarded 1.3 ministries. The d'Hondt rule of division 'decides' allocations when a party's seat share does not authorize a neat whole number of ministries. Doubtless, questions will occur to readers about this example and about the d'Hondt rule. Some of these questions are answered in the Q&A section at the end of this chapter.

The virtues of the d'Hondt rule are that it fills an executive committee – or a cabinet, or a parliamentary committee – automatically and proportionally, according to a rule known in advance. It does so based on levels of support among voters for the respective parties. It eliminates bargaining over how many ministries a party should have, and which party gets to pick which ministry. The same goes for committee places.

The rule is also inclusive. Any party that gets sufficient support can win a ministry – even if all other parties dislike it. Without other rules, no party or bloc can be excluded from their rightful or proportional share. The more ministries there are, the easier it is to win one; the fewer there are, the more difficult it is. The rule is also 'difference blind'. In this example it is impartial across nationalists, unionists, and 'others'.

Unlike controversies over the rules for electing the two first ministers, the d'Hondt rule has not been in the dock to the same degree. When it is questioned it is typically because it is accused of creating a compulsory or mandatory coalition. That is not strictly true, however. It is obligatory to have two first ministers who must cooperate with one another, or the Executive Committee cannot function. That obligatory jointness is integral to the existing model of Northern power-sharing. But under the d'Hondt rule, parties are free to choose not to take up their places in the

Executive. They can go into opposition. Supporting legislation has been passed to facilitate parties which do so – the SDLP and the UUP recently experimented in this role. The price for doing so, however, is letting another party control the portfolio(s) the party might otherwise have had.

When parties do take their ministries, they do not have to agree with their colleagues under strict norms of 'collective cabinet responsibility', unless they all agree to do so. The parties' ministers must accept properly made executive decisions, and implement them, impartially, but they do not have to pretend that they like them. That is among the reasons the d'Hondt rule is appropriate for an historically divided place like Northern Ireland. It's clear, it's fair, it's efficient; it cuts out wasteful bargaining. It allows parties that are very different to share power without pretending that they are in love. The rule can't solve all problems of executive formation, but it has proved its worth.

Q&As on the d'Hondt rule

Q. Is this rule democratic?
A. Yes, parties win ministries in proportion to their strengths in seats won. Their seats won are in proportion to their votes won, provided that the electoral system is proportional.

Q. What would happen in the example in this chapter if, for example, the TUV refuses to pick the ministry to which it is entitled?
A: The tenth ministry would go to the UUP, which has 6.5 seats, the highest remaining total.

Q. Why all this simple division?
A. It achieves a proportional allocation *and* specifies the sequence in which parties win entitlements to ministries.

Q. Could the rule be applied starting with first-preference vote totals instead of seat totals?
A. Yes, but it is better to use seat shares, because these are allocated after votes have been transferred, and seats better represent parties' strengths in the Assembly.

Q. *Is there another rule that would be better for smaller parties?*

A. Yes. There are several. The best known is the Webster or Sainte-Lagüe rule, after the American and European respectively who independently invented it. While the d'Hondt or Jefferson rule uses 1, 2, 3 . . . n as its divisors – successive integers – by contrast, the Webster or Sainte-Lagüe rule uses successive odd numbers, 1, 3, 5, . . . $2n$-1. To see why this rule works better for small parties, consider what would happen if Sinn Féin had 28 seats. When divided by three its seat total is 9.3 recurring, so in the example in the table above, the DUP, the UUP, the SDLP and the Alliance Party would each win a ministry before Sinn Féin won its second ministry. The argument for preferring d'Hondt over Sainte-Lagüe (or Jefferson over Webster) is that it is good to reward parties that win more votes – to discourage parties from splitting, and to avoid having too many small parties.

Q. *Is there a truly fair resolution of multi-party cabinet formation?*

A. Steven Brams has compared the problem of ministerial allocation to cutting a cake fairly in his book *Fair Division*.[20] Being mathematically skilled, he has proposed several resolutions. He thinks d'Hondt may be unfair because a party that is just ahead of another party in the first allocation will always stay ahead of that party. So, if A has more seats than B, a likely allocation sequence will be ABABABAB, in which A always gets a pick ahead of B. He thinks it may be fairer if the allocation went ABBAABBA, resembling the Swedish pop group. He has a point, but it remains a democratic principle – certainly not the only one – that the party that wins more votes should do better in winning and choosing ministries than a party that wins fewer votes.

Q. *Is division by 1, 2, 3, etc.used in order to allocate each party their first, second, and third ministries, etc.?*

A. No, an understandable mistake. Division by 1, 2, 3, etc. is used to achieve proportional allocation; division by 1, 3, 5, etc. would achieve a different proportional allocation. There is not just one way to achieve proportionality.

20.   Realistic cold fusion of voting rules

Irish reunification should not involve one-way traffic. Northern Ireland in some respects has been reformed in ways that should be extended into a united Ireland. Southerners should be educated about these brighter sides of the new North, while Northerners need to register fully the positive transformations of the South, where dramatic progress has not been confined to the economy. Cold political fusion is possible, by which I mean that upgrading to the most improved arrangements or policies should be mutually beneficial without generating extensive political heat. No political explosions need accompany the fusion of electoral arrangements, and in this chapter I outline a number of ways in which the North is often better than the South.

Uniform districting with the single transferable vote system of proportional representation

In Northern Ireland, the extension of universal adult suffrage to local government, 'one person, one vote', and the elimination of egregious gerrymandering* were accomplished before the fall of Stormont Mark I in 1972.[1] Under British direct rule, proportional representation was restored for Northern Ireland elections, and impartial electoral administration was advanced: there is an Electoral Office of Northern Ireland, and a regional branch of the UK Electoral Commission. Registration and voting processes are modernized, and local NGOs and parties remain vigilant to ensure voters do not fall off the register through the shift to the digital age.

The electoral formula used in the North for Assembly elections and local government is the single transferable vote version of proportional

* See Chapter 1, p. 11.

representation (STV-PR), the same as in the South. Successful candidates are returned from multi-member districts. This is the system that the UUP abolished for elections to local government and the Stormont parliament in the 1920s. The Irish Free State kept it, however; it is a legacy of Arthur Griffith's promotion efforts to ensure significant Protestant representation in an autonomous Ireland.[2]

Governing parties and ministers in the South don't like the STV-PR system.[3] Voters do. They have twice rejected efforts to change the system in referendums called by Fianna Fáil governments.[4] Voters rank candidates on the ballot paper in numerical order, expressing as many preferences as they wish. There is a 'fixed post' in STV elections, which candidates must reach to be elected. It is the quota. Both parts of Ireland use the curiously named 'Droop quota' – defined as $[1/(D+1)] + 1$, where D is the number of deputies to be elected. So where five people are to be elected, the quota is one-sixth of the total valid votes plus one. There is an exception to the requirement of meeting the quota: the last-placed candidate(s) may be elected without reaching the quota, when other candidates have been eliminated and a seat (or more) needs to be filled.

In the North, the constituencies elect equal numbers of MLAs. The electorate used to elect six MLAs from each of its eighteen constituencies for Westminster elections ($6 \times 18 = 108$ MLAs), but now it elects five members from eighteen districts ($5 \times 18 = 90$ MLAs). If Northern Ireland's number of Westminster MPs is reduced to seventeen, as has been proposed, then the Assembly would be cut to eighty-five MLAs ($5 \times 17 = 85$).

Elections to the Westminster Parliament, by contrast, take place under a winner-takes-all system in single-member constituencies. This antique UK electoral system is often called 'first-past-the-post'. There is no fixed post, however. Alasdair McDonnell of the SDLP won Belfast South in 2015 with 25 per cent of the vote. In 2017, Emma Little-Pengelly won the same seat for the DUP with just over 30 per cent of the vote. In 2019, Claire Hanna won it back for the SDLP, decisively, with 57 per cent of the vote – aided by Sinn Féin giving her a free run, and by widespread hostility in Belfast South to the DUP's stance on Brexit. The winner's share in these three elections varied from a quarter to a high majority of the ballots cast, vividly demonstrating that there is no fixed post. The winner is the person with the most votes, whose support can range from the highest handful to over 99 per cent.

Drawing Westminster constituency boundaries by independent commissioners nevertheless remains controversial in the North. Belfast constituencies are especially likely to be disputed. In 2019, its four constituencies returned two Sinn Féin MPs, John Finucane and Paul Maskey, one SDLP MP, Claire Hanna, and one DUP MP, Gavin Robinson. The DUP had held three of these seats in 2017. With their standing in Belfast slipping, some unionists have lobbied for the number of Belfast MPs to be reduced to three, or to have Belfast North redrawn and extended along the heavily Protestant northern shore of Belfast Lough towards Carrickfergus – thereby recapturing Belfast North from Sinn Féin. The independent parliamentary commissioners will be watched like hawks to ensure fair districting, and they will want to avoid legal action. Expect the issue to become especially reheated if Northern Ireland's Westminster representation is reduced to seventeen MPs.

All 'electoral districting' is controversial, because the process creates opportunities for politicians to choose their voters rather than the other way around. Northern Ireland's STV districting, however, is currently fairer than that in the South because each constituency in the North elects the same number of candidates, whether for the Assembly or for local government. In the Republic, by contrast, constituency size varies for Dáil Éireann from three to five deputies, so the quota varies from 1/4th + 1 to 1/6th + 1. Currently, three deputies are elected in each of nine constituencies, four deputies in seventeen constituencies, and five deputies in thirteen constituencies:

$$(3 \times 9) + (4 \times 17) + (5 \times 13) = 27 + 68 + 65 = 160 \text{ TDs}$$

This situation is better than it used to be, because all constituencies now return between three and five deputies. But constituencies that vary in size give an advantage to the largest parties, especially in 'three-seaters'. The high quota in such constituencies – one-quarter of the first-preference vote plus one – benefits candidates from the bigger parties. Allowing different-sized quotas reduces proportionality across the country and damages the goal of making each citizen's vote of equal value.

Following reunification, the whole of Ireland should follow Northern practice. In elections to Dáil Éireann, uniform numbers of deputies should be elected in constituencies with populations of eligible voters as equal as possible. This policy would ensure more proportional outcomes.

What number of deputies per constituency would be best? Five is a sweet spot between favouring big and small parties – though six would be acceptable. More seats are better for small parties – the likely fate of parties founded by unionists or ex-unionists across the entirety of a united Ireland. A reunified Ireland could have fifty constituencies, each electing five deputies to a 250-seat Dáil Éireann, with the quota set at one-sixth (16.7 per cent) of the first preference vote plus one. This target provides reasonable opportunities for smaller parties to have their candidates elected, including religious, ethnic, or cultural minority parties, assuming these candidates attract some vote transfers from other parties.

The principle of uniform constituency size and the election of a uniform number of deputies would be transparently fair, ensuring reasonable proportionality across the entire island. All would face the same quota thresholds, including independents. It would, however, mean that it would no longer be possible always to follow existing county and other accepted geographic boundaries. On current and future numbers, this rule would ensure the election of at least one unionist deputy in every future Northern constituency – apart from Belfast West (assuming it remains drawn as it is now). A united 'pan-unionist' party would return between thirty and forty deputies to Dáil Éireann, giving unionists a realistic prospect of being pivotal in the formation of a centre-right coalition government, and with far more sustained influence in Dáil Éireann than unionist MPs have ever enjoyed at Westminster.

At least one further electoral change would be required to improve existing arrangements, and to bring the best of the existing North to the South – and make the South internally consistent. Currently, 'surpluses' in STV elections to Dáil Éireann are distributed by hand and represent the 'physical surplus'. Literally, the surplus consists of the last ballots received by a candidate after the ballot was counted that took her or him to the quota. These surplus ballots, however, cannot be assumed to be a representative sample of the remaining preferences of those who voted for the receiving candidate (the surplus ballots may, for accidental reasons, be different from all the other ballots cast that counted towards the quota). This procedure also means that a recount is unlikely to produce an identical result. There are some further joyous technical difficulties that I will not discuss, so let me say that a better method for managing surpluses is known either as 'Senatorial rules', after its use for most seats in Ireland's Senate elections, or as the 'Gregory method', after its inventor, the Australian mathematician J. B. Gregory. The Gregory method eliminates randomness. Instead of transferring a *fraction* of votes at *full* value, a transfer of *all* votes takes place at a *fractional* value. That is the system that should apply across the country in a reunified Ireland.[5]

Three ways of extending the d'Hondt rule in a united Ireland

The d'Hondt rule, outlined in the previous chapter, could be extended in three ways in a united Ireland. It could be used to elect the first ministers in the North, if Model 1 is followed, *and* in two ways for cabinet formation in a united Ireland, irrespective of which model is followed. Let me deal with each idea in turn.

Extending the d'Hondt rule to elect the two first ministers

It would be simple to extend the d'Hondt rule to electing the Northern premiers, though it would require cross-party consensus and an amendment of the St Andrews Agreement. The parties that win the first two ministries would fill the two first ministers' roles. This rule would be purely 'difference blind' (that is, any party could win the posts). 'Designation' would end, at least for this purpose. That, however, would create the possibility that a party that did extraordinarily well could take both posts. The vista of two nationalists or two unionists winning the two positions, particularly of one party doing so, makes it safe to predict that the existing designation rules are likely to be preferred by the risk-averse.

Using d'Hondt to fill every cabinet post

The d'Hondt rule could also be extended to apply to cabinet formation in the central government of a united Ireland, in either inclusive or minimal ways. Let us first consider the inclusive way: every party with sufficient support gets into the cabinet. In Table 20.1 the d'Hondt rule is used to allocate fifteen cabinet ministries in accordance with the maximum number allowed by the Constitution,[6] and in Table 20.2 twenty junior ministries are added, reflecting the current number. The numbers under the column with '1' at the top are each party's rounded number of first-preference votes in thousands.

	1	2	3	4	5	6	7	8	9	10	ALL
Sinn Féin	760 [1]	380 [4]	250.3 [5]	190 [9]	152 [12]	126.6 [14]	108.6	95	84.4	76	6
Fianna Fáil	485 [2]	242.5 [6]	161.7 [11]	121.3 [15]	97	80.8	69.2				4
Fine Gael	456 [3]	228 [7]	152 [13]	114	91.2	76					3
Democratic Unionists	226 [8]	113	75.3	56.5							1
Greens	175 [10]	87.5	58.3								1
Ulster Unionists	104	52									
SDLP	97	48.5									
Labour	96										
Alliance	73										
People Before Profit	72										
Social Democrats	64										
Aontú	41										
Traditional Unionist Voice	21										

Table 20.1: Hypothetical d'Hondt allocation of ministries in an Irish cabinet

Note: The numbers in square brackets [1]-[15] are cabinet ministries in sequential order of choice. The d'Hondt divisors at the top of the table are 1, 2, 3 . . .

	I1	I2	I3	I4	I5	I6	ALL
Sinn Féin	108.6 [18]	95 [23]	84.4 [26]	76 [28]	69.2 [33]	63.3	5
Fianna Fáil	97 [20]	80.8 [27]	69.2 [34]	60.6			3
Fine Gael	114 [16]	91.2 [24]	76 [29]	65.1 [35]			4
Democratic Unionists	113 [17]	75.3 [30]	56.5				2
Greens	87.5 [25]	58.3					1
Ulster Unionists	104 [19]	52					1
SDLP	97 [21]	48.5					1
Labour	96 [22]	48					1
Alliance	73 [31]	36.5					1
People Before Profit	72 [32]	36					1
Social Democrats	64						0
Aontú	41						0
Traditional Unionist Voice	21						0

Table 20.2: Allocation of twenty junior ministerial posts in an Irish cabinet

Notes: The numbers [16]-[35] are the rank-order in which junior ministerial posts are allocated. The columns and allocation start with the allocation in Table 20.1 completed.

To derive these numbers, I used each party's first-preference votes in the Northern Ireland Assembly elections of 2017 and the Dáil Éireann elections of 2020, adding together the votes of the all-island parties in the two jurisdictions (the Greens, People Before Profit, and Sinn Féin). Since the turnout was very similar in the two elections (64.8 and 62.9 per cent in the North and South respectively), this method provides a defensible guestimate of the votes these parties might win in a unified Ireland if elections were held soon – and if no parties merged or dissolved, and no voters changed their minds (admittedly highly unlikely assumptions).

Under these assumptions, the simulation in Table 20.1 suggests that if the d'Hondt rule was used to fill the fifteen-person cabinet it would consist of six Sinn Féin ministers, four Fianna Fáil ministers, three Fine Gael ministers, one DUP minister, and one Green. Similarly, among junior ministers, the allocation would be: five to Sinn Féin, four to Fine Gael, three to Fianna Fáil, two to the DUP, and one junior ministry each to the Greens, the Ulster Unionists, the SDLP, Labour, Alliance and People Before Profit.

This data also demonstrates the incentives for mergers. If the DUP, UUP, and TUV ran as one party and obtained the same number of votes, and all else remained the same, they would win at least two full cabinet ministries, as of right. Similarly, if Fianna Fáil and Fine Gael decided to merge, and kept their vote totals, they too might do better and would nominate the Taoiseach. Note also that the DUP, UUP, and SDLP ministers and junior ministers would be Northerners, and there would be a significant proportion of Northerners among the Sinn Féin ministers. So, without any fixed quotas, or other devices, allocating the cabinet and junior ministers through the d'Hondt rule would ensure significant Northern representation.

The simulation in Tables 20.1 and 20.2 uses exactly the same system as currently used in the North to compose the Executive.* It would face the standard criticism that there would be no opposition if all parties took up their entitlements. The Social Democrats, Aontú, and the TUV could provide opposition to the parties in the cabinet, and the parties with junior ministries. Admittedly a feeble opposition – on these numbers. *But* this is not the sole way the cabinet might be composed using the d'Hondt rule.

Using d'Hondt for coalitions of the willing

Currently, the norms in the Republic are that the party with the highest number of seats in Dáil Éireann, or the coalition with the highest number of pledged deputies, has the first opportunity to lead coalition formation, and to propose a Taoiseach and cabinet that command the

* See Table 19.1, p. 202.

support of the popular chamber. Typically, parties that have done well seek to form connected coalitions that agree on policy – a 'policy coalition' – or to form a government with the minimum number of parties needed to security a majority – a 'minimum winning coalition'. To succeed, the relevant party leader, or his or her nominee, needs a majority of deputies in Dáil Éireann to back the party's nominee for Taoiseach, and usually a programme of government. As happened after the 2020 election in the Republic, the parties within a prospective coalition might agree to rotate the premiership if both did equally well in the battle for seats.

If these existing norms were extended in a united Ireland, what would happen? Let us imagine that after reunification the total size of Dáil Éireann would be 250 deputies, of which 68 would come from the North, and 182 from the South, according to current proportions.[7] Imagine the seats won by parties are as displayed in Table 20.3. These numbers are my rough guess of what might follow from the first-preference vote totals in Table 20.1, *provided* that no parties merge or disappear, and provided that no parties organize island-wide that had not done so before. No claim is made to precision, and I have made no effort to simulate the consequences of vote transfers. No independents are elected in this scenario. Table 20.3 arranges the parties on a broadly left-right spectrum, showing one possible distribution of seats won.

Left Bloc (93)				Centre Bloc (77)				Right Bloc (80)				
PBP	SF	SD	Lab	GP	APNI	FF	SDLP	FG	UUP	DUP	Aontú	TUV
7	71	6	9	16	7	45	9	43	10	21	4	2

Table 20.3: Possible party configurations in the parliament of a united Ireland on a left-right spectrum, using recent vote totals

The left bloc would have 93 deputies, counting People before Profit, Sinn Féin, the Social Democrats, and Labour as its members. The centre bloc would have 77 deputies, counting the Greens, Alliance, Fianna Fáil, and the SDLP. The right bloc would have 80 deputies. This left-right spectrum simplifies, and the designations are arguable, but simplifications are sometimes helpful. The exact correct placement of parties, or predicting their precise number of seats, is less important than the core point I am about to make.

That point would stand even if we classified the parties differently. Namely, without dramatic change, a united Ireland is unlikely to be dominated by any one party – especially but not only because of our electoral system – or by any one bloc. In this simulation, Sinn Féin would be the largest party, but it could not govern on its own. A secure coalition majority would require 126 deputies (50 per cent of deputies plus one). A left and centre coalition could accomplish a majority with 93 + 77 deputies, and some of the smaller parties could be dropped and the coalition would still have a working majority. A centre and right alliance would have a majority of 157 (77 + 80 deputies) or of 151 (if Aontú and the TUV refused to join it). If the two bigger unionist parties aligned with Fine Gael and Fianna Fáil in an anti-Sinn Féin coalition, then they would need support from among the SDLP, Alliance, or the Greens to have a majority.

None of us knows what would happen in this type of scenario under the existing rules and conventions of the Republic. But any possible coalition that could command the support of 126 deputies would have a serious headache in agreeing the allocation of cabinet portfolios and junior ministries. The d'Hondt rule would provide a workable solution for any feasible coalition, enabling it to allocate the ministerial portfolios rapidly.

Note with emphasis that, in the type of adoption being considered here, the d'Hondt rule would only apply to the parties in the coalition – and to the placement of parties in committees of the Oireachtas. As a bonus, it would prevent small parties (or independents) over-bargaining. The d'Hondt rule could be adopted simply as a convention, but that would mean it would not survive the first hard bargaining. Alternatively, it could be legislated as a rule of coalition formation – to speed the process of government formation in which the larger parties, and the country, would have a profound interest.

What would happen to Northern representation in an all-island cabinet if the d'Hondt rule is *not* used inclusively, i.e. in scenarios where not all parties obtain a proportionate share of cabinet seats and junior ministries, just the parties which are going into the coalition government? In the example just discussed, a centre-right coalition would likely include Northern unionists *and* the SDLP and Alliance. A centre-left coalition, by contrast, could include Alliance, the Greens, the SDLP, and Northern deputies from Sinn Féin, and would therefore have support from some left-wing or liberal Protestants (especially within Alliance and the Greens). So, coalition formation, without any radical modification of existing practice in the South, would likely ensure Northern representation in the cabinet, from both cultural Catholic and cultural Protestant backgrounds, especially if the d'Hondt rule were used within the coalition that forms a government.

There is a negative possibility, however. What if the DUP, the UUP, and the TUV, or their successors, were regarded as taboo partners for any coalition formed by one of the biggest three parties, Sinn Féin, Fianna Fáil, and Fine Gael? Existing norms and conventions could not stop that. True, a grand coalition, or a government of national unity of SF-FF-FG when reunification occurs, is unlikely without an attempt to include the largest of the parties rooted in the historic Ulster unionist community (or their voters). Some may choose to be unconcerned and leave the democratic chips to fall where they may. But if a significant and persistent possibility exists that all unionist parties – and their successors – could be treated as unacceptable partners, then consideration should be given to a territorial quota, at least for a transitional period. For example, it could be legislated that five of the fifteen cabinet ministries, and five of the junior ministerial posts, would have to be allocated among those elected in the six north-eastern counties for twenty years. Of these five ministers, at least two would have to be self-identifying Protestants (a religious and ethnic quota) *or* at least two who identify as British, or as British and Irish (a national and ethnic quota). Such a quota would ensure the proportional inclusion of the North in the first coalition governments after unification.

The immediate point is not whether these institutional possibilities appeal to my readers. The message is that the Republic will have to decide, preferably in advance, which – if any – of its institutions it wishes to keep, and whether to extend any of the newer Northern practices to the whole island, e.g. using the d'Hondt rule for cabinet formation, either fully or just for the parties in a voluntary coalition.

The latter would probably be more palatable, as it is a rule that can be adopted for any coalition that people might like. But an answer will be needed to the British, Protestant, and unionist question in preparation for a referendum: 'Will we be excluded from every Irish cabinet unless we join all-Ireland parties?'

PART SIX

The Economics of Reunification

21. Ireland is ready for economic reunification – and will be readier

Nowhere have the grounds for comparison, North and South, shifted more than in perceptions of the economics of reunification. Unionists used to emphasize, with justification, that Northern Ireland was visibly better off than independent Ireland – in its GDP and income per head, its rate and quality of employment, and in its publicly funded infrastructure, including its health service, roads, and welfare provisions. The argument went that Northern Catholics should be grateful: they were much better off than their Southern counterparts – though such assertions ignored the fact that the Ulster unionist elite generally opposed the post-1945 UK Labour government's benign transformations. The mildly amusing but much weaker nationalist response was that unionists were more loyal to the half-crown than the Crown.

When the dynamism of the Southern economy, especially between 1987 and 2007, became too impressive to ignore, unionist discourse began to shift. No longer was the emphasis placed on the outdated fact that the South could not afford the costs of reunifying with the North while maintaining the North's standards of living. Instead, the new claim became that they would not want to do so. 'We'd cost you too much' became the new unionist line, aimed at tax-conscious Southerners.

These presumed costs were usually 'measured' by Great Britain's 'subvention' of Northern Ireland – an estimate of the difference between what is raised in taxation in Northern Ireland and what is spent there in public expenditure, a subject to which we shall return. There was an intermission in this shifting discourse when *Schadenfreude* erupted among some unionists during the taming of the Celtic Tiger (2008–12), which some may have hoped would be a permanent laming. In that moment, unionists briefly returned to their historic presumption of the superior economic performance of the Union with Great Britain. Yet when the

Republic staged a remarkably resilient recovery, visible by 2014, in the years before the global coronavirus pandemic, the mantra returned that the South would resist reunification because it would be too costly. Unionist pride in their past private-sector prosperity has gone, and the new reflex response has become one of Southern dogs in their mangers.

Who is better off? And who is worse off?

Mature economic analysis of the status quo, and about reunification, should be based on credible evidence. The Dublin economist, broadcaster, and *Irish Times* journalist David McWilliams set the scene in late 2017:

> The Republic's economy is four times larger [than Northern Ireland's], generated by a work force that is only two and a half times bigger. The Republic's industrial output is today 10 times that of the North. Exports from the Republic are 17 times greater than those from Northern Ireland, and average income per head in the Republic, at €39,873, dwarfs the €23,700 across the border. Immigration is a traditional indicator of economic vitality. In the Republic one in six people are immigrants, the corresponding figure for the North is one in a hundred. Dublin is three times bigger than Belfast, far more cosmopolitan and home to hundreds of international companies.[1]

McWilliams's data are robust, and his big-picture contrast is matched by in-depth comparisons of Southern and Northern standards of living by the economists Adele Bergin and Seamus McGuinness of the Economic and Social Research Institute. Bergin and McGuinness surveyed recent independent international data on both parts of Ireland to address the seemingly simple question 'Who is better off?' Their answer is that, in four recent measurements of income, the average person or household in the Republic is significantly better off (see Figure 21.1(a) in the colour plate section). Two separate measures in 2018 of GDP per head, and another measure of 2018 GNI per head, display the Republic's clear lead in conventional international indicators.* However, Bergin and McGuinness prefer a measure of 'disposable household income' – that is, available income after taxes and social transfers are accounted for. They argue persuasively that household disposable income is a reliable comparative measure of relative standards of living. On this measure, the average household in the Republic currently is US$4,600 better off per year than its Northern counterpart.

Figure 21.1(b) in the plate section shows three measures of consumption in which the differences between the two jurisdictions are much less – the Republic is slightly ahead in one, Northern Ireland slightly ahead in the other two. These consumption indicators aim to measure what goods and services – including public services – are enjoyed by individuals and households, but they omit household or individual savings as a measure of comparative income.

These comparisons are useful, but Bergin and McGuinness argue in favour of additional and important comparisons of economic performance and well-being. In both jurisdictions, taxes and transfers reduce inequality, but the Republic is far more effective at reducing relative poverty through taxes and transfers. The tax and welfare system in the Republic 'is much more progressive, and effective in mitigating household poverty risk'.[2] That strongly suggests, all other things being equal, that it is better to be poor in the Republic than in the North – a fact, if better known, which may well affect Northern voting in a future referendum.

Bergin and McGuinness's most startling comparison, however, is in educational enrolment. Education (and subsequent skills-acquisition) reliably predicts future income and opportunity in advanced economies. In 2018, in *all* age ranges, from 3 to 64, the Republic had comparatively more people enrolled in education than there were enrolled in the North. The ratio was nearly two to one among people in their twenties.[3] In the cohort below, those aged 15–19, the Republic had nearly 93 per cent enrolled in education, whereas the North had nearly 74 per cent.[4] In short, over the next decade the Republic's younger cohorts have a baked-in advantage over their Northern counterparts.

---

* For GDP and GNI, see Chapter 4, pp. 58–9, and endnote 12 on p. 337.

Bergin and McGuinness also report that the Northern educational system is 'relatively less effective as a vehicle for social inclusion among students from working class backgrounds and males'.[5] This finding emphasizes that it is vital to improve the width and depth of educational attainment in the North in the decade ahead – especially among Protestant working-class males. And it may also suggest that the Republic's system of education is better suited to the current demands of international and European economies. Educational arrangements should therefore converge on the Republic's system if an integrated Ireland, Model 2, becomes the preferred model of reunification – and perhaps also if Model 1 is chosen.

Bergin and McGuinness also examined other measures of well-being – including health services, housing costs, broadband access, the environment, life satisfaction, quality of jobs, and 'quality of government', the latter measured by perceptions of corruption. The general story here is one of small differences – including in the data they then had on housing costs. Perhaps surprisingly, measures of access to health services suggest no significant Northern advantage. In 2017, the Republic had considerably more physicians per thousand of population, and the Northern advantage in hospital beds was marginal. Northern Ireland had lower unemployment, reflecting a more stable public-sector weighting in its economy. A major turning point, however, is reported by the authors. Since 2005, life expectancy in the Republic has decisively risen over that in the North – including, recently, for those aged 65+.

In his response to Bergin and McGuinness's article, the economic historian John FitzGerald suggested that the quality of health services in the North is superior to that in the South, while agreeing that comparative superiority is reversed in education. FitzGerald argues that cheaper Northern housing should be more fully factored into estimates of household disposable income. He also observes that the Republic will face tougher adjustments in meeting targets for reduced greenhouse-gas emissions, which will lower economic growth in both locations.[6] In their reply to FitzGerald, Bergin and McGuinness stand by their measure of comparative household disposable income. They firmly disagree that health access is superior in the North. The NHS may in principle seem better, but in practice matters are different. Northern Ireland's waiting times are the worst in the UK, and far worse than those in Wales, one rung further up in the UK's hierarchy of health-service performance.[7] The Republic's superior life-expectancy also suggests that the NHS does not repair the North's inadequate economic and educational performance.

Unfortunately, the coronavirus pandemic has provided something of a natural experiment to compare the performance of public health systems across the two jurisdictions in Ireland. The authoritative Johns Hopkins database on the pandemic hosts the official data provided by the UK and the Irish authorities. On 17 February 2022, the cumulative human death toll from the virus in Northern Ireland was 3,169. By comparison, on 18 February 2022 the cumulative human death toll from the virus in the Republic was 6,417.[8] The North's population is roughly 38 per cent of that of the South. So, the North should have expected 2,438 fatalities if it had experienced the same proportion of fatalities as the South. In fact, the Northern death toll was 731 persons (30 per cent) higher, when rounded, than the Southern death toll.

This is a raw comparison. Many other factors may explain these different outcomes – different demographic structures, lockdown policies, public behaviour on vaccinations and mask-wearing in response to governmental advice, levels of public trust in the authorities, levels of consistency in public messaging, different reporting systems, and so on. Nevertheless, in the greatest public health crisis of our lifetimes, the North significantly underperformed when compared with the South. It is, of course, possible to argue that the North would have done worse if it had the Southern system, or that the South would have done better if it had had the NHS, but such counterfactual claims are tougher to assess.

The significance of current and future Irish green growth

Since we are a decade or so from possible reunification referendums, and the world is yet to emerge fully from the pandemic, the importance of the foregoing comparisons must be tempered. Nevertheless, the future pace of growth in the Republic will be decisive in shaping the costs of reunification. 'Green growth' reflects both the historic national colour of Ireland and that of environmentalism. The Republic is now committed to shift from carbon-intensive energy production and use. We must therefore allow for the possibility that the transition to green and softer energy paths will slow the Republic's growth capacity. We must also allow for the possibility that the Russian invasion and attempted conquest of Ukraine, and the western sanctions that have followed, may either slow or accelerate the shift – and its costs.

In the decade ahead, judging by recent performance, Ireland's growth model seems set to outperform Great Britain's – as measured by both GDP and GNI per head. All growth, even if reduced, will increase the Republic's taxation revenues, and its ability to pay down its debts and fund education and other vital public contributors to well-being – including surpassing the North's current health-service standards over the next decade. Simply put, the richer the Republic becomes, the easier it will be to bear the costs of reunification, including the regular setting aside of revenues into the sovereign transition fund recommended elsewhere in this book.*

The unresolved conflict over the Protocol matters. If the Protocol works, then the North, with double-export access opportunities, may perform better than Great Britain – or at least better than it would have without the Protocol. With the Protocol functioning, and the maintenance of an all-island economy in goods, agri-food, and electricity, the North will be better able to track the pace of growth in the Republic. If the Protocol fails, however, and a trade war eventually develops between the UK and the EU, then Great Britain and Northern Ireland will suffer significantly more than the EU – Northern Ireland especially, but damage will also be sustained by the Republic. But even in that bleak scenario, the Republic will not lose its comparative economic advantages over Northern Ireland and Great Britain. It would, however, make reunification more expensive. It is more difficult to

---

* See Chapter 9, p. 115.

assess how Northern voters would react to the breakdown of the Protocol, and its repercussions.

Recent performance suggests good reasons to be optimistic about Ireland's comparative future growth – even if all economies are adversely affected by the war over Ukraine in the next decade. Figure 21.2 shows Ireland's growth trajectory in Gross National Income per head since 2000, compared with the UK and the EU (as a whole). GNI is used rather than GDP to strip out some the consequences of the pricing policies of multinationals in Ireland. Since 2012, Ireland has pulled strongly away from the UK and the EU as a whole. The same data suggest that the EU, despite having weak member-state performers within its ranks, was catching up to the UK before the pandemic and Brexit. If Ireland's performance in the next decade is even close to being as comparatively effective as it has been in the last decade, it will be in robust shape for reunification.

It may be too easy to be impressed with Ireland's recent GDP and

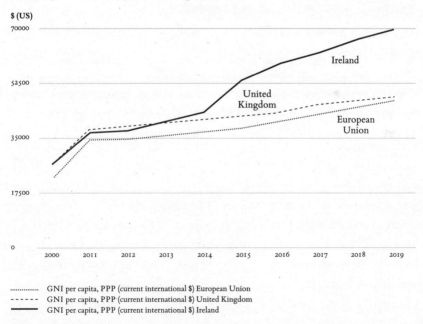

.... GNI per capita, PPP (current international $) European Union
- - - - - - GNI per capita, PPP (current international $) United Kingdom
—————— GNI per capita, PPP (current international $) Ireland

Figure 21.2: Gross National Income performances per head – the EU, Ireland, and the UK, 2000–2019

Source: World Bank database – world development indicators, last updated 28/10/2021

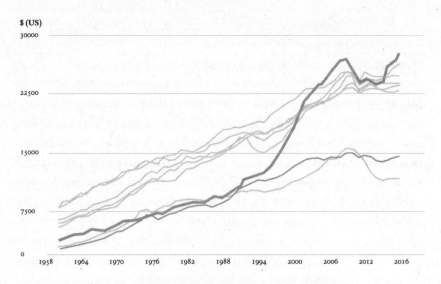

Rank order in 2016: Ireland, Sweden, Netherlands, Denmark, Austria, Belgium, Finland, Portugal, Greece

Figure 21.3: GDP per head performance of Ireland compared with other small western EU democracies that became members, 1958–2016

Note: Ireland's performance is in bold.

Source: Maddison Project Database, version 2018. Jutta Bolt, Robert Inklaar, Herman de Jong and Jan Luiten van Zanden (2018), 'Rebasing "Maddison": new income comparisons and the shape of long-run economic development', https://www.rug.nl/ggdc/historicaldevelopment/ maddison/research (Maddison Project, working paper 10)

GNI per head performances compared to the UK and the EU's five big member-states. Figure 21.3 therefore displays the GDP perform- ance of all the small western EU democracies with populations of over one million – using data from the reputable Maddison Project, covering six decades. The data run from 1958 until 2016, indexed to the 1990 US dollar. The starting year marks Ken Whitaker's plans to open up the Irish economy under Seán Lemass[9] – coincidentally, the year of my birth. The end point is one hundred years after the Easter Rising. By 2016, the Republic had become the group leader of the most dynamic small European trading economies, known as the 'new Hanseatics'.[10] Even during the worst of the austerity, during 2009– 12, Ireland remained among the leading performers of the small democracies, including the Scandinavian countries. The crash did not return Ireland to its pre-Celtic Tiger status. Instead, it fell, temporarily, onto much higher ground.[11] Differently put, Ireland is in a far better place economically than at any point in its history, comparatively and absolutely.[12]

Examine Ireland's bold growth-line in Figure 21.3. Ireland's success cannot simply be attributed to the Whitaker reforms, which may have staved off a further relative decline. The Republic's growth rate from 1958 until 1987 was as miserable as before. Debate over the causation of the lift-off in the late 1980s will likely continue. Focusing on the internal side, some credit the payoff from long-term domestic policies, such as the restructuring and widening of access to education, and low corporate taxation on foreign investment, especially from the United States. Others credit the diffusion of social and economic liberalism – liberating Ireland's people, including its entrepreneurs, from traditionalist conformism. Externally, some focus on membership of the European single market and its payoff in social and regional infrastructure funds, which kick-started a virtuous circle, followed by Ireland's commitment to the Maastricht Treaty that established the European Union and monetary union. An English-speaking democracy with magnificent landscapes, rivers, coasts, salmon fishing, and golf courses is very attractive to multinational executives seeking a secure gateway to the European Union.

Others, more prosaically, emphasize that the Republic simply had a lot of 'catching up to do' after a painful partition and tough start to independence. Catching up included urbanization and the slow reduction in the significance of (low-productivity) small farming, with the EU's Common Agricultural Policy aiding the reduction of the number of farms and of farming in shaping public policy – and the reduction of taxation on the non-agricultural sector.

Cynics suspect all the data, and are tempted to attribute Ireland's 'growth' to accounting manipulations by multinationals in a tax haven. This last perspective, however, does not withstand scrutiny. Seeing is believing. Anyone who journeyed around the entirety of the Republic in 1987 and did the same in 2021 – and that includes me – sees the palpable evidence. The proofs are the physical numbers of people in the island, not just new immigrants; the quality of roads, cars, houses, clothes, schools and universities, shops, and restaurants; and the agglomeration of enterprises – inside and outside the M50.

No single-factor explanation of the sustained Irish growth spurt has so far proven persuasive. Each cause has its partisans. Each plausible cause should be nurtured, to avoid going off the benign path. Ireland now has 'good' problems, a rich country's problems – notably in housing and healthcare.

Avoiding bad government or promoting good government?

In 1992 and 2008, two heads of government of the Republic were driven from office for 'conduct unbecoming' after numerous and embarrassing inquiries into their personal finances, if not precisely because of these inquiries. Charlie Haughey and Bertie Ahern were both leaders of Fianna Fáil. Their irregular personal finances had no obvious negative effect on Ireland's growth rate – though they hardly enhanced the nation's reputation. The two men never won elections that delivered single-party majority governments, however, and that may have helped – Haughey lost the majority he inherited from Jack Lynch.

Having coalition partners makes it slightly more difficult for questionable leaders to stay in office. Since 1981, the Republic has had *only* minority or coalition governments, including minority coalition governments (see Table 21.1). Coalition governments have normally had majority support in Dáil Éireann, whereas minority governments have had to placate other parties or independents. So Irish Governments have been obliged to operate with consensus, which benefits stable economic policymaking. Coalition or minority governments will be even more likely after reunification. They may help to avoid bad government.

Irish political culture is widely criticized, in Ireland, for the vices of clientelism, corporatism, and corruption. Any negative consequences

	TAOISEACH	STATUS OF GOVERNMENT	LEADING PARTY	SECOND PARTY IN COALITION	THIRD PARTY IN COALITION
1981–82	Garret FitzGerald	Minority Coalition	Fine Gael	Labour	
1982	Charles Haughey	Minority	Fianna Fáil		
1982–1987	Garret FitzGerald	Coalition	Fine Gael	Labour	
1987–1989	Charles Haughey	Minority	Fianna Fáil		
1989–1992	Charles Haughey Albert Reynolds	Minority Coalition	Fianna Fáil	Progressive Democrats	
1993–1994	Albert Reynolds	Coalition	Fianna Fáil	Labour	
1994–1997	John Bruton	Coalition	Fine Gael	Labour	Democratic Left
1997–2002	Bertie Ahern	Minority Coalition	Fianna Fáil	Progressive Democrats	
2002–2007	Bertie Ahern	Coalition	Fianna Fáil	Progressive Democrats	Greens
2007–2011	Bertie Ahern Brian Cowen	Coalition	Fianna Fáil	Progressive Democrats	Greens
2011–2016	Enda Kenny	Coalition	Fine Gael	Labour	
2016–2020	Enda Kenny Leo Varadkar	Minority	Fine Gael	Non-party independents	
2020–	Micheál Martin	Coalition	Fianna Fáil	Fine Gael	Greens

Table 21.1: Coalition or minority governments in the Republic since 1981

of these traits would likely be worse under a single-party majority government. Current and future political configurations make that unlikely. Indeed, a further argument in favour of using d'Hondt only for 'coalitions of the willing'* would be that alternation in government is helpful in diminishing opportunities for corruption that tend to arise from long tenure in office by the same ministers of the same parties.

In fact, modern Ireland has recently been hailed by a prominent English political scientist as a democratic 'role-model'.[13] What damaged

---

* See Chapter 20, pp. 211–17.

Ireland in the great crash of 2007–08 was the deeply inadequate regulation of its banking and construction sectors, and the previous closeness of both to successive Governments, especially to Fianna Fáil–led Governments – developers were major funders of the party. Ireland was in international bad company, but the poverty of its regulatory systems exceeded many others.[14] Ireland's bankers were especially outrageous in a global profession that specialized in overextended and risky loans. Inept manoeuvres by the late Minister for Finance Brian Lenihan, and inappropriate conduct by the President of the European Central Bank, Jean-Claude Trichet, jointly left the Irish taxpayer liable for the conduct of Ireland's banks and financial institutions.[15] Ireland's gross government debt doubled, and Irish citizens and residents experienced painful economic administration under the supervision of 'the troika': the European Central Bank, the European Commission, and the International Monetary Fund (see Figure 21.4). Note, however, the remarkable recovery visible from 2014 in Figure 21.3, and the turnaround in public debt in Figure 21.4.

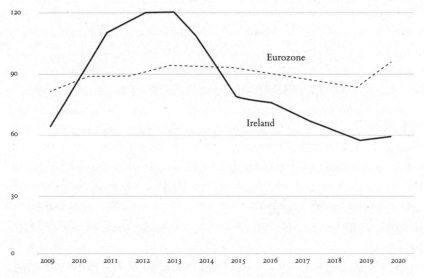

Figure 21.4: Gross Debt to GDP of the Eurozone and Ireland 2009–20 expressed as a percentage

Source of data: Eurostat, 16 November 2021, https://ec.europa.eu/eurostat/databrowser/view/ teina225/default/table?lang=en

Is Ireland really ready?

The fair question for reunification is whether Ireland is vulnerable to a recurrence of this scale of economic catastrophe. Measures have been taken to reduce the risks of wild-west banking and intemperate construction, as the current pain in the housing sector partly demonstrates, though that has complex causation. Eurozone monetary policy is determined and supervised by the European Central Bank, to which Ireland has adjusted, but the Central Bank of Ireland now has an enhanced role to play as a regulator in what is officially called 'macro-prudential regulation': checking that credit expansion is controlled; ensuring that mortgage, business, and personal loans do not get out of control in ways that might damage the overall economy, and that financial organizations are scrutinized, and sanctioned when they misbehave. Free-market ideology has been tempered. Aside from zealots, all now know that both public- and private-sector debt levels require surveillance. New regulations are in place so that banks and 'quasi-banks' that get overextended are quickly dissolved and restructured, with their bondholders having skin in the game – not taxpayers. Banking union at European Union/Eurozone level is yet to be completed, but it would be both astonishing and unfortunate were that not done by 2030. With a full banking union at European level, there would be an operational common resolution system for the orderly dissolution and sell-off of the assets of insolvent banks which pose 'systemic risk' – sparing future taxpayers some of the costs of banking excesses.

Perhaps enough politicians and civil servants have learned these lessons. As a small state with an open trading economy, Ireland does not have the same scope to pursue 'Keynesian' counter-cyclical policies as do bigger member-states. Bigger member-states can usually 'deficit-finance' during recessions and constrain public expenditure during growth phases, but that's more difficult for smaller states. Ireland is too small to manage its own demand entirely through domestic policies. It must expect international turbulence. It must therefore constantly build and replenish a buffer stock of revenues and maintain a strong reputation in the international capital markets. Its public debt policy, legally and politically, has steered and should steer towards Germany's, preferably targeting whatever prescribed rate in relation to GDP that will follow a likely revision to the EU's Maastricht criterion of 60 per cent of GDP, except in genuine crises, such as the pandemic and the Russian invasion of Ukraine, during which this book was finalized.[16] But Ireland must learn the lesson of the Celtic Tiger that private-sector debt can destabilize the economy, whence the need for vigorous macro-prudential regulation.

Ireland is now formally locked in by treaty arrangements, supervised by the European Commission, to inhibit debt expansion and reckless tax cuts. These arrangements were relaxed during the pandemic, and were accompanied by the pooling of EU member-states' borrowing capacity to expand governments' spending capacities amid such crises. The management of the Eurozone will likely continue to land some-where between German and French preferences: the Germans focused on fiscal responsibility and debt reduction; the French wanting to use governmental powers to steer the Euro-economy. No definitive reso-lution of that tension can be expected anytime soon. The Germans may have set the initial rules, but other Europeans will decide how the rules are to be amended and operationalized. The international economic task of Ireland's political governors will be to maintain the country's sovereign standing in the bond market, and hence to steer it towards a status as close to Germany's as possible. Done well, that will facilitate a well-organized reunification.

Unlike monetary policy, fiscal or taxation policy is for Ireland to decide, though subject to domestic and international constraints. If it taxes its citizens too highly, they can emigrate, especially if they are young and skilled – the downside of having linguistic and geographic access to the labour markets of the EU, the UK, the US, and elsewhere. Fear of migration outflows should constrain personal over-taxation. Likewise, if Ireland taxes enterprises too highly then they may disengage and relocate within the EU, or to elsewhere. The Irish state must not cause the geese that lay the golden eggs to fly, but it is not impotent: it need not be the servant of international capital. It can sustain a social contract – better public services in return for comparatively high taxes – but the better services must be credible, and supportive of families, not just the family members in work. Ireland's workers know that the country is vulnerable to international turbulence and are willing to be flexible provided they can trust in governments that deliver on core pledges, maintain high-class educational opportunities, establish and maintain universal healthcare, and oversee pension policies suitable to a world of changing jobs and skill sets. With corporations, the state has a different contract: in return for stable taxation rates, it offers excellent infrastructure and highly skilled graduates. It also must credibly keep itself clean. From this bargain may flow more Irish start-ups, and a ramped-up scale of indigenous enterprise that may partly free Ireland from external dependence.

In 2021 Ireland withstood US and EU pressure to increase its corporate tax rate. In doing so, Ireland sought to protect its existing foreign investors. Later it achieved and supported an international bargain made among OECD members that may be sustainable, and may come into effect in 2023, though it has yet to navigate the US Congress. For enterprises of a certain size, Ireland will have a 15 per cent corporate taxation rate, the new global minimum. For those below that threshold (which will doubtless change), the previous 12.5 per cent rate will apply. Ireland will thereby maintain one of the most attractive rates in the western EU. Either rate, 15 per cent or 12.5 per cent, would make investing in the North after reunification a competitive proposition, given that the current UK rate is higher.[17] Tax revenues from large digital enterprises located in Ireland may also rise. US Treasury Secretary Janet Yellen has kindly declared that Ireland is not a tax haven,[18] so Ireland's special relationships with US digital businesses will continue. Because Ireland's overall tax base is heavily reliant on corporation tax, overall tax revenues are volatile, however. Therefore, Irish Governments, led from the left, right, or centre, must organize, perhaps through legislation, to sustain income and consumption taxes, pay down debt during periods of growth beyond a certain minimum rate, or invest revenues from 'boom times' in sovereign wealth funds – for reunification, public-sector pension funds, or crisis management.

In this chapter I have presumed what I would call the commonplaces of social democratic economics. Free-market libertarians and communist command planners will disagree with my premises, but so be it.

Fortunately, Ireland is headed in this social democratic direction under democratic pressure and responsiveness. No major political party advocates either a nightwatchman state – where the role of central government is restricted to preserving order – or the socialization of all the means of production, and this is a testament to the realism of the public as well as the parties.

22. The benefits and the costs of reunification

A telling indicator of the lack of preparation for reunification is that the Government of Ireland has not regularly commissioned economists, Irish or international, to simulate the possible economic consequences of reunification. That will soon change, however. Dr Alan Barrett and his colleagues at the Economic and Social Research Institute in Dublin plan to organize the data collection required, both North and South, to provide sustained and credible econometric modelling that will be permanently useful, for both the economics of Irish reunification and economic cooperation between the two jurisdictions.

We are not completely in the dark. A pioneering contribution has been issued, worth building upon: 'the first state-of-the-art, data-intensive, recursive dynamic model . . . applied to [reunification]'.[1] In *Modeling Irish Reunification*, Dr Kurt Hübner, Dr Renger Van Nieuwkoop, and KLC Consulting argue that Irish reunification 'would likely result in a sizable boost in economic output and incomes in the North' and a smaller boost in the Republic.[2] They used similar techniques to examine the economic effects of German reunification and possible Korean reunification. Hübner and his colleagues had exploited indirect methods to estimate some of the Northern Ireland data for their simulations, because some data for Northern Ireland are not collected locally.[3]

Dr Hübner and his colleagues first presented their analysis at the Harvard Club in New York at the end of 2015. Invited to attend that event, I conversed and later corresponded with the authors. They modelled three unification scenarios, which I represent graphically in Figures 22.1 (a), (b) and (c) on the following pages so that readers can compare them without worrying about the technicalities. The three scenarios report the annual consequences of reunification over a seven-year period for the former Northern Ireland, the former Republic of Ireland, and a united Ireland, assuming that reunification began on 1 January 2018.

(Yes, we all know that did not happen, and the authors did not predict that it would happen. It was an exercise.) In each graph, the vertical axis lables the simulated effects on GDP per head per year, while the horizontal axis marks the years from 2018 to 2025. It is increased GDP per head that is shown on the vertical axis, not the absolute size of GDP. All the graphs show a boost, followed by a fading of the boost. The authors assumed that the form of a united Ireland would be an integrated Ireland – my Model 2 – and that there would be savings from ending two parallel governments, estimated at 2 per cent of current Northern Ireland public expenditures.

In the first scenario, the lower-bound estimate displayed in Figure 22.1(a), what was the Republic would finance the entirety of Northern Ireland's current budget; reunification would reduce Northern public expenditure by 2 per cent; and joining the Republic's tax regime would have no overall impact on foreign direct investment or productivity in what had been Northern Ireland. Nevertheless, what was Northern Ireland would have an immediate boost in its GDP per head, which would

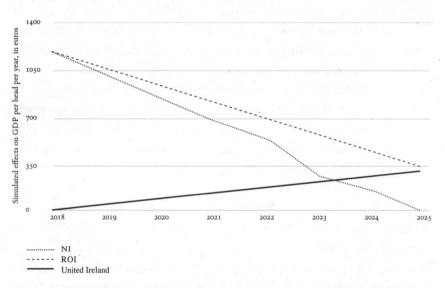

Figure 22.1(a): Scenario 1 – Economic effects of reunification on GDP per head

*Note: Hübner's and Van Nieuwkoop's **conservative simulation of reunification**. Drawn from data in Hübner et al. 2015.*

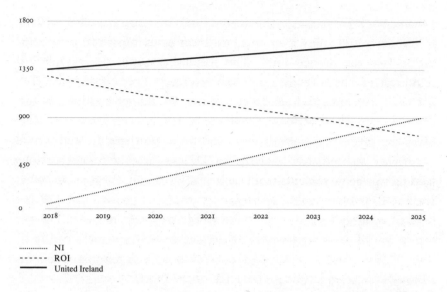

Figure 22.1(b): Scenario 2 – Economic effects of reunification on GDP per head

*Note: Hübner's and Van Nieuwkoop's **middle simulation of reunification**. Drawn from data in Hübner et al. 2015.*

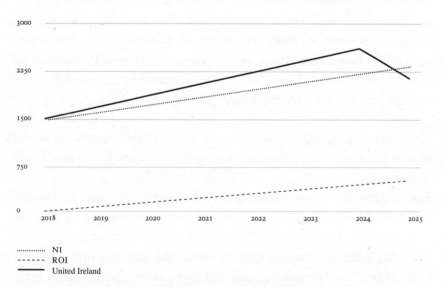

Figure 22.1(c): Scenario 3 – Economic effects of reunification on GDP per head

*Note: Hübner's and Van Nieuwkoop's **most benign simulation of reunification**. Drawn from data in Hübner et al. 2015.*

exhaust itself by 2025 (see the dotted line). By contrast, what was the Republic would enjoy a modest but linear growth path from reunification (see the dashed line). The Republic would be 'paying' for reunification but nevertheless enjoying a modest net boost in its GDP per head. Ireland as whole, the thick bar, would get a growth boost, driven by improved performance in the North, but this too would fade. Over the seven-year period, what had been Northern Ireland would experience a cumulative growth in GDP per head of roughly €5,000 (adding up the increments from each year's growth). By contrast, what was the Republic would experience a cumulative growth in GDP per head of roughly €1,250. And in the whole reunited Ireland, GDP per capita would grow by roughly €6,200, or by €24,800 for a family of four. This scenario is described as conservative, with minimum benefits from reunification but major benefits for the North.

Readers will wonder what produces the hypothetical boost in growth in this exercise. The answer is twofold: currency change and policy changes. By adopting the Euro, at the time of the modelling exercise the North's economy would have enjoyed a competitive devaluation against sterling and other member-states in the EU, and thereby improved its terms of trade and its export performance. These effects would have faded, however, as the graph shows. The policy changes, by contrast, would have longer-term effects, and these are strongly captured in the second scenario, where joining the Republic's tax system (especially its lower corporation tax), and its policies to attract foreign direct investment, transform the North and enable it to converge on the South's productivity levels over fifteen years. That is why the final levels of all three curves in Figure 22.1(b) are much higher in 2025 than in the first scenario. In this second scenario, the North's GDP per head would have had a cumulative boost of nearly €8,000, the South's of €3,800, and a united Ireland's of €11,800, all with a more sustained impact.

In the third and most benign scenario, the upper-bound estimate, Hübner and Van Nieuwkoop assumed that governmental savings from rationalization through reunification would be efficiently reinvested, with the effects displayed in Figure 22.1(c). Here the North would gain a cumulative increase in GDP per head of over €15,000 over seven years, the South just over €2,000, and Ireland as a whole over €17,000.

Irish readers may wonder: what's not to like about the economics of Irish reunification? The exercises of Kurt Hübner and his colleagues strongly suggest overall positive and net benefits to economic reunification, especially if accompanied by appropriate pro-growth and pro-employment policies by the government of a united Ireland. These are honest and professional exercises, free of data manipulation; they are not propaganda. They can help focus our collective thinking. Like all modelling exercises, however, they are only as good as the data put in, as they clearly say, and they have had to infer some Northern Ireland data because it is not specifically collected. Better data is on its way, and we shall have to wait to see how that changes future modelling of reunification scenarios.

Let me make a necessary update to their work before addressing some of the tough questions their exercise raises. The first necessary comment is on currency movements since their exercise was conducted. Figure 22.2 in the colour plate section charts the exchange rate of sterling against the euro since 2012. It shows a major devaluation of sterling after the UK voted in the summer of 2016 to leave the European Union. Sterling has since fluctuated at between €1.08 and €1.20, whereas it was running at between €1.20 and €1.40 in the two years before that act of collective self-harm by the English and Welsh. That change means that the North will probably not enjoy the scale of short-term boost in the terms of trade from reunification that Hübner and his colleagues reasonably suggested in late 2015.

This important update does not mean that their analysis or suggestions are null and void. Before them, no one had credibly argued that Irish reunification could be an Irish win-win, with net benefits to both the North and the South. They clearly maintained that the strongest benefits to economic reunification, as measured by growth in GDP per capita, would accrue to the North, but, importantly, that the South need not experience net losses. Neither unionist mantra – that it's better for the North to be in the UK, and that the South won't want to pay the costs of reunification – holds true. The thing that does the long-term work in this modelling, driving benign impacts from economic reunification, is having common economic policies throughout the island, which would dynamize the North through convergence with the

Republic's tax regime, and make the North as attractive for foreign direct investment as the South. The benefits of enhanced trade and economic specialization within the island, and increased productivity in the North, are both vital. Policy will clearly matter, not just currency-shifts. And, if there are administrative savings to be had from reunification, how efficiently they are allocated would be important – and how transparently, effectively, and with what political sensitivity. Moreover, some benefits of reunification for the North will take much longer than seven years. Turning the Northern education system to mirror that of the South is the work of at least eighteen years.

There are implications for the feasible political models of a united Ireland. Hübner and his colleagues presumed reunification through integration – the abolition of the political institutions of Northern Ireland, and the fusion and rationalization of public administration, North and South. Their work makes a strong economic case for selecting Model 2 of a united Ireland. They did not consider our Model 1, a devolved Northern Ireland persisting in a united Ireland. The inference from their modelling is that a devolved Northern Ireland, compared to an integrated Ireland, would reduce the scale of possible efficiency savings, and the pace of Northern convergence on the Southern growth path and productivity levels. That raises the question of the prospective fiscal transfer from the South to the North. Keeping Northern Ireland would make politically visible the scale of the fiscal transfer from the richer South to the poorer North. It is therefore important to address the 'subvention'.

Subverting the subvention question

A thought-stopping number is often invoked to stop conversation about a united Ireland. The UK subvention of Northern Ireland is the annual gap between what is raised in taxation in Northern Ireland and public expenditure there. It is frequently quoted as £10 billion sterling, or €11.9 billion in November 2021 euros. It is the price tag of reunification for lazy op-ed writers.

It is a big number. Assume that it is right (it was £9.4 billion in

2020). Ireland's GDP in 2020 was US$425.89 billion according to the World Bank, or €377.44 billion (as reported by Ireland's Central Statistical Office). Rounded, that is €377 billion.[4] Simple arithmetic tells us that 11.9 billion divided by 377 billion multiplied by 100 per cent = 3.15 per cent. The question, therefore, *seems* to be whether reunification would annually cost the taxpayers of the Republic 3.15 per cent of their GDP. According to my simple calculation on the same World Bank data, Ireland's average annual growth rate between 2010 and 2020 was 6.23 per cent.[5] So one way to think about the subvention figure, *if the data are correct*, is as follows. Fully absorbing it would cut Ireland's current average annual growth rate by about a half, but still leave it with a positive and respectable rate of 3 per cent. Meeting the total alleged subvention would slow the growth in the South's wealth, but would not impoverish it, or lock it in recession. Recall also that this calculation is just the alleged costs; it does not examine the possible benefits of economic reunification, including the improved performance of the North's economy emphasized by Kurt Hübner and his colleagues.

There are, however, good reasons to question the validity of the £10 billion number as the true ticket price of reunification. My friend and colleague in the Analysing and Researching Ireland, North and South (ARINS) project, political scientist John Doyle of Dublin City University, argues that the number both *underestimates* the taxation revenue that would be collected in a united Ireland and *overstates* the public expenditure that would continue in the North in a united Ireland.[6] The first argument rests partly on the current likely under-reporting of VAT receipts and corporation tax collected in the North, because larger firms report these returns from their London headquarters. The second argument challenges the accuracy of estimates of some 'identifiable' UK expenditure and, crucially, of 'non-identifiable expenditure'. The latter is an accounting notion: it includes Northern Ireland's notional 'share' of UK-wide public expenditure. But often very little of this expenditure takes place in Northern Ireland; or it would not occur in any model of a united Ireland. For instance, the UK's diplomatic services, the UK's military bases in Great Britain and elsewhere, and its Trident nuclear programme would not be questions let alone costs for the Irish

Department of Finance. These caveats must be carefully registered before we consider the subjects of liabilities and assets that would accompany any negotiations following the break-up of the United Kingdom of Great Britain and Northern Ireland.

Liabilities and assets

There are three general ways in which assets and liabilities have been handled internationally in state break-ups or secessions. Firstly, roughly equally sized places split their assets and liabilities 50:50. A second option is usually chosen when there is a significant disparity in population, in which case assets and liabilities may be split proportionally. Lastly, there is the 'zero option'. Here, assets and liabilities are left where they are physically, or financially, often with the successor state. Russia, for example, inherited the debts of the former USSR, and all its other former republics began life debt-free; but Russia also inherited all former Soviet assets on Russian soil.

So, what would be Northern Ireland's liabilities? The largest, at face value, would be pension liabilities. John Doyle correctly suggests that, subject to confirmation in negotiations, Ireland would not be responsible for the UK's public-sector pension liabilities incurred *before* the appointed day on which reunification occurs. That is highly likely, given past precedents – including in the UK's withdrawal from the EU. The next largest item would be Northern Ireland's share of the debt charges on the UK's national debt. But the UK, not Northern Ireland, is legally responsible for the UK's debts, and if in negotiations the UK insisted that Ireland should pay Northern Ireland's share, then Ireland should reasonably counter-bargain for Northern Ireland's share of the UK's total assets. These would include, for instance, royalties and tax revenues from North Sea oil, all the assets of the royal family, the value of the UK's public art collections outside Northern Ireland, and its public properties and assets held outside these islands. It is conceivable that the zero-option would apply: Great Britain would be liable for the UK's total debts, while Northern Ireland would waive its share of UK assets.

Methodically, John Doyle argues that the following annual items, in sterling, should therefore be deducted from the alleged price tag of the subvention:

£3,438 billion	because the UK's pension liabilities up to unification will not be transferred to a united Ireland
£1,600 billion	because a united Ireland will not inherit Northern Ireland's share of the UK's debts
£0.925 billion	because a united Ireland will not inherit Northern Ireland's share of the UK's defence budget (though Doyle allows for a possible 20 per cent increase in Ireland's defence budget)
£0.500 billion	because of the under-reporting of tax collection in Northern Ireland
£0.500 billion	because a united Ireland will not need the same scale of diplomatic and external expenditure
£6,963 billion	**Total** reductions in alleged overall subvention

The *coup de grâce* in Doyle's subversive accounting is to deduct these removed items (£6.963 billion) from the published subvention in 2019 (£9.367 billion). The more realistic subvention that Ireland would have inherited as an obligation on day one of reunification, had it been in 2020, would therefore have been £2.4 billion, or about €2.85 billion in November 2021 prices, one-fifth of the widely quoted price tag. That is about 0.75 per cent of Ireland's GDP in 2020 – not trivial, but close to a rounding error.[7]

As John Doyle correctly suggests, the important questions about the public finances of a united Ireland should not be about the potentially misleading arithmetic of the subvention. They should be about the future economic performance of a united Ireland – including the significant opportunities for expanded tourism in the North, and key policy decisions over education, health, and welfare, and diversifying urban growth-centres beyond greater Dublin. Doyle argues that the subvention does not matter in addressing the *economics* of reunification.

In that, I think he is broadly correct, if slightly excessive. But the subvention does matter *politically*.

Doyle's revised estimate of the subvention is much lower than the figure in UK accounts. If correct, it would suggest that Model 1 of a united Ireland, a persisting devolved Northern Ireland, *is* economically viable. Applied economics, so far, cannot decisively settle which model of a united Ireland should be selected. If one believes, as Hübner and his colleagues appear to do, that a devolved government in the North would be a drag on the performance of both parts of Ireland, then the economic case for Model 2 is stronger. The tacit assumption seems to be that a Northern Executive and Assembly would fail to exploit the opportunities to dynamize the Northern economy. The evidence in favour of that assumption since 1998 or 2007 is strong.

Economic forecasting for a decade ahead is not a mug's game, just exceptionally difficult. The practical economic questions for a united Ireland are straightforward. Will the Republic of Ireland, on average, continue to get richer than the UK? Will Northern Ireland benefit from the Protocol, and will that ease its possible future convergence into the higher-growth economy of the rest of the island? Will Northern Ireland benefit economically from being part of a more dynamic Irish economy? Will the Brexit experiment prove as damaging to the UK's long-run economic performance as currently suggested by most credible economists? The correct answer to all these questions, in my judgement, is 'yes'. But eight years is a long time in economics as well as politics.

PART SEVEN
Securing Ireland

23. Policing, intelligence, and paramilitarism in a united Ireland

The collapse of a state in our times leads to a civil war among militias. The tribe, and its warriors, return as the suppliers of security. Anarchy encourages each family to drill its members to align tribally or face the world defenceless. Having no trusted police or courts brings back the blood feud and blood money – the *weregeld* of the Anglo-Saxons, the *diya* of the Arabs, the *éraic* or honour price of Brehon law, and the world of 'punishment beatings'. Governments must therefore provide order and public security as one of their first duties.

The Irish, and the British in Ireland, should not rely on international bodies – the European Union or the United Nations – to resolve security questions that may arise during Irish reunification. Over the next decade, the Government of Ireland must work vigorously, ideally in cooperation with the British Government, to eliminate residual paramilitarism – both republican and loyalist. That requires patient police work, and the tactical use of carrots and sticks.

The 'carrots' include astute use of provisional amnesties or reduced sentences, rewards, and protection for significant information – including witness protection programmes and worthwhile resettlement prospects for those breaking with paramilitarism.

These policies must be consistent with an Irish public policy that visibly demonstrates how British and Protestant rights and culture would be credibly upheld and sustained in a united Ireland. Recurrent opportunities must be offered to loyalists to engage about their concerns – provided they are peaceful. They don't get a veto, though the Union survives as long as that is the majority will in the North, but not after that majority is lost.

'Sticks' by both sovereign governments in the next decade must include the sustained use of informants, heavy sentences for membership of illegal organizations, the application of normal policing in areas currently left to fester, and the controlled use of emergency legislation. I am not calling for anything new here. At the time of writing, the Tackling Paramilitarism, Criminality and Organised Crime Programme, agreed by the Government of Ireland and the UK, is in the second of two four-year phases that will end in 2024. It identifies forty-three tasks, five of which are co-shared by the two governments. The Northern Executive has similar objectives. 'Community funding' of tacit fronts for militias must end, and before it finally tapers off it must be clearly conditioned on lawful performance, notably by the UVF. It will soon be twenty-five years since the GFA, and as I write, it is seventeen years since the IRA decommissioned its arsenal to the satisfaction of international observers. Republican dissidents have been successfully managed to the point of defeat. Kid gloves must now be replaced by tough love for the loyalist militia. Their communities cannot be in permanent 'transition' – from paramilitarism – and in receipt of grant funding.[1] Indirectly paying paramilitants to secure law and order might seem to be a credible pragmatic policy, at least for a brief period, but paying them without ensuring they uphold their end of the bargain is folly.

Long-term security policy must render extremist goals utterly unviable by making it clear they won't be allowed to happen. Irish strategy must be to persuade sufficient loyalists that they will be equal citizens in a united Ireland, with full political, civil, cultural, and religious rights, and significant prospects of improved prosperity, but at the same time deprive them of any hope that an insurrection against reunification would succeed. British cooperation will help ensure that no external power will recognize a loyalist declaration of independence alleged to be by a 'Northern Ireland majority' or support the sectarian expulsions that would be required to produce a smaller and more homogenous Northern Ireland.

The biggest hope of potential loyalist insurrectionists – covert British military support – is best extinguished by British authorities. Given that even the Conservative-voting English public exhibits indifference towards the Union with Northern Ireland, loyalist hopes of such support are not high. Ireland's US friends and European allies, and constructive diplomatic engagement with the UK Government, should jointly render impossible the forging of a smaller Northern Ireland by loyalist violence.

For its part, Ireland must police away residual pockets of republican paramilitarism over the next decade, to demonstrate impartial hostility towards all paramilitarism and to ensure that only the forces of the Irish state will police any loyalist insurrection. Private republican vigilantes will not be welcome. In the interim, the Irish state must improve its own intelligence-gathering and monitoring of loyalist militia. The Directorate of Military Intelligence must have that as a central goal.

It takes both motivation and resources to start and sustain an insurrection. The object of policy must be both to weaken the motivation – by showing that united Ireland will be attractive, prosperous, and secure for non-Catholics and British people – and to deprive loyalist organizations of resources, particularly trained personnel and weapons.

The British Army no longer directly recruits loyalists – as occurred in the making and development of the Ulster Defence Regiment – so loyalist war-making capacities are radically lower. Lower numbers of British military engagements after Iraq and Afghanistan are also reducing the numbers of combat-trained loyalists.

It is possible that the Police Service of Northern Ireland has small numbers of hidden loyalist militia within its ranks,[2] but it should be possible to incentivize most of the police to follow the legal order, and in due course to respect the referendum outcomes. Potential loss of pay, pensions, and promotion prospects would be the sticks required to ensure police cooperation. A thought-through plan for two police services (in the devolved model) or a fusion of the two (in the integrated model) in a united Ireland should be clearly advertised to display the benefits of following the law, and to remove serving officers' anxiety that they will be unemployed after reunification.

As for resources, intelligence must be gathered on where loyalists obtain their current weaponry, and significant efforts made to ensure the island is as free of private weaponry as possible. That requires a good navy. Public relations and security strategy must highlight that 'loyalist' paramilitary activity is largely narco-gangsterism and parasitic protection rackets, and has been for a long time. That is best done while time thins the ranks of veterans of 'the troubles'. New recruits must not be encouraged by being treated as if they are such veterans.

Given Irish history, especially in the North, the recurrence of significant violence may happen, whatever action or inaction occurs in the South over the next decade. Many may use the threat of violence by others to try to prevent the holding of a referendum, or to block the necessary preliminary planning. As I write, sabre-rattling over the Protocol can be heard, though so far to little effect. Peaceful and democratic change must not be allowed to be blocked by fear, when such fear could itself be reduced by appropriate and open preparation and planning. Blackmail must be expected; it should not be tolerated.

Policing in the North

In September 1999, the Independent Commission on Policing for Northern Ireland,[3] mandated by the Good Friday Agreement, produced the Patten Report, a rigorously researched case for the transformation of policing in the North.[4] *Policing Northern Ireland: Proposals for a New Start*, co-authored by John McGarry and myself, is the most widely cited book in the report.[5] Patten's astute compromise gave the Royal Ulster Constabulary the past, with dignified memorials at police stations, but replaced the RUC with a new Police Service of Northern Ireland (PSNI), the future.

Northern Ireland had begun brutally in policing. The RUC and the B Specials were directly recruited from the first UVF and its Great War veterans. This bad start entrenched itself in institutionalized bias. The RUC and the B Specials killed six of the first eight people who died in 1969[6] – among the reasons why Patten announced a new beginning, though a fresh start had been promised as long ago as 1969, in the Hunt Report.[7] David Trimble, however, had the chutzpah to describe Patten's report as sectarian – though its prime purpose was to de-sectarianize policing and to win cross-community assent for the official police force.[8] For Trimble and many unionists, the RUC had been 'their' police. Letting go of wishful thinking was hard.

Following the establishment of the PSNI, an initially successful programme of affirmative action began: cultural Catholics and cultural Protestants were to be recruited on a 50:50 basis for at least ten years. Significantly reformed police would emerge, with obligatory human rights training, measures to hold them to account, and a code of conduct and ethos suited to a reformed and more peaceful political order.[9] Sinn Féin, with some delayed internal difficulty, accepted and recognized the new police, and added its nominees to the policing board. There are nineteen members of the board. Ten places are allocated to party nominees, according to the d'Hondt rule applied to the number of MLAs each party has in the Assembly. The remaining nine were originally to be nominated by the two first ministers – now they are nominated by the Minister for Justice.

Sadly, however, the return of the Conservatives to power in 2010 was accompanied a year later by a groundless concession to unionist lobbying. The 50:50 recruitment quota, up for review after ten years, was abandoned by Secretary of State Owen Paterson. Ireland's then foreign minister, Eamon Gilmore, opposed the ending of the quota, but support for the change by the Alliance Party's David Ford, the serving Northern justice minister, aided acquiescence.[10] The quota had initially transformed the Catholic participation rate in the police, which had risen steadily from 8 to 30 per cent. But since the quota was abandoned – prematurely, in my view – Catholic participation has slipped back.[11] Though the police are recognizably more representative than before the Patten Report, they are not yet adequately representative. Young Catholics outnumber young Protestants in the population – but, overall, Protestants still significantly outnumber Catholics in the police.

The quota should be restored until parity is attained. To count towards the quota, those who are Catholics and Protestants by background should have been born in Northern Ireland. Catholics recruited by the PSNI who are not Northern Irish should be welcome, but do not achieve Patten's goals. It is the local antagonists who must be reconciled through balanced policing. It would be better if the religious or ethnic origins of police were irrelevant to the successful performance of their roles, but that cannot be so in rebuilding an historically divided place where it is vital to avoid both the perception and the practice of one community policing another.

Policing in the future

If Model 1, a continuing devolved Northern Ireland, is embraced for Irish reunification, then the PSNI could remain as is, accountable to the Northern Ireland Policing Board, funded through the Northern Assembly, and under the jurisdiction of the Northern Minister for Justice. Legislation would need to be drafted to ensure proportional recruitment into the PSNI at a 50:50 ratio of cultural Catholics to cultural Protestants for two decades after unification, possibly with a temporary derogation from the Irish Constitution. Legislation will be needed to define duties and relations between the two Departments of Justice, North and South, and rules of cooperation and coordination between the two policing services and their interactions with European cyber-crime units, Europol, and Interpol. The Garda National Immigration Bureau and the Garda Racial, Intercultural & Diversity Office would now have all-island responsibilities, and would absorb any PSNI officers performing similar tasks, as would the Extradition department of the Garda. It would be better to fuse the Criminal Assets Bureau and its Northern counterpart, the Assets Recovery Agency. Separate Ombudsmen offices would be maintained. In the event that the Northern Assembly failed to function, Ireland's Ministry of Justice would be responsible for policing.

If, by contrast, Model 2, an integrated Ireland, becomes the model of reunification, then the fusion of An Garda Síochána and the PSNI will be required – a more demanding but still feasible transformation. Fortunately, comparative numbers are in the right shape: the Gardaí number roughly twice the number of Northern police, close to the population ratio. The English name of the integrated police might be the Police Service of Ireland or the Policing Service of Ireland (PSI). The Irish name could remain An Garda Síochána. Translations do not need to be exact. Seirbhís Póilíneachta na hÉireann (SPE) would be more literal.

Care should be taken to alternate the early police commissioners after reunification among officers who have served in either the PSNI or the Garda, or both. The current Garda Commissioner is the former Deputy

Chief Constable of the PSNI, so mobility between the two services is already established at the highest levels. Commissioner seems a more appropriate title than Chief Constable, but I confess indifference on the exact title of the chief of police, except that the Irish translation of 'chief' – *taoiseach* – would be unsuitable.

Memorials to officers and to previous policing organizations in both historic jurisdictions should be preserved at functioning police stations: that would include both the Royal Irish Constabulary and the Royal Ulster Constabulary. Following past precedents, pensions for RUC and PSNI officers and administrators (at least the accrued pension liabilities until the appointed moment of reunification) would remain the responsibility of the British Government after the transfer of sovereignty has been accomplished. The all-island police service would take a pledge to respect nationalist, unionist, and other traditions – all those represented in peaceful and democratic organizations – as well as to administer and enforce a suitably modernized code of ethics. The police uniform should be visible but ethnically neutral. It is a fortunate curiosity that the current Gardaí are dressed in blue, while the PSNI are dressed in bottle green, the reverse of expected national stereotypes. The new Gardaí uniforms are relaxed in style.

Under Model 2, a cultural Protestant recruitment quota should operate: one in two officers in the North for two decades – or one in six (or seven) island-wide. Most cultural Protestant police would likely work in the North, but there should be no obligation that they do so. An agreement will be required on the maintenance of existing stations, personnel, ranks, and career prospects until an appropriate management review takes place. All specialist units in both services would be prepared for merger. A commitment to maintain police numbers for an interval of seven years would be appropriate to keep up morale and to backstop the security anxieties that will accompany reunification.

There has been a significant convergence of policing issues and development in both parts of Ireland. Police who faced low crime rates before 1960 subsequently experienced rising challenges from new styles of crime and criminal organization, but policing has begun to match criminals in sophistication. Specialist security units have developed, focused on political security – including the targeting of paramilitary organizations – and on organized criminals engaged in marketing illegal drugs and human trafficking. Immigration has sometimes brought crime, not because all immigrants are criminals, but because organized crime follows immigrant communities to exploit opportunities created by the formation of new diasporas, and it often exploits vulnerable, unorganized migrants, especially illegal migrants.[12] Fair but firm integration of new immigrants is the appropriate policy – including from a policing perspective. The police in both jurisdictions have begun to reverse their indifferent records on domestic violence and their responses to evidence of sexual abuse.

There has been a convergence in forms and modes of policing. Organizationally, both services are unrecognizable compared to their counterparts of sixty years ago. Partial feminization has occurred, North and South: the first female guards graduated in 1959. Specialist skills, the increased prevalence of graduates, and improved thinking about what successful community policing requires, are part of the repertoires of both services.

The Future of Policing in Ireland was published in 2018,[13] though it has not been fully implemented. Known as the O'Toole Report, after its American-born chair Kathleen M. O'Toole, it strikingly resembles the Patten Report in its mode of analysis and recommendations – of which there are fifty. This is not surprising, because Kathleen O'Toole is a former Patten commissioner. Both reports place human rights protection, training, and immersion in rights-culture at the heart of policing. They emphasize that policing should not be a monopoly of the police, and that the police should become a formal profession. Great emphasis is placed on the operational and managerial independence of the senior police officers, and on removing civil service officials from significant roles in the internal management of the police – including pay and promotions. These are tasks for police management. But this emphasis on managerial and operational independence is and should be complemented by a strong emphasis on political accountability.

The O'Toole Report recommends a new and exclusively external oversight body, a Policing and Community Safety Oversight Commission (PCSOC), which would scrutinize policing performance; foster and monitor interagency cooperation in the delivery of community safety; encourage a broad acceptance of community safety as a task for the community as a whole, not just the police; execute inspections or inquiries concerning the delivery of policing services, and advise on and monitor the implementation of recommendations; promote professional policing standards, including human rights standards; support local community policing forums; and aid policy development with robust evidence-based research.

The centenary of An Garda Síochána's formation coincides with the publication of this book.[14] The Guardians of the Peace, the Gardaí, or the Guards, as they are almost universally known, have not had the controversial history of the RUC. Introduced during the civil war, they replaced the Royal Irish Constabulary that had won its 'royal' designation for services against the Fenians, and in 1925 they also replaced the Dublin Metropolitan Police. The Guards were loyal to the new Free State. They have been equally loyal to its successor, the Republic. They had a much easier task than the RUC; they policed a much more homogeneous society. The controversies that have surrounded the Guards usually involve political interference (being too close to ministers), overreach in their efforts to curb republicans, and the episodes of unchecked brutality found among police services everywhere. But the Guards have become better adjusted to the more diverse population produced by the Celtic Tiger and its aftermath, though much remains to be accomplished.

Despite their better historic record and deeper legitimacy, the Guards will have to fuse with the PSNI, and not simply take it over, if reunification on the integrated model is to function successfully. Not least, the amalgamated officers will have to cooperate in eliminating and preventing the recurrence of paramilitarism – loyalist or republican. Intelligence, both on paramilitarism and organized crime, should improve from a well-organized merger.

24. The defence and international relations of a united Ireland

The defence of Ireland requires security forces fit for external security, peacekeeping, and counter-insurgency – with the hope that the latter will never be needed on the island. The security forces also need to be able to aid the civilian authorities in emergencies, as in the recent pandemic. The existing security provision is not currently fit for all these purposes. The Republic's forces minimally need to be incrementally expanded over the next decade to meet existing defence obligations, as well as its European security alliances and UN commitments. They will need more significant expansion if the Russian invasion and attempted conquest of Ukraine is not quickly reversed, and to be ready for any possible security crisis attendant upon reunification.

In a united Ireland, the existing Defence Forces (Army, Naval Service, Air Corps, and Reserves), will be recruited across the island, and provide security impartially throughout it. The military in a democracy must not cause more insecurity than the security they provide, and will therefore need to be infused with the values of the new Ireland and loyal to its Constitution – whether it is an amended version of the current one, or new.

Fórsaí Cosanta, the literal Irish name of the Defence Forces, is acceptable, but the use of the official name, Óglaigh na hÉireann, should be reconsidered. Almost all manifestations of the IRA have claimed that name – with ONH as the abbreviation – and it is still used by 'dissident' republican organizations. Avoiding unnecessary offence should be a prevailing maxim in reunifying Ireland.

International duties

In September 2021, Ireland held the presidency of the United Nations Security Council. The previous year it had been elected to the Council for the fourth time, to serve out the 2021–22 term. This is a position that the Republic wins roughly every twenty years. Ireland's diplomats campaigned on 'partnership, empathy and independence' as the attributes it would bring to UN engagements. With a proud record in the League of Nations, independent Ireland takes seriously 'its devotion to the ideal of peace and friendly cooperation amongst nations founded on international justice and morality'.[1] Small states have a genuine and deep interest in peace, international justice, and morality. Words, however, are not enough.

Past missions by Irish personnel, under UN hats – whether in deploying observers or peacekeepers – have been extensive.[2] Such activities, in partnership with other UN member-states, can be effective: political scientists have demonstrated the worth of UN peace operations.[3] International institutions retain promise, contrary to what 'realists' argue.[4] Ireland is, however, in danger of overdoing its pacific disposition. Among the headlines about the Irish Defence Forces in November 2021 were 'Irish Defence Forces officer warns staffing crisis jeopardising UN overseas missions'. Commandant Conor King, General Secretary of the Representative Association of Commissioned Officers (RACO), maintained that 'inadequate establishment' is undermining Ireland's UN commitments.[5]

Commandant King's complaint should be no surprise. According to a reputable Swedish think tank, Ireland's military expenditure has shrunk from just less than 1 per cent of GDP in 1997 to about 0.3 per cent in 2020 – see Figure 24.1 (next page). Looking at the trajectory of the chart, it appears that the dividend from the Irish peace process was expressed through cuts to Irish security expenditure.[6] A second bout of austerity for the military followed the crash of 2008–09. The apparent rise in 2008–10 shown in the graph is likely owed to the shrinkage in GDP in these years. Cuts took the form of not increasing security expenditure in line with economic growth or inflation. That has had

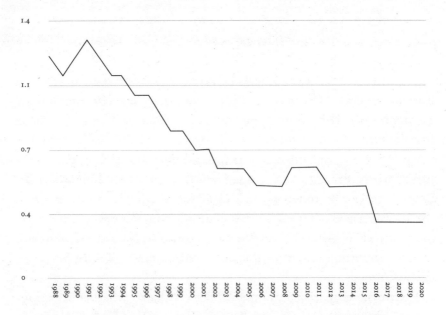

Figure 24.1: Ireland's military expenditure 1988–2020 as a percentage of GDP

Source: Drawn by author from data in SIPRI, https://sipri.org/databases/milex. SIPRI includes all spending on current military forces and activities, both the armed forces, and defence ministries and government agencies engaged in defence projects.

consequences. In the summer of 2021, the *Irish Times* reported retention and recruitment difficulties in the Naval Service: 'There are insufficient crew to operate some vessels . . . Ireland had to rely, earlier this year, on a European Union ship to help patrol its fishing zone.'[7] In early 2022, Russian naval exercises – which we now know were likely part of preparation for the invasion of Ukraine – took place within Ireland's economic zone. It took private fishermen exercising self-help to encourage them to leave Irish waters. On 29 March 2022, over a month after the invasion of Ukraine, the *Irish Times* ran the headline 'One third of Naval Service fleet to be decommissioned.'[8] It described difficulties in recruitment as part of its explanation. Many readers will know that similar tales can be told of the Irish Army: retrenchment, inadequate accommodation, and poor recruitment and retention.

Ireland's security expenditures need to rise, unless Ireland decides overtly to be entirely pacific. These expenditures would have to rise in the mid-2020s in all scenarios, because of the UK's withdrawal from contributions to the EU budget. Ireland as a net contributor to the EU would have to bear some of the burden of some of that shortfall – even if its funding was confined to humanitarian relief.[9]

Is it past time for Ireland to join NATO? After all, Ireland's original objection – partition – is no longer pertinent,[10] because the Good Friday Agreement charts good government for the North if it stays in the UK, and it charts an agreed path to reunification. The question of NATO membership, however, only makes sense if Ireland is ready for it. US administrations frequently scold their European NATO allies for not spending 2 per cent of their GDP on defence. By this criterion, Ireland would have to ramp up its security expenditures sevenfold on 2020 levels and engage in vigorous recruitment across all its security services in order to become a NATO member in good standing. An obvious conclusion follows: Ireland is in no fit condition to become a member of NATO, yet. The suggestion that Ireland should join that alliance is currently of little practical significance. That is likely a row for the more distant future. The question will become more vibrant as and when reunification referendums approach, but before that Ireland will need to have built some genuine security capacity.

Neutrality, its nuances, and its possible termination

Ireland is not a constitutional neutral. The Irish state became neutral by policy choice, as an advertisement of independence, and because military expenditure was cut to the bone after the tragic folly of our civil war. Cynics describe Ireland as 'neutral against Britain'. That is too simple. Ireland was neutral in World War Two because its government and citizens did not want British forces returning to the South less than two decades after they had left – and less than a year since they had withdrawn from the 'treaty ports' – but also because Ireland had little capacity to protect its people against the German air force, navy, or army. Neutrality therefore protected Irish citizens and their property, public and private, better than would the alternative. Ireland was neutral because partition was in place, and because British pledges to support

Irish reunification after the war were not credible, especially when issued by Churchill.[11]

Ireland paid a severe price for this neutrality. Though it benefited from the Marshall Plan, it was blocked by the Soviet Union from joining the UN until 1955. The leading lights in US foreign policy refused to link ending partition to Ireland's entry into NATO. Partition and Northern Ireland's standing as part of the UK were reinforced by World War Two. When Ireland subsequently sided with the post-colonial and non-aligned countries at the UN, it was doing so out of sincere empathy,[12] but also making the best of its isolation. Frank Aiken, de Valera's external affairs minister in the 1950s, was the most enthusiastic supporter of a policy of non-alignment, but neutrality was never proposed for Ireland's Constitution.

The immediate international security question for Ireland in the coming decade is whether it will develop a policy worthy of the name for tough times. Times that have been announced by Vladimir Putin's invasion of Ukraine, and his likely attempt to partition that country if he cannot accomplish an enforced regime change. Ireland's people are not neutral. Ireland was not neutral between the USA and the USSR. Its public, its businesses, its tourists, and its governments are generally pro-American – except when someone resembling Donald Trump is President of the US. We get on with our American cousins, as their employees, as beneficiaries of their investments – and as their employers. That said, Ireland has not approved of most of America's recent 'forever wars'. It is in foreign not domestic relations that Ireland has most resembled the Swedes – as a moral force, as pro-development and pro-peace, distancing itself from great-power imperialism.

Unlike Finland, Sweden, and Switzerland, Ireland does not currently operate a credible policy of 'armed neutrality' – i.e. a policy intended to produce at least a minimal deterrent, by making an invasion costly for those intent on such. Perhaps it has been a virtue that Ireland's young citizens have not been given military training through universal conscription – such a move might have exacerbated recruitment into the IRA and other republican militia after 1950. Low defence expenditures may also have contributed to Ireland's successful model of economic growth. They have been correlated with economic success, but it would be harder to prove causation.

In the immediate future, however, Ireland's formal neutrality and feeble defence expenditures risk becoming increasingly inconsistent with membership in the EU confederation – except as a free-rider. That is partly because some governments in the EU are seeking strategic autonomy from the United States. The Trump administration made the case by its appalling example. The disposition towards strategic autonomy, if it strengthens, will place a strain upon Ireland, which is both pro-American and pro-European. It is, however, possible, as first impressions suggest, that Putin's brutality towards Ukraine will lessen the disposition towards strategic autonomy, as the US and its EU partners in NATO renew their military alliance and as the EU becomes economic sanctioner-in-chief. The dynamics cut both ways, however. If the pursuit of strategic autonomy unfolds, Ireland will be expected to pull its proportionate weight in duties for the EU – consistent with EU and international law. If NATO and the EU act in increased coordination and harmony, Ireland may face isolation and be treated as a free-rider, especially if Finland and Sweden join NATO. (Austria, neutral by treaty, is a special case.)

The Treaty on European Union, in its mutual defence clause, states that, 'If a Member State is the victim of armed aggression on its territory, the other Member States shall have towards it an obligation of aid and assistance by all the means in their power, in accordance with Article 51 of the United Nations Charter. This shall not prejudice the specific character of the security and defence policy of certain Member States.'[13] Ireland is bound by this mutual defence commitment to the EU; Ireland is therefore not formally neutral: it is a partner to a mutual defence agreement. That is qualified, however, by the guarantees given in advance of the second Lisbon referendum in 2009, which are incorporated into Ireland's Constitution,[14] that exempt Ireland from being required to offer military assistance as distinct from other types of aid, e.g. humanitarian aid.

As my colleague in the ARINS project, former ambassador Rory Montgomery, pointed out in a letter to the *Irish Times* on 7 March 2022: 'It is time to abolish [Ireland's] legislative "triple-lock" requirement that the deployment of more than 12 members of the Defence Forces in an international peace support operation requires a UN mandate. It has never made sense that a Government decision endorsed by the Dáil can be stymied by a veto in the Security Council . . . Conversely and illogically, a unanimous EU decision – over which we do have a veto – is not sufficient to authorise Irish participation.'[15]

As Montgomery argues, a UN mandate before deployment would always be desirable, but Ireland need not shackle itself so unbreakably – because, after all, a Security Council veto may be exercised against EU interests, including Irish interests. Ireland's commitment to the EU's mutual defence clause is qualified, as Montgomery says, 'both in the treaty and in the guarantees given to us before the second Lisbon referendum effectively such as to exempt us from actually being required to offer military assistance, as opposed to other types of aid'. While the military assistance Ireland could give to fellow EU member-states is currently meagre – as I have shown at the start of this chapter – it may be potentially useful to a fellow EU member under attack. 'Let us say, Estonia,' writes Montgomery. In those circumstances, 'surely it would be unconscionable for us not to offer' military assistance.

In short, unless Ireland commits to principled pacifism, it will have to rebuild its defence capacities over the next decade. It needs to strengthen the civil emergency capabilities, including the medical capacities, of its Defence Forces, its ability to assist its European allies in their joint maritime operations (both humanitarian and security), *and* to be ready for potential security crises that might accompany Irish reunification. Reunification would be an abject failure if UN or EU peacekeepers were sought, after two successful referendums in favour of ending partition. The best approach to a possible loyalist insurrection, as stated in the previous chapter, is through adequate policing and intelligence resources and policies, impartial law enforcement, and a clear focus on the protection of the rights of British, Protestant, and loyalist people in a united Ireland. But there will also need to be an adequate army in reserve, and an adequate navy to block illegal arms shipments. Adequate security capacity, in and of itself, will reduce the credibility of any loyalist insurrection.

As a central foreign-policy goal, peace is excellent. And Ireland has been fortunate in its neighbourhood: the EU's zone of peace among democratic states. But there remain conditions to sovereign statehood. They include both being able to secure peace at home and being willing to deter potential external aggressors (at least as long as necessary to get help from allies). These conditions can be met through self-help and through alliances. Raising security expenditure to a steady 1.5 per cent of GNI by 2030 would be a feasible target for serious self-help. Full engagement with PESCO will provide the appropriate alliance.

Travelling throughout Ireland in 2021–22, I frequently inquired what people knew of PESCO. Few had an answer. It is not an Italian dish – the most common response. It stands for 'Permanent Structured Cooperation', though Permanent European Security and Co-operation would be more accurate. Allowed for under the Lisbon Treaty of 2009, PESCO encourages EU member-states, including the four historic neutrals – Ireland, Austria, Finland, and Sweden – to opt in and out of diverse defence and security projects and commitments.[16] They include the full array of maritime, air, land, cyber, space, and training domains, and joint actions and operations.

PESCO has taken off since 2017–18 as part of the EU's desire to obtain 'strategic autonomy'; an urge given legs by Russia's annexation of Crimea in 2014 and its subversion of eastern Ukraine. PESCO targets a security expenditure goal of 2 per cent of European GDP – matching the obligations of its NATO members. PESCO is also an embryonic high-tech military-industrial policy that aims to reduce the EU member-states' dependence on non-EU suppliers.

The Government of Ireland initially appeared to treat the 2 per cent figure as the overall goal of the twenty-five EU member-states in PESCO, not as a binding goal for each member-state.[17] That suggested a continued wish to free-ride, and a fear of Irish public opinion. If the Irish public was engaged, however, it could be persuaded to build defence capacities worthy of the name – capable of patrolling Irish seas, handling civil emergencies, deterring potential internal and external subversion (in conjunction with our European allies), and facilitating peacekeeping abroad. Ireland especially needs to have the capacity to withstand cyber-attacks, whether by criminals, governments, or criminal governments, like Putin's. Ireland should not become a garrison state, but it needs to become a European state that is not a free-rider. If it does not correct course, a day of reckoning may follow.

On 8 March 2022, Taoiseach Micheál Martin, speaking in Dáil Éireann, suggested that a citizens' assembly should be convened to discuss the future of Irish neutrality. He said Ireland has a tradition of military neutrality, 'but we have never been politically neutral'. He continued: 'We do need a discussion on this . . . [Though] not right now in the middle of a terrible war when we should be concentrating our resources on helping the Ukrainian people in a practical way.'

He was answering People Before Profit deputy Richard Boyd Barrett, who complained of a 'clamour' to exploit the Ukrainian crisis to 'move Ireland away from its traditional position of military neutrality and to move closer to NATO and . . . European militarization'. Noting that Boyd Barrett had criticized NATO as 'warmongers', Martin declared that there was 'only one warmonger here and that was Russia'.[18]

Scanning the security horizon with confidence is always difficult. A full-scale war over Ukraine was not widely anticipated in 2021. In the same year there was talk of US retreat from Europe, and a renewal of the US's long-promised pivot towards Asia. The security horizon has deeply darkened since then. As a small state, reunified or not, Ireland cannot decide these matters, but it can do its best to look after itself, as ethically as it chooses. PESCO is where Irish commitments currently are, and are likely to remain. Ireland is pledged to the EU by democratically endorsed treaties. Any move to end military neutrality, with or without a referendum, will likely take place in stages: a commitment to the military defence of the EU, followed by the formal opening of the debate over NATO membership, which in my view is obliged by Russian bombardment of European cities and civilians.

European questions going forward

Ireland will not follow Great Britain out of the European Union. There is no significant Irish public appetite for a Lexit – a left-wing exit from the EU – or merely an Irexit – an Irish exit. People Before Profit will win few votes if it persists with such a platform. But if and when reunification occurs, Ireland will acquire a much bigger Eurosceptic constituency – among Ulster Protestants. Not all of them are so inclined, but a significant number are.

They will need to be reintroduced to the merits of the EU, and European-based security. A reunified Ireland will matter a little more in the EU: it will have more MEPs, and its votes in the European Council will have greater weight. It will also allow for some normalization of trade with Great Britain, and free up resources and time that have been dedicated to issues created by Brexit. All that will be reinforced if Ireland pulls its weight in the joint provision of European security. The aspirations of Ireland's Department of Foreign Affairs to specialize in mediation and conflict resolution will also be bolstered if Ireland's security budget contributes a little muscle to a more muscular EU – not an imperial EU, but an EU that can defend and deter in its collective interests.

The Atlantic and beyond

Going forward then, Ireland's foreign and security policy will be shaped by our membership of the European Union, while our special concerns will remain shaped by our Atlantic location, an island behind an island that has hierarchically overshadowed ours: 'The tall kingdom' over our shoulder, as Seamus Heaney described Great Britain.[19] Ireland's policy towards Great Britain should remain governed by the Good Friday Agreement, which resolved most historic and legal legacies – on paper, at least. The successful outworking of the Protocol is in the joint interests of Ireland – North and South – and Great Britain.

After reunification, the British-Irish Council (if Model 1 or 2 is followed) and the British-Irish Intergovernmental Conference (if Model 1 is followed)★ would be appropriate channels for managing Britain and Ireland's joint security interests and avoiding disputes about overfishing waters, waste, and the exploitation of maritime resources. Maintaining

★ See Chapter 19, pp. 192–5.

the Common Travel Area as a zone of freedom of movement and of dual citizenship rights will be an enduring measure of mutual goodwill.

In the decade ahead, before or after reunification, it will be in Ireland's interests to support a British 'return to Europe' – either full membership of the EU or a closer partnership with the EU's customs union or single market, or at the very least a workable détente. While the Irish public will support Scotland's independence, the Irish Government should recall that Ireland's future British citizens among Ulster unionists will not. The Government of Ireland should therefore avoid interfering in self-determination disputes within Great Britain.

One renewed 'British question' will revive, before, during, or after reunification. Should Ireland re-join the Commonwealth? (It has not been the 'British Commonwealth of Nations' for some time.) Interestingly, there may be more public resistance to this idea in the South than to changing the national flag or national anthem.[20] And that makes a case for postponing the question until after reunification. No constitutional amendment would be required for re-entry. The Constitution of Ireland allows for it (Article 29.4.2°). Membership would provide 'a British dimension' to Irish reunification for unionists and the 'others', alongside the birthright British citizenship for Northerners provided by the GFA. Ties to Great Britain, and to the wider British world,[21] matter profoundly to British people on the island. Indeed, all of Ireland has strong affinities with many Commonwealth member-states, including others which shared in national self-determination movements against the British Empire. Many of the 'new Irish' hail from these countries. As a popular bonus, the Commonwealth Games would become available to Irish athletes under an Irish flag, where our medal prospects would be much brighter than in some other contests.

The potential downsides of re-joining the Commonwealth are mostly historic. In the Treaty negotiations of 1921, the Irish Free State was coerced into the British Commonwealth of Nations – a rebranding of the British Empire, coined as the Treaty was being made. A number of the Treaty's clauses – obligatory recognition of the Crown, and the oath imposed on deputies – are still vividly recalled as among the causes of the Irish Civil War. The Commonwealth, then, was a military and foreign policy alliance. It is no longer.

On its website, the Commonwealth declares that '[a] member state that has withdrawn or was expelled from the Commonwealth would need to reapply for membership. Although Commonwealth Heads have not set out any re-joining criteria, it is expected that a country would demonstrate that it continues to uphold the principles and values of the Commonwealth that it espoused when it first joined.'[22] Ireland was not expelled, but its membership had been compulsory, and sustained efforts were made by British authorities to block the Irish Free State from becoming a fully independent and democratic republic. These are hardly principles or values today's Ireland would want to espouse.

Ireland's strong and majority republican tradition may be offended by reapplying for membership. I suspect that is because leaving the Commonwealth is associated with the South's attainment of formal republican status. Yet today the Commonwealth is no longer the *British* Commonwealth. It mostly comprises republics (sixteen of its fifty-four members were monarchies in 2020; Barbados became a republic in 2021, Jamaica's Prime Minister has declared that becoming a republic is a governmental priority, and Belize may follow). The membership rules were changed after Ireland left. India joined as a republic.

In 2007, the heads of government of Commonwealth countries agreed on one symbolic requirement. Applicants for membership would have to 'acknowledge Queen Elizabeth II as the Head of the Commonwealth'.[23] Éamon de Valera would have accepted that. Elizabeth II may not be around by 2030, and though Prince Charles is announced as her successor as the Head of the Commonwealth, that position will not automatically be inherited by Prince William. The position could rotate away from the British head of state in future.

In any case, the Head of the Commonwealth, in that capacity, has no executive, legislative, or judicial authority in any Commonwealth republic. Since loyalty, allegiance, and affection for all things British have been regular features of unionist political culture at least since the 1880s, renewed membership of the Commonwealth would be an accommodation for its British national minority that Ireland's republicans should be willing to consider.

Judge Richard Humphreys has quoted the official biographers of

Éamon de Valera to the effect that the Irish coalition government of 1948–51 merely took 'steps which . . . led the British and the rest of the Commonwealth to conclude that Ireland was not a member'. Humphreys suggests that 'perhaps it may be contended that [Ireland] has been in law a member all along'.[24] Witty though this assessment may be, it seems unlikely that Ireland could simply reanimate its membership and declare that it had never left. The UK's Ireland Act of 1949 treats the Republic's citizens as if they were Commonwealth citizens, but that is not the same as treating Ireland as a member of the Commonwealth. Ireland could grumpily seek to be re-invited to renew its membership by a more contrite Great Britain. Alternatively, Ireland could be more forward-looking and gracious, and proactively reapply as part of our commitment to planning our future reunified nation-state with bi-national accommodations.

I suspect, however, that option will be postponed.

PART EIGHT

Accommodating Diversity

25. Integration is not coercive assimilation

Addressing the Forum for Peace and Reconciliation on obstacles to reconciliation in 1996, Arthur Aughey, a distinguished unionist intellectual and now Emeritus Professor of Politics at Ulster University, was bleak. Of unionist Ulster he wrote, 'To many – and not just the extremists – the prospect of Irish unity still suggests a form of "race death". Any "dynamic" form of cooperation with the Republic would represent cooperation in your own undoing.'[1] Aughey was not mistaken; that view is held among some cultural Protestants in the North. This fear of extinction is not a fear of genocide by physical extermination, but, as Aughey intimates, fear of disappearance through cultural assimilation.

No coercive assimilation

Many unionists believe, mistakenly, that after partition Southern Protestants were expelled en masse, or collectively and coercively assimilated. Proving that such beliefs are almost entirely false or heavily exaggerated will not shift unionist collective psychology anytime soon.[2] They rest on a century of disinformation or conspiratorial thinking. With luck, unionists will realize that a liberal, largely ex-Catholic, and democratic Ireland already exists – before the reunification referendums.

The demographic decline of Southern Protestants was underway long before 1911.[3] Their rate of emigration – often to elsewhere in the British Empire – remained roughly constant thereafter.[4] They had lost proportionally more young men in the Great War, and their community had a lower birth rate long before 1918. Those Southern Protestants who stayed after independence were not coercively assimilated. Parallel and fully funded Protestant schooling was preserved. Notably, Trinity College Dublin remained significantly British and Protestant in character until the 1960s. The high professions, bastions of the Southern Protestants, were neither nationalized nor purged.

Voluntary assimilation occurred through mixed marriages, increasingly over time. The Catholic *ne temere* decree, understood to oblige those who married Catholics to agree to bring their children up as Catholics, was sectarian, but it was papal not governmental policy: the Protestant partner accepted it as the price of marriage to a believing Catholic. This papal sectarianism was matched by taboos on marriage with Catholics among many Protestant churches, though it was in Belfast, as Anthony Hepburn waspishly put it, that the Catholic church and the loyalist working class agreed that the children of mixed marriages were Catholic.

The historical record must be corrected, and I have tried to do so elsewhere, but I have no confidence that this task, even carried out by others, will remove unionist anxieties.[5] Their *fear* of ethnic extinction is real. It is also reciprocated. Cultural Catholics in the North have often feared they would be 'burned out' or forcefully made British.

Model 1 of reunification, the persistence of Northern Ireland as a devolved government within a united Ireland, will make it easier to maintain British and Protestant identifications, modes of being, and symbols in a united Ireland. The power-sharing in the GFA grants unionists veto rights over devolved matters of profound cultural concern to them, notably the primary and secondary educational systems. Power-sharing arrangements, however tweaked – and whether applied within Northern Ireland or across the island – cannot halt the demographic decline of Ulster Protestants, however. But equally, a reunified Ireland in the next decade will neither be Catholic nor Gaelic, and its authorities will have no capacity, and no will, to engage in coercive assimilation.

Wise and just policy would avoid coercive assimilation, but it is also a legal obligation. Ireland is a party to the European Framework Convention for the Protection of National Minorities (1994), which entered into force in 1998. The Oireachtas ratified it in May 1999, as part of the peace process.[6] The Convention explicitly bans coercive assimilation and protects undefined 'national minorities'. Article 4 affirms the fundamental principles of non-discrimination and equality, and clarifies that a state's obligations may require affirmative action. States are to adopt, where necessary, measures to promote 'full and effective equality between persons belonging to a national minority and those belonging to the majority', taking 'due account of the specific conditions' of national minorities. Measures to promote effective equality are not to be considered as discrimination.

Here are extracts from the full text.

Ratifying states agree to:

- promote the conditions necessary for minorities to maintain and develop their culture and identity;
- encourage tolerance, mutual respect, and understanding among all persons living on their territory;
- protect the rights to freedom of assembly, association, expression, thought, conscience, and religion;
- facilitate access to mainstream media and promote the creation and use of minority media;
- recognize the right to use a minority language in private and in public and display information in the minority language;
- recognize officially surnames and first names in the minority language;
- 'endeavour to ensure' the right to use the minority language before administrative authorities and to display bilingual topographical indications in the minority language in areas inhabited by national minorities traditionally or in substantial numbers;
- foster knowledge of the culture, history, language, and religion of both majority and minorities;
- recognize the rights of minorities to set up and manage their own educational establishments and learn their own language;
- 'endeavour to ensure' that there are adequate opportunities to be taught in the minority language, in areas traditionally inhabited by national minorities or where they live in substantial numbers;
- create the conditions necessary for the effective participation of persons belonging to national minorities in cultural, social, and

economic life, and in public affairs, in particular those affecting them;

- refrain from measures that alter the proportions of the population in areas inhabited by minorities; and
- not interfere with the rights to maintain contacts across frontiers and participate in the activities of national and international NGOs.[7]

These are comprehensive obligations. To render the Convention applicable, and to incorporate it in domestic law, it would be necessary to define people who identify as British in the North, and elsewhere, as a British national minority in Ireland; to define Ulster Scots as the language of a national minority; and to define Protestants as an Irish national minority – defined religiously. Many of the Convention's provisions could also, in principle, be drafted to benefit users of Irish, North and South.

The legal point is simple. In international law, the Irish state is not preparing the 'race death' of Ulster unionists. Domestic incorporation of this convention would provide further assurance. The Convention for the Protection of National Minorities offers a script which unionists and loyalists can use before or after the reunification referendums, to score points, or to make reasonable demands for such securities.

Assimilationist policy promises equality: if you become part of us, you will cease to be a structural and possibly disadvantaged minority. But there is a difference between coercive and voluntary assimilation, though the line is sometimes blurred. If two groups wish to tango, assimilation may occur through 'acculturation', where one group's culture (usually the dominant group's) is adopted. The reverse also occurs, especially among conquering migrant minorities, where the dominant group acculturates to the subordinate. Romans assimilated into Greek culture in the Eastern Roman Empire (Byzantium);[8] Mongols became Chinese;[9] and Normans rapidly became French, English, Welsh, Sicilian, and Irish.[10]

Over centuries, the conquered native Irish acculturated to the English language – though retaining affection for and sometimes speaking and reading the Irish language, sometimes aided by institutional efforts at revival. Irish language loss occurred through coercion – and famine – as well as choice. Some native Irish also acculturated to Protestantism through choice, but also through coercion, responding to incentives in the penal laws to become first-class citizens.

There will be no anti-Protestant penal laws if a united Ireland is voted for in the next decade. All but a handful will agree that Ulster Protestants should *not* be obliged to acculturate to the Irish language. Moreover, becoming Catholic in a reunified Ireland will not improve their citizenship status. The ethos that Protestants will experience will be one of political equality with full respect for religious difference and indifference, and with full respect for British people as a national minority.

'Amalgamation' policy, by contrast with acculturation, insists that different people should fuse together to become a novel people – a blend or melt of the previous ingredients. Since Alexander the Great forcibly wedded his Macedonian companions to the princesses of the Persian Empire, ambitious amalgamation strategies have been rare.[11] Amalgamations usually happen organically rather than being planned, as in Spanish-speaking America, where 'the fusion of races' – the formation of Mestizo Americans – took place under the roof of the Catholic church after the conquistadors had done their bloody work. The cultural Catholics of Ireland are arguably an amalgamation of the old English and the Irish Gaels. New forms of amalgamation may happen in Ireland in the very long run, after we are all dead, but they are not advocated here, nor is amalgamation any party's policy. If a deep and thorough novel amalgamation happens, both Irish cultural Catholics and Ulster cultural Protestants will disappear through the choices of their group members: a voluntary double race death, to use Aughey's language. But that is not on anyone's political agenda.

Instead, the prospectus of Irish reunification is currently poised, this book suggests, between two forms of long-term accommodation for British and Ulster unionists: a persistent power-sharing Northern Ireland (Model 1), or an integrated Ireland with extensive minority rights and protections (Model 2). Neither model is programmatically assimilationist. Both would publicly recognize national, ethnic, religious, and linguistic identifications and dispositions among the future minority – British, Scots, English, Welsh, Protestant, and Ulster Scots. The right to dual citizenship now and in the future is already in the GFA and will be embraced in a new Ireland.

'Integrationists', as distinct from assimilationists, seek inclusive and fair institutions, even if such institutions cannot be entirely culturally neutral. For them, the key question is the extent to which the Irish state can be remade, and whether British and Protestant difference can be accommodated under a platform of equality for all.

An Irish nation-state with binational accommodations is a feasible goal. The norm of proportionality, as I have shown in Part Five of this book, can be applied to give Northern Protestants full opportunities to make their votes effective and to be pivotal in government formation. That will give them more access to the exercise of sovereign power than they have had since 1922. Existing institutions could be redesigned to represent the new national minority, and to halt or delay any potential transgressions of its members' rights and liberties. The increased institutionalization of rights and respect given to such rights on both sides of the historic border will aid that redesign.

The growth in respect for rights

Northern Ireland had a decidedly worse record than independent Ireland in protecting human rights after 1923. Ethnic and religious discrimination occurred in employment and housing allocation, in electoral manipulation, in biased policing, and in the failure to protect lives. The governing authorities were not exclusively culpable for the latter, because republican and loyalist militants killed more people – though loyalists often did so in collusion with the authorities. Across the partition line, both police services relied too often on confessions for convictions of politically motivated militants – whose respect for human rights and the laws of war admittedly was often more tarnished than that of those who sought to police them. Emergency legislation was frequently excessive, or too long in force in both jurisdictions – targeted principally but not exclusively at republican militants. Unjustifiable internment without trial and wrongful convictions were too common.

Formal rights standards have improved in both jurisdictions. The European Convention on Human Rights is now part of the domestic law of both jurisdictions, though some Conservative politicians in Great Britain, including former party leaders, threaten to replace this Convention with 'British rights for British people'. The Convention has many merits, though it is weak on anti-discrimination law and regarding equality, which is why it has been bolstered by EU anti-discrimination law, and the Fair Employment Act in the North.

The Northern Ireland Human Rights Commission (NIHRC), established under the GFA, does function, but its two significant efforts to accomplish an agreed bill of rights – part of the pledges in the Good Friday Agreement – have both stalled. The Equality Commission for Northern Ireland functions with greater impact. The Irish Human Rights and Equality Commission (IHREC) in the Republic, and the Joint Committee of the IHREC and the NIHRC operate across the border. These bodies would continue to operate if Model 1, the devolved option of a united Ireland, was followed, but would merge appropriately if Model 2 was chosen.

Whether or not a constitutional convention accompanies Irish reunification, it may be wise to organize a fresh bill of rights for the entire island, preserving the best of Southern and Northern jurisprudence. It need not be radically innovative. It could simply be a work of synthesis, charged with avoiding any diminution in human rights. Independent Ireland is already sold on the merits of a bill of rights from past experience, and it has no conservative party arguing for ending European convention rights or European charter rights. In Northern Ireland, some but not all unionists share English Tory scepticism about bills of rights, but may think differently if they become a minority in a reunified Ireland. In preparation for the reunification referendums, a minimum sketch of a modernized bill of rights – updating the existing rights in the Irish Constitution, and incorporating as appropriate the rights from Ireland's membership of the Council of Europe, the European Union, and the Convention for the Protection of National Minorities – as well as an extension of Northern Ireland's Fair Employment Act should be articulated alongside either the devolved or the integrated model of a united Ireland.

Professor Brice Dickson, a liberal unionist scholar of law who drafted one of the stalled bills of rights in Northern Ireland, has written recently: 'If and when voters in Northern Ireland are asked whether they wish to remain within the UK or to become residents of a united Ireland it is unlikely, I would suggest, that their decision will turn on where they think their human rights will be better protected. Voters would be correct to leave aside this consideration when they go to the polls because, frankly, there are no really significant differences between the human rights regimes in the two countries.' He continues: 'International law, moreover, requires a state which absorbs part of another state to extend to the people in the new portion of the state all the international human rights obligations it already owes to people currently living in the absorbing state. The bottom line for those who will be operationalising a united Ireland should be that on the human rights front there will be no regression for anyone currently living in Northern Ireland.'[12]

Wise counsel; I can't do better than to repeat it.

Figure 18.1: The thirty-one elected authorities in the Republic of Ireland

This map shows the thirty-one elected local authorities in the Republic, consisting of twenty-six county councils, two city and county councils, and three city councils.

Figure 18.2: The eleven Northern Ireland local government districts in 2019

Source: Northern Ireland Assembly

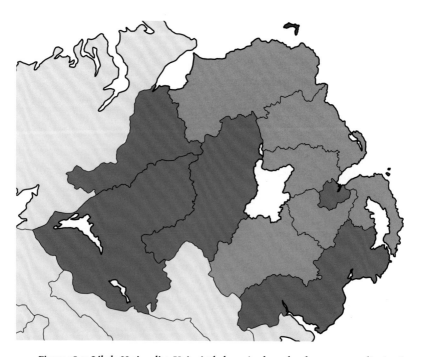

Figure 18.3: Likely Nationalist–Unionist balance in eleven local government districts in the 2020s

Source: Adapted from Local Elections 2019 (Northern Ireland): A Statistical Profile, a joint publication of the Oireachtas Library & Research Service (L&RS) and the Research and Information Service (RaISe) of the NI Assembly

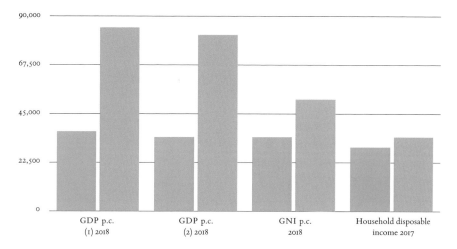

Northern Ireland

Republic of Ireland

Figure 21.1. (a): Who is better off in income in US dollars? This bar chart shows four income indicators of standard of living in which the Republic is ahead of Northern Ireland.

Note: There are two figures for US$ GDP in 2018: the first (1) is in current prices, current PPP; whereas the second (2) is in constant prices, constant PPP.

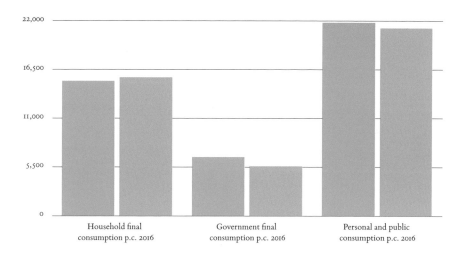

Figure 21.1. (b): Who is better off in consumption in euros? This bar chart shows three consumption indicators of standard of living in which Northern Ireland and the Republic are more evenly matched

Note: The data in Figure 21.1(a) are in US dollars ($) while the data in Figure 21.1(b) are in euros (€). The relevant data are collected and calculated in these respective currencies.

Sources: Adapted from data in Adele Bergin and Seamus McGuinness, 'Who is Better off? Measuring Cross-border Differences in Living Standards, Opportunities and Quality of Life on the Island of Ireland', *Irish Studies in International Affairs*, Volume 32, Number 2, 2021, pp. 143–160

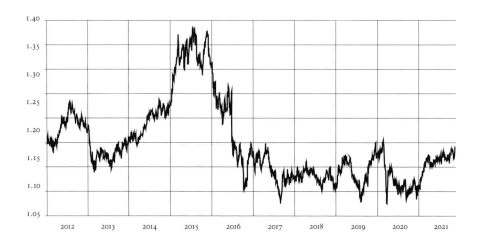

Figure 22.2: The value of Sterling against the Euro, 2012–2021

Sources: European Central Bank online data, accessed 20 November 2021 (https://www.ecb.europa.eu/stats/policy_and_
exchange_rates/euro_reference_exchange_rates/html/eurofxref-graph-gbp.en.html)

 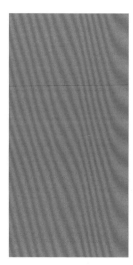

Flag 1: The flag of the Irish state: the republican tricolour. It is intended to be inclusive and integrative; the white symbolizes peace between the green and the orange – rivalrous colours since 1798.

Source: *A History of Irish Flags from Earliest Times*, Gerard Anthony Hayes-McCoy, 1979. (Academy Press: Dublin), pp. 141–8; Shutterstock

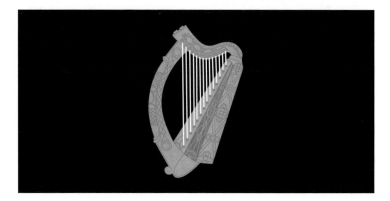

Flag 2: Until the Act of Union, the Kingdom of Ireland had arms with a royal-blue field and a golden harp. The use of the harp in this manner dates back to Henry VIII. When James I of England/James VI of Scotland arranged the arms of his kingdoms, the Irish quarter became a golden harp with a blue field.

Source: Hayes-McCoy, 1979: 22–23; Alamy

Flag 3. Until the Act of Union in 1800, the 'maid of Erin' sometimes fronted the harp. Resurrecting this bare-breasted lady may not win universal approval.

Source: Hayes-McCoy, 1979: 46–47; Shutterstock

Flag 4: Ireland's Presidential Standard has a blue field embossed with a simple gold harp and is plainly modelled on the arms of the Kingdom of Ireland (see Flag 2).

Source: Alamy

Flag 5: The Green Harp Flag, an uncrowned golden harp on a green background, was used by Owen Roe O'Neill in 1642 and the Confederation of Kilkenny, and by the United Irishmen during 1798. Variants were used by Irish troops on the Union side during the US civil war, and by the Irish Republican Brotherhood. The flag predates partition and arguably represents the whole island. It became associated with the Redmondites and was therefore discredited among republicans.

Source: Hayes-McCoy 1979: Ch. 3; Setanta Saki, public domain, via Wikimedia Commons

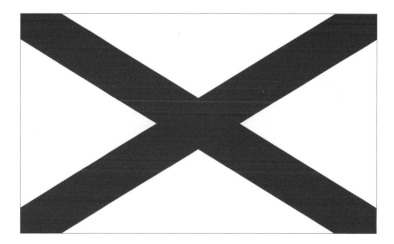

Flag 6: The red saltire of Saint Patrick against a white field, extracted back from the Union Jack, would be unacceptable as the flag of a united Ireland to many – too religious, and too British – though it might in fact be a variant on the Spanish Cross of Burgundy that may have been carried by O'Neill and O'Donnell's forces at Kinsale.

Source: Hayes-McCoy 1979: 36–37; Shutterstock

Flag 7: The historic flag of the four provinces (based on their 1651 flags) would suit an Irish federation constructed around these entities. From the bottom left, clockwise, are the provincial flags of Ulster, Munster, Connacht, and Leinster.

Source: Shutterstock

Flag 8: The Ulster Banner, unofficially the flag of Northern Ireland, is a heraldic banner taken from the former coat of arms of Northern Ireland, consisting of a red cross on a white field, upon which is a crowned six-pointed star with a red hand in the centre.

Source: Shutterstock

26. Secularization, religion, and education

The Holy Roman Catholic and Apostolic Church has been thoroughly displaced from its previous social power in Ireland. One must be a very paranoid atheist or anxious Protestant to anticipate its strong recovery. Though there may be fanatical Catholics intent on that objective, their cause seems doomed. Most Irish Catholic priests will be in their eighties in 2030. More bishops are being ordained than priests.[1] This clerical manpower crisis could be met by female priests – a radical, not to say Protestant, innovation – but more likely it will be met by importing foreign clergy. But their prospective dioceses may not be able to support them, given their dwindling and ageing congregations. The Catholic church is downsizing, leaving, or being driven out of, schools, universities, hospitals, and orphanages. A united Ireland will have a palpable *ex*-Catholic ethos across most of the former Irish Free State. It may be small comfort to Ulster Protestants, but a united Ireland will not involve their Catholicization.

The historic delegation of much of social policy to churches, especially but not only in the South, led to severe human rights abuses in orphanages, schools, 'industrial schools', borstals, and in the maltreatment of so-called fallen women in Magdalene laundries and 'mother and baby homes'. Multi-volume testimonies, histories, and extensive literatures have been and are being written of the cruelty in these religiously run social institutions. Inexcusable cruelties. The Irish, South *and* North, and the British in Ireland – influenced by acerbic interpretations of their respective brands of Christianity – applied harsh disciplinary standards in their own homes and communities, often suppressing evidence of sexual abuse, child abuse, domestic violence, and gender-based violence. They deferred to their clergy and expected their politicians to do the same. Cruelty and denial were no monopoly of public institutions. These abuses prevailed despite the existence of rights protections.

The Free State's and the Republic's record in outlawing divorce, later constitutionalized, was an imposition, by the clergy and the majority, on those Protestants and others with no doctrinal antipathy to divorce. Standard modes of birth control were illegal for decades. Puritanical sexual repression was ubiquitous across the island. As in the second German Reich, a woman's place was seen to be with *Kinder, Küche, Kirche* – children, kitchen, and church.

LGBTQ+ rights and freedoms were suppressed across the partition line. In the North that began to end through the European Court of Human Rights (ECtHR) in 1981[2] and, under British direct rule, through an Order in Council issued in 1982, fifteen years after gay people had been liberated in Great Britain. Had the Democratic Unionist Party had its way, 'Ulster' would have been permanently 'saved from sodomy' by Ian Paisley Sr, who ran a campaign under that brand. In the South, Senator David Norris began his case for gay rights in 1983, having failed before Irish courts, winning vindication before the ECtHR in 1988.[3] Decriminalization followed in legislation in 1993.

Both parts of the island preserved archaic prohibitions on abortion – and the Republic constitutionalized prohibition after a referendum in 1983, when anti-abortionist activists feared the Irish Supreme Court might follow North American and European courts. Both the North and the South contracted out the moral consequences, relying on ferries and planes to Great Britain for the performance of abortions by others.

More recently, the Republic's citizens decisively liberalized social life through referendums amending the Constitution. In 1992, after the infamous 'X case', citizens amended the Constitution to permit information about abortion and travel abroad to have an abortion.[4] In 1996, the right of divorce was made constitutional after a referendum in 1995. In 2015, after an amendment was proposed, the Republic became the first sovereign state to validate same-sex marriage by referendum. In 2018, an amendment repealed the Eighth Amendment of 1983 and legalized abortion, while another passed later in the same year struck blasphemy from the Constitution. The Thirty-Eighth Amendment in 2019 further liberalized divorce regulations. That's a bullet-point summary of an avalanche of liberalization of the rights of women and men, straight and gay.

Derek Scally's *The Best Catholics in the World* (2021) should be read after Tom Inglis's *Moral Monopoly* (1987).[5] Between the publication of these two books, Catholic Ireland imploded. The previous order is sketched by Inglis. The fall is told by Scally. Standard sources of secularization mattered – increased graduate education, urbanization, the diffusion of international knowledge, exposure to comparative global differences through mass media and travel, and science's incremental inroads into magical and religious traditions. Equally important, however, was the Catholic church's record of abuse and its cover-up of abuse – especially by priests and brothers, though nuns were not blameless. Sexual and corporal abuse – and the cover-up of abusive clergy – was consistently exposed, to devastating effect, in the 1990s and after. This was not just an Irish phenomenon, and clerical abuse was not confined to the Catholic church, but its Irish representatives deserved the spotlight that was turned on them. Once a favoured child of the papacy, Ireland became an embarrassing trendsetter in the international exposé of the vices of church personnel. Church officialdom became embroiled in litigation, downsizing properties, and liquidating assets to avoid bankruptcy. Hollowed out, the Catholic church is tolerated or used for ceremonial purposes at funerals, weddings, and perhaps at baptisms. Obliged to retreat to the ethical, where it has lost respect, it will take decades to recover any high ground, and as many decades before being heard beyond its surviving faithful. Indeed, it may never recover moral authority.

Perhaps the culminating disgrace came in 2010 when Cardinal Seán Brady, Primate of All Ireland and Archbishop of Armagh, came under sustained pressure to resign, notably from Deputy First Minister Martin McGuinness in the North and Deputy Róisín Shortall in the South, because of his failure to notify the secular authorities of the results of his investigations into the abusive activities of a paedophile priest, Brendan Smyth. In 1975, as a young canon lawyer, Brady had sworn to secrecy the young victims of Smyth he had interviewed. He found the priest guilty, and notified his bishop, but took no further action, even though Smyth continued to abuse new victims, North and South – which may have numbered in the hundreds according to Smyth's own confession. Putting the church's reputation first ended in its reputational collapse.[6] In 2011, Taoiseach Enda Kenny publicly admonished the Vatican in Dáil Éireann after the Cloyne Report documented its continuing role in covering up the rape of children by clergy.[7] Between 2011 and 2014, Ireland closed its embassy to the Holy See as part of public retrenchment, an act of biting cultural significance.[8] Brady resisted resignation until 2014, dragging out the disgrace.

Unionists once argued that 'Home Rule' would mean 'Rome Rule'. They forgot that Irish home rule would have been within Westminster's legal jurisdiction, which would have inhibited Catholic clerical dominance. It is fairer to argue that partition facilitated Rome rule in the south, notably in family law, marriage, and the regulation of women's bodies and rights. As the socialist revolutionary James Connolly had predicted in March 1914, partition would facilitate a 'carnival of reaction'.[9] Without partition, a secular bloc, along with cultural Protestants, would have found it easier to emerge and to restrain the Catholic church's ambitions for moral hegemony. But whatever the verdict on that historical debate, today's Ulster Protestants can visibly see, if they choose to, that cultural Catholics in the South, by their own efforts, have decisively denounced, repudiated, and politically subordinated their clergy.

Liberal Protestants therefore have nothing to fear, religiously, from a future united Ireland. Any Catholic revival would be led by a humbled church. They can be confident of full and equal citizenship. Theologically and socially conservative Ulster Protestants – largely represented by the DUP and TUV – may think that their position will be worse: they may regard a liberal Ireland as even worse or not much better than a Catholic Ireland. Yet they must have noticed that their surroundings have changed. Great Britain no longer has an active Protestant majority. It too has been socially liberal. Socially conservative Ulster Protestants find themselves surrounded throughout the isles by social liberalism – or what they might deem 'paganism and atheism'. Staying in the UK won't help them.

In the North, the Alliance Party, the SDLP, and Sinn Féin are socially liberal, and jointly constitute a political majority. They are supported in social liberalism by a significant swathe of the Ulster Unionist Party. In the South, Aontú and sections of Fianna Fáil articulate traditional conservative Catholic values, especially over abortion, but they are a minority. Ironically, therefore, Southern liberals will be anxious that in a united Ireland social conservatism will be reinforced by the arrival of Northern evangelicals, and less liberal cultural Catholics. That fear, however, assumes that the North will stop changing over the next decade, which seems unlikely. It is quite possible that conservative Protestants and Catholics may make alliances in a reunified Ireland, as they have done elsewhere in Europe, and they may think they can harvest votes among some of the more socially conservative new Irish.

The Constitution always formally separated church from state by not permitting endowment, but making that formality actual is now well advanced, if incomplete. The process started in 1972 with the repeal of the 'special position' of the Catholic church, once recognized in the original Article 44.2.[10] The end of blasphemy occurred in 2018. Article 44.1 remains one of the last fortresses of overt religious thought in the Constitution: 'The State acknowledges that the homage of public worship is owed to Almighty God. It shall hold His Name in reverence, and shall respect and honour religion.'[11] Respect should be owed to all religions, provided they earn it, but respect is also owed to the non-religious, on the same terms. The full separation of church and state, a standard republican aspiration, will be realized with or without Irish reunification.

Nevertheless, the religious will and should have their rights protected, as indicated by existing rights provisions in the GFA. There will be no latter-day equivalent of the French Revolution targeted at clerics of either Catholic or Protestant persuasion. Rather, the religious question will become the extent to which religious influence persists in primary and secondary education.

Educational questions in a United Ireland

The secularization of schools in the South is underway. There, irrespective of whether reunification occurs, the debate over the relationships between state and churches in education has already arrived. Should denominational education – Catholic, Protestant, Jewish, Hindu,

Muslim – be supported by the Irish state in publicly funded schools? Or should all children be educated together, with no role for religious clergy or lay religious, albeit with respect for differences in religion among the children's families – or their irreligion, as the case may be?

There is a related debate underway over the extent to which, if at all, the Irish state should subsidize private schools. Those in favour of ending public support for private schools are usually not arguing for the wholesale abolition of private schools, which would be unconstitutional and against existing European human rights standards. Indeed, they are usually at pains to emphasize that they are not targeting Protestant schools per se. The debate they want to raise is about social class: why should the taxpayer, including relatively poor taxpayers, subsidize private schools, mostly populated by children from better-off parents? Shouldn't such resources be spent upon improving publicly funded schools, especially in more deprived areas? These debates are unlikely to be resolved by 2030.

The two feasible models of a united Ireland have different implications for education policy. Under Model 1, a continuing Northern Ireland, three consociational principles would be likely to be maintained. Namely, schooling according to the principles of parity, proportionality, and autonomy. Each set of schools is already regarded as equal, and since 1992 has been equally funded, whether Protestant, Catholic, or integrated. Existing de facto Catholic, Protestant, and integrated schools would remain in receipt of capital and salary budgets in proportion to their pupil numbers.[12] Autonomy is currently reflected in each sector's different lines of authority, and to whom its schools seek to be attractive. In the administrative terminology of Northern Ireland, Protestant schools are 'controlled', that is, managed by a board of governors, under the relevant education authority; Catholic schools are 'maintained', with their own boards of governors under the authority of the CCMS, the Council for Catholic Maintained Schools; and integrated schools are run by their own boards of governors, under the Ministry of Education. I use *de facto* rather than *de jure* because no legal prohibition prevents Catholics attending Protestant schools or vice versa – and that happens, with varying accommodations offered by the relevant schools.

If this consociational pattern persists, it would disappoint those who want to see more integrated education and an end to voluntary segregation. If the 'others' expand politically and socially in sufficient numbers, that will generate demand for an increased supply of integrated schools. And under Model 1, if a cross-community consensus developed to end denominational education, that would be legislated for.

An arguably more contentious feature of existing Northern education is selection, especially selection based on intelligence tests to get into grammar schools – whether Catholic, Protestant, or integrated. Though the Northern Ireland-wide 11+ examination no longer exists, each grammar school applies its own selection policy, usually with variations on intelligence tests. Under Model 1 this feature, 'academic selection', may persist, at least until there is cross-community consensus to end it.

Under Model 1, Protestant-controlled and integrated schools in particular may wish to keep the existing system of preparing pupils for Northern Ireland's current educational credentials (GCSEs and A levels) or for examinations run by British examination boards. That will ease the access of their pupils to universities in England and Wales. (Scottish 'Highers' are very close to the Irish Leaving Certificate.)

By contrast, if Model 2 of a united Ireland prevails, an integrated education system will need to be developed, island-wide. It is more difficult to predict its evolution and precise contours. A key feature of the Southern system has been the elimination of selection by intelligence tests and fees. It approximates what is widely known as 'comprehensive education'. That would mean an end to formal academic selection for publicly funded schools in Northern Ireland. Under any integrated model, in a united Ireland it will be necessary to reach accommodations with private religiously oriented schools – on the basis of equality, and respect for a substantively common curriculum, accomplished through the common Junior and Leaving Certificates and such reforms as may occur to these certificates in future. Not all Ulster Protestants will be happy with secular education, though some will. But they will be unhappier if they have no choice but to send their children to schools with a palpable Catholic ethos, or a strikingly not-so-ex-Catholic ethos. That is an entirely avoidable scenario. Any considered national reunification plan will avoid it. The full divestment of Catholic-owned schools will be advanced by many in the South in the decade ahead.

Model 1 would thus see the persistence of two educational models, with the Southern one secularizing faster. Model 2 would pose greater difficulties, though its pay-off, in preparing people for participation in the modern Irish economy and its pluralist society, may be very high.

The incorporation of the European Convention for the Protection of National Minorities may play a crucial role in designing policy in this domain. The Irish state is pledged to 'recognize the rights of minorities to set up and manage their own educational establishments' and 'promote the conditions necessary for minorities to maintain and develop their culture and identity'. These pledges would be expressly met if adequate provision for schooling with a British and Protestant ethos were made available by the Government for those who want it.

27.   Language policy

Language controversies will also certainly arise in future reunification debates. In the Good Friday Agreement, the British Government pledged to take 'resolute action' to promote Irish in the North – guided by the European Charter for Regional or Minority Languages – and to facilitate education through the medium of the Irish language.[1] But at St Andrews in 2006, Tony Blair surreptitiously gave the DUP a veto over the development of language rights by devolving the decision-making on language policies. He thereby sweetened the DUP's acceptance of the new order. The DUP then persistently used that veto to block changes to language rights, contributing to Martin McGuinness's resignation and the collapse of the Northern Assembly in 2017. In the New Decade, New Approach agreement, issued by the British and Irish governments in 2020 and accepted by the five main parties in the North, a resolution was promised, including language legislation and language commissioners for Irish and Ulster Scots. That has yet to be delivered.[2] As I write, another promised deadline for putting legislation through Westminster has been missed by the current Northern Secretary of State, Brandon Lewis.

If this part of the Good Friday Agreement is not fulfilled before the referendum campaigns on reunification begin, the Irish Government will have to indicate what language polices will apply after reunification. If Model 1 prevails, then the commitments in the GFA will have to be legislated in Dáil Éireann. Unionists could then reasonably be granted a devolved veto over any further extensions of language rights, or support. It would not be fair, however, to keep the unreformed status quo of pre-1998. If Model 2 prevails, then fresh all-island language laws must be made – but, importantly, these should allow for local variation, perhaps to the level of each school.

Coercive efforts to revive the Irish language failed after independence, marring Kathleen Ni Houlihan's educational record.[3] No programme of imposing Gaeilge/Irish is now articulated by any political party, South or North, though there is also little drive to make Irish an optional subject in most schools. Sinn Féin passionately advocates public recognition and support for the Irish language in the North – responding to past injustice and representing a devoted community of Irish speakers, including those who want to expand instruction in Irish, especially at primary level. But it only demands what was pledged in the Belfast Agreement. Facts may help reduce fear. Gaelscoileanna (Irish immersion schools) account for 8 per cent of primary pupils in the South, and less in the North. They account for 4 per cent of secondary schools in the South, and just 1.5 per cent in the North. Neither Sinn Féin nor the SDLP argue for the imposition of Irish on Ulster Protestants. Making Irish optional in schools would be consistent with their preferences.

In a devolved Northern Ireland, Model 1, schools will decide whether to provide Irish as a modern language – or instruction in Irish in some subjects, as now. 'Protestant' and integrated schools will also have that option, but not that obligation.

Public signage and public spaces

In Northern Ireland there has been controversy over street signage, and the naming of institutions. This question raises some of the ire and anxiety attached to symbolic matters that we shall address in the next chapter. There is a simple power-sharing formula readily available, which should be applied irrespective of whether Model 1 or 2 is chosen as the road map for reunification. Only three languages are in contention for public signage – English, Irish, and Ulster Scots. Local demand should be decisive here, except for the naming of nationwide infrastructure (where the case for all three languages would be strong in the North, and for Irish and English in the South). Local demand could be decided by local governments. The existing arrangements in the Gaeltacht, the results of past negotiations, should be honoured – they do not affect those living in the North.

Both the Northern Assembly and Dáil Éireann have shown that the use of both English and Irish by speakers can work without severe difficulties in comprehension. The usual courtesy has been for the Irish speaker to switch into English when addressing technical complexities or substantive matters. The house rules should decide on such usage and whether translation services should be provided.

The Constitution

If Model 2, the integrated united Ireland option, is followed, then Article 8 of the Constitution will be questioned: it states that 'the Irish language as the national language is the first official language', that the English language is recognized as a second official language, and that provision may be made by law 'for the exclusive use of either of the said languages for any one or more official purposes, either throughout the State or in any part thereof'.[4]

This article was symbolic, aspirational, and outmoded when written. Though laced with Irish idioms and influences, English is the predominant language of the existing Irish nation and most of the people on the island. It is the language of all British people in Northern Ireland, and of all Ulster Protestants – though a minority are fluent in Ulster Scots, as are some Northern Irish Catholics. The special recognition of Irish is clearly appropriate on cultural, historical, and national grounds. There is also a case for a more localized recognition of Ulster Scots.

Let me suggest the following wording to amend Article 8, which would be more suited to an integrated Ireland:

8.1. The Irish language and the English language are the two official and national languages of the State.

8.2. The Irish language is a unique and living legacy of Irish national tradition and culture and the State shall take special care to nurture and encourage its voluntary use.

8.3. The Ulster Scots language is a unique and living legacy of the British tradition and culture in Ireland, and the State shall take special care to nurture its voluntary use in those Ulster counties where sufficient demand exists.

8.4. Provision may be made by law to regulate language usage in public life, in public administration and correspondence, in state-funded education, in the Gaeltacht, and in those parts of Ulster where there is sufficient demand for Ulster Scots.

Some would argue that 'where sufficient demand exists' should also be added to qualify Article 8.2, but clearly Irish is in better shape, in usage and standardization, than Ulster Scots.

The full details of language regulation would be addressed in legislation governed by these principles. It would be necessary, however, to end the supremacy of Irish text in judicial interpretation of the Constitution. Legal parity of the English and Irish languages is an entirely viable option – after all, the EU's courts function with the parity of multiple languages.

If, by contrast, Model 1 is followed and Northern Ireland persists, two separate language regimes could operate on the island, subject to mutual adjustment, though because of the existence of a common central government Article 8 would still need to be amended.

28. Citizenship, identity, and symbols

This chapter addresses three topics likely to provoke some minimal controversy: citizenship, identity, and public symbols. They need not, however, disable the project of reunifying Ireland.

Citizenship and identity

We have seen that the parties to the Good Friday Agreement affirmed that it is 'the birthright of all the people of Northern Ireland to identify themselves and be accepted as Irish or British, or both, as they may so choose, and *accordingly* confirm that their right to hold both British and Irish citizenship is accepted by both Governments and would not be affected by any future change in the status of Northern Ireland.'★

So, whether Model 1 or 2 applies in Irish reunification, Northerners will have an enduring birthright to identify as British or Irish or both, as they do now within the United Kingdom. They will also have the right to dual citizenship, and two passports, though standard international tax treaty conventions will apply, and they will have to pay their taxes where they are ordinarily resident.

So far so good. There will be no change. But do these requirements suggest that a constitutional amendment would be required to give such British citizens the right to vote on constitutional amendments and presidential elections in a united Ireland, without becoming Irish citizens?[1] I have answered that question in Chapter 12, and want to amplify that answer here.

Much depends on the meaning of 'accordingly' and of accepting someone's chosen identity in the above passage from the GFA. If

---

★ Italics are mine.

'accordingly' simply means 'therefore', does the right to identify and be accepted as Irish or British, or both, imply that the two states in their citizenship laws must recognize unqualifiedly equal rights for the three choices: British, Irish, or both? Professor Oran Doyle suggests that a rigorously impartial Irish Government would have a treaty obligation under the GFA to give these British citizens, in a united Ireland, identical rights to Irish citizens (without these British citizens having to become dual citizens).

However, that is not exactly what the relevant passages say. They say that the two governments must accept the right of people who identify as British or Irish or both to hold both citizenships, *not* that they have the right to hold only one citizenship in all circumstances and thereby be assured of identical rights in all circumstances. If 'accordingly' means 'appropriate to the circumstances' rather than 'therefore', that would mean that the recognition of the right to be identified as Irish or British or both is appropriately reflected in both governments' commitment to allow the Northern Irish to hold both citizenship entitlements. So, the two governments in 1998 were simply confirming the previous status quo. This seems to me the most plausible reading. If my reading is correct, there is no obligation for Ireland to give British citizens born in the North the right to vote on constitutional amendments or in presidential elections.

There is, of course, an overwhelming political case for giving them another incentive to add Irish citizenship to their British citizenship in a united Ireland. On top of other incentives, Irish citizenship and an Irish passport command attractive travel, educational, and work opportunities, as well as voting rights elsewhere in the European Union's other member-states – opportunities and rights now lost to British citizens. These are among the practical benefits of Irish citizenship.

Holders of diverse identities and traditions must, according to the GFA, experience rigorously impartial administration by the incumbent sovereign. Identities and traditions are not citizenships, however. Citizenship rights are not in the text of the GFA in express terms: they must be read into it as the summation of 'civil, political, social and cultural rights'.

Perhaps full respect for the equality of the named rights implies that people should be able to refuse such rights (and obligations), and therefore refuse Irish citizenship. But does it follow that there is an obligation, through some other means, to grant such persons the rights that they have refused? Freedom from discrimination certainly must apply to all citizens under the sovereign government, and there must be parity of esteem and just and equal treatment of collective identities, ethe,* and aspirations. However, the GFA does not say 'citizens', and the preceding clause, which does discuss citizenship, expressly protects only dual citizenship.

My opinion therefore is that Ireland is obliged to recognize singular, dual, or fluid *identity* (Irish, British, or both), and to facilitate British and/or Irish *identities* through its citizenship laws, but how Ireland is obliged to do that by the GFA is by allowing dual citizenship. Political equality will be adequately respected once Northerners are able to choose the Irish citizenship or Irish *and* British citizenship that entails full franchise rights. Adding a citizenship does not necessarily detract from an existing citizenship, nor from an identity. One can be an Irish citizen and identify as British. One can be a British citizen and identify as Irish. That is clearly allowed for.

The Northern Irish, whatever their identity, tradition, or ethos, will have a birthright entitlement to British citizenship, which Ireland must respect. Should that right be constitutionalized? Perhaps, if unionists want it, but British citizenship is not Ireland's to *grant*, merely to *recognize*, so a constitutional duty of recognition might be considered. British citizenship, however, must be maintained in British law, and by the continuation of the Union of Great Britain, neither of which will be in Irish control.

Reflection on the right to elect the head of state, and of eligibility to be so elected, may persuade people to accept the merits of my reading of these admittedly complex matters. Would it be reasonable to argue that someone who is not an Irish citizen should be eligible to stand for the presidency of Ireland? Must Ireland, because of the GFA, accept a

* The plural of 'ethos'.

presidential candidate who only identifies as British, and is only a British citizen, albeit born in the North? If these rhetorical questions do not persuade, a reciprocal test may do the business. Is the continuing existence of the Protestant monarchy of Great Britain and Northern Ireland a violation of the UK's obligation to govern Catholic people, especially in Northern Ireland, with rigorous impartiality under the GFA? Did the UK Government effectively agree to that idea in international law in 1998? That would be news to the lawyers of Her Majesty's Government.

Now consider the Irish Constitution: Article 16.1.1° and Article 18.2 restrict eligibility for election to Dáil Éireann and to Seanad Éireann to Irish citizens. In making the GFA, the Government of Ireland did not agree to open membership of the Oireachtas to non-citizens. After reunification, existing law would ensure that all birthright Northern British Protestants in Ireland could vote in all elections, but to vote on constitutional amendments or for the President, and to run for the presidency or the legislature, they would need to be Irish citizens. That is reasonable.

I am suggesting that no constitutional amendments are absolutely required before or after reunification regarding citizenship and rigorous impartiality. Ireland already respects dual citizenship. A duty of constitutional recognition to welcome British and unionist people into a united Ireland would be a good idea. But people in the North with British citizenship, who wish to vote in future referendums on constitutional change in Ireland, or to stand for office in the chambers of Ireland's National Parliament or vote in elections for the President, should accept, *in addition*, the Irish citizenship to which they will be automatically entitled.[2]

These matters need to be resolved. It would be bizarre to have 900,000 or so people in a reunified Ireland without the right to vote for the President or on future constitutional amendments – which may be numerous following reunification – albeit through their own choices. My view is that, in its reunification bill, the Irish Government should legislate to make them Irish citizens while recognizing their British identity and right to dual citizenship.

Names

A United Ireland would be a nation-state with binational accommodations. An academic phrase, from this academic. What might it mean for names, symbols, flags, the anthem, and emblems?

The names of political institutions are culturally important, North and South. They need not be officiously changed. In the Constitution the name of the state and the island is 'Ireland'. That should remain the state's English name if the island is politically unified, not the 'Republic of Ireland'. To emphasize the victory of the republican over the monarchical form would be gratuitous. It is easier for Ulster Protestants and British people in the island to identify with Ireland, as they do with its rugby team, than with the Republic of Ireland.

Every official political institution in the South has both an English and an Irish name – though the Constitution specifies Irish names in English for key offices. Both English and Irish names should be used in public media and be permissible in our National Parliament – the English title of the Oireachtas. It should be just as acceptable to refer to Prime Minister Martin as to Taoiseach Martin. In the North, Ulster Scots versions of these titles should be equally recognized.

Renaming has occurred in many post-colonial countries. Ireland was less thoroughgoing than some. To name but a few organizations, the Royal Irish Academy, the Dublin Horse Show hosted by the Royal Dublin Society, the Royal Irish Yacht Club, and the Royal Dublin Golf Club retain their titles. By contrast, Collins Barracks, O'Connell Street, Parnell Square, Pearse Street, and Connolly Station in Dublin, Wolfe Tone Bridge in Galway, Markiewicz Park in Sligo, and De Valera Street in Youghal honour Ireland's democratic and revolutionary heroes and heroines. A glut of renaming should be avoided upon reunification. It would be foolishly provocative to attempt to rename Belfast's Royal Avenue as Bobby Sands Avenue, or Queen's University as McGuinness University, or to insist that Londonderry never be used or be applied solely to the county. Where there are two existing names, both should be kept and respected. Craigavon has not successfully merged Lurgan and

Portadown, but its name should be left alone unless its local council agrees a name change with cross-community consent. Streets which reflect the British imperial heritage should have their names left alone – whether or not the Irish majority at the time celebrated the pertinent battles. Churchill Street in the New Lodge should stay, as should the Royal Victoria Hospital. As far as I can tell, there is no Lloyd George Street in Belfast. Dual names or three names for new streets and public places should be decided at local government level and without rancour. Scrubbing heritages is not typically useful in political accommodation.

Symbolic public holidays

All symbols can be politicized, but they can also be depoliticized, though usually that happens more slowly. St Patrick's Day, 17 March, is Ireland's globally known national holiday. St Patrick is recognized by both the Church of Ireland and the Catholic church. The Friendly Sons and Daughters of St Patrick, as they are now called in the United States, have avoided sectarian identification since before the American revolution. They set a good example. It might just be possible, eventually, to make 17 March 'Irish Unity Day'. Personally, I would prefer 10 April, the day the Belfast/Good Friday Agreement was finalized. But by far the best day would be the day on which the referendum processes on Irish reunification are completed – or, in the alternative, the day the new constitution of a united Ireland is ratified. No unity can be expected around Orangemen's Day on 12 July in the North, or in commemorating the Easter Rising. But both Easter Monday and 12 July should be public holidays, whether or not Northern Ireland persists in a united Ireland. And they should be public holidays throughout Ireland.

Flagging the flag questions

The flag of the Irish state is republican, a tricolour. It is intended to be inclusive, and integrative. The white in the middle symbolizes peace between the green and the orange. Thomas Francis Meagher, leader of the Young Irelanders, designed it.[3] It would be sad for many of us to see it replaced, but sadness would slowly shrivel if a replacement flag could be agreed. Whatever the Orange Order's views on the incorporation of their colour into the Irish flag, many socialist, liberal, and conservative unionists, and most among the 'others', insist that the orange in the Republic's flag does not represent them. But then, what would?

Some historic flags of Ireland are available in the colour plate section. Flags with crowns will not be welcome to any Irish nationalist, North or South, nor will any variant on the Union Jack. Until the Act of Union, the Kingdom of Ireland had a flag with a royal-blue field and a golden harp. The bare-breasted maiden who fronts the harp on the flag of the Kingdom of Ireland is unlikely to win universal approval. The harp, however, is a genuine and unobjectionable Irish symbol, though a little upper-class – maybe. So, should it be accompanied by a flute, a bodhrán, and a fourth instrument – a Lambeg drum? Ireland's presidential standard has a blue field embossed with a simple gold harp, echoing the old Kingdom of Ireland. Making that the national flag would be a sacrifice most Presidents would accept for reunification.

Would a plain gold harp on a green background win greater support? That, however, would be the flag of the seventeenth-century Catholic Confederacy, though it is also the flag of the Irish Naval Service. The red saltire of Saint Patrick, against a white field, extracted back from the Union Jack, would be unacceptable to many – too religious, and too British.

The historic flag of the four provinces would suit an Irish federation constructed around these entities.

This cursory review suggests that there is no easy or obvious replacement for the tricolour. Perhaps a new design could be commissioned after reunification, through a competition among the artists of Ireland? Two polls in late 2021 suggested that little flexibility exists on the question of a new flag in the South. But context matters: these polls were not taken amid serious planning for reunification or with imminent referendums afoot, or with a freshly designed new flag.[4]

The anthem

The Irish national anthem is rousing, and the music moving – at least to my ears. Perhaps we could keep the music, please? It is no accident that, on official occasions – including sporting events – the song is sung in Irish, as 'Amhrán na bhFiann', and not its original title, 'A Soldier's Song'. For those who need reminding, here are the lyrics in English. The second and third verses are not typically sung when the anthem is presented:

> Soldiers are we, whose lives are pledged to Ireland,
> Some have come from a land beyond the wave,
> Sworn to be free, no more our ancient sireland
> Shall shelter the despot or the slave;
> Tonight we man the bearna baoil
> In Erin's cause, come woe or weal
> 'Mid cannons' roar and rifles' peal,
> We'll chant a soldier's song.
> . . .
> In valley green, on towering crag,
> Our fathers fought before us,
> And conquered 'neath the same old flag
> That's proudly floating o'er us;
> We're children of a fighting race,
> That never yet has known disgrace,
> And as we march, the foe to face,
> We'll chant a soldier's song.
> . . .
> Sons of the Gael! Men of the Pale!
> The long watched day is breaking,
> The serried ranks of Inisfail
> Shall set the Tyrant quaking;
> Our campfires now are burning low,
> See in the east a silv'ry glow,
> Out yonder waits the Saxon foe,
> So chant a soldier's song.

There are some myths here. 'The same old flag'? We have had a few. And there's certainly poetry. 'Inisfail' is a beautiful synonym for Ireland, and I appreciate 'ancient sireland' rhyming with 'Ireland'. Even if 'sireland' is masculine, it makes a change from calling Ireland a motherland, as in the dirge-like 'Ireland, Mother Ireland'. There's some inclusivity in the lyrics too. The diaspora is recalled – those from 'beyond the wave'. The Gaels unite with the 'men of the Pale' (the old English). It's the song our revolutionaries sang. Singing it, we swear to be free and shelter no despot and reject slavery – good democratic and republican values. But we also sing against 'the Saxon foe', which is hardly diplomatic. The Gaels and the Palemen were Catholics, and it's clear the soldiers doing the singing are all men. The United Irishmen don't figure – neither Protestants nor Dissenters. Do we want to insist that we remain the 'children of a fighting race'? The 'fighting Irish' is an excellent brand for the University of Notre Dame American football team, but is that how we wish to represent ourselves abroad? Even in the lyrics of Phil Coulter's 'Ireland's Call', while we are standing 'shoulder to shoulder' we're clearly fighters – albeit less lethal, as rugby warriors. Lastly, there's that easily misunderstood beginning to the anthem's lyrics. The Irish version begins with 'Sinne Fianna Fáil'. The untutored ear hears a partisan celebration of Sinn Féin and Fianna Fáil. These lyrics shouldn't be cancelled, they're part of our history, but perhaps others could be composed to go with the music.

Changing the national anthem will not be easy, but the possibilities should be discussed. Let me, however, put in a pre-emptive bitter word against 'Ireland, Mother Ireland'. How many of us could reach the high notes demanded for closing with 'Ever shall we hold you / Dearest – best of all'? A national anthem has to be 'singable' by those who cannot sing; it should not resemble the American 'Star-Spangled Banner'. I have detected little enthusiasm for 'Ireland's Call' as a replacement anthem. Two polls in late 2021 suggested that little flexibility exists among Southerners on the question of a new anthem in the South. I repeat, however, that context matters. These polls were not taken amid serious planning for reunification or with imminent referendums afoot, or with any alternative lyrics or song on offer, or with a process to determine new versions.[5]

The political management of symbolic questions

It might seem easier to settle these potentially heated symbolic questions if a devolved Northern Ireland persisted in a united Ireland, Model 1. Each place would keep its symbols, songs, and monuments. However, the whole country would still have to have a national flag, and because the North remains internally polarized over these questions, a policy of accommodation is necessary. In 2016, the Commission on Flags, Identity, Culture and Tradition (FICT) was formed, with representatives of all five main parties in the Northern Ireland Assembly. They were to make recommendations on these contested subjects. The FICT report was belatedly presented to the Executive in July 2020, with forty-five recommendations.[6] For a while it seemed lost in the Executive Office, blocked by the DUP. The Commission had tough questions to address. As Paula Bradshaw of the Alliance Party argues, there is no current lawful authority for the display of flags and emblems on public property, or for the constructing of memorials. Flags promoting paramilitarism are illegal under the Terrorism Act 2000, but the police do not systematically enforce the act. The display of flags, emblems, and memorials often ignores the effects on businesses, tourism, and relations within neighbourhoods.[7] Flags have been knowingly raised to promote the unmixing of mixed neighbourhoods.

Flag, anthem, and emblem disputes can be more temperate in a reunified Ireland provided an accommodationist ethos is adopted. If FICT had produced a workable consensus, that could have guided our future. But the report's publication on 1 December 2021 proved a disappointment.[8] Numerous 'remaining challenges' were diplomatically identified on all the key questions. The Commission could not deliver the DUP, or the DUP could not deliver loyalists.

In the absence of consensus, key power-sharing principles should apply in a reunified Ireland. Parity, especially parity of esteem, is difficult, but each national flag needs to be respected – both the republican tricolour and the Union Jack (or the Ulster Banner, as shown in the colour plate section). Neither the Union Jack nor the Ulster Banner can be the flag of a united Ireland, but one of them should be permitted to fly beside every public building in the North – so long as the tricolour flies beside it. Two flags or none should be the public policy, especially in Model 1. Proportionality should be applied in both senses of the concept. Flags should be erected on public occasions on governmental buildings, but not all the time. Those who tiresomely insist on flying flags constantly may curb their enthusiasm if both flags must fly together. A little less flag-waving would, of course, be helpful, and aid a stable accommodation, but that can't be guaranteed. As John Hume's father told him, 'You can't eat a flag, son.' Autonomy should also matter. Private bodies – football clubs, for example – will have their own flags. They should, however, respect both national flags, or none. Outlawed militia should have no right to display their flags or emblems.

The Parades Commission established by Mo Mowlam continues to operate, with surprising success.[9] Had the management of parades been part of the interparty negotiations in 1997–98, there might not have been a Good Friday Agreement. The Parades Commission should stay, under either Model 1 or Model 2. The fine line between peaceful parading in public places and the invitation to riot needs to be regulated, with the cooperation of the affected parties, at local level. Unlike the Victorians, a reunified Ireland should not ban the Loyal Orders. Those of us who are Irish might also bear in mind the advice given in 2021 by Patrick Kielty, the comedian whose father was murdered by the UDA. He remarked, 'It's way easier to sing a rebel song about a united Ireland than to decide not to sing one in order maybe to have one.'[10] The remit of the Parades Commission might be extended to the public display of flags and emblems, and the construction of monuments.

Managing citizenship, identity, and symbols within a reunified Ireland will not be easy, but a decided improvement on the status quo is possible.

Conclusion: Closing the case

Having shown that a united Ireland may materialize is not the same as saying it should happen. As David Hume would have said, 'Is does not prove ought.' *Ought*, however, implies *can*. A united Ireland can happen. Ought it?

A united Ireland should not happen because Sinn Féin advocates it. True, most of Sinn Féin's voters, North and South, want reunification to happen, and their voters deserve the same respect as every other party's voters in both jurisdictions. In the first week of April 2022, when the final manuscript of this book was completed, averaging all polls suggested Sinn Féin was the leading party in the South with a steady level of intended support in first-preference votes of 33 per cent. A Lucid Talk poll in late March 2022 had Sinn Féin as the lead party in the North at 26 per cent. Very impressive numbers, by historic standards, but even if they were realized or exceeded in subsequent elections, they will leave the party well short of a 50 per cent plus one majority in both jurisdictions. Getting to that threshold before 2030 is unlikely.

A united Ireland, to succeed, must therefore be a multi-party project. It cannot be just that of a party deeply distrusted in both quarters, and too prone to premature calls for a referendum before the moment is ripe. If a united Ireland happens it will be helped to referendum victory by Sinn Féin voters, but they will not be pivotal. In the South, the decisive votes will be cast by those who currently support Fianna Fáil or Fine Gael, or other political parties, currently nearly two-thirds of the electorate. In the North, the decisive votes will be cast by SDLP and Alliance voters, and the neither/nors, those who 'don't know' right now, and by people who have ceased to be unionists.

A united Ireland should occur if it is voted for, North and South, by majorities in both jurisdictions. That is the democratic argument, and the constitutional status quo. Northern Ireland should not be part of the UK because a local minority prefers that status. And a united

Ireland should not occur without the majority consent of the citizens of the Republic of Ireland – because the changes required, after a partition of one hundred years and more, are momentous. Jointly, of course, these two majorities would be a majority of those who vote across the entire Ireland. The best and most powerful argument for a united Ireland will be that it reflects the will of the people of Ireland, North and South respectively. Suggestions that a qualified majority or a parallel majority should be required in the North were rejected here, because they would unjustly allow a minority to prevail after a century of pledges that Northern Ireland's union with Great Britain rests solely on the consent of a local majority in the six counties, not on British strategic interests.

Should a narrow majority prevail in either jurisdiction? Yes, because the alternative is that a narrow *minority* should prevail. The possibility of a narrow majority in either jurisdiction is an argument for adequate preparation to begin now – to inform the public debates fully, as and when the referendums are called. Leavers won in the UK in 2016 with 52 per cent of the vote, but there are reasonable doubts about whether that referendum was adequately prepared, informed, or conducted. The lesson here is not to outlaw referendums. After all, the legitimacy of the Constitution of Ireland and of the Belfast Agreement rests on past referendums. The lesson is to have adequately prepared, informed, and well-conducted referendums, according to the norms laid out in this book.

Should there be two referendums in the North before the transfer of sovereignty takes place – one to vote on the principle, the second to vote on the new arrangements? No, because the vote on principle should be decisive. Any second vote on new arrangements should take place within a united Ireland. That procedure properly incentivizes voters to turn out in the North, the two sovereign governments to prepare the transfer of sovereignty, and also obligates the Government of Ireland to prepare in advance the necessary new arrangements which should be decided according to the model or the process solemnly offered, in full detail, in published and video form in the two referendums.

All other arguments for a united Ireland are secondary to the democratic argument just advanced – even though many secondary arguments will matter in the referendums and may decide its outcome. From the perspective of traditional Irish nationalism, this democratic argument takes for granted an historic concession. Traditional nationalists and republicans argue that there was an all-island majority for sovereignty and against partition in 1920 – and that majority has persisted. They are factually correct. Many of them believe that an all-island referendum, without separate consent processes for North and South, would be more just. That is not agreed. The Good Friday Agreement displaced that argument. Since 1998, agreed procedures effectively give both the North and the South a veto over reunification – though they do not give a veto to unionists or nationalists, or Protestants or Catholics, over Northern Ireland's sovereign status. That veto is granted rather to majorities in both jurisdictions.

The majority consent principle on the change of sovereign status is appropriate, because it flows from previously negotiated and ratified agreements, and because it is consistent with international norms. They should be respected. That does not mean, however, that a united Ireland should be a majoritarian dictatorship. The required accommodations and securities, or at least some of those which should be considered, have been identified in this book. Credible commitments to these accommodations may ease unionists' and loyalists' possible loss in the future Northern referendum. Such accommodations, and variations on them, should be pursued because they are right and prudent. It is right to protect human rights and minority rights – including the rights of national, religious, and linguistic minorities. It is right to accommodate minority identifications – symbolically and substantively – as well as dual citizenship rights. It is appropriate to consider power-sharing carefully given past antagonisms – preserving the arrangements in the North, perhaps, or instead considering new ones in an integrated Ireland. It is prudent to avoid provoking a loyalist insurrection, and equally prudent to be prepared to defeat one.

There are important secondary arguments in favour of a united Ireland. It would return Northern Ireland to the European Union, with its own MEPs who can vote on EU law, along with Irish ministers. The Protocol could then be replaced, by agreement, with one border between the UK and the EU, running along the North Channel and the Irish Sea. The island would benefit from being one regulatory and customs unit within the EU, and from being a bigger and slightly more powerful actor within EU institutions. It may benefit from some assistance to facilitate infrastructural improvements to sharpen connectivity, especially in the west of Ulster and the island. Though there may be some short-term transitional costs from reunification, both parts of Ireland will benefit from a larger national market, more closely integrated into the European single market and attractive to US foreign investment – all as part of the most dynamic and largely English-speaking economic unit in the western EU. The North will benefit most, but the South would make net gains too if the economic modelling described here is broadly correct. A united Ireland may also be judged a comparatively better democracy than its immediate neighbour. The Republic is a more modernized, liberalized, secularized, law-abiding, tolerant, and pluralist polity than that governed by the Westminster Parliament. Its Constitution constrains majority rule, and its proportional representation system ensures that governments are formed with genuine majorities. Northern Ireland will benefit politically from integrating with the Republic. It will improve its democratic life, and all its citizens will have more influence in an all-island polity than they do within the UK; and if counsel given here is heard, some of the best Northern practices will follow them.

May 2022 and the decade ahead

The May 2022 elections to the Northern Ireland Assembly were underway when this book was finalized. When these close, a widespread display of mutual goodwill and warm cooperation is not to be anticipated. Sinn Féin seems set to top the poll in numbers of first-preference votes and seats, and will thereby earn the right to nominate the First Minister. Unionists, split between three parties, may win a smaller proportion of seats than their total first-preference votes – compared to nationalists, who are split between two parties. Yet a nationalist plurality in seats – or votes – is not a majority, and neither may happen, especially if Alliance comes in third behind Sinn Féin and the DUP, the order suggested by recent polls. A poor performance for the SDLP would have the same effect. Even if there is a nationalist plurality in seats, a call from Sinn Féin to have a referendum in 2022–23 would be a mistake – unless it had the support of Alliance and the SDLP and a sustained majority of voters in opinion polls, and unless the South was properly prepared.

A change in the rules of government formation in the North occurred before the elections. If a new Executive cannot be formed immediately after, then six months may elapse in which previous ministers may stay on as caretakers. When this book is published, the DUP may be trying to block the installation of a Sinn Féin First Minister or refusing to form an Executive unless the Protocol is scrapped – or both. There are suggestions, however, that the DUP and the TUV might prevent the Assembly from agreeing speakers or approving a caretaker Executive. In turn that might lead to fresh elections in or after September 2022, or a British-Irish effort to produce a new local formula, or even to the restoration of direct rule.

All scenarios in which the Northern Assembly and Executive fail – especially if the DUP is held culpable for that – would make Model 1, as outlined in this book, far less likely to become the chosen form of a united Ireland. The DUP, the party that was once more in favour of devolution than its UUP rival, may yet bring about the death of devolution in another self-defeating move.

The rest of the decade will contain unknown surprises. The decade began with the global pandemic of 2020–22 (a hopeful dating) and the Russian invasion of Ukraine in February 2022. The final data on the pandemic, I have suggested, will show that Ireland managed it better than Great Britain, and the Republic better than the North – measured in 'excess deaths'. Not flawlessly, but better. That assessment will not settle whether a united Ireland should be accompanied with socialized medicine throughout the island, but the data on this subject may become part of the repertoire of arguments in favour of all-island political coordination.

The negative economic costs of the Russian war against Ukraine, however long it lasts, affect both parts of Ireland. The longer-term political impact may well be a sustained revision of Ireland's military neutrality, especially if Finland and Sweden, both familiar with the Russian navy, do the same. Building better security capacity is part of Ireland's obligations towards its European economic, diplomatic, and democratic allies – and ourselves. Neither the pandemic nor the Russian war in Ukraine, however, will determine the outcome of reunification referendums held between 2028 and 2032.

Thales of Miletus, an ancient Greek, claimed that 'the past is certain, the future obscure'. In fact, the past is not certain; it is constantly debated, sometimes appropriately. Good history is what the evidence obliges us to believe, and evidence and its interpretation may change. What is certain is that we cannot go back into the past to alter what really happened – though bad-faith efforts to rewrite history will continue, and cannot be stopped. The future is not entirely obscure. We could not live our lives without the hypothesis that tomorrow will resemble today. Yes, big and small change will happen, of which we have no foreknowledge, but a united Ireland is not in that category. Would it were done, then best it were done well. Not quickly, nor violently, but peacefully, through ballot papers – and after sustained reflection, debate, and mature preparation.

Acknowledgements

I would like to thank Michael McLoughlin of Penguin Random House Ireland for commissioning this book after hearing me on a podcast hosted by Hugh Linehan of the *Irish Times*. Talking often has unexpected consequences. Patricia Deevy of Penguin Sandycove and Storyline's Brian Langan were vital developmental editors of the manuscript. Thanks too to Gemma Wain for highly supportive copy-editing and fact-checking. Isabelle Hanrahan of Penguin Sandycove facilitated the transfer of graphics, figures, and maps and the colour plate section.

Special appreciation is owed to the US-Ireland Fulbright Commission, notably Sonya McGuinness and her colleagues in Dublin. A Fulbright fellowship to the National University of Ireland-Galway in the academic year 2021–22 gave me the time to compose this book. Distinct acknowledgement is owed to John Garry of Queen's University Belfast with whom I have elaborated Models 1 and 2 over several years, including testing reactions to them in mini-deliberative forums. At the University of Pennsylvania I owe deep appreciation to the former chair of my department, Nicholas Sambanis, and to his successor Michael Jones-Correa for the continuation of his kindness, as well as to Deans Steve Fluharty and Emily Hannum. Leonard Lauder's endowment of my chair enabled me to travel and conduct meetings and interviews, without which this book would be very different.

My hosts and friends in Galway were Dan and Sue Carey, Breandán and Katharine MacSuibhne, Niall and Carol Ann Ó Dochartaigh, and Pól and Geraldine Ó Dochartaigh. Despite the constraints of the pandemic they were truly hospitable critics – in the best sense of that noun. Our friends Paul and Carol McAlister and Zandra and Paddy McLoughlin in Cushendall, and Pat and Maria Conway of Belfast and Glynsk, kept us grounded and informed. Our landladies in Cushendall and Galway, Helen McGowan and Liz O'Byrne Mannion respectively, catered for all our needs, and enabled Lori Salem, my wife – as well as me – to have perfect all-weather writing conditions. My personal thanks to the authorities at Temple University for allowing Lori to work online in Ireland.

Breandán, Dan, Niall, and Pól kindly gave me detailed readings. In alphabetical order of surname, the following friends also scrutinized the entire manuscript: Nicholas Canny, John Coakley, Oran Doyle, David Edgerton, Brian Feeney, John Garry, Steven Greer, John A. Hall, Abby Innes, Tom Lyne, Paul Magill, Christopher McCrudden, John McGarry, Jack Nagel, Oliver O'Connor, Khaled Salih, and Etain Tannam.

Technical questions were answered by my friend Professor Bernie Grofman of the University of California, Irvine and Professor Nic Tideman of Virginia Tech. Very useful research assistance at different junctures was provided by Jan Nowak, then at the University of Pennsylvania, and by Samantha Twietmeyer of Queen's University Canada. Through correspondence and their publications, Micha Germann of Bath University and Matt Qvortrup of Coventry University improved my knowledge of referendums in world history. For specific help on historical and current matters through correspondence, or for recent or past in-person conversation, I would like to thank Ambassadors Barbara Jones, Rory Montgomery, and Sean Ó hUiginn, as well as Martin Mansergh, Joanna Murphy, Rita O'Hare, and Quentin Thomas. Memorable conversations with President Michael D. Higgins, Laurence Marley, Máirín Ní Dhonnchadha, and Gearóid Ó Tuathaigh, all of Galway parish, were spurs to completion. As was a rewarding conference in Derry, partly spent at the Guildhall, where along with others I was courteously hosted by Graham Warke, the DUP mayor of Derry City and Strabane District Council.

I had begun what became this book independently but was aided in clarifying my thoughts by my membership of the Working Group on Unification Referendums on the Island of Ireland. I would like to thank its principal organizers, Alan Renwick and his secretariat Conor Kelly and Charlotte Kincaid, as well as those in the group whom I have not already named above – that is, Paul Gillespie, Cathy Gormley-Heenan, Katy Hayward, Robert Hazell, David Kenny, and Alan Whysall. We did not always agree, and our joint work was the better for that. Arthur Aughey is also owed a shout-out.

Some fellow participants in the ARINS project, a joint initiative of the Royal Irish Academy and the University of Notre-Dame, have been exceptionally helpful for many years. Among those not already named are Shelley Deane, Pauric Dempsey, John Doyle, Jennifer Todd, Catherine Wilsden, and especially Patrick Griffin, the specialist in 'the people with no name', allegedly. Lastly, profound thanks are owed to my daughters, and to my siblings and their respective families.

Some materials here were initially presented during 2021–22 as lectures at the National University of Ireland Galway, hosted by Niall Ó Dochartaigh, and at its Moore Institute, run by Dan Carey; at IBIS at University College Dublin, hosted by Dawn Walsh and Paul Gillespie; at Princeton University, hosted by Paul Muldoon and Fintan O'Toole; at the University of Notre Dame, hosted by Lisa Caulfield; and at Villanova University, hosted by Cera Murtagh. Though these were often virtual presentations, all lines of questioning proved helpful.

Any named here should be absolved of any responsibility for remaining errors of fact or judgement. They are, however, individually and collectively guilty of improving my health and happiness.

Books and articles cited

[The Belfast or Good Friday Agreement] (1998), 'The Agreement: Agreement Reached in the Multi-Party Negotiations', 30.

Adams, T. W. (1966), 'The First Republic of Cyprus: A Review of an Unworkable Constitution', *Western Political Quarterly*, 19: 475.

Akenson, Donald H. (1975), *A Mirror to Kathleen's Face: Education in Independent Ireland, 1922–1960* (Montreal: McGill-Queen's University Press).

Altman, David, T. Donovan, R. Hill, N. Kersting, C. Morris, and Matt Qvortrup (2014), 'Appendix A: Referendums Around the World', in Matt Qvortrup (ed.), *Referendums Around the World: The Continued Growth of Direct Democracy* (Basingstoke: Palgrave Macmillan), 252–99.

Amaral, Joana (2018), 'Do Peace Negotiations Shape Settlement Referendums? The Annan Plan and Good Friday Agreement Experiences Compared', *Cooperation and Conflict*, 53: 356–74.

———(2019), *Making Peace with Referendums* (Syracuse, NY: Syracuse University Press).

Anthony, Gordon (2022), 'The Protocol in Northern Ireland Law', in Christopher McCrudden (ed.), *The Law and Practice of the Northern Ireland–Ireland Protocol* (Cambridge: Cambridge University Press), 118–28.

Aristotle (1996), *The Politics and The Constitution of Athens* (Cambridge: Cambridge University Press).

Armitage, David (2007), *The Declaration of Independence: A Global History* (Cambridge, MA: Harvard University Press).

Aughey, Arthur (1996), 'Obstacles to Reconciliation in the South', in Forum for Peace and Reconciliation (ed.), *Building Trust in Ireland: Studies Commissioned by the Forum for Peace and Reconciliation* (Belfast: Blackstaff Press), 3–51.

Bahcheli, Tozun (2000), 'Searching for a Cyprus Settlement: Considering Options for Creating a Federation, a Confederation, or Two Independent States', *Publius*, 30: 203–16.

Balinski, Michel L., and H. Peyton Young (1982), *Fair Representation: Meeting the Ideal of One Man, One Vote* (New Haven, CT: Yale University Press).

Barnier, Michel (2021), *My Secret Brexit Diary* (Cambridge: Polity Press).

Barrett, Alan (2021), 'Debating the Cost of Irish Reunification: A Response to "Why the Subvention Does Not Matter" by John Doyle', *Irish Studies in International Affairs*, 32: 335–37.

Bartlett, Robert (2000), *England Under the Norman and Angevin Kings, 1075–1225* (Oxford: Clarendon Press).

Bergin, Adele, and Seamus McGuinness (2021a), 'Quality of Life: A Reply to John FitzGerald', *Irish Studies in International Affairs*, 32: 164–65.

———(2021b), 'Who is Better Off? Measuring Cross-border Differences in Living Standards, Opportunities and Quality of Life on the Island of Ireland', *Irish Studies in International Affairs*, 32: 143–60.

Besley, Timothy, and Hannes Mueller (2012), 'Estimating the Peace Dividend: The Impact of Violence on House Price in Northern Ireland', *American Economic Review*, 102: 810–33.

Blair, Tony (2011), *A Journey: My Political Life* (New York: Vintage).

Bose, Sumantra (2003), *Kashmir: Roots of Conflict, Paths to Peace* (Cambridge, MA: Harvard University Press).

Bradford, Roy (1981), *The Last Ditch* (Belfast: Blackstaff Press).

Brady, Conor (1974), *Guardians of the Peace* (Dublin: Gill & Macmillan).

———(2014), *The Guarding of Ireland: The Garda Síochána & the Irish State 1960–2014* (Dublin: Gill & Macmillan).

Brams, Steven, and Todd Kaplan (2004), 'Dividing the Indivisible: Procedures for Allocating Cabinet Ministries to Political Parties in a Parliamentary System', *Journal of Theoretical Politics*, 16: 143–73.

Brams, Steven J., and Alan D. Taylor (1996), *Fair Division: From Cake-Cutting to Dispute Resolution* (Cambridge: Cambridge University Press).

Brams, Steven J., and Daniel L. King (2005), 'Efficient Fair Division: Help the Worst Off or Avoid Envy?', *Rationality and Society*, 17: 387–421.

Brown, Malcolm (1973), *Sir Samuel Ferguson* (Lewisburg, Bucknell University Press).

Bulmer, Elliot (2021), 'Opposition and Legislative Minorities: Constitutional Roles, Rights and Recognition' (Sweden: IDEA).

Bunreacht na hÉireann (1937), *Constitution of Ireland, as amended* (Dublin: Office of the Attorney General).

Burke, Sara, Sarah Barry, Rikke Siersbaek, Bridget Johnston, Meabh Ní Fhallúin, and Steve Thomas (2018), 'Sláintecare – A Ten-year Plan to Achieve Universal Healthcare in Ireland', *Health Policy*, 122: 1278–82.

Cahillane, Laura (2016), *Drafting the Irish Free State Constitution* (Manchester: Manchester University Press).

Callaghan, James (1981), 'Speech in the House of Commons during the Northern Ireland (Emergency Provisions), 2 July', cols. 1046–53 (Westminster: Hansard).

Campbell, John L., and John A. Hall (2017), *The Paradox of Vulnerability: States, Nationalism & the Financial Crisis* (Princeton, NJ: Princeton University Press).

Cassese, Antonio (1995), *The Self-Determination of Peoples: A Legal Reappraisal* (Cambridge: A Grotius Publication, Cambridge University Press).

Chambers, Anne (2014), *TK Whitaker: Portrait of a Patriot* (Dublin: Transworld Ireland).

Charlemagne (2013), 'The New Hanseatic League', *The Economist*, 30 November, section 'Europe'.

Coakley, John (2016), 'British Irish Institutional Structures: Towards a New Relationship', in John Coakley and Jennifer Todd (eds.), *Breaking Patterns of Conflict: Britain, Ireland and the Northern Ireland Question* (London: Routledge), 76–97.

Coakley, John, and Jennifer Todd (2020), *Negotiating a Settlement in Northern Ireland, 1969–2019* (Oxford: Oxford University Press).

Cochrane, Feargal (2013), *Northern Ireland: The Reluctant Peace* (New Haven, CT: Yale University Press).

Collins, Liam (2017), 'Brendan Smyth's Evil Deeds Can Never Be Forgotten', *Irish Independent*, 23 July.

Conley, Richard S. (2013), 'The Consociational Model and Question Time in the Northern Ireland Assembly: Policy Issues, Procedural Reforms and Executive Accountability 2007–2011', *Irish Political Studies*, 28: 78–98.

Connelly, Tony (2017), 'The Brexit Veto: How and Why Ireland Raised the Stakes', RTE.ie.

'Consolidated Version of the Treaty on European Union' (2012), Official Journal of the European Union [English edition].

Cornford, Francis Macdonald (1993) [1908], *Microcosmographia Academica* (Cambridge: MainSail Press).

Council of Europe (1994), 'Framework Convention for the Protection of National Minorities and Explanatory Note' (Strasbourg: February 1995).

Coyle, Diane (2015), *GDP: A Brief But Affectionate History* (Princeton, NJ: Princeton University Press).

Crick, Bernard (1982), 'The Sovereignty of Parliament and the Irish Question', in Desmond Rea (ed.), *Political Co-operation in Divided Societies: A Series of Papers Relevant to the Conflict in Northern Ireland* (Dublin: Gill & Macmillan), 229–54.

Cronin, Sean (1985), 'The Making of NATO and the Partition of Ireland', *Eire-Ireland*, 20: 6–18.

Darby, John (1986), *Intimidation and the Control of Conflict in Northern Ireland* (Dublin: Gill & Macmillan).

Darby, John, and Geoffrey Morris (1974), 'Intimidation in Housing' (Belfast: Northern Ireland Community Relations Commission).

Davies, Rees R. (1990), *Dominion and Conquest: The Experience of Ireland, Scotland and Wales, 1100–1300* (Cambridge: Cambridge University Press).

Davis, Richard P. (1974), *Arthur Griffith and Non-Violent Sinn Féin* (Dublin: Anvil Books).

Dent, Martin (1988), 'The Feasibility of Shared Sovereignty (and Shared Authority)', in Charles Townshend (ed.), *Consensus in Ireland: Approaches and Recessions* (Oxford: Oxford University Press), 128–56.

Dicey, Albert Venn (1915), *Introduction to the Study of the Law of the Constitution* (London: Macmillan).

Dickson, Brice (1996), 'A Unionist Legal Perspective on Obstacles in the South to Better Relations with the North', in *Building Trust in Ireland: Studies Commissioned by the Forum for Peace and Reconciliation* (Belfast: Blackstaff Press), 53–84.

———(2021), 'Human Rights in a United Ireland' (Dublin: Royal Irish Academy-ARINS).

Donoughue, Bernard (1987), *Prime Minister: The Conduct of Policy under Harold Wilson and James Callaghan* (London: Jonathan Cape).

Doyle, John (2021a), 'Why the "Subvention" Does Not Matter: Northern Ireland and the All-Ireland Economy', *Irish Studies in International Affairs*, 32: 314–34.

Doyle, Michael W., and Nicholas Sambanis (2006), *Making War and Building Peace: United Nations Peace Operations* (Princeton, NJ: Princeton University Press).

Doyle, Oran (2018), *The Constitution of Ireland: A Contextual Analysis* (Oxford: Hart).

Doyle, Tim (2021b), *Changing of the Guard: Jack Marrinan's Battle to Modernise An Garda Síochána* (Dublin: Currachbooks).

Egan, Timothy (2016), *The Immortal Irishman: The Irish Revolutionary Who Became an American Hero* (Boston, MA: Houghton Mifflin Harcourt).

Elster, Jon (1983), *Sour Grapes: Studies in the Subversion of Rationality* (Cambridge: Cambridge University Press).

European Commission for Democracy Through Law (Venice Commission) (2018) [2007], 'Code of Practice on Referendums adopted by the Council for Democratic Elections at its 19th meeting (Venice, 16 December 2006) and the Venice Commission at its 70th plenary session (Venice, 16–17 March 2007), revised and corrected version in English' (The Venice Commission of the Council of Europe).

Evans, Bryce, and Stephen Kelly (eds.) (2014), *Frank Aiken: Nationalist and Internationalist* (Dublin: Irish Academic Press).

Evans, Geoffrey, and Anand Menon (2017), *Brexit and British Politics* (Cambridge: Polity Press).

Evans, Richard J. (1997), *Rereading German History: From Unification to Reunification 1800–1996* (London: Taylor & Francis).

Fanning, Ronan (1979), 'The United States and Irish Participation in NATO: The Debate of 1950', *Irish Studies in International Affairs*, 1: 38–48.

Farrell, Brian (1970a), 'The Drafting of the Irish Free State Constitution I', *Irish Jurist*, 5: 115–40.

———(1970b), 'The Drafting of the Irish Free State Constitution II', *Irish Jurist*, 5: 343–56.

———(1971a), 'The Drafting of the Irish Free State Constitution III', *Irish Jurist*, 6: 111–35.

———(1971b), 'The Drafting of the Irish Free State Constitution IV', *Irish Jurist*, 6: 345–59.

Feeney, Brian (2002), *Sinn Féin: A Hundred Turbulent Years* (Dublin: The O'Brien Press).

FICT (n.d.), 'Commission on Flags, Identity, Culture and Tradition: Final Report'.

Fisk, Robert (1985), *In Time of War: Ireland, Ulster and the Price of Neutrality, 1939–45* (London: Paladin Books).

FitzGerald, Garret (1991), *All in a Life: Garret FitzGerald, an Autobiography* (Dublin; New York: Gill and Macmillan).

———(2003), *Reflections on the Irish State* (Dublin: Irish Academic Press).

FitzGerald, John (2021), 'Thoughts on Quality of Life, North and South: A Response to "Who is Better Off?" by Adele Bergin and Seamus McGuinness', *Irish Studies in International Affairs*, 32: 161–3.

FitzGerald, W. (1982), *Irish Unification and NATO* (Dublin: Dublin University Press).

Fitzpatrick, David (2014), *Descendancy: Irish Protestant Histories Since 1795* (Cambridge: Cambridge University Press).

Fitzsimmons, Paul A. (1993), *Independence for Northern Ireland: Why and How* (Washington DC: The Juris Press).

Flanagan, Marie Therese (1989), *Irish Society, Anglo-Norman Settlers, Angevin Kingship: Interactions in Ireland in the Late Twelfth Century* (Oxford: Clarendon Press).

Forum Report (1984), 'Report' (Dublin: Stationery Office).

Frame, Robin (2012) [1981], *Colonial Ireland 1169–1369* (Dublin: Four Courts Press).

Gallagher, Michael (1987), 'Does Ireland Need a New Electoral System?', *Irish Political Studies*, 2: 27–48.

———(2005), 'Ireland: The Discreet Charm of PR-STV', in Michael Gallagher and Paul Mitchell (eds.), *The Politics of Electoral Systems* (Oxford: Oxford University Press), 511–32.

Garry, John (2009), 'Consociationalism and Its Critics: Evidence from the Historic Northern Ireland Assembly Election 2007', *Electoral Studies*, 28: 458–66.

Garry, John (2016), *Consociation and Voting in Northern Ireland* (Philadelphia PA: University of Pennsylvania Press).

Garry, John, Kevin McNicholl, Brendan O'Leary, and James Pow (2018), *Northern Ireland and the UK's Exit from the EU: What Do People Think? Evidence from Two Investigations: A Survey and a Deliberative Forum* (Belfast: ESRC/The UK in a Changing Europe).

Garry, John, Brendan O'Leary, Kevin McNicholl, and James Pow (2020), 'The Future of Northern Ireland: Border Anxieties and Support for Irish Reunification under Varieties of UKEXIT', *Regional Studies,* 55:9, 1517–27.

Garry, John, Brendan O'Leary, Paul Gillespie, and Roland Gjoni (2022), 'Public Attitudes to Irish Unification: Evidence on Models and Process from a

Deliberative Forum in Ireland', *Irish Studies in International Affairs*, 33 (2): 246–86.

Garry, John, Brendan O'Leary, John Coakley, James Pow, and Lisa Whitten (2020), 'Public Attitudes to Different Possible Models of a United Ireland: Evidence from a Citizens' Assembly in Northern Ireland', *Irish Political Studies*, 35 (3): 422–50.

Garry, John, James Pow, John Coakley, David M. Farrell, Brendan O'Leary, and James Tilley (2021), 'The Perception of the Legitimacy of Citizens' Assemblies in Deeply Divided Places: Evidence of Public and Elite Opinion from Consociational Northern Ireland', *Government and Opposition*, 1–20. doi:10.1017/gov.2021.4.

Ginnel, Laurence (1919), *The Irish Republic: Why?* (New York: The Friends of Irish Freedom).

Gonssolin, Emmanuel (1921), *Le Plébiscite dans le droit international actuel* (Paris: Librairie Générale de Droit et de Jurisprudence).

Gordon, David (2010), *The Fall of the House of Paisley* (Dublin: Gill & Macmillan [Kindle edition]).

Government, HM (1998), *The Northern Ireland Act 1998* (United Kingdom: HMSO).

Government of Ireland & Government of the United Kingdom (1995), *Frameworks for the Future* (Dublin).

Government of the United Kingdom (1998), 'The Agreement: Agreement Reached in the Multi-Party Negotiations', 30.

Griffith, Arthur (2003) [1904], *The Resurrection of Hungary: A Parallel for Ireland* (Dublin: University College Dublin Press).

Guadani, Marco, Ugo Matteo, John Murray, and Brendan O'Leary (1998), 'A Draft Constitutional Charter for the State of Puntland' (Garowe, Somalia: UNDOS Consultants' Report).

Hain, Peter (2012), 'From Horror to Hope: Northern Ireland Breakthrough', in *Outside In* (London: Biteback), 310–53.

Hamilton, James R. (1973), *Alexander the Great* (London: Hutchinson University Library).

Hand, Geoffrey J. (1973), 'MacNeill and the Boundary Commission', in F. X. Martin and F. J. Byrne (eds.), *The Scholar Revolutionary: Eoin MacNeill, 1867–1945, and the Making of the New Ireland* (Shannon: Irish University Press), 201–75.

————(ed.) (1969), *Report of the Irish Boundary Commission 1925* (Shannon: Irish University Press).

Hanley, Brian, and Scott Millar (2009), *The Lost IRA: The Story of the Official IRA and The Workers Party* (Dublin: Penguin Ireland).

Hayes-McCoy, G. A. (1979), *A History of Irish Flags from Earliest Times* (Dublin: Academic Press).

Heaney, Seamus (1975), *North* (London: Faber & Faber).

Hepburn, Anthony C. (1996), *A Past Apart: Studies in the History of Catholic Belfast* (Belfast: Ulster Historical Foundation).

Heseltine, Michael (2022), 'Why the Panic among Boris Johnson's Allies? Because They Know Brexit Is Unravelling', *The Guardian*, 16 February.

Hix, Simon (2020), 'Remaking Democracy: Ireland as a Role-Model, the 2019 Peter Mair Lecture', *Irish Political Studies* 35:4.

Hopkinson, Michael (1988), *Green Against Green: The Irish Civil War* (Dublin: Gill & Macmillan).

Hübner, Kurt, Renger Van Nieuwkoop, and KLC Consulting (2015), *Modeling Irish Unification* (Vancouver, BC: KLC Consulting).

Humphreys, Richard (2009), *Countdown to Unity: Debating Irish Reunification* (Dublin: Irish Academic Press).

————(2018), *Beyond the Border: The Good Friday Agreement and Irish Unity After Brexit* (Dublin: Merrion Press).

————(ed.) (2021) *Reconciling Ireland: Fifty Years of British–Irish Agreements* (Dublin: Irish Academic Press).

Inglis, Tom (1987), *Moral Monopoly: The Catholic Church in Modern Irish Society* (Dublin: Gill & Macmillan).

Isaacharoff, Samuel (2013), 'Courts, Constitutions and the Limits of Majoritarianism', in Joanne McEvoy and Brendan O'Leary (eds.), *Power-Sharing in Deeply Divided Places* (Philadelphia, PA: University of Pennsylvania Press), 214–30.

Israel, Jonathan I. (2014), *Revolutionary Ideas: An Intellectual History of the French Revolution from The Rights of Man to Robespierre* (Princeton, NJ: Princeton University Press).

Jarausch, Konrad H. (1994), *The Rush to German Unity* (Oxford: Oxford University Press).

Joyce, James (2022) [1922], *Ulysses* (London: Penguin Random House).

Kampfner, John (2021), *Why the Germans Do it Better: Notes from a Grown-up Country* (London: Atlantic Books).

Kane, Alex (2020), 'Northern Ireland Needs a Pro Union Group That Will Help Prepare for Any Border Poll', *News Letter*, 23 October.

Kennedy, Liam (1986), *Two Ulsters: A Case for Repartition* (Belfast: Queen's University of Belfast).

———(1990), 'Repartition', in John McGarry and Brendan O'Leary (eds), *The Future of Northern Ireland* (Oxford: Oxford University Press), 137–61.

Kennedy, Michael (2000), *Division and Consensus: The Politics of Cross-Border Relations in Ireland, 1925–1969* (Dublin: Institute of Public Administration).

Kenny, Anthony (1986), *The Road to Hillsborough: The Shaping of the Anglo-Irish Agreement* (Oxford: Pergamon Press).

———(1990), 'Joint Authority', in John McGarry and Brendan O'Leary (eds.), *The Future of Northern Ireland* (Oxford: Oxford University Press), 219–41.

Ker-Lindsay, James (2011), *The Cyprus Problem: What Everyone Needs to Know* (Oxford: Oxford University Press).

Ker-Lindsay, James, Hubert Faustmann, and Fiona Mullen (2011), *An Island in Europe: The EU and the Transformation of Cyprus* (London: I. B. Tauris).

Knaus, Gerald, and Felix Martin (2004), 'Lessons from Bosnia and Herzegovina: Travails of the European Raj', *Journal of Democracy*, 14: 60–74.

Kyridikes, S. (1968), *Cyprus: Constitutionalism and Crisis Government* (Philadelphia, PA: University of Pennsylvania Press).

Laffan, Michael (1999), *The Resurrection of Ireland. The Sinn Féin Party, 1916–1923* (Cambridge: Cambridge University Press).

Laponce, Jean (2001), 'National Self-determination: The Case for Territorial Revisionism', *Nationalism and Ethnic Politics*, 7: 33–56.

———(2004), 'Turning Votes into Territories: Boundary Referendums in Theory and Practice', *Political Geography*, 23: 169–83.

———(2010), *Le référendum de souveraineté: comparaisons, critiques et commentaires* (Québec: Les Presses de l'Université Laval).

———(2012), 'Language and Sovereignty Referendums: The Convergence Effect', *Nationalism and Ethnic Politics*, 18: 113–28.

Laver, Michael, (1996), 'Notes on an Irish Senate', in Constitution Review Group (ed.), *Report of the Constitution Review Group* (Dublin: Stationery Office). 531–37.

Leahy, Pat (2013), *The Price of Power: Inside Ireland's Crisis Coalition* (Dublin: Penguin Ireland).

————(2022), 'Citizens' Assembly Should Consider Ireland's Neutrality, Taoiseach Says: Martin Tells Dáil Ireland Not "Politically Neutral" as Opposition TD Criticises NATO', *Irish Times*, 8 March.

Leerssen, Joep (2006), *National Thought in Europe: A Cultural History* (Amsterdam: Amsterdam University Press).

Loizides, Neophytos G. (2015), *Designing Peace: Cyprus and Institutional Innovations in Divided Societies* (Philadelphia, PA: University of Pennsylvania Press).

Longford, Lord, and Thomas P. O'Neill (1970), *Eamon de Valera* (Dublin: Gill & Macmillan).

Lynch, David J. (2010), *When the Luck of the Irish Ran Out: The World's Most Resilient Country and Its Struggle to Rise Again* (New York: Palgrave Macmillan).

Lyne, Thomas (1990), 'Ireland, Northern Ireland and 1992: The Barriers to Technocratic Anti-Partitionism', *Public Administration*, 68: 417–33.

Mac Cormaic, Ruadhán (2017), *The Supreme Court: The Judges, the Decisions, the Rifts and the Rivalries that Have Shaped Ireland* (London: Penguin Random House).

Maguire, Martin (1993), 'A Socio-Economic Analysis of the Dublin Protestant Working Class', *Irish Economic and Social History*, 20: 35–61.

Mallon, Seamus and Andy Pollak (2019), *A Shared Home Place* (Dublin: Lilliput Press).

Matthews, Kevin (2004), *Fatal Influence: The Impact of Ireland on British Politics, 1920–1925* (Dublin: University College Dublin Press).

Maume, Patrick (1995), 'The Ancient Constitution: Arthur Griffith and His Intellectual Legacy to Sinn Féin', *Irish Political Studies*: 125–37.

————(1999), *The Long Gestation: Irish Nationalist Life 1891–1918* (New York: St Martin's Press).

McAllister, Ian (1977), *The Northern Ireland Social Democratic and Labour Party: Political Opposition in a Divided Society* (London: Macmillan).

McBride, Ian (1997), *The Siege of Derry in Ulster Protestant Mythology* (Dublin: Four Courts Press).

McBride, Sam (2019), *Burned: The Inside Story of the 'Cash-for-Ash' Scandal and Northern Ireland's Secretive New Elite* (Dublin: Merrion Press).

McClements, Freya (2021a), 'Twenty Years of the PSNI', *Irish Times*, 6 November.

————(2021b), 'Jeffrey Donaldson: Talk of a United Ireland Is "Premature" When the North Is Not United', *Irish Times*, 25 September.

McCrudden, Christopher, Robert Ford, and Anthony Heath (2004), 'Legal Regulation of Affirmative Action in Northern Ireland: An Empirical Appraisal', *Oxford Journal of Legal Studies*, 24: 363–415.

McCrudden, Christopher, Raya Muttarak, Heather Hamill, and Anthony Heath (2009), 'Affirmative Action Without Quotas in Northern Ireland', *The Equal Rights Review*, 4: 7–14.

McCrudden, Christopher, John McGarry, Brendan O'Leary, and Alex Schwartz (2016), 'Why Northern Ireland's Institutions Need Stability', *Government and Opposition*, 51: 30–58.

McCrudden, Christopher (ed.) (2022), *The Law and Practice of the Ireland–Northern Ireland Protocol* (Cambridge: Cambridge University Press).

McDonagh, Sunniva (ed.) (1992), *The Attorney General v. X and Others: Judgments of the High Court and Supreme Court with Submissions Made by Counsel to the Supreme Court* (Dublin: Incorporated Council of Law Reporting for Ireland).

McDowell, R. B. (1970), *The Irish Convention, 1917–1918* (London: Routledge and Kegan Paul).

McEvoy, Joanne (2006), 'The Institutional Design of Executive Formation in Northern Ireland', *Regional and Federal Studies*, 16: 447–64.

———(2013), ' "We Forbid!" The Mutual Veto and Power-Sharing Democracy', in Joanne McEvoy and Brendan O'Leary (eds.), *Power-Sharing in Deeply Divided Places* (Philadelphia, PA: University of Pennsylvania Press), 253–77.

———(2015), *Power-Sharing Executives: Governing in Bosnia, Macedonia and Northern Ireland* (Philadelphia, PA: University of Pennsylvania Press).

McGarry, John (2004), 'Policing Reform in Northern Ireland', in *Essays on the Northern Ireland Conflict: Consociational Engagements* (Oxford: Oxford University Press).

———(2017), 'Centripetalism, Consociationalism and Cyprus: The "Adoptability" Question', *Political Studies*, 65(2): 512–29.

McGarry, John, and Brendan O'Leary (1990a), 'Conclusion. Northern Ireland's Options: A Framework and Analysis', in *The Future of Northern Ireland* (Oxford: Oxford University Press), 268–303.

———(1995), *Explaining Northern Ireland: Broken Images* (Oxford: Blackwell Publishers).

———(2015), 'Power-sharing Executives: Consociational and Centripetal Formulae and the Case of Northern Ireland', *Ethnopolitics*, 15: 497–520.

————(ed.) (1990b), *The Future of Northern Ireland* (Oxford: Oxford University Press).

McGuinness, Seamus, and Adele Bergin (2019), 'The Political Economy of a Northern Ireland Border Poll', *Cambridge Journal of Economics*, 44: 781–812.

McKay, Susan (2021), *Northern Protestants on Shifting Ground* (Newtownards: Blackstaff Press).

McKittrick, David, Seamus Kelters, Brian Feeney, and Chris Thornton (2008), *Lost Lives: The Stories of the Men, Women and Children Who Died as a Result of the Northern Ireland Troubles* (Edinburgh: Mainstream Publishing).

McNamara, Kevin (2009), *The MacBride Principles: Irish America Strikes Back* (Liverpool: Liverpool University Press).

McWilliams, David (2017), 'Northern Ireland and the Trip Advisor Index of Economic Vibrancy', *Irish Times*, 2 December.

Mearsheimer, John J. (1994), 'The False Promise of International Institutions', *International Security*, 19: 5–49.

Mendez, Fernando, and Micha Germann (2016), 'Contesting Sovereignty: Mapping Referendums on Sovereignty over Time and Space', *British Journal of Political Science* 48(1): 141–65.

Menon, Anand, and Geoffrey Evans (2017), *Brexit and British Politics* (Oxford: Oxford University Press).

Miller, David W. (1978), *Queen's Rebels: Ulster Loyalism in Historical Perspective* (Dublin: Gill & Macmillan).

Montgomery, Rory (2022), 'Letter: War in Europe–Russia's Assault on Ukraine', *Irish Times*, 7 March.

Moravcsik, Andrew (1998), 'The Choice for Europe: Social Purpose and State Power from Messina to Maastricht' (Ithaca, NY: Cornell University Press).

Morel, Laurence, and Matt Qvortrup (eds.) (2017), *The Routledge Handbook to Referendums and Direct Democracy* (London: Routledge).

Morris, Ian, and Walter Scheidel (eds.) (2009), *The Dynamics of Ancient Empires: State Power from Assyria to Byzantium* (Oxford: Oxford University Press).

Murray, Gerard, and Jonathan Tonge (2005), *Sinn Féin and the SDLP: From Alienation to Participation* (Dublin: O'Brien Press).

Murray, Paul (2011), *The Irish Boundary Commission and Its Origins, 1886–1925* (Dublin: University College Dublin Press).

New Ulster Political Research Group (1979), 'Beyond the Religious Divide'(Belfast: New Ulster Political Research Group).

O'Brien, Conor Cruise (1980), *Neighbours: Four Lectures Delivered by Conor Cruise O'Brien in Memory of Christopher Ewart-Biggs* (London: Faber & Faber).

———(1998), *Memoir: My Life and Themes* (London: Profile Books).

O'Connell, Hugh (2015), 'Ireland Says NO in Presidential Age Referendum', *thejournal.ie*, 23 May.

O'Duffy, Brendan, and Brendan O'Leary (1995), 'Tales from Elsewhere and an Hibernian Sermon', in Helen Margetts and Gareth Smyth (eds.), *Turning Japanese? Britain with a Permanent Party of Government* (London: Lawrence & Wishart), 193–210.

O'Leary, Brendan (1989), 'The Limits to Coercive Consociationalism in Northern Ireland', *Political Studies*, 37: 562–88.

———(1993), 'Sovereignty, Joint Authority and Shared Authority', in Brendan O'Leary, Tom Lyne, Jim Marshall, and Bob Rowthorn (eds.), *Northern Ireland: Sharing Authority* (London: Institute of Public Policy Research), 136–38.

———(1995a), 'Britain's Japanese Question: Is There a Dominant Party?' in Helen Margetts and Gareth Smyth (eds.), *Turning Japanese? Britain with a Permanent Party of Government* (London: Lawrence & Wishart), 3–8.

———(1995b), 'Afterword: What is Framed in the Framework Documents ?', *Ethnic and Racial Studies*, 18: 862–72.

———(1999a), 'The Nature of the Agreement', *Fordham Journal of International Law*, 22: 1628–67.

———(1999b) 'A Bright Future and Less Orange (Review of "A New Beginning" by the Independent Commission on Policing for Northern Ireland)', *Times Higher Education Supplement*, 19 November.

———(1999c), 'The Nature of the British-Irish Agreement', *New Left Review*, 233: 66–96.

———(2007), 'Analyzing Partition: Definition, Classification and Explanation', *Political Geography*, 26: 886–908.

———(2009), *How to Get Out of Iraq with Integrity* (Philadelphia, PA: University of Pennsylvania Press).

———(2011), 'Debating Partition: Evaluating the Standard Justifications', in Kurt Cordell and Stefan Wolff (eds.), *The Routledge Handbook of Ethnic Conflict* (London: Routledge), 140–57.

———(2012), 'Partition', in Thomas M. Wilson and Hastings Donnan (eds.), *A Companion to Border Studies* (Oxford: Wiley-Blackwell), 29–47.

————(2016a), 'The Dalriada Document: Towards a Multinational Compromise that Respects Democratic Diversity in the United Kingdom', *Political Quarterly*, 87: 5618–33.

————(2016b), 'Power-Sharing and Partition Amid Israel-Palestine', *Ethnopolitics*, 15: 345–65.

————(2020a), *A Treatise on Northern Ireland, Volume 3: Consociation and Confederation* (Oxford: Oxford University Press).

————(2020b), *A Treatise on Northern Ireland, Volume 1: Colonialism* (Oxford: Oxford University Press).

————(2020c), 'The Nature of the European Union', *Research in Political Sociology*, 27: 17–44.

————(2020d), *A Treatise on Northern Ireland, Volume 2: Control* (Oxford: Oxford University Press).

————(2021), 'Getting Ready: The Need to Prepare for a Referendum on Reunification', *Irish Studies in International Affairs*, 32: 1–38.

————(2022), 'Consent: Lies, Perfidy, the Protocol, and the Imaginary Unionist Veto', in Federico Fabbrini (ed.), *The Law and Politics of Brexit* (Oxford: Oxford University Press), 231–50.

O'Leary, Brendan, Bernard Grofman, and Jorgen Elklit (2005), 'Divisor Methods for Sequential Portfolio Allocation in Multi-Party Executive Bodies: Evidence from Northern Ireland and Denmark', *American Journal of Political Science*, 49: 198–211.

O'Leary, Brendan, Tom Lyne, Jim Marshall, and Bob Rowthorn (1993), *Northern Ireland: Sharing Authority* (London: Institute for Public Policy Research).

O'Leary, Brendan, John McGarry, and Khaled Salih (eds.) (2005), *The Future of Kurdistan in Iraq* (Philadelphia, PA: University of Pennsylvania Press).

O'Rourke, Kevin Hjortshøj (2017), 'Independent Ireland in Comparative Perspective', *Irish Economic and Social History*, 44: 19–45.

O'Toole, Fintan (2010), *Ship of Fools: How Stupidity and Corruption Sank the Celtic Tiger* (New York: PublicAffairs).

————(2021), 'Other Countries Yearn for the Good Old Days. Not Ireland', *Irish Times*, 13 November.

O'Toole, Kathleen, Noeline Blackwell, Johnny Connolly, Vicky Conway, Tim Dalton, Peter Fahy, Eddie Molloy, Tonita Murray, Antonio Oftelie, Donncha O'Connell, and Helen Ryan (2018), 'Commission on the Future of Policing in Ireland' (Dublin: online).

Parades Commission (2022), 'Encouraging Resolution Through Local Dialogue' Available at www.paradescommission.org.

Parsons, Craig (2003), *A Certain Idea of Europe* (Ithaca, NY: Cornell University Press).

Patten, Christopher (1999), *A New Beginning: The Report of the Independent Commission on Policing for Northern Ireland* (Belfast: Independent Commission on Policing for Northern Ireland).

Peel, Lord (1937), *Report of the Palestine Royal Commission (The Peel Report)* (London: HMSO).

Pickvance, T. Joseph (1975), *Peace Through Equity: Proposals for a Permanent Settlement of the Northern Ireland Conflict* (Birmingham: The author).

Pinker, Steven (2011), *The Better Angels of Our Nature: Why Violence Has Declined* (New York: Penguin).

———(2018), *Enlightenment Now* (New York: Viking Penguin).

Plunkett, Horace (1918), 'Report of the Proceedings of the Irish Convention' (Dublin: HMSO) [Google digitalized edition from the University of Michigan].

Pocock, J. G. A. (1982), 'The Limits and Divisions of British History: In Search of an Unknown Subject', *The American Historical Review*, 87: 311–36.

———(1999), 'The New British History in Atlantic Perspective: An Antipodean Commentary', *The American Historical Review*, 104: 490–500.

———(2005), *The Discovery of Islands: Essays in British History* (Cambridge: Cambridge University Press).

Qvortrup, Matt (2012), 'The History of Ethno-National Referendums 1791–2011', *Nationalism and Ethnic Politics*, 18: 129–50.

———(2014a), *Referendums and Ethnic Conflict* (Philadelphia, PA: University of Pennsylvania Press).

———(2014b), 'Referendums on Independence, 1860–2011', *Political Quarterly*, 85: 57–64.

———(2016), 'Referendums on Membership and European Integration 1972–2015', *Political Quarterly*, 87: 61–68.

Qvortrup, Matt, Brendan O'Leary, and Ron Wintrobe (2018), 'Explaining the Paradox of Plebiscites', *Government and Opposition* 55(2): 202–19.

Rea, Desmond (ed.) (1982), *Political Co-operation in Divided Societies: A Series of Papers Relevant to the Conflict in Northern Ireland* (Dublin: Gill & Macmillan).

Regan, Anthony (2008), 'Resolving the Bougainville Self-determination Dispute: Autonomy or Complex Power-sharing?', in Marc Weller, Barbara Metzger, and Niall Johnson (eds.), *Settling Self-Determination Disputes: Complex Power-Sharing in Theory and Practice* (Leiden, Boston: Martinus Nijhoff), 125–59.

———(2019), *The Bougainville Referendum: Law, Administration and Politics* (Canberra: Department of Pacific Affairs, Australian National University).

Renwick, Alan, Oran Doyle, John Garry, Paul Gillespie, Cathy Gormley-Heenan, Katy Hayward, Robert Hazell, David Kenny, Christopher McCrudden, Brendan O'Leary, Etain Tannam, and Alan Whysall (2021), *Final Report of the Working Group on Unification Referendums on the Island of Ireland* (London: Constitution Unit, University College London).

Ritter, Gerhard Albert (2011), *The Price of German Unity: Reunification and the Crisis of the Welfare State* (Oxford: Oxford University Press).

Roser, Max, and Mohamed Nagdy (2014), 'Optimism and Pessimism', https://ourworldindata.org/optimism-pessimism.

Ross, Shane (2010), *The Bankers: How the Banks Brought Ireland to Its Knees* (Dublin: Penguin Ireland).

Rourke, John T., Richard P. Hiskes, and Cyrus Ernesto Zirakzadeh (1992), *Direct Democracy and International Politics: Deciding International Issues through Referendums* (Boulder, CO: Lynne Rienner).

Rowan, Brian (2021), *Political Purgatory: The Battle to Save Stormont and the Play for a New Ireland* (Dublin: Merrion Press).

Saunders, J. J. (1972), *The History of the Mongol Conquests* (Philadelphia, PA: University of Pennsylvania Press).

Saunders, Robert (2018), *Yes to Europe! The 1975 Referendum and Seventies Britain* (Cambridge: Cambridge University Press).

Scally, Derek (2021), *The Best Catholics in the World: The Irish, the Church and the End of a Special Relationship* (Dublin: Sandycove/Penguin Random House).

SDLP (1972), *Towards a New Ireland: Proposals by the Social Democratic and Labour Party* (Belfast: SDLP).

Seligman, Martin E. P. (1995), *Abnormal Psychology* (New York; London: Norton).

Şen, İlker Gökhan (2015), *Sovereignty Referendums in International and Constitutional Law* (Berlin: Springer).

———(2017), 'Sovereignty Referendums: People Concerned and People Entitled to Vote', in Laurence Morel and Matt Qvortrup (eds.), *The*

Routledge Handbook of Referendums and Direct Democracy (London: Routledge), 210–26.

Shipman, Tim (2016), *All Out War: The Full Story of How Brexit Sank Britain's Political Class* (London: HarperCollins).

Simms, Katharine (1989), 'The Norman Invasion and Gaelic Recovery', in Roy F. Foster (ed.), *The Oxford Illustrated History of Ireland* (Oxford: Oxford University Press), 53–103.

Sinn Féin (1971–72), 'Éire Nua' (Dublin: Kevin Street).

———(1979), 'Éire Nua: The Sinn Féin Policy. The Social, Economic and Political Dimensions' (Dublin), reproduced at https://cain.ulster.ac.uk/issues/politics/docs/sf/sinnfein79.htm.

Spruyt, Hendrik (1994), *The Sovereign State and Its Competitors: An Analysis of Systems Change* (Princeton, NJ: Princeton University Press).

Staunton, Denis, and Pat Leahy (2017), 'Brexit Summit: EU Accepts United Ireland Declaration: Way Clear for North to Automatically Become Part of EU if Its People Vote for United Ireland', *Irish Times*, 29 April.

Steinberg, Jonathan (2015), *Why Switzerland?* (Cambridge: Cambridge University Press).

Sudan, Government of, and Sudan People's Liberation Movement (2005), *The Comprehensive Peace Agreement between the Government of the Republic of Sudan and the Sudan People's Liberation Movement, Sudan People's Liberation Army* ([Khartoum?]: National Federation of Sudanese Youth).

Sutton, Malcolm (1994), *Bear in Mind These Dead: An Index of Deaths from the Conflict in Ireland, 1969–1993* (Belfast: Beyond the Pale Publications).

Szporluk, Roman (1991), *Communism and Nationalism: Karl Marx versus Friedrich List* (New York: Oxford University Press).

Taylor, Rupert (ed.) (2009), *Consociational Theory: McGarry and O'Leary and the Northern Ireland Conflict* (London: Routledge).

Thomas, Hugh M. (2003), *The English and the Normans: Ethnic Hostility, Assimilation and Identity 1066–c.1220* (Oxford: Oxford University Press).

Trimble, David (2000), 'Stop Patten's Sectarian Plan', *Daily Telegraph*, 28 July.

Vertovec, Steven (2009), *Transnationalism* (London: Routledge).

Vertovec, Steven, and Susanne Wessendorf (eds.) (2009), *The Multiculturalism Backlash* (London: Routledge).

Vile, Maurice J. C. (1982), 'Federation and Confederation: The Experience of the United States and the British Commonwealth', in Desmond Rea (ed.),

Political Co-operation in Divided Societies: A Series of Papers Relevant to the Conflict in Northern Ireland (Dublin: Gill & Macmillan), 216–28.

Wall, Martin (2020), 'EU Defence Plan to Present Ireland with "Significant" Costs', *Irish Times*, 9 November.

———(2021), 'Defence Forces Pay Issue Affects Broader Government Wage Policy', *Irish Times*, 26 July.

Walsh, Dawn (2017), *Independent Commissions and Contentious Issues in Post-Good Friday Agreement Northern Ireland* (Basingstoke: Palgrave Macmillan).

Wambaugh, Sarah (1920), *A Monograph on Plebiscites, with a Collection of Official Documents* (New York: Oxford University Press).

———(1933), *Plebiscites Since the World War, with a Collection of Official Documents* (Washington, DC: Carnegie Endowment for International Peace).

———(1940), *The Saar Plebiscite, with a Collection of Official Documents* (Cambridge, MA: Harvard University Press).

Whitaker, T. K. (1973), 'From Protection to Free Trade. The Irish Experience', *Administration* 11: 405 ff.

White, Robert W. (2006), *Ruairí Ó Brádaigh: The Life and Politics of an Irish Revolutionary* (Bloomington, IN: Indiana University Press).

Wilkinson, David (1997), ' "How Did They Pass the Union?" Secret Service Expenditure in Ireland, 1799–1804', *History*, 87: 223–51.

Winters, Rory (2022), 'Hundreds of PSNI Officers in Protestant Fraternal Groups and Freemasons', *thedetail*, 31 March.

Wolff, Stefan (2003), *Disputed Territories: The Transnational Dynamics of Ethnic Conflict Settlement* (New York: Berghahn Books).

Woodall, D. R. (1982), 'Computer Counting in STV Elections', *Representation*, 23: 4–6.

Youn, Miryang (1997), 'Women in Two Nations and Four States: A Comparative Study of the Impact of Political Regimes and Culture on the Status of Women in the two Koreas and the two Germanies, 1945–89', PhD Thesis (London: The London School of Economics and Political Science).

Young, Robert A. (1997), 'How Do Peaceful Secessions Happen?', *Canadian Journal of Political Science*, 27: 773–94.

Zelikow, Philip, and Condoleezza Rice (1995), *Germany Unified and Europe Transformed: A Study in Statecraft* (Cambridge, MA: Harvard University Press).

Endnotes

Part One: Why We Are Here

1. Six into twenty-six won't go – or will it?

1 For a detailed analysis of the conflict, its dating, and the killings, and injuries, and a review of all the databases and analyses, see O'Leary 2020b: Chapter 1.

2 O'Leary 2021.

3 O'Leary 2020b and Miller 1978. The first Pale described the zone of English colonial settlement around Dublin; the barbarous Irish lived 'beyond the Pale'.

4 For a crisp account, see McBride 1997.

5 McDowell 1970; Plunkett 1918.

6 Walter Long, who drafted the partition act, reported that the people in the inner circles of unionism favoured six rather than nine counties because that would prevent their supremacy from being seriously threatened. See O'Leary 2020b: 338, n. 94.

7 The Ulster Banner was the flag of the Government of Northern Ireland between 1953 and 1972. See the plate section: Flags of Ireland and Ulster.

8 Susan McKay 2021 describes Northern Protestants as living on 'shifting ground'.

9 Sinn Féin, founded in 1905, and with numerous offshoots, is translated literally as 'We Ourselves', or 'Ourselves Alone'. I have also seen it translated as 'Self-determination'. On the party's history, see Feeney 2002; on the early party, see Laffan 1999. The SDLP is the Social Democratic and Labour Party of Northern Ireland, whose most famous leader was the late John Hume. For an assessment of its rivalry with Sinn Féin, see Murray and Tonge 2005; on the party's early years, see McAllister 1977.

10 Hepburn 1996.

11 Nobel Lecture Trimble 1998, https://www.nobelprize.org/prizes/peace/1998/trimble/lecture/.

12 Kevin McNamara wrote a PhD thesis on the subject, published in McNamara 2009.

13 See McCrudden, Ford, and Heath 2004; McCrudden et al. 2009.

14 In 2018–19 there were 20,865 students (49.5 per cent) from a Catholic background attending Queen's and Ulster universities, compared with 13,145 (31.2 per cent) from a Protestant background. There were 8,150 (19.3 per cent) students defined as 'others' – including 'other', 'unknown', or 'no religion'. Even if the smaller portion of each of these 'others' are of cultural Catholic origin, cultural Catholics comprise a majority of this student cohort.

15 O'Leary 2020b: Chapter 1.

16 Darby and Morris 1974; Darby 1986.

17 'Ulster and the Union: the view from the North', Lord Ashcroft Polls, December 2021: https://lordashcroftpolls.com/wp-content/uploads/2021/12/LORD-ASHCROFT-POLLS-Ulster-and-the-Union-1.pdf.

18 All data and quotations from the Ashcroft polls cited in the endnote above.

19 O'Leary 2020a: Chapter 2.

2. The comeback of reunification after 2016

1 Frame 2012 [1981].

2 That kingdom, previously a 'lordship', was a dependent polity: a colony, subordinate to metropolitan England, but territorially unified. See O'Leary 2020b: Chapters 2–4. The Act of Union was bought through multiple forms of patronage and secret service bribes, see Wilkinson 1997.

3 Article 12, Articles of Agreement for a Treaty between Great Britain and Ireland, 6 December 1921.

4 My full treatment of these institutions may be found in O'Leary 2020a.

5 Feargal Cochrane 2013 writes of a 'reluctant' peace.

6 McBride 2019.

7 Evans and Menon 2017.

8 O'Leary 2020a.

9 Staunton and Leahy 2017.

10 O'Leary 2016a.

11 For largely legal evaluations of the Protocol, see McCrudden 2022; for a political account of early Irish diplomacy, see Connelly 2017: Tony Connelly broadcasts regular updates in RTE's podcast *Brexit Republic*. For the calm memoir of the EU's principal negotiator of the Protocol, see Barnier 2021.

12 O'Leary 2022; McCrudden 2022: 153.

13 O'Leary 2022.

14 Anthony 2022.

15 So did Jeffrey Donaldson, also briefly: see this Twitter link, https://twitter.com/ChasMooney1/status/1489576552719343616.

16 NIQB 64, Justice Colton, 30 June 2021.

17 NI Court of Appeal, 14 March 2022.

18 'DUP Minister Accused of Racism', *Irish Times*, 6 August 2009, https://www.irishtimes.com/news/dup-minister-accused-of-racism-1.844432.

Part Two: Lessons from Elsewhere

3. The failed reunification of Cyprus

1 No distinguished books or articles comparing unifications after partitions are available. There are excellent studies of partitions, and I drew on these in two articles, O'Leary 2007, 2011, summarized in another, O'Leary 2012. There are some good studies of reunifications: Zelikow and Rice 1995; Jarausch 1994; Ritter 2011.

2 On Kashmir, see Bose 2003.

3 See Peel 1937.

4 Bose 2003.

5 My views on resolving Israel/Palestine may be found in O'Leary 2016b. The idealism of those who advocate a 'one state' solution may be admirable, but it is neither emergent, nor politically feasible … yet. A confederation would be more workable.

6 Youn 1997.

7 Annex IX, 1 of the Annan Plan, http://www.hri.org/docs/annan/AnnexIX/AnnexIX.pdf.

8　Conversations with Professors Tozun Bahcheli and Neo Loizides, Turkish and Greek Cypriots respectively, and advocates of reunifying Cyprus, albeit in different ways. See Bahcheli 2000, Loizides 2015. My close friend Professor John McGarry is an authority on Cyprus, having advised the UN mediation on Cyprus since 2008; see McGarry 2017. Professor James Ker-Lindsay of the London School of Economics and Political Science is another authority: Ker-Lindsay 2011; Ker-Lindsay, Faustmann, and Mullen 2011.

9　John McGarry tells me that the simultaneity of the two referendums avoided giving one side the chance of voting 'Yes' after the other had voted 'No'; suggesting extraordinary levels of mutual distrust.

10　The application of the *acquis communautaire*, the accumulated body of EU law is suspended in the lands of the TRNC.

11　They had, however, accepted a similar judiciary before. See Adams 1966; Kyridikes 1968.

12　In fact, EU law is not prescriptive or applicable regarding freedom of movement *within* member-states, as opposed to *between* them. Had the converse been true, the UK's Prevention of Terrorism Act, which blocked freedom of movement between Great Britain and Northern Ireland, would have violated EU law.

13　Equally, there would have been no atonement by Greek Cypriots for the events of 1963–64, which some have labelled Cyprus's first partition.

14　[The Belfast or Good Friday Agreement] 1998: Constitutional Issues: 1 (i).

15　Amaral 2018; the book-length version of the argument is in Amaral 2019.

16　Garry et al. 2021.

4. The successful reunification of Germany

1　Berlin was incorporated as a city-state, a status shared with Hamburg and Bremen.

2　https://www.bundesregierung.de/breg-en/chancellor/basic-law-470510. The Preamble to the basic law and some of its articles were amended. The 'fundamental law' might, I think, be a better translation. It was approved and came into force in May 1949, and was intended to be 'temporary', until Germany was sovereign – and united.

3　Zelikow and Rice 1995. The US Senate *unanimously* ratified the treaty of the final settlement.

4 One American scholar thinks German unification did not modify the prospects of European monetary integration: Moravcsik 1998. His critics are more persuasive, see Parsons 2003.

5 Evans 1997: see especially Part V.

6 'Scotland Decides', BBC, https://www.bbc.co.uk/news/events/scotland-decides/results.

7 Kampfner 2021: 80.

8 Rory Winters, 'Council Plans for Mackie's Site in West Belfast', *thedetail*, 24 April 2020, https://thedetail.tv/articles/council-plans-for-mackie-s-site-criticised-amid-calls-for-social-housing-in-west-belfast.

9 Germany is not Europe's largest country by area: Ukraine, France, Spain, Sweden, and Norway are larger. It is the fourth-largest EU country. Its centrality to the European continent, its population and its power, make many of us think Germany is the largest state.

10 World Bank data, 'GNI per capita, PPP'. GNI = Gross National Income in PPP (Purchasing Power Parity) in a common international dollar index; this index is sometimes more useful for Ireland than GDP figures, which can be distorted by the extensive roles of multinational investment in Ireland, and their foreign tax-reporting.

11 Eurostat, *Key Figures on Europe – Statistics Illustrated*, 2019 edition, 31.

12 GDP measures total output, income, and expenditure within an economy. Calculated correctly, the figures for output, income, and expenditure should be the same. An accessible guide to the development of the concept, and controversies over its merits, may be found in Coyle 2015.

13 Eurostat News Release, March 2020. Such comparisons likely strongly undervalue the contribution of the German *Sozialstaat* (welfare state) to German living standards.

14 Derek Scally, 'Germany Will "Never Forget" Ireland's Help', *Irish Times*, 29 April 2010, https://www.irishtimes.com/news/germany-will-never-forget-ireland-s-help-1.658399.

15 For why dictators pursue absurd levels of support in referendums, see Qvortrup, O'Leary, and Wintrobe 2018.

16 See the work of the German scholar and founding director of the Max Planck Institute at the University of Göttingen, Vertovec and Wessendorf 2009; Vertovec 2009.

17 Apologists for the churches maintain they provided the safety nets that governments failed to provide; that forgets the role of the churches in seeking to monopolize such provision.

18 East Germany also acted as a military and political vanguard for the projection of Soviet power in the third world, providing military support and police training to Soviet allies, notably in the Horn of Africa and in southern Africa.

19 Ritter 2011.

5. Lessons from our past

1 On the varieties of Sinn Féin, see Laffan 1999, Feeney 2002, Hanley and Millar 2009.

2 Griffith 2003 [1904].

3 Hopkinson 1988.

4 Davis 1974; Maume 1995, 1999.

5 Leerssen 2006.

6 For an illuminating comparison of the thought of Friedrich List with that of Karl Marx, see Szporluk 1991.

7 O'Rourke 2017.

8 Central Statistics Office, Statistical Release, 15 February 2022.

9 The IRA's campaigns to force a British withdrawal, as well as being ineffective, were unconstitutional in 1939, 1956, and after 1971. The original Articles 2 and 3 had been drafted to win the consent of Seán MacBride and others to accept the constitutional supersession of the Irish Free State. That worked with the bulk of the old IRA.

10 Brown 1973.

11 Joyce 2022, [1922], [12] 1190–1200: 266–67.

12 [The Belfast or Good Friday Agreement] 1998: Declaration of Support.

6. Lessons from other referendums

1 Laponce 2001 and Şen 2015 count over 150 and over 300 respectively, while Mendez and Germann 2016 count 602 between 1776 and 2012. Germann 2019 more recently counts 360 'self-determination referendums'. The different estimations partly flow from different definitions. Some authors, for

example, count EU integration referendums as votes on the 'transfer' of sovereignty, but they could often be considered as merely enabling the 'delegation' rather than the irrevocable transfer of constitutional authority. The different estimates also flow from decisions over whether to count only lawful or authorized referendums, or only referendums held under secret ballots of the electorate.

2 Sudan and Movement 2005; Regan 2008, 2019.

3 In some writings, such referendums go under the title of 'annexations', but in ordinary usage the latter means the incorporation of territory without any necessary popular consent.

4 In both countries, the vote for unification, when rounded, was 100 per cent. Despite this apparent enthusiasm, Syria seceded in 1961. In 1971, Libyans, Egyptians, and Syrians created the Federation of Arab Republics, with three referendums in which each electorate displayed percentage support in the high 90s. This federation failed to form.

5 Alaska held a referendum in 1946 demanding statehood: it was obliged to wait until 1959. Hawaii held a referendum to confirm the statehood bill passed by Congress. Following the 'Tennessee Plan', US territories have unilaterally used referendums and constitutional drafting to petition Congress to elevate their status to statehood: Tennessee (1796) was followed by Michigan (1837), Iowa (1846), California (1850), Oregon (1859), Kansas (1861), and Alaska (1946). New Mexico (1850), however, failed to be admitted until 1912.

6 The American Declaration of Independence and the French Revolution initiated a key aspect of the principle of self-determination, viz. the freedom of a people to choose its government. Armitage 2007; Cassese 1995.

7 Mendez and Germann 2016 correct the under-reporting of 'sovereignty referendums' in North America.

8 Jean Laponce thinks this is the key distinction among 'sovereignty referendums': in Avignon (in 1791) people voted to change their sovereign; whereas in Schleswig in 1920 people voted not only on whether to change their sovereign, but also to draw a new border, see Laponce 2001. Though Laponce refers to this type as one in which voters choose sovereigns *and* borders, that is not quite accurate. Rather, the relevant arbiters or commissioners drew the final boundaries largely in alignment with popular preferences – but also using other criteria. The cases of North and South

Schleswig (Sønderjylland) in 1920 and Upper Silesia in 1921, administered by the League of Nations, fit this description.

9 Cassese 1995: 11 ff.

10 Wambaugh 1920: 3 identified a precursor in Burgundy in 1527, and in 1552, when the cities of Metz, Toul, and Verdun resolved to stay within France, though the voting method was likely by acclamation. İlker Gökhan Şen, 2015: 17, cites a precedent from Geneva in 1420, when the male citizens unanimously rejected annexation to Savoy – his sources are Gonssolin 1921, and Rourke, Hiskes, and Zirakzadeh 1992.

11 An instructive account may be found in a recent intellectual history of the French Revolution, Israel 2014: 316–44, The 'General Revolution' from Valmy to the Fall of Mainz (1792–93). In the initial draft of the Constitution of 1793, under the leadership of Condorcet, it was declared that 'The French Republic . . . solemnly renounces the reincorporation of foreign places in its territory, if not according to the freely expressed wish of the majority of the inhabitants.' (My translation of a passage cited in Cassese 1993: 11.)

12 In 1948, Newfoundland and Labrador was under modified direct rule by Britain ('commission government'). In the first referendum, voters chose between three options: (i) Responsible Government (i.e. a return to dominion status, held before bankruptcy in 1933), (ii) joining the Canadian Confederation (in fact, a federation), and (iii) Commission Government (continued rule for five years by a commission dominated by the London government). These options respectively won 44.6, 41.1, and 14.3 per cent of the vote. A run-off referendum was held between the two top options. Union with Canada won by 52.3 per cent on an 85 per cent turnout. The confederation side, led by Joseph Smallwood, argued that their option was the British and Protestant union. The President of the Responsible Government League was Francis M. O'Leary. The League was favoured by Catholics of Irish descent, some of whom preferred joining the United States. The US option was not put on the ballot paper, partly because of US disinterest – its military bases were already established – and because both the London and Ottawa governments were against it.

13 Dicey 1915, The Nature of Parliamentary Sovereignty: 3–35.

14 Wambaugh 1920, 1933, 1940; Laponce 2001, 2004, 2010; Altman et al. 2014; Qvortrup 2014a, 2014b, 2016; Morel and Qvortrup 2017; Şen 2015, 2017;

Qvortrup 2012; Mendez and Germann 2016; and numerous encyclopaedias.

15 See note 12 above.

16 Young 1997.

17 Saunders 2018.

18 UK legislation could be passed, after consultation in the BIIGC, to exclude the UK Electoral Commission from having any role in the question-setting: after all, it did not exist when the Good Friday Agreement was made and ratified. Good intergovernmental cooperation should render such a step unnecessary.

19 For the inside dope on the Brexit campaign, see Shipman 2016; for the best immediate scholarly treatment, see Menon and Evans 2017.

20 Heseltine 2022.

Part Three: How Reunification May Happen

7. Referendum matters

1 The Good Friday Agreement: Constitutional Issues (ii) and (iii), https://www.dfa.ie/media/dfa/alldfawebsitemedia/ourrolesandpolicies/northern ireland/good-friday-agreement.pdf.

2 The Good Friday Agreement: Constitutional Issues, Annex A.

3 The Northern Ireland Act 1998 (UK Public General Acts 1998 c. 47, Part 1, Section 1), https://www.legislation.gov.uk/ukpga/1998/47/section/1.

4 There are legal subtleties here. Under Irish and UK law the GFA does not bind Irish and UK institutions. But legislation in the Oireachtas and at Westminster is necessary – under international law – to allow Ireland and the UK to meet their obligations under the GFA. If either parliament failed to enact the necessary legislation to give effect to reunification – in the event of approval by referendum, North and South – then its state would be in breach of international law. (Thanks to Oran Doyle.)

5 The Vienna Convention on the Law of Treaties requires states to fulfil their treaty obligations. Article 62 allows such obligations to be avoided if there is a fundamental change of circumstances, but this exception is very

narrowly drafted, and has never been successfully invoked before a court, Renwick et al. 2021 4.9: 65.

6 The Irish version, the Agreement between the Government of Ireland and the Government of the United Kingdom of Great Britain and Northern Ireland, Treaty Series, 2000, No. 18, entered into force on 2 December 1999. Four other treaties entered into force that day registering the creation of the British-Irish Council, the British-Irish Intergovernmental Conference, the North South Ministerial Council, and the implementation bodies.

7 Agreement on the Withdrawal of the United Kingdom of Great Britain and Northern Ireland from the European Union and the European Atomic Energy Community, 2019, p. 92, EU version. The European Union (Withdrawal Agreement) 2020 is the UK's legislation giving effect to leaving the EU.

8 This point is legally true, but in the political world no Secretary of State would initiate a referendum without at least informal discussions with the UK Prime Minister and Cabinet colleagues.

9 19th Amendment of the Constitution Act, 1998: https://www.irishstat utebook.ie/eli/1998/ca/19/schedule/enacted/en/html#sched-parti.

10 Article 6 of the Irish Constitution declares that all powers of government derive from the people 'whose right it is – in final appeal – to determine all matters of national policy'. Taking Articles 3 and 6 together, 'the people' who decide in Article 3 can't be reduced to one of the organs of government, and one can't imagine a question of national policy more important to the people. My thanks to Oran Doyle.

11 Former Taoiseach Bertie Ahern (RTE News, 6 April 2017, https://www. rte.ie/news/brexit/2017/0406/865735-brexit/), former and likely future Taoiseach Leo Varadkar (*Irish Independent*, 2 April 2017, https://www. independent.ie/irish-news/politics/sinn-feins-push-for-border-poll-alarming-says-varadkar-35585809.html), and Seamus Mallon (2019), the late Deputy First Minister of Northern Ireland, proposed changes to the key GFA rule in 2017–19.

12 Two books by Richard Humphreys merit continuing attention (Humphreys 2009, 2018). He argues for the full transfer of the Good Friday Agreement (2018: 93); I disagree with his thesis that it is obligated.

13 The curious requirement of 55 per cent support for independence in a referendum on a turnout of over 50 per cent, eventually agreed in Montenegro's secession from Serbia on the suggestion of an EU mediator, was unique, and a bad precedent. It was completely ad hoc, emerging from negotiation, not principled argument. Both sides imagined they would win under these numbers! The Serbs erred, but not by much.

14 European Commission for Democracy Through Law (Venice Commission) 2018 (2007) III. 7: 14.

15 Annex A: Schedule 1 of the Agreement, also found in the Northern Ireland Act 1998: Schedule 1: Government of the United Kingdom 1998, p. 3; and Government 1998: Schedule 1.3. These are pledges by the UK Government, endorsed by all the parties to the Agreement.

16 The Québecois have twice lost secession referendums; the second very close defeat appears to have sapped the appetite to leave Canada.

8. Three expressions that will still matter

1 Compare *A New Framework for Agreement*, Government of Ireland & Government of the United Kingdom 1995: para. 16 Constitutional Issues, which reiterates 'alone' and 'without external impediment'. *Frameworks for the Future* did not name the two governments as the authors.

2 Aristotle 1996: IV, 91–92. Written in the 4th century BCE, Aristotle's *Politics* begins by stating that the science of government 'has to consider what government is best and of what sort it must be, to be most in accordance with our aspirations, if there were *no external impediment . . .*'

3 Since the 1990s I have had historical documents of Irish provenance on self-determination – not private – originally made available to me by Seán Ó hUiginn, including Ginnel 1919.

4 E-mail correspondence 2021.

5 Resolution 2625 (XXV), UNGA Declaration 1970, p. 8, https://www.refworld.org/docid/3dda1f104.html.

6 In his celebrated account of the customary international law of self-determination, Antonio Cassese placed special emphasis on the 1970 Declaration and its predecessor, the 1960 Declaration Granting Independence to Colonial Countries and Peoples. See Cassese 1995.

7 Fergus Finlay has written in the *Irish Examiner* that there would have been no successful peace process without Seán Ó hUiginn, https://www.irish examiner.com/opinion/columnists/arid-20439400.html.

8 Seán Ó hUiginn had a classical education, and is formidably erudite. Professor Breandán Mac Suibhne of National University of Ireland-Galway identified the link to Aristotle.

9 Ó hUiginn emphasizes that his focus was on achieving an agreement on British procedural neutrality in a future referendum.

10 This understanding is common to Irish officials and SDLP figures who were pivotal in the making of the Joint Declaration for Peace, the Framework Documents of 1995, and the Good Friday Agreement. It may also have been critical to the decision-making of the IRA's Army Council.

11 The drafting history matters. In late November 1993 the British negotiators, led by the UK Cabinet Secretary, attempted a fresh start on a joint text, proposing to set aside the Irish draft submitted by Taoiseach Albert Reynolds. In the proposed British redraft, 'external' was deleted before 'impediment', rendering the phrase simply 'without impediment'. Reynolds gave the UK Cabinet Secretary 'hell' when he produced this alternative draft. Coakley and Todd 2020: 268–9; see also 234.

12 Mansergh went on, in a response to a neutrally phrased question from me, to write, 'I understand it simply to mean that the British would not externally impede a concurrent exercise in Irish self-determination, some of the conditions for which are set out in the GFA. I don't believe it would be legally construed in a court as meaning that they were undertaking to be politically neutral in the event, say, of a border poll, just that they would not prevent one taking place as part of the larger exercise in concurrent self-determination, if the condition for necessitating the holding of one were satisfied.' I argue in the text that this reading is too minimalist.

13 McGarry and O'Leary 1995: 409; the entire text may be found at 408–13.

14 Irish officials may have passed on documents in which the 'persuader' demand was included, but they expected British officials to reject them.

15 McGarry and O'Leary 1995: 48.

16 Readers will be spared discussion of whether the absence of commas in the phrase has material significance.

17 In the Joint Declaration for Peace, 'without external impediment' was more immediately linked to giving effect to necessary legislation to implement the future agreement, though also linked to the exercise of self-determination.

18 The insertion of 'ethos' is another expression attributable to Seán Ó hUiginn. I attributed it to an Irish official in O'Leary 1995b. Compare *A New Framework for Agreement*, Government of Ireland & Government of the United Kingdom 1995: para 19 Constitutional Issues, and para. 6 by the Taoiseach of the Declaration on Peace (1993).

19 Rory Montgomery, a former Irish Ambassador to France and a senior advisor on Brexit to the Irish Government, wrote to me upon receipt of a previous draft of this chapter that 'I entirely agree with your interpretation of "without external impediment" as requiring neutrality on the part of the British Government not just on the timing of the referendum, but also in its conduct. Indeed, I would go further and (relying in particular on the position of the phrase [in the GFA]) argue that it would also apply to all aspects of the implementation of a vote in favour of (re-)unification.'

9. Preparation: planning, deliberation, and polling

1 Roser and Nagdy 2014.

2 Cited in Elster 1983.

3 Seligman 1995.

4 This view has been persuasively defended in Pinker 2011, Pinker 2018.

5 Burke et al. 2018.

6 Shared Island Initiative, https://www.gov.ie/en/campaigns/c3417-shared-island/.

7 Kane 2020.

8 Constitution of Ireland Preamble, https://www.irishstatutebook.ie/eli/cons/en/html.

9 The manifestos may be found online, or at the website of Professor Michael Gallagher of Trinity College Dublin.

10 OECD, 'The 0.7% ODA/GNI Target – A History', https://www.oecd.
    org/dac/financing-sustainable-development/development-finance-standards/
    the07odagnitarget-ahistory.htm.
11 Cornford 1993 (1908): 29.
12 My exposure to this idea first came through supervising the PhD thesis of
    Miryang Youn (1997).
13 See Renwick et al. 2021: Chapter 12, drafted by Oran Doyle, David Kenny,
    and Christopher McCrudden.

Part Four: Models and Process

10. A critical choice: offering a model, or a process to pick a model?

1 This chapter and the next three draw extensively on joint work with John
   Garry and several other colleagues: Garry et al. 2018; Garry, O'Leary,
   McNicholl and Pow 2020; Garry, O'Leary, Coakley, et al. 2020; Garry et
   al. 2022.
2 Here I draw on materials in O'Leary 2020a.
3 E-mail correspondence with Kieran Bradley, whose biographical details
   can be found here: https://curia.europa.eu/jcms/jcms/a1_209257/en/.
4 Isaacharoff 2013.
5 Brice Dickson, Professor of International and Comparative Law at Queen's
   University Belfast, refers to 'a little known provision peculiar to Northern
   Irish law' that requires judges in the North 'to know the law of the Republic of Ireland' as well as that of England and Wales, but not Scotland's,
   Dickson 1996: 79. This provision could have been designed for a pattern of
   Irish reunification in which Scotland has seceded from Great Britain!

11. Model 1: A continuing Northern Ireland

1 Richard Humphreys in Humphreys 2009 and 2018 maintains that the GFA
   obliges the full transfer of the existing devolved arrangements. But no provisions of the text *oblige* the maximalist interpretation. When I was
   intimately engaged in policy analysis and development between 1987 and
   1999, it was clear that some leading figures in the South had the idea of a

'swing constitution' – one that would fit Northern Ireland whether the UK or Ireland was sovereign. I called this idea 'dual protection', see O'Leary 1999a, 1999c. It can be 'read into' the text of the agreement but cannot be found there 'in terms', as lawyers say, or in the treaties which protect it, or in its UK legislative enactment. In 1998 unionists were not, any more than they are today, intent on negotiating their rights in a possible united Ireland.

2 Constitution of the Irish Free State, https://www.irishstatutebook.ie/eli/1922/act/1/enacted/en/print.

3 Farrell 1970b, 1970a, 1971a, 1971b; Cahillane 2016.

4 Currently defined in the Northern Ireland Act (1998) Schedules 2 and 3.

5 Article 15. 2.2°, https://www.irishstatutebook.ie/eli/cons/en/html#part4.

6 E-mail correspondence with Professor Oran Doyle; his biographical details may be found here: https://www.tcd.ie/law/people/ojdoyle.

7 That is the opinion of Oran Doyle in correspondence.

8 'What is the West Lothian Question?' BBC, 25 September 2014, https://www.bbc.co.uk/newsround/29355003.

12. Model 2: An integrated Ireland

1 In principle, policing could be decentralized (or deconcentrated) and attached to local governments, but I suspect security concerns will override those willing to commence such an experiment.

2 Told to me by Professor Sid Noel, Professor Emeritus of Political Science at the University of Western Ontario, Canada (his biographical details may be found here: https://www.tjcentre.uwo.ca/about/faculty/sid_noel.html).

3 McClements 2021b.

13. Questions for both models

1 The Good Friday Agreement Constitutional Issues, 1 (v).

2 The Good Friday Agreement Constitutional Issues, 1 (vi).

3 Our studies were reported in *Irish Political Studies and Regional Studies*, Garry, O'Leary, Coakley, et al. 2020; and one is forthcoming in *Irish Studies in International Affairs*, Garry et al. 2022.

4 ARINS (Analysing and Researching Ireland, North and South) is a joint initiative of the Royal Irish Academy and the University of Notre Dame. I am a founding member, on its steering committee, and the chair of its survey committee.

5 Garry et al. 2022.

14. What won't happen: an independent Northern Ireland, confederation, and repartition

1 Government of the United Kingdom 1998: 1 (i), p. 2.

2 For the argument that the political decolonization of Ireland was accomplished in 1998 when both parts of Ireland endorsed the Belfast or Good Friday Agreement, see O'Leary 2020b, 2020d, 2020a: *passim*.

3 Several discussions and listings of secession and independence referendums exist: Laponce 2010, 2012; Qvortrup 2014b. A longer list may be constructed from the database in Mendez and Germann 2016.

4 New Ulster Political Research Group 1979, Callaghan 1981. Callaghan may have been influenced by discussions of 'dominion independence' under his predecessor's premiership, Donoughue 1987.

5 Paul Arthur reviewed 'Independence' in Rea 1982. Margaret Moore and James Crimmins took on the task of making the best case for negotiated independence in McGarry and O'Leary 1990b. Fitzsimmons 1993 volunteered the perspective of a US lawyer.

6 The late Conor Cruise O'Brien once effectively advanced this argument, O'Brien 1980. As a young diplomat O'Brien had been an ardent supporter of reunification. In the last phase of his life he became a candidate for Robert McCartney's UK Unionist Party. In his memoir he advocated that unionists should support a united Ireland provided that they could keep the RUC: O'Brien 1998.

7 Bradford 1981.

8 It figured briefly in the New Ireland Forum Report 1984.

9 O'Leary 2020c.

10 Matthews 2004; Murray 2011; Hand 1969, 1973.

11 Kennedy 1986, 1990.

12 As young men, John McGarry and I considered that the threat of repartition could concentrate minds in favour of power-sharing: O'Leary 1989;

McGarry and O'Leary 1990a. That was mistaken. The threat of joint or shared authority is better suited for these purposes, and much less risky.

15. An increasingly improbable model: shared sovereignty

1 O'Leary 1993. My dynamic former PhD student Professor Stefan Wolff has analysed the instances of joint sovereignty (Wolff 2003).
2 SDLP 1972; FitzGerald 1991.
3 Among their number were the Quaker thinker T. J. Pickvance; Martin Dent, an academic at Keele University and former colonial administrator in northern Nigeria; Bernard Crick, a political scientist who did not believe in political science; the humane philosopher and a president of the British Academy, Anthony Kenny: Pickvance 1975, Dent 1988, Crick 1982, Kenny 1986, 1990. According to Tom Lyne, the idea of an EU commissioner went down like a 'lead balloon' in Brussels.
4 It was close to the conclusions in McGarry and O'Leary 1990b.
5 O'Leary et al. 1993.
6 Hain 2012.

16. An Irish federation?

1 On Bosnia, see Knaus and Martin 2004; on Kurdistan and Iraq, see O'Leary, McGarry, and Salih 2005, and O'Leary 2009; on Puntland in Somalia, see Guadani et al. 1998; and on Nepal, see Upreti, Bishnu Raj, Nicole Topperwien and Marcus Heiriger 2009, *Peace Process and Federalism in Nepal* (Kathmandu, Nepal: South Asia Regional Coordination Office, Swiss National Centre of Competence in Research (NCCR) North–South.)
2 The Interim National Constitution of Sudan of the Republic of Sudan (2005) under the Comprehensive Peace Agreement had this innovative feature: https://www.refworld.org/pdfid/4ba749762.pdf, Schedule E.
3 Sinn Féin 1971–72, 1979. For a vivid biography of Ó Brádaigh, built from his papers, see White 2006.
4 My friend, the late Jonathan Steinberg, wrote the most accessible guide to Switzerland for the general reader, revised in Steinberg 2015.
5 Vile 1982.
6 Vile 1982.

Part Five: The Government of a United Ireland

17. The central government: separating and sharing powers

1 A referendum in 2015 defeated an amendment to lower the age of eligibility for the presidency from thirty-five to twenty-one, by a ratio of three to one: O'Connell 2015.

2 Bunreacht na hÉireann 1937, Article 12.2.

3 Bunreacht na hÉireann 1937, Article 12.8.

4 My wife and I, who are not religious, used Quaker 'self-uniting' rules to marry at the Constitution Center in Philadelphia. No vows or oaths were made, and no clergy or public officials were present; Quaker rules are effectively secular.

5 Northern Ireland Executive, Ministerial Code, 1.4.

6 Bunreacht na hÉireann 1937, Article 13.4.

7 Bunreacht na hÉireann 1937, Article 13.6.

8 Bunreacht na hÉireann 1937, Article 31.

9 Bunreacht na hÉireann 1937, Article 13.9.

10 Bunreacht na hÉireann 1937, Article 35.

11 Bunreacht na hÉireann 1937, Article 24.

12 Bunreacht na hÉireann 1937, Article 27.1.

13 Bunreacht na hÉireann 1937, Article 26 1.1.

14 Bunreacht na hÉireann 1937, Article 12. 20.

15 Bunreacht na hÉireann 1937, Article 13.1.

16 Bunreacht na hÉireann 1937, Article 12.4.ii.

17 Bunreacht na hÉireann 1937, Article 14.

18 That is not obliged by the GFA. Richard Humphreys thinks otherwise. His arguments are the same as those of Oran Doyle discussed in Chapter 12, except that Humphreys believes that the GFA actually requires the maximum transfer model of the GFA, so that a devolved Northern Ireland is already the (sole) required mode of unification: Humphreys 2018: 201–06.

19 Leahy 2013: 94; Doyle 2018: 53–54.

20 Doyle 2018: 54.

21 Doyle 2018: 68.

22 Laver 1996: 532.

23 Here I follow the arguments of Laver 1996, modified for a reunified Ireland.

24 Laver 1996: 536–37.

25 This section is significantly informed by the *International Idea Primer for Constitutional Designs*, Bulmer 2021.

26 Sweden, Instrument of Government, Chapter 2, Article 22.

27 Constitution of Denmark, Article 41.3; Bulmer 2021.

28 Bulmer 2021: 36.

29 Technically what I am doing here is proposing liberal rather than corporate consociational mechanisms.

30 Constitution of Denmark, Article 42; Bulmer 2021: 36 ff.

31 An emergency provision enables a bill to receive royal assent immediately after it has been passed by Parliament (without waiting for three days) but it is to be repealed if voted against in a referendum: Bulmer 2021.

32 The Constitution of Latvia also has a minority-veto referendum rule. The president may within ten days of the adoption of a bill by parliament suspend the bill for a period of two months. A referendum is held if, during those two months, a public petition is received signed by 10 per cent of the voters. Several such referendums have been held, including on citizenship laws (1998), on security laws (2007), and on pensions (1999 and 2010). Information from Bulmer 2021.

33 Here too I benefit from Bulmer 2021.

34 The net effect may be to compel meetings of the Council of State; currently only the President can convene them.

35 A readable account of the Irish Supreme Court may be found in Mac Cormaic 2017.

18. Local government

1 Local Government Facts and Figures, see https://lgiu.org/local-government-facts-and-figures-ireland/.

19. Repurposing the institutions of the Good Friday Agreement

1 British-Irish Council, Summits, https://www.britishirishcouncil.org/bic/summits.

2 Coakley 2016.

3 See, for example, that released after a conference at Dublin Castle in June 2021, https://www.dfa.ie/news-and-media/press-releases/press-release-archive/2021/june/joint-communique-of-the-british-irish-intergovern mental-conference-.php.

4 On the quiet history of North–South cooperation between 1925 and 1969, as well as the better recalled clashes, see Kennedy 2000. On Seán Lemass and his successors' pursuit of 'technocratic anti-partitionism', see Lyne 1990.

5 The North/South Interparliamentary Association does not meet when the Executive and Assembly are suspended or not functioning: https://www. oireachtas.ie/en/inter-parliamentary-work/northsouth/.

6 As first demonstrated by Professor Conley 2013. See also McCrudden et al. 2016. Professor Jonathan Tonge extended and confirmed Conley's point in his Statement to the Houses of the Oireachtas Joint Committee on the Implementation of the Good Friday Agreement, 13 July 2021.

7 Leeds Castle Proposals, 8 December 2004, para. 9, https://www.peace agreements.org/viewmasterdocument/124; see Humphreys 2021: 253–71.

8 *New Decade, New Approach*, Part 2.9 & 2, Annex B, 2.2.3: https://www.dfa. ie/media/dfa/newsmedia/pressrelease/New-Decade-New-Approach.pdf; Humphreys 2021: 411–67.

9 See Tonge, note 6 above.

10 See Garry 2009; Garry 2016 and Conley 2013.

11 McBride 2019.

12 The author of *Political Purgatory*, a study of the restoration of the institutions, believes that New Decade, New Approach is Stormont's last chance, Rowan 2021.

13 See, among others, McEvoy 2006, 2013, 2015; McCrudden et al. 2016; McGarry and O'Leary 2015; O'Leary, Grofman, and Elklit 2005; O'Leary 2020a; and the contributions in Taylor 2009.

14 The 1998 Agreement obliged all participants to 'use any influence they may have to achieve the decommissioning of all paramilitary weapons within two years following endorsement in referendums North and South of the agreement and in the context of the implementation of the overall settlement', The Good Friday Agreement, Section 7, Para. 3. The date to complete decommissioning became 22 May 2000, an obligation on Sinn Féin and the loyalist parties. But Mandelson suspended the institutions in February 2000,

while his delays and failures to implement the Patten report meant that the overall settlement was not being implemented by the UK Government. He pleaded necessity, and that Trimble forced his hand.

15 The St Andrews Agreement 2006, Section 8, (4) and (5), https://www. legislation.gov.uk/ukpga/2006/53/section/8.

16 The Northern Ireland Act 1998, Section 16C, https://www.legislation. gov.uk/ukpga/1998/47/section/16C.

17 For an account of the end of Paisley's premiership, see Gordon 2010.

18 Thomas Jefferson had invented the rule significantly earlier to apportion congressional seats proportionate to population for the US House of Representatives. See Balinski and Peyton Young 1982.

19 Blair 2011.

20 Brams and Taylor 1996; see also Brams and Kaplan 2004; Brams and King 2005.

20. Realistic cold fusion of voting rules

1 In an infamous example of gerrymandering, Londonderry Corporation was gerrymandered so that twelve unionist councillors compared to eight non-unionists were elected in 1967, even though non-unionist voters outnumbered unionists by over three to two. See O'Leary 2020d: 44–45.

2 Gallagher 2005.

3 Garret FitzGerald 2003 endorsed the conventional criticism that the system is tough on ministers, who may face the loss of their seats to internal party rivals, not just to candidates from other parties. Many deputies spend a large portion of their time nursing their constituencies and offering their services. That need not be a bad thing. Civil servants are already obliged to do what many deputies harass them to do, so there is an element of showmanship in deputies' conduct. Greater decentralization might reduce wasteful interactions among citizens, deputies, and central ministries as voters learn to lobby their local councillors.

4 O'Duffy and O'Leary 1995; O'Leary 1995a.

5 Those mathematically competent may decide whether to propose the Meek method to supersede the Gregory method – it resolves the transfer of surpluses by computer methods. Gallagher 1987 provides a robust defence of STV-PR and proposes using the Gregory method for Dáil

Éireann elections. For an explanation of the Meek method, see Woodall 1982. My thanks to Bernie Grofman and Nic Tideman.

6　Bunreacht na hÉireann 1937, Article 28.1 restricts the Government (cabinet) to fifteen members. Junior ministers are excluded from the cabinet. For a discussion of constitutional practice, see Doyle 2018: 52–56. The Taoiseach would be the first minister allocated through the d'Hondt rule.

7　The electorate in Northern Ireland in 2019 was 1,330,905. The electorate in the Republic was 3,509,969. So the North's electorate is 37 per cent of the Republic's. The total Irish electorate is 4,840,874, so the North would be entitled to 68 deputies in a Dáil Éireann of 250 deputies.

Part Six: The Economics of Reunification

21. Ireland is ready for economic reunification – and will be readier

1　McWilliams 2017.

2　Bergin and McGuinness 2021b: 151. 'Taking the more extreme poverty line of 50% of average household income, the proportion of individuals at risk of poverty in NI was 14.3% compared to 8.9% in the RoI based on the most recently available data', ibid., 159.

3　Bergin and McGuinness 2021b: 153, Table 3, row 6: 29 per cent to 15.2 per cent.

4　Bergin and McGuinness 2021b: 153, Table 3, row 5: 92.6 per cent to 73.6 per cent.

5　Bergin and McGuinness 2021b: 154.

6　FitzGerald 2021.

7　Bergin and McGuinness 2021a; see also McGuinness and Bergin 2019.

8　RoI data at https://covid19ireland-geohive.hub.arcgis.com; https://coronavirus.data.gov.uk/details/deaths?areaType=nation&areaName=Northern%20Ireland (accessed 19 February 2022).

9　See Whitaker 1973; Chambers 2014.

10　For the rise and fall of the early modern Hanseatic League of Northern European trading cities, see Spruyt 1994. The phrase 'the new Hanseatics' may be owed to *The Economist*, but in a telling oversight it did not include Ireland when the magazine first ran with the idea: Charlemagne 2013.

11 Luxembourg is excluded from the comparison because of its much smaller population – about a third of Northern Ireland's. It outranks Ireland in GDP and GNI per head.

12 As Fintan O'Toole advises, reporting 2021 Ipsos Global Trends data, the Irish of the Republic are among the least nostalgic peoples in the world, for good economic reasons: O'Toole 2021.

13 Hix 2020.

14 Campbell and Hall 2017.

15 See Ross 2010; O'Toole 2010; Lynch 2010; Campbell and Hall 2017.

16 The Fiscal Compact treaty was incorporated through an amendment in 2012.

17 PWC, Corporate Tax Summaries, https://taxsummaries.pwc.com/united-kingdom/corporate/taxes-on-corporate-income.

18 Peter O'Dwyer, 'Yellen: Historic Global Tax Consensus "Likely to Prove Durable" ', *Business Post*, 31 October 2021, https://www.businesspost.ie/extra-interviews/yellen-historic-global-tax-consensus-likely-to-prove-durable-c4d51e0e.

22. *The benefits and the costs of reunification*

1 Hübner et al. 2015: 22.

2 Hübner, Van Nieuwkoop, and KLC Consulting 2015. The full report is available on the CAIN website.

3 Cautionary remarks on their data are found at Hübner et al. 2015: 6.

4 Central Statistics Office, Modified GNI, https://www.cso.ie/en/interactivezone/statisticsexplained/nationalaccountsexplained/modifiedgni/.

5 World Bank, 'GDP growth (annual %) – Ireland', https://data.worldbank.org/indicator/NY.GDP.MKTP.KD.ZG?end=2020&locations=IE&start=1971&view=chart.

6 Doyle 2021a. John Doyle partly credits the work of Senator Mark Daly and others in the Oireachtas for facilitating his exploration of this question. Senator Daly deserves credit for his bravery and clarity in advancing public debate.

7 Alan Barrett of the ESRI is more cautious on the question of whether a London government would be such a benign actor on pension liabilities and UK debt liabilities, see Barrett 2021; he rightly suggests that the

Scottish case will have a bearing on the behaviour of any London governments. Doyle's political judgements are nevertheless sound, and the historic
precedents on pension and debt liabilities favour his calculations.

Part Seven: Securing Ireland

23. Policing, intelligence, and paramilitarism in a united Ireland

1 https://www.executiveoffice-ni.gov.uk/articles/communities-transition-
   background.
2 In March 2022, *thedetail* reported that at least 168 Protestant officers of the
   PSNI were members of exclusively Protestant groups – the Orange Order,
   the Royal Black Institution, the Apprentice Boys of Derry, and the Independent Orange Order – compared to two Catholic members of the Ancient
   Order of Hibernians and the Knights of Saint Columbanus: Winters 2022.
3 Independent commissions established under the GFA have a mixed record,
   see the superb study by Dr Dawn Walsh, Walsh 2017.
4 Patten 1999; reviewed in O'Leary 1999b. Before the report was published,
   I had a constructive meeting with its named author in London. The principal drafter was the late Senator Dr Maurice Hayes.
5 Barry White of the *Belfast Telegraph* wrote, 'What really surprised me was
   the number of times Patten refers to a book by two academics, John
   McGarry and Brendan O'Leary, *Policing Northern Ireland*. Its summary
   makes 10 points, most of which find their way into the report in some
   form': 'Patten . . . finding the gems in the detail', 18 September 1999.
6 McKittrick et al. 2008; Sutton 1994; https://cain.ulster.ac.uk/sutton/
   chron/1969.html.
7 Report of the Advisory Committee on Police in Northern Ireland, https://
   cain.ulster.ac.uk/hmso/hunt.htm
8 Trimble 2000.
9 McGarry 2004.
10 'Concerns Raised as PSNI Ends 50/50 Recruitment Policy', *Irish Examiner*,
   22 March 2011, https://www.irishexaminer.com/news/arid-30498261.html.
11 The intake of new cultural Catholic recruits amounted to just 24 per cent
   of the total in 2020, with the cultural Catholic proportion of the front-line

service at 32 per cent. The civilian staff of the PSNI retains a four-to-one ratio of Protestants to Catholics: McClements 2021a.

12 See the work of Dr Gemma Dipoppa on the movement of organized crime across Europe: https://politicalscience.stanford.edu/people/gemma-dipoppa.

13 O'Toole et al. 2018.

14 For its history by the long-serving *Irish Times* correspondent and editor, see Brady 1974 and Brady 2014; and for part of the story of its internal modernization, see Doyle 2021b.

24. *The defence and international relations of a united Ireland*

1 Bunreacht na hÉireann Article 29.

2 Irish Defence Forces, 'Past Missions', https://www.military.ie/en/overseas-deployments/past-missions/. Irish observers or peacekeepers have been in Cyprus, Lebanon, Iran, El Salvador, Haiti, Angola, Chad, Central African Republic, Congo, Côte d'Ivoire, Ethiopia and Eritrea, Liberia, Somalia, West Iran, India-Pakistan, Cambodia, and Timor.

3 Doyle and Sambanis 2006.

4 For an eloquent statement of the contrary view, see Mearsheimer 1994.

5 'Irish Defence Forces Officer Warns Staffing Crisis Jeopardising Overseas Missions', *The Journal*, 23 November 2021, https://www.thejournal.ie/defence-forces-officers-un-mission-5609423-Nov2021/.

6 For the argument that the peace dividend in the North was felt in rising house prices, see Besley and Mueller 2012.

7 Wall 2021.

8 Conor Gallagher, 'One Third of Naval Service Fleet to Be Decommissioned', *Irish Times*, 29 March 2022.

9 Wall 2020.

10 For discussions, see Fanning 1979; FitzGerald 1982; Cronin 1985.

11 Fisk 1985; O'Leary 2020d.

12 Evans and Kelly 2014.

13 'Consolidated Version of the Treaty on European Union' 2012, Article 42. This mutual defence clause should be distinguished from the 'solidarity clause' in Article 222 of the Treaty on the Functioning of the European Union (https://eur-lex.europa.eu/legal-content/EN/TXT/?uri=

LEGISSUM:solidarity_clause). The solidarity clause enables the EU and EU countries to act jointly; to prevent a terrorist threat in the territory of an EU country; and to provide assistance to another EU state which is the victim of a natural or man-made disaster.

14 The 28th Amendment to the Constitution, amending Article 29, in particular Part Two, 9°, https://www.irishstatutebook.ie/eli/2009/ca/28/schedule/enacted/en/html#sched-part1.

15 Montgomery 2022.

16 Malta's position awaits developments: its constitution obligates neutrality.

17 Constitutionally neutral Malta, and Denmark, a NATO member, have not opted in to PESCO.

18 Leahy 2022.

19 'Act of Union' in Heaney 1975.

20 *Sunday Business Post*, Red C poll, 28 November 2021; *Irish Times*/Ipsos MRBI, 11 December 2021.

21 Pocock 1982, 1999, 2005 provide eloquent songs to 'greater Britain' from New Zealand.

22 The Commonwealth, 'Joining the Commonwealth', https://thecommonwealth.org/about-us/joining-the-commonwealth.

23 'Joining the Commonwealth'.

24 Humphreys 2009: 192, quoting Longford and O'Neill 1970: 433.

Part Eight: Accommodating Diversity

25. Integration is not coercive assimilation

1 Aughey 1996: 23.

2 Elsewhere, I have tried to provide a fair summary of controversies over the fate of Southern Protestants. See O'Leary 2020d: Chapter 2.3, especially pp. 85–103.

3 On working-class Protestants in Dublin, see Maguire 1993.

4 On Protestant demographic decline, and for a critical undermining of Peter Hart's theses, see the concluding chapters of Fitzpatrick 2014.

5 For a survey of controversies over the fate of Southern Protestants, see O'Leary 2020d: Chapter 2.3.

6 Dáil Éireann debate, 22 April 1999, https://www.oireachtas.ie/en/debates/debate/dail/1999-04-22/3/.

7 Council of Europe 1994.

8 Morris and Scheidel 2009.

9 Saunders 1972.

10 Flanagan 1989; Thomas 2003; Bartlett 2000; Davies 1990; Simms 1989.

11 Hamilton 1973.

12 Dickson 2021.

26. Secularization, religion, and education

1 Sara Mac Donald, 'Irish Church in "Vocations Crisis"', *The Tablet*, 18 August 2020, https://www.thetablet.co.uk/news/13266/irish-church-in-vocations-crisis-.

2 European Court of Human Rights, Case of Dudgeon *v.* The United Kingdom, Application No. 7525/76, Judgment, Strasbourg, 22 October 1981 (accessed 17 October 2021).

3 Norris *v.* Ireland, Application no. 10581/83, Council of Europe: European Court of Human Rights, 26 October 1988 (accessed 17 October 2021).

4 On the X case, see McDonagh 1992.

5 Scally 2021; Inglis 1987.

6 Disputes over the extradition of the same priest led to the fall of the coalition government of Fianna Fáil and Labour: 'How a Government Sailed into a Storm over Clerical Abuse', *Irish Times*, 23 August 1997. For a brief account of Brendan Smyth's record of abuse, see Collins 2017.

7 https://www.youtube.com/watch?v=mo5MXrqbDeA.

8 Labour was happy with the decision, Fine Gael less so; see Leahy 2013: 161.

9 Connolly's prediction was made in March 1914, when he condemned Asquith, Devlin and Redmond for contemplating (temporary) partition: https://www.marxists.org/archive/connolly/1914/03/laborpar.htm.

10 Referendum (Amendment) Act 1972, https://www.irishstatutebook.ie/eli/1972/act/23/enacted/en/print.html.

11 The lack of respect for full female equality and the historic provisions on the family have patriarchal sources that are older than Christianity.

12 Department of Education, 'Information on School Types in Northern Ireland', www.education-ni.gov.uk/articles/information-school-types-northern-ireland.

27. Language policy

1 The Good Friday Agreement, Economic, Social and Cultural Issues, para. 4.
2 Annex E: Rights, language and identity, especially para. 5 and following.
3 Akenson 1975.
4 Bunreacht na hÉireann 1937, Article 8 – under the heading of the State.

28. Citizenship, identity, and symbols

1 My friend Oran Doyle was influential in pressing this reading in Renwick et al. 2021, 4.30: 70, of which I am a co-author. Now I'm not so sure.
2 British citizens who were not born in Northern Ireland but were resident there for three to five years before reunification should be entitled to Irish citizenship, and any period of residence in Northern Ireland should count towards meeting Irish citizenship requirements.
3 His biography has been written by Timothy Egan: Egan 2016.
4 *Sunday Business Post*, 28 November 2021, Red C poll, and *Irish Times* Ipsos MRBI poll, 11 December 2021.
5 *Sunday Business Post*, 28 November 2021, Red C poll, and *Irish Times* Ipsos MRBI poll, 11 December 2021.
6 *Irish News*, 22 November 2021.
7 Flags, Identity, Culture and Tradition, Private Members' Business, in the Northern Ireland Assembly, 22 March 2021, https://www.theyworkforyou.com/ni/?d=2021–03–22.
8 FICT, n.d.
9 Parades Commission 2022.
10 Address to the Shared Ireland Forum, December 2021, https://www.youtube.com/watch?v=wXAZgfHtvdc.

Index of Names

Index